The Emperor of Nature

The Emperor of Nature

Charles-Lucien Bonaparte
and His World

PATRICIA TYSON STROUD

University of Pennsylvania Press

Philadelphia

10 9 8 7 6 5 4 3 2 1

Published by

University of Pennsylvania Press

Philadelphia, Pennsylvania 19104-4011

Library of Congress Cataloging-in-Publication Data

Stroud, Patricia Tyson

The emperor of nature : Charles-Lucien Bonaparte and his world / Patricia Tyson Stroud

    p.   cm.

Includes bibliographical references and index

ISBN 0-8122-3456-0 (alk. paper)

1. Bonaparte, Charles Lucian, 1803-1857. 2. Ornithologists—France—Biography.
3. Ornithologists—Italy—Biography. I. Title

QL31.B637S77 2000

598'.092—B21   00-026157

CIP

Designed by Carl Gross

Frontispiece: *Charles-Lucien Bonaparte* (1803–1857)
by T. H. Maguire, 1849. Stipple engraving.
Courtesy of the American Philosophical Society

For Sandy

CONTENTS

List of Illustrations   ix

Preface   xiii

1. A Turbulent Youth   1

2. The New World   33

3. An Author's First Campaigns   61

4. Sorties to Familiar Shores   83

5. International Correspondents   99

6. The Naturalist in Italy   123

7. The Napoleon of Peace?   147

8. Prince of Canino   163

9. The Network   183

10. Legacies of Trouble   201

11. The Prince and the Pope   217

12. A Prince in Political Trenches   235

13. The Dean of French Exiles   259

14. Paris   279

15. A Race Against Death   301

Notes   317

Genealogical Chart   348

Bibliography   351

Index   359

ILLUSTRATIONS

FIGURES

1. *Napoleon in His Study*, David   3

2. *Portrait of Joseph Bonaparte*, Lefèvre   5

3. *Portrait of Alexandrine de Bleschamps Bonaparte*, Fabre   7

4. *Charles-Lucien Bonaparte as a Child*, Wicar   12

5. *Lucien Bonaparte and His Family*, Wicar   13

6. *Lucien Bonaparte with Charles-Lucien and other members of his ménage*, de Châtillon   16

7. *Padre Maurizio, Dr. de France, and Charles-Lucien Bonaparte*, Wicar   20

8. *Padre Maurizio da Brescia*, Wicar   20

9. *Portrait of the Family of Lucien Bonaparte*, Ingres   22

10. *Lucien Bonaparte and His Family at the Villa Rufinella*, de Châtillon   25

11. *Julie Clary Bonaparte, Queen of Spain, and Her Daughter Zenaide*, Lefèvre   26

12. *Charles-Lucien Bonaparte as a Young Man*, de Châtillon   28

13. *Manor House of Joseph Bonaparte*, Bodmer   35

14. *Joseph Bonaparte*, Peale   39

15. Bust of Charles-Lucien Bonaparte, Trentanove   44

16. *Thomas Say in the Uniform of the Long Expedition*, Peale   47

17. *Titian Ramsay Peale* (self-portrait)   53

18. *Audubon*, Syme   57

19. *Great Crow Blackbird*, Audubon and Rider   65

20. *Burrowing Owl*, Peale   69

21. Two views of *U.S.S. Delaware*   94-95

22. *Villa Paolina*, Charlotte Bonaparte   103

23. *Georges Cuvier*, Rembrandt Peale   113

24. *1. Bufo vulgaris 2. Bufo calamita*, Quattrocchi   125

25. *Louis Agassiz*, Stuart   131

26. *Letizia Ramolino Bonaparte*, Gérard   133

27. *Garden of the Palazzo Serristori*, Napoleone   142

28. *Charlotte Bonaparte*, Robert   152

29. *1. Vespertilio bonapartii, Savi; 2. Vespertilio albo limbatus*, Quattrocchi   169

30. Presentation copy of *Iconografia della fauna italica*   170

31. *Charles-Lucien Bonaparte*, Liverati   171

32. Sketch of Musignano, Lear, 1839   205

33. *Princess Zenaide Bonaparte*, Bonaparte   207

34. *Julie Bonaparte, marchesa del Gallo di Roccagiovine*, Belloli   226

35. *Alessandro, marchese del Gallo di Roccagiovine*, Belloli   227

36. Uniform of the Roman Republic   252

37. *Zenaida Dove*, Audubon   266

38. *Luciano Bonaparte*, Belloli   277

39. *Coenraad Jacob Temminck*   282

40. "Arrivo d'un Diplomatico Importuno: Sbarco a Civitavecchia"   288

41. "Arrivo a Roma"   289

42. *Portrait of Napoleon-Joseph-Charles-Paul Bonaparte*, Flandrin   292

43. *Emperor Napoleon III*, Winterhalter   294

44. *Rachel*, Dubufe   297

45. *Joseph Bonaparte*, Belloli   303

46. *Prince Charles-Lucien Bonaparte*, Bocourt   313

COLOR PLATES

1. *"Universal Murderer of Domestic Happiness, or the Fraternal Tyrant"*

2. *Lucien Bonaparte*, Fabre

3. *Alexandrine de Bleschamps Bonaparte*, Viganoni

4. *Charles-Lucien Bonaparte*, de Châtillon

5. *Charles-Lucien Bonaparte with Zenaide at the Harp*, de Châtillon

6. *Point Breeze on the Delaware*, Birch

7. *The Sisters Zenaide and Charlotte Bonaparte*

8. *Wild Turkey, Meleagris Gallopavo, male and female*, Titian Peale

9. *1. Swallow tailed Flycatcher, . . . ,* Titian Peale

10. *Atrium of the Villa Paolina*, van den Abeele

11. *The salon of the Villa Paolina*, van den Abeele

12. *1. Hyla viridis 2. Rana esculenta 3. Rana temporaria*, Quattrocchi

13. *Acridotheres roseus*, Quattrocchi

14. *1. Serranus hepatus 2. Anthias sacer 3. Anthias buphthalmus*, Ruspi

15. *1. Aulopus filamentosus 2. Chlorophthalmus agassizi 3. Sternoptyx mediterranea*, Quattrocchi

16. *Bonaparte's Gull*, Audubon

PREFACE

WHY IS IT THAT NO ONE till now has written a biography of the leading ornithologist of the nineteenth century? Charles-Lucien Bonaparte is mentioned in countless works of natural history and studies of the history of science. During his lifetime, friends such as John Godman and William Swainson dedicated their books to him; Swainson even christened a small black-headed sea bird "Bonaparte's Gull" in his honor. Yet, aside from a comprehensive chapter devoted to him in Erwin Stresemann's *Ornithology from Aristotle to the Present* and a long article on his works by Elie de Beaumont, a colleague of Bonaparte's, no one has delved into his life.

One answer to this conundrum may be that Bonaparte was essentially a man without a country. No nation claimed him as a native son whose accomplishments could be celebrated as a credit to his homeland. He was born in France and raised in Italy and England; for less than five years he was a visitor to the United States. His return to Italy lasted for an extended period, but culminated in self-appointed exile to England and Holland. His final years were spent in France. France, the great center for natural science at the time, would seem the most likely candidate to claim him (particularly because of his relationship to Napoleon), but he actually only spent seven years there. For most of his life he had been exiled from France, first by Napoleon himself, then by Louis XVIII, Charles X, and Louis-Philippe, and last by his cousin Louis-Napoleon.

Italy has not had the impact of France or England on the recent history of science, which might explain why Bonaparte, and other important naturalists working in Italy, have been known only to experts. It is also curious that writers on the Risorgimento, on Mazzini and Garibaldi, have left Bonaparte almost completely out of their accounts, considering the important role he played in the assembly of the newly formed Roman republic. His ideas, expressed in his speeches, were so progressive that even as we enter the second millennium we applaud his concern for political equality, women's rights, religious tolerance, and prison reform, and his attacks on many inequities of the time. These speeches, delivered of course in Italian, are only available, as far as I could find, in French translations that appeared in newspapers. Perhaps because of his aristocratic standing—in the Roman republic all aristocrats were held in some disdain—and his theatrical personality, he was not taken seriously.

In England, Bonaparte stood beside the naturalists Huxley, Gould, and Owen in the public mind, but these were all Englishmen, while he was thought of as French and thus was associated with the traditional enemies of the English. (The name Bonaparte was particularly open to scorn and ridicule.) As for the United States, he was only in the country a relatively short time, and, although his continuation of Alexander Wilson's *American Ornithology* was a noteworthy contribution, the work has been completely overshadowed by that of Audubon. Ironically so, because in his own time, Audubon, although thought of as a great artist, was not considered a trustworthy naturalist by his peers. It was Bonaparte who was elected to the prestigious American Philosophical Society and the Academy of Natural Sciences of Philadelphia (in 1824) and honored as a scientist, while Audubon was refused admission to these august institutions for another ten years. Audubon himself considered Bonaparte his superior in ornithology, in fact his mentor. Yet later the disciple completely eclipsed the master in the public mind.

It has been something of a task, then, to find Charles-Lucien Bonaparte. I spent much time reading his voluminous scientific correspondence at the Jardin des Plantes in Paris and his personal letters at the Fondazioni Primoli in Rome. Other repositories of letters are the National History Museum in London, the Houghton Library at Harvard, the Beinecke Rare Book and Manuscript Library at Yale, and, in Philadelphia, the American Philosophical Society, the Academy of Natural Sciences, the Library Company, and the Historical Society of Pennsylvania. Bonaparte also left traces of himself in private family archives in Europe that I was privileged to examine.

The Museo Napoleonico in Rome has a marvelous collection of paintings, drawings, sculptures, and artifacts pertaining to Charles-Lucien Bonaparte's family. American museums have such treasures as the exquisite drawing of Alexandrine and her children by Ingres at Harvard's Fogg Museum, and two portraits by David: *Napoleon in His Study* at the National Gallery in Washington and *Zenaide and Charlotte Bonaparte* at the Getty Museum in California.

Bonaparte's letters to and from his family were always written in French, as were those to and from scientists from Switzerland and Germany, such as Agassiz and von Humboldt, and explorers, such as Prince Maximilian of

Neuweid. The majority of his correspondence with other naturalists, however, was with British and American colleagues and was therefore in English. Most of the documents relating to the Risorgimento are in Italian. I take full responsibility for all translations from both French and Italian. A number of proper names that occur frequently (notably Jérôme, Napoléon, Zénaïde) would require accents if spelled properly in French. They have been rendered in English form in the text, as have names of cities. The full forms are included in the Index and in the genealogical chart.

It is truly wonderful that so much material has been carefully saved and archived over the nearly century and a half since Bonaparte's death. Historians of today's great men and women will have a much more difficult time than I did finding their subjects because so much of our communication is ephemeral—phone calls, e-mail—and never appears in tangible form,

That so many eminent scientists of the time kept in regular contact with Bonaparte, and that they preserved so many of his letters, attests to the esteem in which they held him. This esteem and the life that inspired it have been buried in libraries for generations. It is my hope that this book will bring Charles-Lucien Bonaparte back into the light of day.

... to find in your position a man so nobly and continually
attached to science who has given his name a new renown so different
from that which one would expect by the amazing
chance of his birth near a throne.

Isadore Geoffroy Saint-Hilaire to Charles-Lucien Bonaparte,
Paris, 26 May 1839

After you left here the impression lived on of your profound
simplicity of character, of an erudition as solid as varied,
of an ardor of talent and of action worthy of the great name you carry.
Hurry again to visit us another summer in Hyères
at the far end of beautiful Italy.

Alexander von Humboldt to Charles-Lucien Bonaparte,
Berlin, 22 September 1844

Among people I have met, the few whom I would term "great"
all share a kind of unquestioned, fierce dedication; an utter lack of
doubt about the value of their activities (or at least an internal
impulse that drives through any such angst); and, above all,
a capacity to work (or at least to be mentally alert for unexpected
insights) at every available moment of every day of their lives.

Stephen Jay Gould,
"The Man [Buffon] Who Invented Natural History"

I

A TURBULENT
YOUTH

"... the ambitious tiger who overshadowed my childhood."

Charles-Lucien Bonaparte to Lucien Bonaparte,
Rome, 4 October 1822

CONTENTION SURROUNDED Charles-Lucien-Jules-Laurent Bonaparte almost from the moment of his birth on 24 May 1803. The arrival of a new Bonaparte was problematic to the infant's uncle, Napoleon, and the real fireworks exploded five months later, when the First Consul learned that his brother Lucien had made this child legitimate by marrying the mother, Alexandrine de Bleschamps Jouberthou de Vamberthy. He received Lucien's letter announcing the marriage in the midst of a concert at Malmaison. As he read the note, he flushed with rage, stopped the concert, shouted that he had been betrayed, and at once sent Joachim Murat, his brother-in-law, to tell Lucien that he would not recognize the union.[1] He had not objected to the hasty religious ceremony the day after the birth because it was not binding under French law. But this unwelcome news of the legal marriage destroyed his dynastic plans for Lucien, who was the most naturally ambitious of Napoleon's brothers, the most avid for money, properties, and honors, and, with his intelligence, the most capable and obvious candidate for the succession. The First Consul of France would soon be emperor, and his plans for consolidating his empire by means more binding than diplomacy were based on strategically marrying his brothers and sisters into the royal houses of Europe. He envisioned each sibling seated on a throne, a network of royal Bonapartes stretched across Europe. That a son had been born to Lucien and his mistress, this commoner, Alexandrine de Bleschamps Jouberthou, was one thing; that he had married her was something else entirely.

Napoleon's anger might have been tempered had he known that in manhood his nephew would emerge as an esteemed scientist. The First Consul had a deep respect for knowledge and for savants. Only four years earlier, on his Egyptian campaign, he had taken along more than one hundred scholars, artists, and scientists to improve the infrastructure, education, and social conditions of Egypt and to record its great antiquities. Once, while viewing the pyramids with Napoleon, the young naturalist Etienne Geoffroy Saint-Hilaire overheard the general lament that he had not devoted his own life to science: "I found myself a conqueror in Europe, like Alexander. It had been more to my liking to march in the footsteps of Newton."[2]

Napoleon Bonaparte's political empire stretched across Europe; Charles Bonaparte's empire of nature, specifically the collection, study, and ordering of birds, would span oceans as well as continents. He would study and classify the birds of North and Central America, Europe, Africa, and Australia. In many ways, his life's undertaking would be as vast as his famous uncle's, and more

Figure 1. *Napoleon in His Study* by Jacques-Louis David, 1812. Oil. The Samuel H. Kress Collection, Board of Trustees, the National Gallery of Art, Washington, D.C.

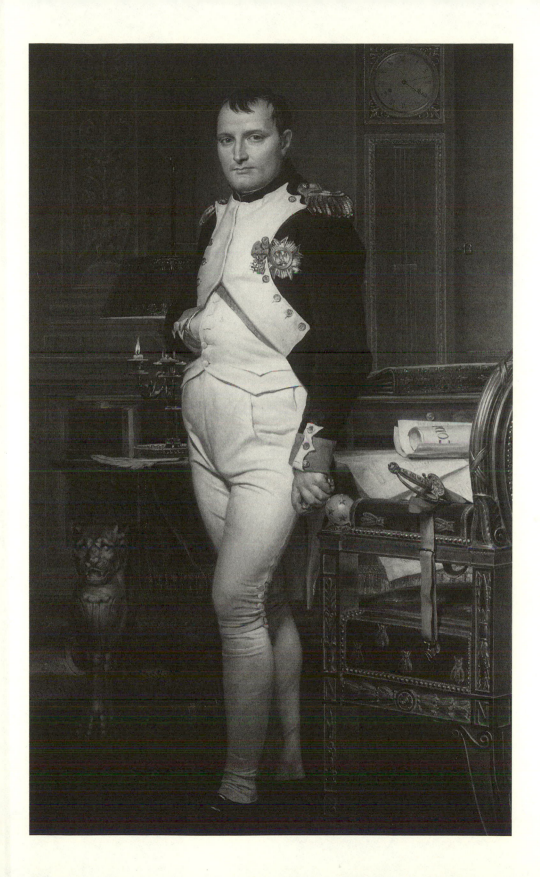

beneficial to humanity, for he helped to lay the foundation for the modern science of ornithology, upon which Darwin based his theory of evolution.

Scarcely a month after Charles's birth, Napoleon, disregarding Lucien's illegitimate child and its mother, had conspired to put Lucien on the throne of Etruria, the central Italian kingdom created by France. A marriage was to take place between this brother and the recently widowed queen, the Spanish infanta Marie Louise—in spite of contemporary opinion that she was singularly ugly. As ambassador to Spain, Lucien had signed the Franco-Spanish treaty establishing Etruria's boundaries. As king of Etruria, he would rule from Florence, the original home of the Bonapartes; from there in the sixteenth century they had emigrated to Corsica, where Napoleon and all his siblings were born. To Napoleon's exasperation, Lucien rejected the scheme.[3] Annoyed, he sent him instead to his Rhineland territories with instructions to select a district to represent as senator and to purchase a home. In July, Lucien selected the beautiful château of Poppelsdorf, near Bonn, as his official residence. The property would bring in a large rent, but he would never actually live there.

As the summer wore on, an all-important issue increasingly occupied all five Bonaparte brothers. A year earlier, Napoleon had been named First Consul for life, thus replacing the insecurity of his position as a self-appointed ruler with the guarantee of a dynastic succession. For this, however, he needed an heir. Since his wife, Josephine, had been unable to produce one, the succession question consumed his impetuous, eager family. Because his oldest brother, Joseph, had only daughters and Lucien's son was illegitimate, Napoleon planned to name the son of his third brother, Louis, to succeed him. Louis's wife, Hortense, was Napoleon's beloved stepdaughter—a good reason to make her son his successor.

Clearly it was time for Lucien to stake out a claim for his own son. (Only if the baby were a boy had he agreed to marry Alexandrine in the first place.) He therefore went through the formality of a civil ceremony on 26 October 1803 at Chamant-Plessis, his estate near Senlis.[4] At the time it was suspected that Alexandrine's debt-ridden husband, Gian Francesco Ippolito Jouberthou de Vamberthy, pursuing some dubious business venture in Santo Domingo, was still alive, but Lucien later produced a death certificate for Jouberthou, issued at Port au Prince on 15 June 1802.[5]

When Joseph heard of the marriage, he was as angry as Napoleon. He wanted to know how Lucien thought the Bonapartes could press through their plan of hereditary succession with this child of a commoner as one of the

Figure 2. *Portrait of Joseph Bonaparte* by Robert Lefèvre, 1805. Oil.Inv. LM74766, neg. CO3130. Coutesy of the Swiss National Museum, Zurich.

claimants to the future throne of France?[6] Here was yet another example of Lucien's willfulness and hardheaded determination.

In many ways as brilliant as Napoleon, Lucien had a history of angering and opposing his militant brother. It was said he had "no idea of a superior, and Napoleon could not bear the thought of an equal."[7] Four years earlier, as president of the Council of Five Hundred, he had played a major role in the coup d'état of the 19th Brumaire (10 November 1799) that elevated Napoleon to his position as First Consul of France. But an ardent republican, at times even a Jacobin, Lucien opposed Napoleon's increasing centralization of power. According to Laure, duchesse D'Abrantes, wife of General Andoche Junot, Lucien had stated in her presence that, "if the men who surround my brother in the government choose to assist him in measures oppressive to the country, I shall not increase their number; and on the last day of the liberty of the republic, I shall go and seek another country."[8] His words were prophetic. Lucien was a man of sharp contrasts, and in spite of his high-sounding rhetoric he had handled affairs as minister of the interior (from 1799 to 1800) in a somewhat shady manner. Napoleon dismissed him and sent him to Spain as the French ambassador. While there, Lucien took every opportunity to enrich himself by inducing the Spanish king to lavish on him gifts of diamonds and paintings by old masters in gratitude for his efforts to effect a peace treaty with France.

One of his major accomplishments was in negotiating the treaty with Spain, signed in 1801, returning Louisiana to France. This was the vast territory that Thomas Jefferson would buy two years later from Napoleon, much to Lucien's bitter resentment.[9] Lucien's treaty, ironically, would have special significance for his son Charles, because the book that launched his career in natural science dealt largely with newly discovered species of birds from the western portion of the Louisiana Territory.

As full of contrasts as his son would be, Lucien's lust for riches was combined with a fierce adherence to the principles of the French Revolution. He saw with dismay that Napoleon was gradually deviating from these ideas, and he believed the root of their discord was as much this departure as Napoleon's opposition to his marriage. Lucien's devotion to republicanism—in his youth he had assumed the name Brutus from the founder of the first Roman republic (509 B.C.)—would be passed on to his son Charles, the cause of his rift with Napoleon. The First Consul refused to countenance this boy standing in the line of succession to the highest position in France. And Charles-Lucien was second eldest of the nephews. Only Louis's and Hortense's son Charles-Napoleon, born seven months earlier on 10 October 1802, stood closer to the throne that the Bonapartes hoped to establish.

Figure 3. *Alexandrine de Bleschamps Bonaparte* by F.X. Fabre, 1808.
Oil. Collection of Giuseppe Primoli. Courtesy of the Museo
Napoleonico, Rome.

An added and more subtle reason for Napoleon's intense opposition to
Lucien's marriage may have been Alexandrine's intelligence, beauty, vivacity,
and strength of character, which, when combined with the drive of her ambitious husband, might create formidable opposition to Napoleon himself.[10] In
spite of her reputation as a near courtesan, Alexandrine was from a well-born
royalist family in St. Malo and related to the poet Lamartine.[11] Napoleon had no
objection to her as his brother's mistress, but demanded that Lucien divorce
her, promising him wealth and power should he comply. However, much to his
credit, Lucien refused to sacrifice Alexandrine and their son to his own ambi-

tion, a decision that had enormous implications for Charles-Lucien's future life.

Another difficult decision for Lucien was whether to leave Paris under these uncomfortable circumstances. Leaving would mean abandoning the magnificent Hôtel de Brienne, the large Parisian mansion decorated in the fashionable Adamesque Etruscan style that provided such a handsome backdrop for his priceless art collection. A German traveler described his warm reception there in early 1804, when Lucien, carrying his infant son in his arms, conducted him through the spacious rooms, pointing out Raphael's *Holy Family* and David's *Belasarius*, among over one hundred other masterpieces.[12] The collection included a Perugino, a da Vinci, and several paintings by Guido Reni, representatives of the Italian, Dutch, and French schools, and many canvases Lucien had accepted from King Carlos IV of Spain.[13] Several were by the popular seventeenth-century religious painters Bartolomé Esteban Murillo and José de Ribera; others were stunning works by the contemporary artist Francisco José de Goya. It was indeed a discriminating collection for a young man to have assembled, but then Lucien had shrewdly taken to Madrid the painters Eugène Lethière and Jacques Sablet as advisers.[14] While in the Spanish capital, in order to appear even more erudite, he had distributed visiting cards engraved with the laurel-crowned heads of Homer, Raphael, and Gluck.[15]

For Charles Bonaparte's passionate father there would be no compromise with Napoleon over his situation. He was steadfast in his determination to be his own man and never to be ruled by his strong-minded brother, regardless of what he might lose. That winter he settled his affairs. In early spring he gathered together his entire family—his wife and their infant son Charles; Charlotte and Christine, his two daughters by his first wife Christine Boyer; Anna Jouberthou, Alexandrine's daughter by her previous marriage; and a number of servants—and set off for Italy. Before leaving Paris, he admonished Joseph: "Do not do anything during my absence to make peace for me with the First Consul. I am going away with hatred in my heart."[16]

In Rome, where he arrived with his large retinue in mid-April, Lucien put himself and his family under the protection of Pope Pius VII. The pontiff was grateful to the charismatic Frenchman, who as minister of the interior had facilitated a resurgence of religious freedom and the reopening of churches in France, closed because of Revolutionary anticlericalism. Financially, Lucien was independent. He had at his disposal not only the riches he had amassed during his rise to power—through his "gifts" from the Spanish crown, his salary as a senator, and the largesse bestowed on Napoleon's family by the French Senate, for example—but also the booty that had come his way from financing "corsair" (pirate) operations with Joseph. Both men had risked arrest in 1798 for pursuing this flourishing trade in Corsica, but had managed to elude the authorities and come off with millions of francs to divide between them. (Some of this lucre helped pay for Napoleon's Italian campaign.) By 1804 Lucien had become the richest member of the Bonaparte clan.[17]

At first Lucien and his family lived with Cardinal Fesch, his mother's half-brother, in the Palazzo Lancelotti. This arrangement was unsuccessful because of his relations with the cardinal, and he purchased the immense Palazzo Nuñez (today Palazzo Torlonia) in the Via Bocca di Leone, near the Piazza di Spagna, and spent as much again on renovations.[18] In the private theater he constructed there, plays, operas, and concerts were performed, employing the best actors and musicians available. It was essential to have the finest talent, because his guests included members of the local aristocracy, cardinals, ambassadors, the scientist/explorer Alexander von Humboldt, and the sculptor Antonio Canova, who had earlier immortalized his sister Pauline Borghese in marble as Venus Victrix, reclining half-naked on a couch.

Lucien also bought the Villa Rufinella at Frascati, built in 1578, the grounds of which had once belonged to Cicero. Ruins of the Roman orator's once-extensive house remained, including several archways, a suite of rooms, and a terrace. On a mountain summit nearby sat the stately Villa Rufinella, with a magnificent view on every side: the vestiges of a Roman aqueduct, the town of Tivoli, in the distance Rome, and forty miles away the glittering sea. Chateaubriand, the French author and politician, lived nearby for ten years. Archaeology being one of Lucien's passionate interests, he excavated his property and in the process dug up several Roman busts and a well-preserved, full-length statue of the emperor Tiberius. He transformed the hillside behind the villa into a Mount Parnassus, with fountains and grottos "populated by statues."[19] Rufinella was not only a place to visit for study and contemplation but a thriving farm producing white wine, potatoes, chestnuts, onions, beans, and large crops of corn. It had vineyards and woodlands and, everywhere, wonderful views and pleasant walks.[20]

In 1806 Pope Pius VII needed a large loan and Lucien offered to back him. The pontiff refused but suggested that Lucien instead purchase Canino. Lucien agreed. Canino, not far from the town of Viterbo, had formerly belonged to the Farnese family and afterward became the domains of the Apostolical Chamber as a dependency of the duchy of Castro. The land was situated on a spur of volcanic lava surrounded by pastures, vineyards, olive groves, and valleys crossed with streams. This extensive property included, among many smaller buildings, a manor house built within the remnants of an old castle in the center of the town of Canino. Since it was much neglected and badly laid out, Lucien set about transforming it into a handsome residence.[21] About three miles west of the town, and also included in his domain, were the ruins of an old convent, part of which had been converted into a granary. On an elevated site commanding a clear view of the far-off sea and bordered by a large stream, the ancient edifice, called Musignano, was ideally situated, and Lucien set about transforming it into a comfortable house. It was first of all a favorite spot for picnics, often followed by horse races, dancing, and "other amusements."[22] A mile beyond lay several ancient Etruscan sites. In one, hot springs bubbled up, and nearby, in a forest of olive trees, were the remains of the associated baths, an extensive Roman structure with a hundred cells or bathing rooms. It was the perfect place for a swimming pool in one of the baths, where the family dog, Mustapha, joined Alexandrine and the children on warm summer days.

Lucien established extensive vineyards and supervised the cultivation of his fertile fields. He was especially interested in growing cotton and brought peasants from southern Italy to teach his local employees how to do it. He also refurbished an iron smelting foundry and imported ore from Elba. In addition to these pursuits, he continued writing his poem *Charlemagne*, a long epic celebrating the papacy of the great eighth-century pope Leo III as the source of all civilization in Europe. In the poem, a fictional emperor puts his sword at the service of the Holy See—a thinly veiled critique of Napoleon's intention of dominating the pope. (At his coronation in December 1804, Napoleon had even taken the crown of France out of the hands of Pius VII and placed it on his own head, instead of waiting for the pontiff to do it, as was traditional.[23])

In Rome, hundreds of miles from France, Lucien believed he could finally live as he pleased. Napoleon needed his clever brother, however, and was determined to overpower his resistance without making the compromise of acknowledging his wife. The emperor arranged a meeting at Mantua on the evening of 12 December 1807, where he offered to make Lucien an imperial prince and to grant him a crown somewhere in his empire. In addition, he would bring about a marriage for the fifteen-year-old Charlotte with the prince of the Asturias, heir to the Spanish throne, and recognize Charlotte and Christine as his nieces. Alexandrine he would make duchess of Parma, with Charles as her heir. In return, Lucien would have to divorce her and accept that Napoleon would never recognize Charles as in line for the succession. Napoleon confided that Josephine's barrenness might compel him, for reasons of state, to divorce her, and it would lessen the public impact if his brother would make a similar sacrifice. Lucien turned him down on all counts. The offer had been tempting—almost any kingship on the continent over which Napoleon had control—but the price was too high. Again, he refused to renounce Alexandrine and Charles for Napoleon, or for France.

Napoleon wrote Joseph after the meeting: "it appeared to me there was in Lucien's mind a contest between opposite feelings, and that he had not sufficient strength to decide in favor of any one of them. I exhausted all the means in my power to induce him, young as he is, to devote his talents to my service and to that of the country." "Tell Lucien," he had added with a note of compassion not usually associated with the emperor, "that I was touched by his grief and by the feelings which he expressed toward me; and that I regret the more that he will not be reasonable and contribute to his own comfort and to mine."[24] Charles would remember his father telling him that until Napoleon himself had a son he, Lucien, was never at peace.[25]

Back in Rome the pressure continued. Shortly thereafter the youngest Bonaparte brother, Jerome, allowed Napoleon to annul his legal marriage to the American Elizabeth Patterson so he could marry a German princess, and on that occasion Lucien received a long letter from Cardinal Fesch urging him to divorce Alexandrine. (The cardinal, by toadying to Napoleon, was amassing a fortune.) With fury and indignation, Lucien replied, "Have you forgotten all honor, all religion? I wish you would at least have sufficient common sense not to think I am like Jerome and to spare me the useless insult of your cowardly advice. In a word, don't write to me again until religion and honor that you are now trampling under foot have dissipated your blindness. At least hide your base sentiments under your purple robes, and follow in silence your own path along the highway of ambition."[26]

Lucien was a brilliant orator with a flair for theatrical displays, a characteristic he would pass on to his son. But his temperament was somewhat unscrupulous and amoral, and, though resembling Napoleon in many respects, he lacked his great calculating and organizing brain. Charles would inherit his father's tempestuous personality and ambition as well as his zeal for revolutionary politics, but unlike Lucien, whose interests were multifarious, he would funnel his enthusiasms into natural science. And he would show himself more honorable, though often just as arrogant in dealing with his colleagues. He was conscientious in his pursuit of scientific truth and meticulous in his classifications and descriptions.

Ironically for Napoleon, who categorically rejected this nephew as his relation, Charles bore an uncanny resemblance to him in face and physique. Like Napoleon, he was short and increasingly stout as he grew older, and he also had his uncle's handsome facial features. Lucien, on the other hand, was "tall, ill-shaped," with a small head and a squint from bad eyesight, according to Laure D'Abrantes. Nevertheless, she said, he was attractive to women, which Charles also appears to have been.[27]

As a child in Rome at the Palazzo Nuñez, Charles lived at a time when the estrangement of the two ruling powers of France and Italy was growing daily. In 1803, when war broke out between France and England and Napoleon planned to invade the British Isles, Pope Pius VII refused to close his ports to English ships in compliance with Napoleon's blockade. The pontiff maintained that as a man of peace he could not be an enemy to any Christian nation. Charles, then about six, figured inadvertently and rather amusingly in this tense situation. His mother had designed for him two miniature officer's uniforms, one for the French infantry and one for the Roman cavalry. Prophetic of his later involvement with the Risorgimento and the Roman republic, the second of these was his favorite—probably because it was richly embroidered—and he often wore it when out walking with his tutor. On one of these occasions, the commander of the French garrison in Rome observed the young cavalryman and thought it too serious a matter to ignore. He therefore "felt it his duty" to inform the French minister at Milan that the pope was preparing means of defense and that Senator Lucien, in order to give the appearance of greater importance to His Holiness's troops, had made his son an honorary colonel of cavalry. The French authorities demanded an explanation.[28]

Figure 4. *Charles-Lucien Bonaparte as a Child* by J. B. Wicar. Pencil drawing. Courtesy of the Museo Napoleonico, Rome.

Napoleon's feud with the pope culminated in his seizing the pontiff's lands, annexing them to the French empire, and in July 1809 removing Pius himself to France to live in exile. The emperor sent one of his generals to take command of Rome. With the Eternal City under the jurisdiction of France, and an order in hand from Napoleon to leave Rome because he did not want his recalcitrant brother in any part of his empire (the passport for Alexandrine was issued insultingly in the name of Jouberthou), Lucien moved his family to Canino, since Tuscany was then without a government and not under Napoleon's jurisdiction. He attempted to lead a normal life, continuing his excavations and writing his poem, but the close surveillance of the French authorities became intolerable and he made plans to emigrate to the United

Figure 5. *Lucien Bonaparte and His Family: Alexandrine, Charles, Letizia, and Jeanne* by J. B. Wicar. Pencil drawing. Courtesy of the Museo Napoleonico, Rome.

States. In frustration and anger he wrote Napoleon: "I am aware that your fury is capable of making you commit fratricide."[29]

After obtaining passports from the minister of police—Napoleon must have known of his brother's request but did nothing to stop him—Lucien asked Joachim Murat, king of Naples and his sister Caroline's husband, to charter an American ship. Murat, at odds with Napoleon for reasons of his own, released the U.S. merchantman *Hercules*, held at Naples for violating the continental blockade. The ship sailed for Civitavecchia to pick up its prominent passengers.

Many of Lucien's great art works were left with his banker in Rome, but a quantity of others, including family portraits and a bust of the pope, were loaded onto the ship. On 7 August 1810, he and his retinue of forty-six set sail aboard the *Hercules*. The party included his wife and their four children, Charles, then seven, Letizia, Jeanne, and Paul; the children's half-sisters Charlotte, Christine, and Anna; Count Charles de Châtillon, a penniless artist and Lucien's intimate friend, who had followed him to Rome; a chaplain, the Capuchin Padre Maurizio da Brescia (Fortunato Antonio Malvestiti); a French doctor, Henri de France; Lucien's nephew-by-marriage André Boyer; a secretary with his wife and son; the children's tutor; and thirty servants.

The captain of the *Hercules* weighed anchor in spite of contrary winds. But, as he may have suspected and feared before leaving, a tremendous storm blew up shortly after the ship lost sight of land. A frightening pitching and swaying ensued, with the fierce winds showing no signs of abating. Since his entire family was seasick, Lucien reluctantly agreed with the captain to put in at the port of Cagliari, Sardinia; reluctantly because the island was under English jurisdiction. However, because of the circumstances—their flight from Napoleon—they were bound to find leniency. Count Châtillon went ashore to request permission of the Sardinian minister to land the party. He also delivered a letter from the pope recommending Lucien to the protection of any sovereign on whose territory he found himself. Had such a letter recommended anyone else, the minister might have agreed to protect him, but Napoleon's brother? He referred the matter to the British envoy, who lost no time in placing the ship's passengers under arrest—so much for their idea of leniency.

After two weeks, a tedious, seemingly interminable interlude passed by being shunted back and forth between the lazaretto—the quarantine station required of all foreign vessels—and the ship, Lucien persuaded his captain to leave secretly. Scarcely a mile outside the harbor, however, two English frigates awaited them, having witnessed their preparations for departure. Captain Barry of HMS *Pomona* fired a warning shot and commanded the *Hercules* to lay to. Since there was no response, he launched his tender and approached the American ship. The enraged captain of the *Hercules* whipped out his own pistol and would have shot Barry, had not Lucien knocked the gun from his hand. The Englishman placed the entire party under arrest and forced the American ship to sail for Malta to await the fate befitting a captured Bonaparte.

Before leaving Cagliari, Lucien had entrusted Charles with a bag of large pearls for safekeeping, believing that should the family be captured the authorities would not think to search a child. He had found these treasures (so he said) sewn up in the lining of a Goya painting he had acquired in Spain. Once underway to Malta, he asked Charles for the precious package, but the little boy had no idea where it was.[30] Coincidentally, this incident would be the first of many misunderstandings and disputes over money between father and son in the future.

On 24 August Lucien disembarked his wife and children on Malta, the mid-Mediterranean island that Napoleon, en route to Egypt eleven years earlier, had bombarded and captured, only to lose it again to the British. An American on Malta wrote to a countryman at Cadiz: "Last night arrived here the American ship Hercules detained by Hill, Frigate Pomona, with *Lucien Bonaparte & family* on board, 15 days from Rome & 3 from Cagliari—the captain was to receive $10,000 to carry him to America—on being boarded Lucien formally surrendered himself."[31]

After three days' quarantine, the prisoners were taken to the forbidding Fort Ricasoli and consigned to rooms almost unfurnished and without other essentials. These had to be purchased by an outraged Lucien, who protested heatedly to the civil commissioner, Lt. General Hildebrand Oakes. Oakes replied coolly that the senator was being treated in conformity with his status as a prisoner of war. Word eventually arrived from London, however, that Napoleon's brother and his family were to have the best possible accommodations, so they were transferred to the palace of San Anton (formerly the country seat of the Grand Master of the Knights of St. John, now the official residence of the president of Malta). A detachment of infantry was placed on guard.[32] The entire experience must have been thrilling to a child who possessed the courage and imagination Charles would reveal in later life.

Three months passed during which frantic letters crossed between Malta and Downing Street. The decision, as expected, was that Lucien and his family were refused permission to proceed to the United States and instead were to board a man-of-war headed for England. HMS *President* was adapted to receive the large party and armed to repel a French attack.

Because the ship had to avoid the coast of France, the journey lasted nearly a month. The *President* was continually battered by heavy winter gales, and, as if this were not enough, on the evening of its arrival in Plymouth the wind was so violent it caused the hapless vessel to drag its anchors. The following day,

Figure 6. *Lucien Bonaparte with Charles-Lucien and other members of his ménage aboard the English frigate "The President"* by Charles de Châtillon, 11 December 1810. Pencil drawing. Charles-Lucien, far right, watches his father play backgammon with the ship's captain while his sisters and others look on. Courtesy of the Museo Napoleonico, Rome.

when the ill and exhausted group of distinguished refugees came on deck to see England for the first time, they were amazed and somewhat disconcerted that so many people were watching from the dock. On going ashore, the cheering throng crowded about and insisted on accompanying them to the King's Arms, where they were to stay for a few days. Much to the Bonapartes' surprise, the townspeople regarded Lucien as a hero for defying Napoleon, their country's great enemy. So intense was the hatred of the English for the French emperor that damning and belittling cartoons of him appeared almost daily in the newspapers and on posters. There would soon be a cartoon entitled "Universal Murderer of Domestic Happiness, or the Fraternal Tyrant." It showed a messenger from Napoleon presenting Lucien (surrounded by his terrified wife and children) with an ultimatum: "Kick your wife and children out of doors, I shall marry you to a Princess and make you King of Rome. Comply immediately or dread the vengeance of your Brother Napoleon." Lucien says: "He seems determined to make me a villain! But I am determined there shall be one honest man in the family, and will fly to that Country where character is respected." Behind him, one of the girls speaks up, "Then let's go to England Father for that is the only place where Honor and Virtue find partizans."[33]

At the comfortable English inn, Lucien received messages of welcome and hospitality from many distinguished people, including Lord Powis, who offered to lease him at a nominal fee his country seat in Shropshire, Dinham House, near Ludlow.[34] The English papers called the arrival of Napoleon's brother "a triumph" for England, for it proved the emperor was such a tyrant his own family had to flee from him.[35] True to this characterization, when Napoleon learned that Lucien had settled in England he cut off any revenues his brother was still receiving from France, including his income from Poppelsdorf in Belgium and his salary as a senator, and forbade him, his wife, and his children to enter French territory. Along with the rest of the family, Charles Bonaparte at the age of seven was an outlaw.

After six months at Dinham House, Lucien purchased the rambling estate of Thorngrove in Worcestershire, where he arranged his art treasures: pictures, statues, bronzes, archaeological artifacts from his excavations at Canino and Frascati, cabinets of gems, and portfolios of engravings. With financial help sent secretly from his mother—he was always considered her favorite—he and his family were soon leading a life of comparative luxury and leisure. He continued to write *Charlemagne* (in French), which Lord Byron saw and admired. Monsieur Châtillon made a series of illustrations for the work, and the chaplain translated it into Italian.[36] After meeting and corresponding with the astronomer John Herschel, Lucien became so interested in studying the stars that he mounted a telescope in a small observatory at Thorngrove. In his memoirs, he said that because of all the intellectual stimulus he found in England his children were better off growing up there, even as prisoners of war, than in France under their uncle's regime.

Certainly Charles did not suffer from his so-called imprisonment. He later remembered that the men in whose custody the family was placed were always polite and kind. He cited for special praise the last custodian, a Colonel Sighton, who gave him an English copy of Linnaeus's *Systema vegetabilum*. It was through this book that he first discovered his love of natural history.[37] In his enthusiasm for the subject, he also read works of the naturalists Buffon, Valmoux, and Barnave. He trained birds, collected butterflies and mounted them in boxes, hunted snakes and birds, which he skinned and preserved, and cultivated a vegetable garden. Absorbed also in the study of fish, he made lists of their vernacular names (supplied by the family cook) and kept a small collection in a garden pond. Monsieur Châtillon drew detailed pictures to document his specimens, and when a fish died Charles and his artist-teacher held short funerals and sang hymns in French. Although Lucien did not look with favor on his son's enthusiasm for natural history because he did not regard it as intellectual, Charles was strongly encouraged by the family doctor, Henri de France, who gave him the excellent advice, to follow his heart.[38] Dr. de France would die in Viterbo in 1820, when Charles was seventeen, but Charles remembered him forever as a model for the right way to live. He willed Charles his repeating watch, which the young man treasured and kept for the rest of his life.

Charles had a tutor, Father Charpentier, but the most important influence on the boy during this period was Padre Maurizio, the family's chaplain and music teacher. This learned man took an interest in every topic Charles questioned him about and was especially his companion in the study of natural history. In later years, Padre Maurizio met the writer Stendhal at Canino and so impressed him that he used him as a model for the noble character Don Blanes in *The Charterhouse of Parma*.[39]

Perhaps the influence of Dr. de France and Padre Maurizio caused Charles to develop certain sensibilities and ideals of right behavior he could never have gotten from his parents, who had grown up under quite different circumstances than his. They had known revolution, tremendous social upheaval, and poverty in youth, been obliged to survive as best they could, and clawed their way to prominence through craft and cunning. The finer character traits were not in their makeup, but they were sharply intelligent and had inquiring minds and unlimited energy. But Charles would later reflect that his most important teacher and "master" was always his own will.[40]

In addition to astronomy and poetry, politics was at all times a serious concern of the household in which he grew up. When news arrived of

Figure 7. *Père Maurizio, Dr. de France, and Charles-Lucien Bonaparte* by J. B. Wicar. Pencil drawing. Collection of Luigi Primoli and Giuseppe Primoli. Courtesy of the Museo Napoleonico, Rome.

Figure 8. *Père Maurizio da Brescia* (1778–1865) by J. B. Wicar. Pencil drawing. Collection of Luigi Primoli and Giuseppe Primoli. Courtesy of the Museo Napoleonico, Rome.

Napoleon's disastrous defeat in Russia in 1812, his father contacted the English government in an attempt to persuade them to back his brother Joseph as emperor of France should Napoleon be deposed. But Parliament regarded all Bonapartes as parvenus and was not interested.

Then, in the spring of 1814, Napoleon was defeated by the allied powers of England, Prussia, and Russia, forced to abdicate, and sent in exile to Elba. Lucien and his family were free to return to Italy. Their exile and "imprisonment" had been far from unpleasant, but after four years of virtual house arrest the prospect of returning to Rome was joyful; they left as soon as possible. Since France was forbidden territory, they landed at Ostend and traveled by easy stages through Belgium and Switzerland to Italy.[41]

A year later, during the hundred days between Napoleon's escape from Elba and the Battle of Waterloo, Lucien, in the manner of a true Corsican clansman, returned to Paris to close ranks with his beleaguered brother. He acted as the unofficial envoy of Pius VII, who had given him the papal title prince of Canino on his return to Rome in 1814, for his loyalty to the papacy and to the Catholic Church. Lucien had seen Napoleon brought down by the great powers of Europe and believed that, so humbled, he would now be a true republican leader; if so, Lucien was eager to offer assistance.

On his arrival in the French capital, Lucien was at once reconciled to Napoleon, as he had anticipated. He was decorated with the Legion of Honor, reinstated as a senator, and assigned the Palais Royal as his residence. Charles Bonaparte would never live at that splendid palace, however, since the Battle of Waterloo, where Napoleon's army was finally crushed by the allies, was only two months away. After the defeat it was to Lucien, as his advisor and scribe, that Napoleon dictated his letter of abdication. Shortly thereafter, as a prisoner of the British, the fallen emperor was taken to the remote island of St. Helena for the rest of his life. Lucien attempted to rejoin his family in Italy but was arrested en route and detained for some months in Milan.

In the summer of 1815, while her husband was still in custody, Alexandrine assembled her growing family in Rome for a group portrait by the French artist Jean-Auguste-Dominique Ingres. The portrait, one of the most exquisite drawings of the nineteenth century, includes nine individual studies. Alexandrine, pregnant with her son Pierre, is seated in the midst of her children and stepchildren. Behind her, her stepdaughter Charlotte plays the harpsichord, while Letizia rests her arms on the back of Charlotte's chair. Charlotte's sister Christine stands beside her. Charles, in the center of the picture, leans against his mother, with a protective arm draped around her. Little Louis-Lucien, later to become a learned philologist, stands at her knee pointing to something in a book, while Paul sits at her feet with his toy Punchinello. Jeanne sits on a stool with a basket of flowers in her lap, while behind her, holding a lyre, is Anna Jouberthou, Alexandrine's daughter by her first husband. Lucien, not being present, is represented by a marble bust in the background, as is his mother, designated "Madame Mère" by Napoleon, on the right side of the picture. The mood of the drawing is deceivingly tranquil for a family who had passed through such turbulence and for whom so much more still lay ahead.

With the Bourbon monarchy reestablished in France, the Bonapartes were once more forbidden to enter the country. This was not of great importance to Charles's family, however, since the prince of Canino, being a favorite of the pope, was comfortably, even luxuriously, resettled in Rome. He and Alexandrine resumed their lives, rich in social and intellectual pursuits, while Charles, a precocious twelve-year-old, pursued his favorite subject and fast became a knowledgeable naturalist. In his memoirs, Lucien described his son as

Figure 9. *Portrait of the Family of Lucien Bonaparte* by Jean-Auguste-Dominique Ingres, 1815. Graphite on white wove paper. Bequest of Grenville L. Winthrop, the Harvard University Art Museums.

"a very interesting child, capable of great application to his studies, and remarkably intelligent."[42] By his teenage years Charles was bilingual in French, the language spoken within the family, and Italian, and could read and communicate in English. He could also read and write Latin. In Rome he had an Irish tutor who tried to interest him in literature, but without success. It was botany, with Dr. Sebastiani, then with Father Leandro Ciuffa and with Father Eugenio di Homburg, a neighbor in Frascati, that captured his imagination. Under their direction, he drew up a *Sistema plantario* (a kind of chart) showing how plants made fruits. Insects were also of particular interest to him, especially leaf and tortoise beetles and scarabs.[43]

Charles successively studied plants, insects, animals, and birds.[44] This last subject became his passion, and he pored over the *Manuel d'ornithologie* by the great Dutch ornithologist Coenraad Jacob Temminck. In his late teens he decided to write his own book on birds, an *Ornitologia Romana* (Roman Ornithology). Unable to identify one bird he had shot in the Roman Campagna, he sent it to Professor Temminck in Leiden. The species, the moustached warbler, was new to science. Temminck, with credit given to the "jeune prince de Canino," would include it in his *Planches coloriées* of 1823 as *Sylvia [Acrocephalus] melanopogon* (plate 244).[45]

In early November 1817, bandits viciously assaulted the Bonapartes' summer home, the Villa Rufinella at Frascati and took Count Châtillon and a visiting prelate hostage. They were later freed, but the incident persuaded Lucien to move his family to Rome more or less permanently, and he sold the villa in 1820.[46] In the Eternal City Charles applied himself to his studies with fervor, often reading quietly in the ancient Church of Aracoeli on the Capitoline Hill. To his dismay, however, his father enrolled him in the Collegio Clementino, a boarding school where he was miserable, in spite of the opportunity it gave him to have long talks with a priest he described as a "genius in science." Though Charles was first in his class, Lucien thought his son was wasting his time with all his attention drawn to natural history, and had him tutored at home in history and geography. Studying the globe became one of his passions, for he was keenly interested in the distribution of animals, especially birds. His knowledge of geography would be a great aid in his study of natural science.[47]

Partly for economy, but according to Charles more for a change of scene, his father moved the family yet again, to rural Canino. It was not a move calculated to please his son, for Charles was decidedly bored at the remote location where he was unable to pursue his intellectual interests with learned tutors. He later said that two of the best years of his life were wasted in the idleness of country activities: horseback riding, hunting, and shooting. Nevertheless, he continued to study botany and made a small zoological museum.[48]

Figure 10. *Lucien Bonaparte and His Family at the Villa Rufinella* by Charles de Châtillon, 1815. Sepia drawing. Courtesy of the Museo Napoleonico, Rome.

Several years later, Charles's life changed dramatically from that of a young man at loose ends to that of a mature individual who set out with courage to pursue his own dreams. After seemingly endless negotiations between Lucien and his oldest brother over financial arrangements, on 29 June 1822, in Brussels, Charles married his cousin, his Uncle Joseph's daughter, Zenaide-Letitia-Julie Bonaparte.[49] According to their agreement, Joseph sent Lucien the rather excessive sum of 730,000 francs—Lucien's villa in Rome had cost only 150,000—that he had demanded as Zenaide's dowry.[50] Such a marriage had been in Joseph's mind for a long time; he had suggested it to his wife when Zenaide was only five. The idea was to carry on the Napoleonic succession (a return to power was always anticipated) by marrying his two daughters to sons of two of his brothers.[51] Shortly before he died on St. Helena a year earlier, Napoleon had said to General Bertrand that, "only Roman princes were worthy of them."[52] Charles qualified on both counts, since he was Roman and a prince.

Two years older than her cousin, Zenaide had been even more closely involved with the great events surrounding their common uncle. At twelve she had played a part in Napoleon's plan to force the abdication of her father—

Figure 11. *Julie Clary Bonaparte, Queen of Spain, and her daughter Zenaide, the Future Princess of Canino* by Robert Lefèvre, 1805. Oil. Musée National du Château de Versailles et Trianon.

whom he had made king of Spain—and to restore Ferdinand VII to the throne. Joseph was determined not to give up his Spanish kingship (he had been a disaster as king because the Spanish people were so opposed to a Frenchman as their sovereign), but without waiting for him to comply Napoleon signed the Treaty of Valençay, which recognized Ferdinand as king of Spain. He also agreed to arrange a marriage for Ferdinand with Zenaide. In return Ferdinand was to use his influence to secure peace between Spain, Great Britain, and France. But when Joseph learned of this plan he would have none of it.[53]

Joseph was unable to be at his daughter's wedding to Charles because he had been living in America since his escape from France in 1815. His wife, Julie Clary Bonaparte, professing ill health as a reason for not crossing the Atlantic to join her husband, had found asylum for herself and her two daughters first in Frankfurt, then in Brussels. It was there that she and her daughters met the great French painter Jacques-Louis David, Napoleon's former court painter, living in self-imposed exile.

Since Charles and Zenaide had never met, in December 1821 Julie sent a painting of Zenaide to Rome. It was a double portrait by David, commissioned during the winter of 1821, depicting Zenaide and her sister Charlotte.[54] The anxious prospective bridegroom wrote his aunt that he awaited it with impatience.[55] From Brussels, Zenaide, having just received news that her father had approved the marriage agreement, enclosed a letter with the portrait saying how much she looked forward to embracing her aunt and uncle (never having met either one). Modestly, she asked them to assure Charles of her "affectionate feelings" and of her desire to make his acquaintance.[56]

Charles would see in David's painting a confident, intelligent, determined-looking young woman who somewhat resembled himself. With her dark, curly hair, large brown eyes, straight nose, and prominent lower lip she was clearly a Bonaparte. In the picture Zenaide, nicely rounded and full-bosomed, sits erect, staring out past the viewer. Charlotte is less self-assured: she peeks out from behind her older sister, a reticent expression on her plain but sensitive and interesting face. Both girls are petite and exquisitely dressed. In her left hand Zenaide holds a letter obviously from their father, since "Philadelphie" is legible in the upper right-hand corner. Was this detail a clever hint to Charles and his father of Zenaide's plan to visit Joseph in America? Although the painting was executed in the early months of 1821, the idea of such a visit may have been around much longer. Charlotte had, in fact, been there since December 1821.

Since they were not allowed to enter France, Charles and Lucien traveled to Brussels for the wedding by way of Austria and Germany. After a short visit, the young couple were married with surprisingly little fanfare, perhaps because

Figure 12. *Charles-Lucien Bonaparte as a Young Man* by Charles de Châtillon. Pencil drawing. Courtesy of the Museo Napoleonico, Rome.

Julie was outraged at the unreasonable size of the dowry, which had strained her resources as well as those of her husband.[57] After the ceremony, Lucien returned to Italy alone, while the bride and groom took their time traveling back, so that Charles could visit various naturalists along the way. Before leaving Brussels, Professor Pierre-Augustin-Joseph Drapiez told the budding scientist the best books to buy and what museums to visit. In Frankfurt Charles visited the natural history museum, and later, in Munich and Milan, he met many prominent naturalists. After a delightful interlude in Venice, the newlyweds stopped for a three-day visit in Bologna to see Charles's family at the Villa Croce del Biacco, the elegant house Lucien had recently bought. Their reception was surprisingly cool. Perplexed, they shortly departed. Zenaide had never visited the Eternal City and was excited at the prospect of seeing it and their common grandmother, Madame Mère, even though this would also mean an encounter with their great-uncle Cardinal Fesch, invariably described by Charles as his "ever implacable enemy [*sempre implacabile nemico*]."[58]

Charles and Zenaide spent the winter at Lucien's Roman palace in the Via Bocca di Leone, where Charles de Châtillon sketched the happy couple in pencil. Zenaide sits at her harp with Charles standing behind her. In his left hand he holds a drawing of a butterfly, an allusion to his interest in science. Charles took great delight in showing his bride the impressive ruins and monuments of the Eternal City: the Colosseum, the Roman forum, and the ancient Church of Aracoeli on the Capitoline Hill that he had frequented as a boy. But most important, he prepared for a trip to America to visit Zenaide's father.

Throughout this time in Rome, as the young couple were enjoying each other and prospering in their arranged marriage, a curious dark cloud of parental disapproval hung over them. Charles was shaken when he received an angry letter from his father in early October, full of accusations, particularly against Zenaide.[59] It seems that Lucien held her responsible for all Charles's most recent actions (delaying his return to the family), attitudes (calling himself "prince"), and decisions (to leave Italy and stay with Joseph in America), which certainly accounted for the couple's cold reception in Bologna. The young man at once leaped to his wife's defense, saying he would "combat the prejudice" his father had demonstrated "against the best of wives and daughters."[60] He asked that he alone be blamed because his bride was innocent, having been guided by his own desires and intentions. Also, as a typically obedient son of the period, who had been totally under the sway of a dominant, demanding father, he asked how he could pursue a career "diametrically opposed" to his father's wishes. Charles was probably referring to his decision to study natural history—which his father considered a waste of time—and to expand his knowledge of birds by visiting his father-in-law in North America for an extended time. Lucien undoubtedly blamed Zenaide for this idea of putting thousands of miles between him and Charles—anathema to a father who had always kept such strict tabs on his eldest son.

Lucien was angry with Charles for a number of other reasons as well. Why had it taken him and Zenaide so long to reach Rome after their marriage? In Charles's defense, one can speculate that it must have been blissful for this young man, brought up by the most authoritarian of fathers, to have been free at last, at the age of nineteen, for a few months of unsupervised travel, sight-seeing, and visiting. From what can be surmised from existing documents, he was probably a virgin until his marriage and was thrilled with his pretty young wife, who returned his enthusiastic affection. "I would be lying," his letter continues, "if I said this freedom you promised me and which you can be sure I would not abuse, knowing my character—has not caused me one of the great pleasures of my life. It pleases me to think that you have rendered justice to my character and to my good sense, perhaps more walled-up than other young people." This freedom had flattered his self-esteem and, far from abusing it, he promised to "make a great effort to be even more dutiful than before."

However, he complains bitterly at the cold reception Zenaide had received at Bologna. In Brussels they had left an adoring mother, who was sick and alone, in order "to fly to the arms of his family." But, though a young bride who comes into a new household for the first time is ordinarily celebrated (*fêtée*) and each member hastens to surround her with "carpets of flowers," his wife had found only tears of distress at their treatment of her. "Ah, my dear Papa," Charles says, "you know I have always been a submissive son, and you have always been for me the best of fathers, why save me all your anger when I most need your love, since I must share it with the best part of myself?" He continues more passionately, with an obvious reference to Napoleon: "Why, if you wish to persecute me, did you defend me from the ambitious tiger who over-shadowed my childhood? Why did you not leave me to be suffocated by his hirelings? If my wife was to be a victim, why did I marry her? Why choose my poor Zenaide for a victim? Does one choose the sweet dove for a sacrifice of expiation?" He asks his father to excuse his despair, which would indeed be great without the consoling knowledge that nothing can separate him from his Zenaide. One sees in this letter the same passion Lucien had exhibited in his letter to Cardinal Fesch about his own marriage to Charles's mother.

After all, Charles says, his father has given him such an example of conjugal protection that he never would have believed he needed to protect his own wife from her father-in-law, especially since Charles had received Zenaide from Lucien's hands, as it were. "What a portrait you make of my Zenaide," he exclaims, adding that there is only one possible explanation: "You do not know her!" In Bologna, his father had taken it as a "crime" that Zenaide did not kiss her mother-in-law's hand. But think, she never kisses her own mother's hand! Of course, both the young couple knew she would have to perform this obeisance to Madame Mère when they visited her, and Zenaide did so. But Charles never thought his mother worried about such things. "Leave us free, my dear Papa," he pleads, "and enjoy our freedom and *voluntary* submission and dependence."

In a statement guaranteed to arouse Lucien's ire, Charles says that his "excellent uncle" and aunt (Joseph and Julie) have wanted them to escape their "masters [*maîtres*]." His aunt had told him he would be less free living with his mother than with her and he had been angry with her for saying that, but now he repents those feelings and sees that Julie lives only for their happiness. How chagrined Joseph would be if he knew how his daughter was suffering. "Would the ocean be a barrier for him?" The most beautiful time of their lives has been poisoned, and why? Are their crimes so enormous? "You ask me my decisions, it is up to you, my dear Papa, to state them. You know better than I do what will make us happy, and you have proved it by emancipating us of your own free will." He asks his father to believe in his good intentions, and to realize that, after contracting a marriage under all the terms Lucien desired (the enormous dowry), he, Charles, now feels as unhappy as if he were a fugitive from his home who had made a choice unworthy of both him and his father.

Lucien was particularly furious at his son's insistence on calling himself and his bride the prince and princess of Musignano. "You have no right to titles that I forbid you to take," he writes. The problem concerned the fact that Zenaide was a princess in her own right, since her father had been king of Spain, and Charles insisted he would not demote her by calling himself a count and her a countess. He did not care for honors, he told his father, and it was not because of inferiority (because she had a title) that he used the title prince, since he did not think that feeling of rivalry could exist between husband and wife, above all when they were from the same family. It was, rather, to appear equal before others that he allowed himself to be called prince. To another angry letter from his father, he replied with dignity: "The respect I have for you hinders me from responding to the accusations of cowardice you lavish on me."[61]

Lucien fired back that Charles could not take his wife's title; she could only take his. If this injures his wife's happiness, it could only mean "you and she are mad with vanity." "I forbid you to allow your wife to call herself princess, and put an end to these stupid pretensions. I tell you for the last time to take the title of Count and Countess of Musignano—if you persist in disobeying I tell you in return I will no longer consider you as my son." Charles's right to the future title of prince depends on his will alone to allow it. "Open the eyes of your wife," he says, revealing the real object of his resentment. In a postscript, he adds that he does not want to receive any more letters because he refuses to be outraged by "a disobedient child." "Put your house in order [*Fixe votre sort*]," Lucien commands.[62]

Charles's pursuit of natural science was an ongoing point of contention between him and his father—just as exasperating as the question of titles, if not more so. It was perhaps to follow his star, as Lucien had once followed his by moving to Rome, that Charles decided to leave for the United States, where the young couple could live in relative peace with Zenaide's father on his estate, Point Breeze. Joseph had repeatedly asked them to come, and her sister Charlotte was there.

With conviction, moral courage, and that mastery of his own will he had already shown as a child, Charles wrote to his father in early February 1823 to announce the move. "Nothing, not contrary winds nor *physical* force can prevent me from being at Point Breeze toward the end of May, to pass some time, as I have given my word to my uncle and to my aunt before and after my marriage, a thing I was right in doing after your positive consent."[63] Aside from the point of honor involved in keeping his word and his need to put some distance between himself and Lucien, Charles undoubtedly relished the prospect of studying firsthand the rich flora and fauna of the New World, much of it still unknown to European science. Professor Drapiez had confirmed his decision in an encouraging letter written from Brussels at the end of the month. "Continue, Prince, to follow the beautiful career that you have begun . . . and pursue natural history in every particular . . . because in the present state of growth of the sciences it is possible to be immensely useful."[64]

In spite of his father's opposition, Charles and Zenaide left Rome in May 1823. On their way north, they stopped off in Bologna to bid his family goodbye, but, much to Charles's dismay, Lucien was not there to give his blessing for the long voyage that lay ahead. Charles left a note saying that he had at last taken the title of "Count of Musignano," and to prove that he did so not merely to travel incognito, or temporarily to placate his father, he had taken out his passport under that name.[65] He and Zenaide then traveled to Brussels to bid her mother farewell and in the summer sailed from Antwerp aboard the American ship *Falcon*. Charles had only recently turned twenty.

2

THE

NEW WORLD

"O, heureuse pays qui possède ce qui la
pauvre Italie est si loin de posséder

Charles Bonaparte to Alexandrine Bonaparte,
Point Breeze near Philadelphia, 1 November 1823

IT WAS CONSIDERED NEWSWORTHY when Napoleon's nephew Charles-Lucien Bonaparte and his wife Zenaide, with "their suite of 8 persons," arrived in New York from Antwerp on Tuesday, 8 September 1823, aboard the American ship *Falcon*, and took lodgings at the City Hotel.[1] Charlotte, who went to New York with her father to meet the ship, had written her mother in Europe that according to the papers the *Falcon* had left Plymouth, England on 9 July and she feared that the exceedingly long journey would be a repetition of her own unpleasant crossing.[2] That Zenaide was pregnant would make it so much worse. "It was frightful," Bonaparte wrote to Temminck in Holland, "as we took 75 days from Antwerp to New York. We were in Plymouth for 11 days but had 51 days of *tribulations* from Plymouth to New York—we had altogether 3 or 4 tempests. It did not bother me but my wife suffered constantly so you can judge my sad situation aboard the ship."[3]

To make matters worse, the American captain and the ship's English doctor, John Stokoe—hired by Joseph to accompany Zenaide because she was pregnant—fought continually, even challenging each other to a duel when they landed. Bonaparte had little sympathy with the "very coarse" captain and quite a lot with the "excellent" English surgeon, who had been assigned by the British to treat Napoleon during his final illness. Dr. Stokoe had shown his patient such kindness that he was court-marshaled by the British and dismissed from service.[4]

In spite of all the unpleasantness aboard ship, Bonaparte had been fully occupied. He had pursued his chosen profession with the zeal that would only increase with the years, catching and studying fish, turtles, and birds. Four species of petrels he would later describe scientifically in an American journal. Leach's Storm Petrels (*Oceanodroma leucorhoa*), a few of which he brought down near the Banks of Newfoundland, he found less common as the ship approached the American coast. He thought the bird must be new to science, since Professor Temminck had written that it was only found on St. Kilda, the remote island off the western coast of Scotland's Outer Hebrides, while Charles himself had observed it over much of the ocean.

Still another petrel, differing only in a yellow spot on the membrane of its feet, was clearly common on the coast of North America and apparently unknown to Temminck. Bonaparte would later name it Wilson's Storm Petrel (*Oceanites oceanicus*) after the man who, although deceased, would become his American mentor. Alexander Wilson was the Scottish poet/naturalist who came to live near Philadelphia in the late eighteenth century and wrote and illustrated the first systematic study of American birds. In his book Wilson described the petrels as "solitary wanderers of the deep skimming along the surface of the wild and wasterful ocean; flitting past the vessel like swallows, or following in her wake, gleaning their scanty pittance of food from the rough and whirling surges."[5] According to the eminent French naturalist, the Comte de Buffon (cited by Wilson), the bird's peculiar ability to stand and even to run on the water's surface had suggested the name of "petrel" to him, after the apostle Peter, who was said to have walked on water, in Matthew 14: 28–29.

Because petrels were known to appear in greater numbers before a storm, Wilson said that for years they had been blamed by the superstitious for violent weather. They were called witches, or "Mother Carey's chickens," perhaps after some particular sorceress. "It is the business of the naturalist and the glory of philosophy," he wrote, "to examine into the reality of these things, to dissipate the clouds of error and superstition wherever they begin to darken and bewilder the human understanding, and to illustrate nature with the radiance of truth."[6] Written sometime between 1810 and 1813 (the year of Wilson's death), only some ten or twelve years before Charles

Figure 13. *Manor House of Joseph Bonaparte near Bordentown* by Karl Bodmer. Joslyn Art Museum, Omaha, Nebraska; gift of Enron Art Foundation.

Bonaparte's arrival in America, the passage illustrates the primitive state of ornithology at the time Bonaparte began his career.

After spending several days in the city so Zenaide could regain her strength, the family proceeded to Bordentown, New Jersey. They traveled by stagecoach to Trenton, then across the Delaware River by ferry to Point Breeze, the mansion Joseph had built on a high bluff overlooking the Delaware, about twenty-five miles north of Philadelphia. The location had been chosen at the advice of Napoleon, who once told him that should he ever have to flee to America he should reside somewhere between the seaports of Philadelphia and New York, so that news from abroad could easily reach him.[7] The house Joseph originally built at Point Breeze had burned to the ground in 1820. During the fire the local villagers of Bordentown had rescued the contents, including vast treasures of antique furniture, paintings, rugs, silver, and jewelry. The "Count of Survilliers"—as Joseph called himself in America, in an attempt to be incognito—unused to the "barn-raising" mentality of the young republic, had been astonished and pleased to learn that not a single item had been stolen and had placed a grateful letter to that effect in the local paper. To his chagrin, his benefactors were deeply offended that he should have been surprised at their honesty.

Joseph then built on the same site a large white three-story house, with a central block and two perpendicular wings, somewhat resembling the château in Prangins, Switzerland, that Joseph had bought after Napoleon's exile to Elba. It was at this splendid new residence that Charles and Zenaide arrived in 1823. The surrounding grounds were magnificent and the interior as elegant as that of Lucien's villa in Rome. Large heavily carved folding doors opened onto a grand hall and staircase. In the central salon, on walls hung with blue merino, were paintings by François Gérard of Napoleon, of Joseph as king of Spain, and of Julie and the children, along with Vernet seascapes and Neapolitan landscapes by Denis. Heavy chandeliers, tapestries, and gold- and silver-fringed draperies hung in the principal rooms, and intricately sculpted marble mantels graced the fireplaces. Liveried servants lent an air of foreign elegance on a scale unknown to most Americans.[8] A fine lawn stretched out to a marble balustrade overlooking the Delaware River. Centered on the balustrade, a life-size Apollo-like statue in white marble stood on a tall pedestal, its back to the house, and gazed out at the river, giving the scene a sense of serenity. In spring there were garden parties, where the inevitable menu of early Bordentown and Philadelphia—strawberries and shad—was varied by fancy concoctions dreamed up by Joseph's chef.[9]

Reuben Haines, a wealthy young gentleman farmer whom Charles would meet later at the Academy of Natural Sciences, described in a letter to a cousin the wonder of his visit to the estate in the summer of 1825:

I partook of royal fare served on solid silver and attended by six waiters who supplied me with 9 courses of the most delicious viands, many of which I could not possibly tell what they were composed of; spending the intermediate time in Charles' private rooms looking over the Herbarium and Portfolios of the Princess, or riding with her and the Prince drawn by two *Elegant Horses* along the ever varying roads of the park amidst splendid Rhododendrons on the margin of the artificial lake on whose smooth surface gently glided the majestic European swans. Stopping to visit the Aviary enlivened by the most beautiful English Pheasants, passing by alcoves ornamented with statues and busts of Parian marble, our course enlivened by the footsteps of the tame deer and the flight of the Woodcock, and when alighting stopping to admire the graceful form of two splendid Etruscan vases of Porphyry 3 ft. high & 2 in diameter presented by the Queen of Sweden [Joseph's sister-in-law Désirée Clary Bernadotte] or ranging [?] through the different apartments of the mansion through a suite of rooms 15 ft. in [height] decorated with the finest productions of the pencils of Coregeo [sic]! Titian! Rubens! Vandyke! Vernet! Tenniers [sic] and Paul Potter and a library of the most splendid books I ever beheld.[10]

Another visitor described one of the principal reception rooms at Point Breeze where the family often gathered: "A door led out of the vestibule into the billiard room, in which the proprietor and his guests spent much of their time, richly furnished also with heavy mahogany chairs and sofas and many paintings, among which Joseph had hung in the most prominent place the picture, painted by David for the Emperor himself, of Napoleon crossing the Alps [one of three copies oredered by Napoleon]. There were also other canvases notably by Rubens and Vernet. The curtains were white bordered with green; with a carpet upon the floor of red and white."[11] It must have been in this room that, as Zenaide wrote to her mother, the family played dominoes or read every evening. Zenaide reported that after dinner Charles and the others soon gave up the game and fell asleep because they were tired from their activities of the day, which consisted mostly of riding and hunting on the seventeen-hundred-acre estate.[12]

Much of the land at Point Breeze had been fashioned into a park, laid out by Joseph, the ex-king of Spain, to resemble the grounds of the Escorial, Philip II's sixteenth-century palace. Philip's dictum to his architect had been "nobility without arrogance, majesty without ostentation."[13] Joseph seems to have adhered to this motto when planning his own estate. Twelve miles of carriage roads and bridle paths wound through groves of pines and oaks and over stone bridges gracefully arching across twisting streams and gullies. Rustic gazebos, bowers, and benches provided shelter from rain showers and places to sit and contemplate the surrounding beauty. Several knolls were crowned with statuary.

Across the lower end of a lagoon, Joseph built an embankment that dammed Crosswicks Creek, a tributary of the Delaware, thus forming a lake two hundred yards wide and nearly a mile long. Several islands, dotted with velvet grass, rare small trees, and shrubs, added interest to the picturesque scene, as did the European swans gliding serenely on the water's surface. A fleet of swan-shaped "pleasure-boats" was moored in a small cove.[14] In winter, the lake swarmed with local skaters to whom Joseph had his servants roll out on the ice oranges and tangerines—rare treats shipped from Florida and Spain. At all times, neighboring children were allowed to play hide and seek among the marble gods and goddesses on the estate and to use the iron deer, lions, and dogs in the gardens as hobby horses.[15] Joseph's nephew had the same generous spirit, as he would show throughout his life by filling his friends' and colleagues' requests for books and natural history specimens.

Near the lake Joseph had built a three-story guesthouse for his daughter and her husband that the family called the Maison du Lac (Lake House). John Watson, who visited Charles there several years later, wrote in his diary, "The Porter when we called there introduced us into a large & elegantly carpeted Parlour. The Floors richly carpeted, the Walls hung round with large & expensive paintings by the great masters of Europe. The largest was the Escape of Europa drawn in great spirit, but with little regard to female modesty."[16] Despite low ceilings and rather small windows, the charming white cottage with green lattice shutters was quite spacious. A long covered walkway faced with latticework connected it with the main house, and there was also an underground passage for communication in bad weather and for the coming and going of servants.[17] It was an idyllic setting, and Charles and Zenaide settled in for an indefinite visit.

Joseph may not have installed them in the Lake House strictly for their own privacy, however. From the beginning of 1823, the lovely and vivacious Emilie Lacoste, a French émigré, had been staying at Point Breeze with her husband, but soon after their arrival Joseph had sent Félix Lacoste to Santo Domingo on business for an extended period. In the spring of 1825 Emilie Lacoste gave birth to a baby boy, whom she named Félix-Joseph.[18] Although Joseph Bonaparte and his wife never ceased to be friends, they lived apart throughout most of their married life. Joseph had a series of mistresses over the

Figure 14. *Portrait of Joseph Bonaparte* by Charles Willson Peale. Oil. The Historical
Society of Pennsylvania.

years and had already had several in America. Once, when he was at dinner with
his friend Nicholas Biddle, another guest, the Portugese ambassador José
Francisco Correa da Serra, had noted that in the United States there was "much
happiness, but little pleasure." Biddle observed that Joseph had pointedly disagreed with the last part of the ambassador's statement.[19] A visitor to Point
Breeze in the mid-1830s described Joseph's "suite of sleeping apartments" as
hung with light blue satin trimmed with silver. Bed draperies and chair covers
were all in the same material. Each room contained a large mirror, with an espe-

cially fine one on the ceiling over the bed and another above the bath. Oil paintings of nude young women covered the walls.[20] It was not without reason that
the count of Survilliers, ex-king of Naples and Spain, was described as, "at heart
a *sardanapale*, a lover of palaces, a patron of art, an Assyrian voluptuary."[21]

The New World to which Charles Bonaparte came in the early fall of 1823
differed markedly from the Old World he had left. The democratic mode of life
was proudly proclaimed in the local newspapers. *Niles Weekly Register* in
Philadelphia announced in December 1822 that "Lucien Bonaparte [meaning
Charles] and his family, and Achille Murat, oldest son of the ex-king of Naples"
(Charles's cousin) had been granted permission to depart for the United States.
"If they are willing to *work* to get an honest living," the paper states, "we shall
be glad of their arrival—but we have consumers enough already."[22] Here would
be no catering to members of France's former imperial family.

Philadelphia, the city where Bonaparte would spend most of his time, was
a bustling seaport on the Delaware River, a hundred miles from the Atlantic
Ocean, with a population roughly the same as Rome, about 136,000 people.
According to the historian Edwin Wolf 2nd, "early in its history Philadelphia
had dreamed of becoming the Athens of America. In the early decades of the
nineteenth century it came close to that hope, mixed in good American fashion
with Quaker prudence, Calvinist respect for earned wealth, and Yankee ingenu-
ity."[23]

The city's geographical location between two rivers, the Schuylkill and the
Delaware, provided abundant waterpower for running mills and other manu-
factories. A series of canals linked the metropolis to the western suburbs and to
the interior parts of Pennsylvania, in order to bring in agricultural products as
well as iron ore and anthracite coal. It was also at that time the American center for book publishing, which would be of paramount importance for Charles
Bonaparte.

Culturally there was much to recommend the city. The American
Philosophical Society, founded by Benjamin Franklin, listed among its members the most prominent citizens in all fields of endeavor. Thomas Jefferson had
served simultaneously as president of the society and president of the United
States. The newly rebuilt Chestnut Street Theater, resplendent with gas lighting,
hosted plays produced primarily by English companies and frequent concerts
sponsored by the newly founded (1820) Musical Fund Society. The
Pennsylvania Academy of the Fine Arts displayed its collections of paintings,
engravings, and classical sculpture and held an annual exhibition for artists
modeled after that of the Royal Academy in London.[24] Zenaide's artistic sister
Charlotte had already shown her work there several times.

Entertaining instruction in natural history could be found at Charles Willson Peale's Philadelphia Museum, one of the city's biggest attractions. Inside the museum one could see the famous giant mastodon skeleton and stuffed animals of all kinds, and outside, a display of live creatures—often exotics, such as South American giant rats and the two grizzly bears brought back from the West by Zebulon Pike in 1808. The bears were only legendary when Charles Bonaparte arrived in Philadelphia, however, for they became too large and ferocious and Peale had been forced to shoot them in 1812. Peale's exhibits were housed in the long room on the second floor of the State House (now Independence Hall), the seat of the federal government until its move to Washington in 1800. The venerable Peale, eighty-three years old in 1823, was still ingenious in devising ways of attracting the public to the museum. Taking advantage of the general fascination with exotic species, both plant and animal, he placed a notice in the newspaper in July 1823, stating that "a very curious and singular plant known by the name of the Night Blooming Cereus (*Cactus grandiflorus*)" would be in flower in a few evenings and promising that the precise time would be advertised.[25] For the serious study and discussion of natural history, the Academy of Natural Sciences, founded in 1812, provided its members with a meeting place, a library, and collections of minerals, insects, shells, and other natural objects for examination and comparison. Weekly meetings allowed for discussions of all topics pertaining to natural science.

Philadelphia was indeed a cosmopolitan and lively city, where merchandise from all over the world was trumpeted daily in the local newspapers: Russian goods for sale by the wealthy importer Stephen Girard, Joseph Bonaparte's banker and friend; "a 100 lbs. of Opium, superior quality, and 3 cases of Naples sewing silks just received and for sale by Ralson & Lyman of Front Street"; "35 logs of Mahogany from the south side of San Domingo now landing at the upper side of Chestnut Street wharf"; Chinese tea, Havana "segars," and English cheese.[26] Young women advertised themselves as wet nurses, and occasionally young blacks of both sexes were put up for sale as indentured servants, with as much as sixteen years ahead of them in bondage. The papers were also filled with accounts of pirate attacks on shipping and spectacular sightings of sea serpents. From abroad came news that Lord Byron was setting out for Greece to assist in the fight for independence, a cause that also attracted Bonaparte's younger brother Paul. A short piece on Beethoven, "considered one of the most celebrated of living composers," noted that there was about his compositions something very new in the history of music: "the gigantic harmony which he wields, enables him to excite by sounds, a terror, hitherto unknown."[27]

As soon as Charles Bonaparte arrived in the United States, his enthusiasm for natural science took priority over all other activities. Nearly every day he collected plants, insects, and, especially, birds that were new to him. He was thrilled when given a rattlesnake ("Serpente a sonagli," as he described it in his memoirs, written in Italian), but was thoroughly chastened when he attempted to capture a skunk. While horseback riding one afternoon, he spied the strange little black and white creature scurrying along the path ahead of him, and jumped off his horse to grab it by its tail! Afterward, he reported having tried everything he could think of to rid himself of the smell, including hot baths, strong perfume, even cutting off his hair. But he lamented, "nothing worked, except time."[28]

Charles wrote to his mother about the lovely house on the artificial lake his father-in-law had built and furnished especially for them. In his letter, written in French as is all his correspondence with his family, he tells her of the immense park, with sassafras and tulip trees as numerous as the willows and oaks at her own home (probably Bologna), and that she would be immensely pleased by a large rhododendron in front of their house. He has collected seeds of *Diospyros virginiana* (persimmon), a tree peculiar to America with a taste all its own, and he will send them to her, along with several sweet potato plants. The park is divided by three or four creeks, abounding in fish—you just throw in your line to catch one—and the hunt is equally rewarding. In the course of the hunt, he finds great pleasure in discovering animals, especially birds, unknown to him, and already his collection of natural history specimens is remarkable. To give her an idea of the richness of nature that surrounds him, he will take an example of the part she loves best—the trees—and tell her there are twenty-five species of oaks (*Quercus*), many of which are always green, and eight species of walnuts.[29]

"America is an admirable country," he continues, extolling the republicanism of the New World, "the government is the most perfect of all those that have ever existed, without excepting those of Athens, Sparta and Rome." It would be necessary to be near the workers of this great machine (American society) to appreciate them for herself. There will shortly be an election (the one in which John Quincy Adams was elected president) and he is amazed at the importance each citizen attaches to his vote which he would not dream of selling as one does in England. In order to be rich in America, it is necessary to work, because skilled craftsmen, servants, houses, and everything but essentials like bread and meat are three times more expensive than in Europe.

His uncle has been wonderful to them, he says, and seems happy that they are with him. Joseph, too, admires America and shares Charles's feelings about the American way of life. Nicholas Biddle quoted Joseph in his journal as saying that, "if the question were raised as to what country in the world the majority of the Nation enjoyed the greatest happiness, certainly this one would be named."[30] He said that his ideas had been formed by the French Revolution—liberty, equality, fraternity—and that he was an American "even more than you Americans are." Biddle remembered Joseph stating that he had been opposed to the formation of the French Empire. Joseph was an educated man, with a special love for tragic drama. According to his nephew, he could recite whole passages from memory, with a voice of extraordinary power. Often after dinner everyone took part in reading Racine, Corneille, or Voltaire. Charles tells his mother he wishes she were with them, because she is so good at dramatic reading and could take one of the great roles. As for his sister-in-law, Charlotte, whom he had met for the first time on his arrival, she is the most amiable creature on earth—it would be impossible to see a more perfectly compatible trio than this excellent sister, his wife, and himself.[31]

A few days earlier he had read his father's "Ode on America" to an assembled group of Americans. They were all enchanted with it, particularly Louisa Catherine Adams, wife of John Quincy Adams the minister of foreign affairs (secretary of state), who had heard Lucien's name mentioned among those "heroes of independence"(presumably Franklin, Washington, and Jefferson). "Oh, happy country," Charles says, "which possesses that which poor Italy is so far from possessing!"[32] The seeds of his future passion and activity on behalf of Italian independence and unity were already sown.

Charles Bonaparte was a passionate young man, energetic, dedicated, unquestionably bright, yet often arrogant, perhaps to compensate for his short physique. John Watson, who came to Point Breeze with Reuben Haines, described Charles as "a peculiar man in his appearance—of middle height—a general fatness on small bones—broad shoulders—features & face possessing that round plumpness which marked Napoleon's pictures when he became corpulent. The eyes of Prince Charles are dark, full & expressive—fine teeth & a pleasing smile." Watson also noted that Charles was "very affable, republican, & frank in his manners; & puts his Plebian acquaintance quite at their ease."[33] Full of contrasts in his personality, his contemporaries held a wide range of opinions concerning him and could agree on only one thing: his facial resemblance to the handsome Napoleon.[34] Unlike Napoleon, though, he sported a full beard for many years, not a common sight in the United States at the time. Certainly his quick-flaring disposition was inherited from his mother. Alexandrine's temper has been described as "naturally hot and violent" and could only be restrained by constant vigilance: "Frequent fits of passion, occasional rudeness, and a haughty demeanor often betrayed the inward mind."[35] In spite of Charles's tendency to take and give offense easily, he was a loyal friend. Many who knew him might have sided with the scientist in Frankfurt

Figure 15. Bust of Charles-Lucien Bonaparte by R.
Trentanove. Signed and dated "Roma 1827." Marble.
Courtesy of the Museo Napoleonico, Rome.

who once told a colleague: "I believe that the prince, with his fiery enthusiasm,
would please you."[36]

That winter of 1823, galvanized by the excitement of his new environment,
Bonaparte compiled careful lists of all the mammals, birds, and reptiles he saw
at Point Breeze with their Latin names. The birds' names were accompanied by
notes on who gave him the specimen, specifically who killed it. Many entries
mention two servants, Jean and Alphonse. Joseph also shot birds for him, as did
Mary (a maid?) and the cook, and Charlotte gave him a Belted Kingfisher taken
in the park. But he shot the great majority himself. These included (amazingly)
falcons, woodpeckers, ducks, grebes, rails, cardinals, wood thrushes, flickers,
catbirds, mockingbirds, robins, peewees, goldfinches, bluebirds, and passenger
pigeons (*Columba migratoria*, now extinct).[37] Bonaparte preserved the tiny
bodies—probably with arsenic, the usual method at the time—and studied
them with intense scientific scrutiny. In 1826 Watson described Bonaparte's
study in the Lake House as "finely carpeted—& all round the high walls were

beautiful glass cases exposing Birds, beasts & reptiles, prepared & stufed by himself in fine condition. His collection & display of Butterflies, spread in glass plates, was beautiful. He had much passion for natural history & especially for *ornithology.*"[38]

Bonaparte also closely observed the flora of Point Breeze. His notebook of May 1824 catalogues 174 different plants, including trees, bushes, and wildflowers that grew in the woods and around Lake House and the manor. He jotted down only native American plants; he had no interest in those introduced from foreign countries. Bluets, veronica, and forget-me-nots grow in great quantities around the boathouse, he notes. Creeping wood sorrel is in the grass, in the woods, and around the aviary, and there are columbine, wood anemone, cranesbill, ranunculus, solomon's seal, tradescantia, and birdsfoot violet in the little woods on the edge of the lake. Stargrass surrounds the "fountain Hopkinson" (presumably named after his father-in-law's close friend Joseph Hopkinson), and there is sheep sorrel in the lawn between the Lake House and the great house. The woods are full of may-apple, a plant, he observes, that has great uses in medicine and whose fruit is yellow and agreeable to the taste. *Andromeda racemosa* grows near the "fountain Claudine," and there are numerous bushes of *Philadelphus* (mock orange), *Rhododendron maxima*, and *Viburnum prunifolium*, of which a superb specimen grows near the main house.[39]

The trees on his list are legion: beech, chestnut, ash, American white birch, sweet gum, black walnut, pitch pine, willow, honey locust, red cedar, and dogwood in great quantity in the park and in the woods. Red mulberry also grows in the woods and at "the bridge of savages" (native Americans), a site where a number of Indian relics had been found when the foundations of the manor were dug. There are black cherries at "old Point Breeze" (the site of the burned-down house) and around the mansion, and hawthorns, black locusts, sycamores, and oaks of every variety. Tulip trees are to be found in the woods, at the "fountain of the tulips," at the aviary, and on the way to the kitchen house, and a superb one grows in the park.

Bonaparte was overflowing with ornithological questions and sent a long list of them to Professor Drapiez in Brussels. Is the *Fringilla purpurea* (Purple Finch) a *Pyrrhula*? He doesn't think so himself. Is the *Fringilla albicollis* (White-throated Sparrow) not a true *Emberiza* (a term no longer used), as the naturalist Vieillot has said? And shouldn't the *Troglodytes* (wrens) be formed into a separate genus from the *Sylviae* (gnatcatchers and kinglets, today called *Sylviidae*)? What did Linnaeus mean by "falco Americanus"? And is the *Corvus hudsonius* (a crow) truly distinct from the *Corvus picus*? He asks the professor to send him a number of European specimens of birds to use for comparisons.[40]

All these questions and requests were carefully copied by Zenaide into her husband's notebook. She seems to have been a willing amanuensis throughout much of their marriage. Since their arrival in America she had helped him as much as she could, but in the winter of 1824 her time had been otherwise occupied. The young couple had moved for the winter to the John Dunlap house, between Market and Chestnut Streets on Eleventh, which Joseph rented in Phialdelphia, and there, on 13 February, after "fourteen hours of suffering" (as her father wrote his wife in Brussels), Zenaide gave birth to a large baby boy.[41] Charles was ecstatic at the birth of his first son, Joseph-Lucien-Charles-Napoleon. He noted in his memiors, in regard to the child's name, that it was his "own everlasting wish" to keep the memory of the older Napoleonic generation in the family.[42] The Roman Catholic bishop of Philadelphia, the Rt. Rev. Henry Conwell, a friend of Madame Mère's, baptized the infant at St. Joseph's Parish.

While in Philadelphia, Charles accompanied his uncle to meetings of the American Philosophical Society and himself became a member in May 1824. He probably joined Joseph at the Wistar parties, weekly soirées begun by Dr. Caspar Wistar, a prominent physician, and continued by his friends after his death (1818).[43] Joseph Bonaparte, a popular figure in Philadelphia, was included in almost all the social and intellectual gatherings of the city. Nicholas Biddle said he was by far "the most interesting stranger" he had ever known in America. He described Joseph as "free and communicative" and said he spoke of "all the great events and the great persons of his day with a frankness which assures you of his good nature as well as his veracity."[44]

At the meetings of the Philosophical Society and the Wistar parties, Charles Bonaparte sought out the leading naturalists, whose interests he shared so earnestly. He could have met the eminent zoologist Thomas Say, since Say was a curator at the Philosophical Society and often frequented the Wistar evenings. The tall, dark naturalist and explorer, who in recent years had crossed a large part of the great plains as far as the Rocky Mountains, and the more northern parts of the United States and southern Canada, was dignified and learned. His modest, quiet manner, markedly different from, yet complementary to, Bonaparte's enthusiasm and exuberance, and combined with a subtle sense of humor, appealed at once to the young foreigner. Bonaparte was particularly sympathetic with Say's dedication to republicanism, both men having reformist backgrounds. Say's family was Quaker and had emigrated from England in the late seventeenth century because of religious persecution. During the American Revolution his father and others had broken with the pacifist Yearly Meeting of Friends, as the organization was officially called, to found the Free, or Fighting, Quakers. Say himself disdained all forms of religion

and was fiercely democratic. More than anything else, however, it was his passion for natural science that Bonaparte shared so completely. He therefore
accepted on the spot when Say invited him to visit the Academy of Natural
Sciences, the institution Say had been instrumental in establishing twelve years
earlier, in 1812.

Figure 16. *Thomas Say in the Uniform of the Long Expedition, 1819–1820* by Charles
Willson Peale, 1819. Oil. The Ewell Sale Stewart Library, the Academy of Natural
Sciences of Philadelphia.

Charles Bonaparte's name first appears in the Academy's minutes for 13 January 1824, when Say read Bonaparte's paper on storm petrels to the other members. The essay was subsequently referred to George Ord, vice-president of the Academy, Titian Ramsay Peale, the twenty-four-year-old son of Charles Willson Peale, and Say to review for possible publication in the Academy's *Journal.* The following week the committee reported favorably, and when the article came out it was illustrated with engravings of the petrels after drawings by Peale.[45] Several weeks later the minutes record that "Charles, Prince of Canino"—was he using his father's title in defiance of his parent and because no one back home would know the difference?—had presented to the library a beautiful copy of *Insectes en Afrique & en Amérique* by Palisot de Beauvois. This may have been a gesture of thanks to Say, who was primarily an entomologist. On 24 February 1824, the minutes state that "on motion of Messrs. Say and [Charles-Alexandre] Lesueur, Charles Bonaparte of this city was duly elected a member of the Academy."[46] He attended the next meeting.

Founded in 1812 by a group of seven friends for the purpose of "occupying their leisure occasionally, in each other's company, on subjects of natural science, interesting and useful to the country and the world, and in modes conducive to the general and individual satisfaction of the members, as well as to the primary object, the advancement and diffusion of useful, liberal, human knowledge,"[47] the Academy was by this time a well-established and thriving institution, by far the most important center of natural history studies in the New World. Bonaparte must have been impressed with the number of eminent foreign correspondents the academy had acquired, especially the French savants Henri Ducrotoi de Blainville, Pierre-André Latreille, Jean-Baptiste de Monet de Lamarck, Georges Cuvier, Antoine-Laurent de Jussieu, and Etienne Geoffroy de Saint-Hilaire.[48] They had all been proposed for membership by Lesueur, a native of Le Havre, who had distinguished himself as a naturalist/artist on a four-year "expedition of discovery" to Australia sent out by Napoleon in 1800. Lesueur had come to the United States in 1816 employed as an artist by the geologist William Maclure.

Say had only recently (October 1823) returned from a six-month expedition by horseback, raft, and canoe to the St. Peter's (Minnesota) River, the Lake of the Woods in Canada, and across the top of Lake Superior. His collections from this journey were confined almost exclusively to insects and mollusks, but from a previous, much longer expedition to the Rocky Mountains (1819–20) he had brought back a number of interesting birds entirely new to science. Because birds were not Say's specific field of study and there was no one in America qualified at the time to describe them, these discoveries had remained unknown to science. For Bonaparte it was a golden opportunity: he was in the right place at the right time.

He must have worked feverishly during January and February, because on 9 March, only two weeks after he was elected to membership, he read at an Academy meeting the first part of a long essay, "Observations on the Nomenclature of [Alexander] Wilson's Ornithology."[49] This was the beginning of his major work in the United States: to revise Wilson's nomenclature and add to the body of scientific knowledge all the American birds discovered—principally by Say—since 1813, when Wilson died, at only forty and at the height of his career. Wilson's had been the first book on American birds published in America, and Bonaparte's would be the second. It was an ambitious endeavor for a twenty-one-year-old foreigner for whom English was a third language.

In the first paragraph of his paper Bonaparte states that he will give his opinions regarding the identity or dissimilarity of American and European species. (This was a subject that, as a European who was studying American birds, he was presumably in a position to know more about than his colleagues.) He says that many of Wilson's mistakes were due to a lack of scholarly resources and opportunities for comparison. Since libraries—except for a few private ones—and museums were then virtually nonexistent in the New World, Wilson had little to go on but his own experience. Bonaparte had the wherewithal to acquire the ornithological books he needed, which the poverty-stricken Wilson did not. Also, since Bonaparte had left for America from Antwerp, he may have gone to Holland to see his mentor Coenraad Jacob Temminck at Leiden and to study the Dutch museum's large collection of birds from all over the world. Such an opportunity had not been possible for Wilson.

Many of the mistakes Bonaparte finds in Wilson's book have to do with different states of plumage, that is, changes resulting from age or seasonal molting. He thinks, for example, that a particular species of owl named by Wilson is the same as another to which he had given a separate name: one specimen was simply older than the other, and its feathers had altered with age. In order to decide this point beyond a doubt, Bonaparte was keeping a living red owl and observing how its plumage changed in the course of its life cycle. Bonaparte also distinguished females and young birds that had been wrongly identified as separate species.

Some of the birds Wilson catalogued had already been named by European naturalists and, according to the protocols of the field, priority ruled. The original name, however misleading, always took precedence over any other. For the most part Bonaparte ferreted out these originals. In the case of the Orchard Oriole (*Icterus spurius*), he said that Wilson had no right to change the name Linnaeus had given the bird. On the other hand, Bonaparte himself, for perhaps the only time, tried to change a name: the bird Louis Pierre Vieillot had called *Bombycilla cedrorum* (Cedar Waxwing). It actually feeds on the berries of juniper, not cedar. The original name has stuck, however. As for the Red-breast-ed Nuthatch, Vieillot had called the bird *Sitta sulta* (sulta meaning "foolish" in Latin), a name based on the "ridiculous assertion that the bird is so stupid as to be easily knocked down from the sides of the tree with one's cane." Wilson had rightly rejected this notion with contempt, Bonaparte felt, and he agreed with Wilson's renaming the bird *Sitta varia*, though he would himself have called it *Sitta canadensis* (the name it bears today).[50]

It was a tricky business correcting Wilson at all, because of George Ord. A member of the Academy, Ord had been a close friend of Wilson's, had finished his *Ornithology*, and was fiercely defensive of his reputation. That June, after Bonaparte began his book continuing Wilson's work,[51] Ord sent him a note of warning, prefaced by cautionary remarks for his health. "The present sultry weather is the bane of ornithologists; I presume that you hardly dare venture among the thickets, especially as the passenger birds have almost all departed. As you are not yet *acclimated*, I would advise you to beware of our summer sun, for should you once get that disease, which American shooters are liable to, the *coup de soleil* [sunstroke], you may never perfectly recover from it." After this solicitous opening, he gets to the point: "there was present [at an Academy meeting] an Englishman, recently *come over*, who cannot see the propriety of a Frenchman's attempting, or presuming, to meddle with the nomenclature of Wilson's Ornithology. I should suppose that so long as that *Frenchman* [Bonaparte] does not presume to review Wilson's poetry [Wilson was also known as a poet], our fastidious critic (who, by the by, represents himself as an ornithologist) would be satisfied."[52] Ord had found a convenient mouthpiece in the English visitor.

Several days later, he followed up with a long dissertation on the use of "Mr." in America. Bonaparte had apparently reproved Ord for addressing him in this way. No doubt he was reluctant to relinquish the designation of "prince" he had so recently purloined from his father (he never used the title "count" that supposedly appeared on his passport). Ord explained that he had thought Bonaparte would be better pleased with "our homely Mr." than the title to which he was accustomed in his own country. He had arrived at this conclusion after speaking with Say, who told him that he had spoken to Bonaparte on the subject of how his name should appear in the *Journal*, and that Bonaparte had objected to the inclusion of his title. Ord continues, "the President of the United States is entitled by law to the title of Excellence; but when he retires from office, and becomes again one of the people, he is not allowed to retain the badge of distinction, it devolves to his successor; and he contents himself with plain Mr." As for the other extreme, Ord says "nothing excites [his] abhorrence more than the practice of the Quakers of addressing everyone by his Christian name. This leveling system I never will subscribe to." But he assures Bonaparte that in future he will endeavor "to make amends" for his misconception of Bonaparte's views: "with respect to yourself I am tolerably easy, but I am pained to believe that I shall have occasioned mortification in the breasts of your family, particularly the Princess, who will be apt to consider me a Goth."[53]

Disregarding Ord's advice, and continuing to sign himself "Prince of Musignano"—a variation perhaps less offensive to his father?—Bonaparte nevertheless worked as hard as any day laborer. His object was to build up as large a collection of specimens as possible, in order to compare anatomies and thus to ascertain and record the different variations that occurred in particular species. His supplier of specimens was the merchant James Forester in New York, who wrote in early January that he was sending "your grace" a pair of breeding canaries.[54] He instructs Bonaparte to feed them "hens' eggs boiled hard and mixed with stale bread grated fine." They must have two boxes in their cage, three inches square, and deer's hair to nest in. "I have ordered the Captain [of the Delaware steamboat] to bring these birds to you, [so that] if any of them should die by the way he may not say they flew away and perhaps keep them: we are in Yankee land, and must keep a lookout." Forester says he has been too busy going to school in the daytime and at night to inquire about the prices of "Parrots, Robins, Yellow Birds [Goldfinches?], Rice Birds, Indigo Birds, Baltimore Birds, Mocking Birds etc. etc.," all of which are very high priced and are in the hands of those who will only part with them at "something extraordinary." He adds that New York is "the dearest place in the United States, almost for everything." "Mocking Birds" in their cages can be purchased for ten or twelve dollars apiece, "according to their goodness," and robins, without a cage, for three dollars. He is amazed at Bonaparte's industry: "My dear Sir, you astonish me when you say that you have already stuffed more than 100 species of Birds, your Grace has not been idle, I do not know where you have found so many species at this season of the year. The birds must be more plenty [sic] in your part of the country than they are with us."

When Bonaparte requested a crossbill, Forester replied that he had lived in the states of New Jersey and New York since the year 1794 but had never seen "an American cross bill flying about. I have not one of them in my collection, if I had it would be at your service. And as for the other bird, you mention in your letter, viz. Loxia? I cannot find out what bird you mean and will be very happy if in your next letter you will write it more plain." (*Loxia* is simply the Latin name for the crossbill.) He adds that if "your Grace" can find more "pinnated grouse" on the pine barrens of New Jersey than needed, please to send him several.[55]

A few months later Forester wrote that his son "the physician" had just returned from France and had brought two hundred pairs of crystal birds' eyes for the prince at seven and a quarter cents a pair. These are to be used in the birds he is mounting. He also requests a favor—one that would be asked by many others—"would your Grace send any trifling thing that once belonged to your deceased uncle, the late emperor of France; if it were only a button from his coat it would satisfy me." Forester also wants to know whether Bonaparte has succeeded in raising "mule birds" from the American Goldfinch and the Canary.[56]

Bonaparte's friends sent him specimens as well. Reuben Haines wrote that while in New York Dr. (James Ellsworth) DeKay had given him a bird for Bonaparte that he had hoped to deliver to Point Breeze on his way home. But "as the tide was down" it was not possible to land. Haines adds that one of his neighbors had brought him a Red-Winged Hawk to give to Bonaparte. "I hastily took out the body this morning before breakfast, but had not time to skin the legs and wings, and thought it unnecessary as the weather is so cool. I shall place it in the hands of the steward of the Steam boat for thee."[57]

The prince was trying to preserve animal specimens, but apparently without success. In September, Forester complained that the ground hog he had just received from Bonaparte was not in "as good order" as he would have wished; actually, the smell was "very disagreeable." "It is true the weather lately has been damp and heavy, but my Dear Sir," he says, "the head, the nose, and mouth of this animal, at this season of the year, must often have to be scraped very clean, or it without doubt will putrefy."[58]

Although giving some attention to animals new to him, Bonaparte was concentrating primarily on birds. Because of the wealth of new and undescribed bird specimens he found at the Academy of Natural Sciences, particularly the large and important collection brought back by Say from the Rockies, and as a natural outgrowth of his long article on Wilson's nomenclature—a word he is credited as the first to use in this context—he decided, with his usual flair for attempting the seemingly impossible, to write and publish a book on American birds.

Since Wilson had not been to Florida, Bonaparte saw that a serious gap still remained in American ornithology. This lacuna included not only the permanent avian residents of Florida but birds from Cuba and other Caribbean islands that might frequent the southern part of the peninsula and thus should be included as American. Therefore, in order to secure new specimens to describe in his book, he hired Titian Ramsay Peale to make an expedition to Florida during the winter of 1824–25. Peale had already established his reputation as an expert hunter and taxidermist, as well as an artist of some skill, on

Figure 17. *Titian Ramsay Peale* (self-portrait). Oil. Neg. 323811. Courtesy of the American Museum of Natural History, New York.

the Long Expedition with Say five years earlier. In the fall, Peale sailed for Charleston, South Carolina, where he spent time at the local natural history museum making sketches. Toward the end of November, he embarked for points farther south and eventually arrived at St. Augustine, Florida, in mid-December.[59] While in Florida, he stayed for a time with Bonaparte's cousin, Achille Murat, who had settled there on a farm. He returned to Philadelphia in April 1825 with a number of previously unknown birds, and Bonaparte set to work at once on their description and classification.

It was an all-absorbing study, and Bonaparte never did things by halves. The technical problems surrounding ornithology at the time were fourfold: distinguishing between varieties and species, establishing genera, constructing a natural system rather than the artificial one set up by Linnaeus, and standardizing nomenclature.[60] All the time Bonaparte was encountering a great wealth of new bird species, both in the woods around Point Breeze and in the specimens sent to him. In a letter to his father a year later, he said that during his stay in the United States natural history had entirely occupied his moments of leisure.[61] Since he was not working for a living such "moments" were plentiful, an advantage that most of his colleagues lacked. He was far ahead of them in the breadth of his education as well. Louis Agassiz would write in 1846 that "American science lacks the scope which is characteristic of higher instruction in old Europe." American naturalists lacked "neither zeal nor knowledge," he said; what they needed was leisure.[62]

During the first half of the nineteenth century, the study of natural history was the dominant scientific endeavor in America.[63] Men of science at the time were amateurs in the sense that no paid positions in their fields existed. They had to draw their livelihood from other sources. Many were physicians interested in the anatomy of living creatures other than man or in the medicinal properties of plants; others were clergymen who studied nature for metaphysical reasons. A few, like Bonaparte, who had the means, and Say, who did not, were wholeheartedly devoted to natural science for its own sake.

In just ten years, between 1815 and 1825, scientific societies in America, such as the Academy of Natural Sciences, tripled in number, and during this time, many scientific journals were launched to publish the papers presented at meetings of these societies. The *Journal of the Academy of Natural Sciences* had been founded in 1817, at the instigation of William Maclure. Maclure was a farsighted man who knew that to broaden the scope of the institution it was necessary to publish original articles on all major aspects of natural history and to exchange the publication for the journals of the principal societies abroad. Maclure saw clearly what Jefferson expressed in a letter written several years later: "Science is more important in a republican government than in any other.

And in an infant country like ours, we must depend for improvement on the science of other countries, longer established, possessing better means, and more advanced than we are."[64] After a brief, unsuccessful attempt to use the services of a professional printer, Maclure bought a printing press and set it up in his own house. Here the academy's publishing committee, headed by Say, printed the *Journal* themselves for several years.

The *Journal*'s mandate, as set forth in the first issue, was to communicate to the public "such facts and observations as, having appeared interesting to [the members of the academy] and are likely to be interesting to other friends of science." The members proposed to exclude entirely all papers on theory and to confine their communications as much as possible to facts.[65] This emphasis on facts and empirical observations was typical of the pragmatism that characterized early American science. Benjamin Franklin had laid the foundation for it with his inventions and his investigations into the nature of electricity, and Jefferson had continued it with his weather charts, experiments in horticulture, farming innovations, and accomplishments in architecture. Jefferson once wrote his mentor George Wythe that he wished those who explored the West for fossil remains would make "exact descriptions" of what they saw instead of weaving theories about them. The moment a person forms a theory, his imagination sees in every object only the traits that favor that idea, said Jefferson. The time for forming theories had not arrived, "we must wait with patience until more facts are collected."[66]

The founders of the *Journal* were also aware that the love of science was not always associated with leisure and superfluous wealth. Thus they intended to make their publication as simple and inexpensive as possible.[67] If this was the attitude of the entire academy, and presumably it was, it is no wonder that the members, predominantly Quakers or of Quaker descent—a sect that abhorred ostentation to such an extent they would not permit painted portraits of themselves, only silhouettes—were not enthusiastic about the flamboyant Frenchman who attended one of their meetings as Bonaparte's guest and showed them the enormous watercolors of American birds he intended to publish.

Bonaparte had met John James Audubon in the spring of 1824, through a mutual friend, James Mease. Newly arrived in Philadelphia, Audubon was clearly a gifted and fascinating man of enormous energy.[68] He had none of the advantages of education and leisure that had been Bonaparte's birthright, but instead was entirely self-taught and self-supporting. Born in Santo Domingo (now Haiti), the bastard son of a French father who was a merchant, planter, and slave trader, and a serving girl who died shortly after his birth, Audubon was raised in France by his stepmother. His father sent him to America in 1803, when he was only eighteen, to make his own way in the world and to look after Mill Grove, a family property outside Philadelphia. When Bonaparte met Audubon, he was thirty-nine and still completely unknown as an artist. After a life of hardship and hard work on the frontier, he had returned east to seek a publisher for the large portfolio of bird paintings he had been accumulating for years.

As Napoleon's nephew, Bonaparte was certainly used to ostentation, but dissension awaited Audubon from the moment he set foot inside the academy's door. Aside from any feelings the other members may have had about the arrogant foreigner, he had to contend with the formidable opposition of George Ord. Ord, who had not only completed Wilson's unfinished opus with a ninth volume, published posthumously, but was about to bring out a supplement, at once saw a threat to his favorite project and had no intention of allowing this "uncouth upstart" to supplant the work of his friend. He pronounced Audubon's art "absurd" and "pretentious" and successfully blocked his membership in the academy.[69] Audubon's fellow French artist Lesueur, however, recognized his genius, sympathized with his ambition to publish his work, and suggested he go to Europe for the purpose. In the meantime, Lesueur offered to find him a temporary job giving art lessons at the same school for young girls where he himself taught.

Bonaparte was immensely impressed by the magnificent array of paintings Audubon showed him—life-size depictions of numerous species of birds. But though Audubon had closely observed the habits of birds in the wild, he did not have the scientific background Bonaparte could lay claim to. A perfect collaboration of talents appeared in the offing. Bonaparte took Audubon to meet Alexander Lawson, the engraver of Wilson's *American Ornithology*. "I saw Audubon when Bonaparte brought him to see father," Lawson's daughter said years later, "he looked like the backwoodsmen that visit the city. His hair hung on his shoulders and his neck was open."[70] Whether it was Audubon's open collar or his somewhat extravagant manner, the gruff Scotsman took an instant dislike to him. He surveyed the paintings and told Bonaparte to go ahead and buy them but he would not engrave them. "Ornithology requires truth and correct lines—here are neither!" When Audubon boasted that he had studied under Jacques-Louis David, Lawson snapped: "Then you have made some bad use of your time."[71] Audubon, in any case, was lying, and it was a particularly dangerous lie to tell in front of the prince, whose wife and sister-in-law had been painted by David only two years before. Charlotte, moreover, was David's student in Brussels and knew him well. Bonaparte made a mental note to follow up on the remark, and later, when it suited him, established its falsehood.[72] But Lawson's hostility to Audubon's work probably had less to do with aes-

Figure 18. *Audubon* by John Syme, 1826. From John James Audubon, *Birds of America*, edited by Roger Tory Peterson and Virginia Marie Peterson (New York: Abbeville Press, 1981). Courtesy of the White House, Washington, D.C.

thetics or science than with personal loyalty. Lawson took great pride in his engravings of Wilson's bird paintings and, like Ord, did not want to see them surpassed by anyone. Undoubtedly, his friend Ord had already warned him away from Audubon. Besides, he was a successful and sought-after engraver who did not need the work.

Collecting information on American birds, classifying them, writing articles on them for the *Journal*, and planning his book were Bonaparte's main occupations. But he was also increasingly concerned with money matters. On the question of Zenaide's dowry, he was caught in the middle between his uncle and his father. Lucien, in financial difficulties because of his lavish lifestyle, had kept the entire sum and in addition had taken out a mortgage on the property at Canino. Charles had expected to receive the interest payments, but nothing had been sent. In a letter to his father in the fall of 1824, Bonaparte quotes his uncle as always complaining that he has done too much for his daughters, considering his moderate means. He says the large dowry he gave Zenaide obliges him now to do the same for Charlotte, which is financially inconvenient. (Charlotte was engaged to marry her cousin Napoleon-Louis, the eldest living son of Louis Bonaparte, whose firstborn son Charles-Napoleon had died in childhood. This child had been the only Bonaparte of his generation older than Charles and the one designated by Napoleon to be his successor before his own son was born.)

Charles tells his father that in the end, his uncle cannot or will not ("which comes to the same thing") do anything for him and Zenaide. "What is more," he continues, "he signified to us that if, during our visit here, you do not pay us more of the interest on the dowry that you promised in the contract, he would want to see us leave sooner rather than later." He has tried to persuade his uncle that his father's financial problems are temporary, but his uncle claims to have heard from many quarters that Lucien never intended to pay his son and daughter-in-law a cent while they were living with Joseph. "You understand, knowing my character, that the day when that [the fact that Lucien had no intention of paying them anything] is proved to me I will not stay 24 hours with him."[73]

Around the same time, Zenaide wrote to her mother, Julie, who had moved for the time being from Brussels to Rome. Zenaide asks whether her father should come to join Julie in Italy. "I believe he is a little disgusted [*un peu dégoûté*] with this country, if I am not mistaken, his health and the isolation he finds here, your distance from him most of all, and the absence of Charlotte [who had returned to Europe in early 1824 to prepare for her marriage] makes him want to return to Europe. He will tell you all this himself, if I am right in my suppositions, although I am mixing myself up in what is not my business." She cautions her mother not to take what she says too seriously, because it mostly comes from her own great desire to see them all together in the same country. Since her mother cannot come to America and finds it agreeable in Italy, it must be in Italy that the family reunion will take place. Given Joseph's rather obvious affair with Madame Lacoste, Zenaide seems to be deluding herself, her mother, or both. She says quite openly that life has been busy with

Monsieur Lacoste (newly returned from Santo Domingo) and Madame always there. They are all going to spend December in Philadelphia, because it is already so cold at Point Breeze. Her baby is strong and happy, but she doesn't want to have any more children until she is with her mother again.

It has been a busy household, she continues, with guests coming and going. The young Monges girls, daughters of a French doctor, have just left with James Carret (Joseph's American interpreter), and the son of a Dr. Wise has been there for awhile. The young man had planned to leave the previous day, but he missed the steamboat because of a misfortune while hunting with Charles and Monsieur Lacoste. Attempting to follow them, he had lost his way and got mired up to his neck in a swamp. "The poor little devil was so exhausted from the experience he couldn't get up at six o'clock to leave."[74]

In addition to Joseph Bonaparte's friends, many important men of the day came to visit him at Point Breeze. The politicians Daniel Webster, Henry Clay, and John Quincy Adams; Generals Winfield Scott and Thomas Cadwallader; Commodore Richard Stockton; Joseph's lawyer, Joseph Hopkinson, a neighbor in Bordentown, whose father was a signer of the Declaration of Independence; the banker Nicholas Biddle; and a number of French generals who had served under Napoleon, including Bertrand Clausel, Emmanuel de Grouchy, Charles Lallemand, and Charles Lefebvre-Desmouettes.[75] But there was no more exciting guest than General Lafayette, who came to America in 1824, at the invitation of the nation for a triumphal tour of the country he had helped to liberate from the British nearly half a century earlier.

Joseph, the count de Survilliers, with a group of distinguished friends—of course including Charles and Zenaide—descended the Delaware in a large and handsome sixteen-oared barge, presented to Joseph by Stephen Girard, to meet the steamboat carrying General Lafayette to Bordentown. The party boarded the vessel for the last part of the journey with the barge taken in tow.[76] At Point Breeze, Lafayette was lavishly entertained. There was the famous art collection to see, carriage rides in the park, and perhaps a row on the lake in the small swan-shaped boats Joseph had imported from Europe. At the sumptuous meals, waiters with mustaches and long beards—a striking anomaly among servants in America—wearing black broadcloth liveries and white gloves, served the concoctions prepared by Joseph's French chef.[77]

As much as he enjoyed the pomp and prestige of welcoming distinguished visitors, Bonaparte was always eager to return to his work, to the vast body of knowledge he was assembling for his book on American ornithology. Whenever possible, he escaped to his study in the Lake House, where he could work undisturbed. Natural history was, as ever, the overriding passion. Historians have frequently remarked that during the first half of the nineteenth century students of natural science tended not to specialize.[78] Charles Bonaparte was perhaps ahead of his time in restricting his studies, at the time, almost exclusively to that of avian anatomies and the descriptions and classifications of birds. Later, he would include bats, amphibians, and fish in his work.

3

AN AUTHOR'S
FIRST CAMPAIGNS

"I am afraid even of an English *comma* when not
approved by my *guardian angels*."

Charles-Lucien Bonaparte to Isaac Hays,
Point Breeze, probably August 1824

BONAPARTE WROTE TO SAY in October 1824, "I am very glad to hear you have finished with all I sent you, but am afraid you are mistaken [that it was all], since you have besides Sylvia Celata and Fringilla Grammaca two others to copie or correct and the preface!"[1] Say had been helping Bonaparte with his book for some time, since the prince thought his command of English was inadequate. The two birds he mentioned to Say, the Orange-crowned Warbler (*Sylvia celata*, today called *Vermivora celata*), and the Lark Finch or Lark Sparrow (*Fringilla grammaca*, today *Chondestes grammacus*), were brought back by Say on his expedition with Major Long to the Rocky Mountains. Both birds had been shot along the Missouri River and until then were unknown to U.S. naturalists.

In later years Bonaparte would be considered the father of descriptive ornithology in America because of the scientific approach of his book [2]—surprisingly, since he was a foreigner. "As an ornithologist Bonaparte was by far the most celebrated [of his day]," wrote another famous ornithologist in 1899, "and though only twenty-two . . . had already published the first volume of American Ornithology and laid the foundations for the study of nomenclature and synonymy which has to this day developed to such formidable proportions."[3]

In his preface, Bonaparte explains that "a love for the same department of natural science, and a desire to complete the vast enterprise so far advanced by Wilson's labours" has induced him to publish all the new discoveries that had been made in American ornithology since Wilson's landmark study. Wilson's classifications of various species and the synonyms that had been assigned to them were more or less accurate for his day, but because science has advanced considerably since then, his work must be updated. Bonaparte acknowledges the great deal of help he has received in this enterprise and in particular thanks his friends Thomas Say and John Godman "for the care they have bestowed in preventing the introduction of foreign expressions, or phrases not idiomatic, into my composition."[4]

Say also assisted him with papers he gave at Academy meetings. "Notwithstanding *not to keep you idle*," Bonaparte wrote him from Point Breeze, "I sent you some more things to correct; you will observe they have nothing to do with my work [his book], but I must proceed with my observations [a paper he was writing]; those d[amn] . . . Muscicapas [finch-like birds] have given me a devilish trouble [in classifying them] and I am anxious to get rid of them; as soon as you will have sent them [his observations] back to me I shall come in town the next Tuesday to read them at the Academy."[5]

It was a tedious job sorting out the various names given to different birds over the years, mostly by Europeans who, at best, had only dried specimens and more often than not only drawings to work with. Bonaparte cited a particular instance where Buffon took the description of a bird—the Great Crested Flycatcher—from Mark Catesby's drawing of it, and later, when he was given a specimen of the same bird, described it as new, not recognizing it as the same one in Catesby's picture.[6] Even Wilson was faulted for adopting William Bartram's name for the Eastern Pewee in preference to the one "consecrated" by "the fathers of the science," that is, Linnaeus, John Latham, and Vieillot, even though Bonaparte thought Bartram's name more "elegant, expressive, and appropriate." "If authors are to be permitted to change specific names under the excuse of improving them," Bonaparte wrote in a *Journal* article, "there will be no end to their alterations, and our systems will be involved in utter chaos."[7] He told Temminck, who sent him European specimens, that to him the naming of birds was a "Tower of Babel."[8]

The question of names got him into a full-scale battle with Ord, who was furious that Bonaparte should correct his classification of the Boat-tailed Grackle. On his return from a trip to Florida with Say and Maclure in 1818, Ord had written an article for the *Journal* about this large, handsome blackbird. Some six years later, in a paper read at the Academy, Bonaparte challenged the older man's nomenclature and Ord reacted predictably. Bonaparte asked a colleague, Dr. Isaac Hays, to tell Say that if he found him too severe with Mr. Ord he might tell him that he, Bonaparte, had only intended to correct him, not to hurt his feelings (if it were possible to do one without the other). It was very likely, he continued, that he had written in English what he would not have in Italian from the difficulty of selecting the wording. In short, he always wanted Say's help, but above all in predicaments such as this one.[9]

When the proofs of Bonaparte's book were circulated the following year, the prickly Ord again took offense at Bonaparte's remarks on the same subject. Meticulous and exacting in his science, the latter had merely said that Ord, in an attempt to correct Wilson, had used the wrong names of two allied species of Crow Blackbird in a *Journal* article.[10] But this would have been quite enough to infuriate the older man. According to his contemporaries, he was a particularly contentious individual. Alexander Lawson's daughter described him as "a very singular person, very excitable, almost of pure nervous temperament." She said he would often "speak rudely to gentlemen, and more than once father was consulted as to whether Mr. Ord should receive a challenge for what he said, but father was always the peacemaker."[11]

As for Bonaparte, Miss Lawson observed that "the advent of the Prince of Munsigno [sic.] set the whole Academy by the ears. He appeared to make warm friends and equally warm enemies." She said that he would come to see her father and tell him in "high glee" of the last "war-whoop" and its effect, laughing heartily. For a while he seemed to take a "boyish delight" in challenging his peers.[12] Perhaps this was not so surprising in view of his youth.

At a meeting of the Academy toward the end of May, Bonaparte read a continuation of his "Observations on the Nomenclature of Wilson's *Ornithology.*" Again it contained remarks pointed at Ord, accusing him of giving an ungrammatical name to a certain bird and of excluding the Golden Plover from Wilson's book. Ord was apparently not present at the meeting to hear Bonaparte's words, because it was not until early September when the paper appeared in the *Journal*, that he reacted as Bonaparte might have predicted, and with great pomp:

> And now my good Prince, I am going to find fault with you, for the disrespectful manner in which you, in the last number of the Journal, treated my article, in Wilson's seventh volume, on the supposed Golden Plover. We are all liable to error; but when we honestly err, we are not willing that our fault should be magnified into a crime. A gentleman, accustomed to the courtesies of life, cannot but be hurt at any conduct which wears the appearance of asperity or inurbanity . . . allow me to say, that the temper in which your criticism was written, was what the occasion did not call for, and what my character ought to have repressed; the abrupt manner in which it begins shows a disposition to enforce your opinion at all hazards; and your passing over the important facts upon which my determination was grounded, should seem to prove that the spirit of contradiction has been allowed to prevail over the sense of justice, and the love of truth. Unless you can disprove the positive assertions of my paper, your gratuitous opinion must go for naught.[13]

Bonaparte did disprove Ord's assertions, and Ord withdrew. But the incident would end all correspondence between the two men for the next sixteen years. The prince of Musignano did not take such criticism of his character lightly.

Meanwhile, the same Great Crow Blackbird that had sparked discord between Bonaparte and Ord came between Bonaparte and Audubon as well. Bonaparte's book was due to come out in the summer of 1825, with illustrations by Titian Peale, and supposedly one by Audubon. In April, Audubon wrote him from Louisiana that he was somewhat piqued by the doubts Bonaparte had raised concerning Audubon's sizing of the bird in question. He declared that he had always been especially careful in every particular of natural history:

> I will here assure you that all the drawings of birds I have made for upwards of

Figure 19. *Great Crow Blackbird*, drawn from nature by J. J. Audubon and A. Rider. From Bonaparte, *American Ornithology; or, The Natural History of Birds Inhabiting the United States not given by Wilson*, vol. 1 (Philadelphia: Carey, Lea & Carey, 1825). Author's collection. Photo credit: Lisa Tyson Ennis.

twenty years have all been so exactly measured with the compass in all their parts & even feathers, that when you say that you have received lately from Georgia [presumably from Peale] beautiful individuals of both sexes of Gracula Barita, females less and males larger than in my drawing I feel inclined to ask if they are *Live Birds*? If not have they been measured before being skinned? If neither, I shall be sorry as long as I live that any alteration should have been made to my Drawing by such a person as Mr. Lawson who you well know is by no means *My Friend*.[14]

Audubon wrote to their colleague Reuben Haines that he often thought the prince doubted his words, but he would have to bear it until he could vindicate himself. Since he did not want to cause dissension where he believed "the closest amity and mutual support ought to exist," he would drop the subject of the *Gracula barita*.[15] Bonaparte, on the other hand, could not drop it because his conscience bothered him. On his way to see Niagara Falls at the end of July, he stopped at Saratoga, where it was a "stifling 99 degrees," and from there wrote Audubon—in French as usual—to inform him that the first volume of his *Ornithology* had at last appeared and he would send him a copy at once. However, he had been "tormented" by the plate of the Great Crow Blackbird and by the way he, Bonaparte, had proceeded with it. He felt the need to explain himself in terms Audubon could accept. The problem was that he had never compared his specimen with the drawing Audubon had made for him. He had described the bird on the basis of the specimen alone, and only after the text of his work was published did he discover that the dimensions he had cited did not accord with the drawing.

We must attribute this mistake to the *bar-keeper* of the City Hotel [who apparently neglected to give him Audubon's description along with the drawing], because had I the notes that were to accompany the drawing I would at once have seen the difference. But it was impossible to give a figure in contradiction to my text and [the drawing] was too large for the copper [plate], something I found hard to believe since you had the measurement exactly. Your figure was larger than my individual, Lawson was repugnant to do it, and so I resolved then to have another drawing made & I did not wish to charge Mr. Peale with this task (I hope you appreciate this) so that Mr. Rider, an artist well known & considered by all the world, who [had] the nature [the specimen] & your work before his eyes made the outline after which Mr. Lawson engraved the plate which according to me is the best of the work.

Bonaparte explained that, though Rider had made an entirely new drawing, he had "taken much" from Audubon's picture, and therefore, after consulting Audubon's friends, particularly Lesueur, it was decided that the two names should appear jointly under the plate. That was how it was done in Paris among all the artists: they often appeared as collaborators on the same work. He added that if Audubon wished it he would give a full explanation of the affair in his second volume. He hoped "the excellence" of the drawing was such that Audubon would not "find it bad" to have his name attached to it.[16]

On a more comfortable subject, Bonaparte was delighted to hear of Audubon's project of publication. "We will hope then that your magnificent drawings will not be long ignored by artists & savants. It is in making them known that you render a veritable service to Science." The brilliant description Audubon has given him of the beginning of spring in Louisiana makes him want to visit the region, but he is not sure this will be possible. His wife is delighted with the offer Audubon made her of one of his "little masterpieces," which she will hang in her study, and requests the drawing he made of Lesueur and herself. Bonaparte concludes with the news that Peale has returned from Florida with many bird specimens. "He wished to imitate your manner of drawing but he has completely failed. I believe that it is only you in the world who can manage the pencil thus & Peale would do well not to use it any more."

By this time Bonaparte was disillusioned with Peale, who did not deliver drawings when they were needed. Nevertheless, he published descriptions of all Peale's principal discoveries from Florida in the Academy's *Journal.*

That fall the affair of the blackbird drawing was finally put to rest. Audubon was not one to burn his bridges. He was chiefly annoyed that the accuracy of his drawing had been questioned and cared not at all about the appropriation of his name. "I am sorry you should have felt so much anxiety about reproducing the Gracula either from my drawing or that of any other person whatever," he wrote to Bonaparte, "yet I can vouch the size of *Birds Drawn by Me* as correct, and thus I call *Gracula Barita* [correct]." He added, however, that "whatever you have done or wrote employing my name is received thankfully by me."[17] Although his name appeared in print under the *Gracula*, Audubon must have been disappointed, because his own picture of the blackbird would have been the first he ever published. It must have been at least somewhat upsetting to see "drawn from Nature by John J. Audubon and A. Rider" under an inferior artist's rendering. Under normal circumstances, Peale would have been asked to re-do the drawing in question. Bonaparte had selected Peale as his illustrator, with Lawson's approval, probably because Peale had been the main artist for Say's *American Entomology*, published shortly before. But Peale and Audubon did not get along, so Bonaparte engaged Alexander Rider—an alcoholic, employed by Lawson principally to color the plates drawn by Peale—to re-do the dubious blackbird. Ironically, it was Rider, actually a competent artist, who eventually produced the majority of drawings for Bonaparte's book and thus became by default, his chief illustrator.

Audubon says in the same letter that he looks forward to receiving Bonaparte's continuation of Wilson's *American Ornithology*, which has not yet arrived. "It would be difficult for me to express my thanks to you as I feel them for your friendly presentation of the first volume of your work; believe me My Dear Sir I very seldom in my life felt a greater pleasure." Still smarting from his negative reception at the Academy the previous winter, he adds that he is glad his account of the Wild Turkey has been useful: "I assure you I never expected *you* to publish any portion of it, from reports made me of the little influence my Word had either with *you* or the Scientific Academicians of Philadelphia." He has finally decided to go to England to "exhibit" his drawings, and if not successful in London, he will go to the continent, to Paris, where he fervently wishes the "Great Napoleon" still existed. He reminds Bonaparte of his offer to give him letters of introduction and hopes the prince thinks him "still worthy such attentions." He concludes, pointedly, "My work proceeds as fast as can be under the efforts of an humble Citizen destitute of many advantages derived by others better situated."

Bonaparte answered him: "I see with pain from your letter my dear Sir that you have entirely false reports of me and that you do not believe in me any more than in the savants of the Academy." He has been Audubon's warm defender (*chaud defenseur*), and has never doubted the reports sent back by Audubon of the customs and habits of the birds he observed during his long sojourns in the woods. "In truth, your history of the *dindon* [turkey], which has been of great use to me perhaps serves as an example, and the publication of your work will be an epoch in the history of ornithology." He will send letters of recommendation to the two people who would be the most helpful to Audubon in Europe: Temminck, who is "the man of the century in ornithology," and Drapiez, who knows everyone in Paris—savants, booksellers, ornithologists, and "powerful men [*hommes puissants*]." Drapiez is "already prejudiced in your favor by my letters, and awaits you with impatience."[18]

If Bonaparte's relations with Audubon were often fluctuating and uncertain, with Say his friendship was steady and unambiguous. He had great respect for the mentor who assisted him in so many ways with his work. Say's aim was to promote American science by having American scientists name and describe their country's fauna, so he was pleased when Bonaparte—who, although French, was working on New World science—was given specimens of ten different species of South American birds to describe. But after Bonaparte had read his descriptions at an Academy meeting the donor withdrew the birds in order to send them to Europe for the same purpose. Say was furious. As principal editor of the *Journal*, he insisted on publishing Bonaparte's paper anyway, which meant his nomenclature would have priority.[19]

Bonaparte reciprocated in kind. When he described the small, robin-like Western Phoebe, he called it Say's Flycatcher (*Muscicapa saya*, now *Sayornis saya*), and wrote: "We now introduce into the Fauna of the United States a species which is either a non-descript, or one that has been improperly named; and I dedicate it to my friend Thomas Say, a naturalist, of whom America may justly be proud." A specimen had been shot by Peale in 1820 near the Rocky Mountains.[20]

He described three other birds discovered by Say on this same expedition to the Rocky Mountains, the Lazuli Finch (*Fringilla amoena*), now called the Lazuli Bunting (*Passerina amoena*), the Band-tailed Pigeon (*Columba fasciata*), and the Burrowing Owl (*Strix cunicularia*, now *Athene cunicularia*), which is diurnal and lives in the ground in abandoned prairie dog holes. The description of the latter, the most unusual bird Say brought back, afforded Bonaparte the opportunity to express his deeply felt admiration for his mentor and friend:

The votaries of natural science must always feel indebted to the learned and inde-

Figure 20. *Burrowing Owl*, drawn from nature by Titian R. Peale. From Bonaparte, *American Ornithology; or, The Natural History of Birds Inhabiting the United States not given by Wilson*, vol. 1 (Philadelphia: Carey, Lea & Carey, 1825). Author's collection. Photo credit: Lisa Tyson Ennis.

fatigable Say, for the rich collection of facts he has made whenever opportunities have been presented, but more especially in the instance of this very singular bird, whose places of resort, in this country, are too far distant to allow many the pleasure of examining for themselves. We feel doubly disposed to rejoice that the materials for the history of our bird, are drawn from his ample store, both on account of their intrinsic excellence, and because it affords us an opportunity of evincing our admiration of the zeal, talents, and integrity, which have raised this man to the most honorable and enviable eminence as a naturalist.[21]

Bonaparte tried often to persuade Say to visit him. He ended one letter: "[I] live always in the hope of seeing you at Point Breeze before the day of judgement."[22] He also entreated their mutual friend, Hays, another editor of the Academy's publication, to "please be after Say in order, 1st that he might come to see me, 2nd that he might not loose [sic] time in rendering my scratches fit for your journal."[23]

Bonaparte knew how deeply involved Say was with his own work. He wrote Temminck, in Holland, that he had passed along Temminck's letter to Say, but warned, "it is necessary for me to tell you that this learned naturalist and worthy man [*digne homme*] is a very bad correspondent; his own collection takes all his care & time & I doubt that you would ever obtain from him a single fly, but I have occupied myself with Entomology & my collection is in a perfect state so that I could send you what you desire."[24] Perhaps Bonaparte was trying to protect Say from extraneous demands on his time—or perhaps he was disingenuous by forwarding his own career. In fact, Say was always eager to exchange his specimens with foreign naturalists and corresponded regularly with them.

Bonaparte told Temminck, somewhat immodestly, that the first volume of his "great work [*grand ouvrage*]" had just been published and that it could be justly compared to Wilson's. In any case, the plates were on a par with those of Buffon. He had once considered writing it in French and had consulted Professor Drapiez on the subject. The professor replied that it was difficult to say which language Bonaparte should use: if he was writing for special localities, he should probably use the idiom of the country, but if he intended his book for the world, he must use French, "which for naturalists is the conventional language, as Latin was once."[25] Bonaparte had of course chosen the idiom of the United States.

In spite of the gratitude Bonaparte felt for the help he was receiving from his American colleagues, a tone of arrogance occasionally crept into his letters. He could be quite irascible and dictatorial at times. One evening he sent a note to Hays—a busy physician—concerning an essay he had asked Hays to review in galley: "According to your promise I watched with impatience each & all the four boats that are now plying between Philadelphia & this place! . . . but it was in vain . . . & I am really disappointed to the utmost. . . . My steward *Fedeli* will bring you the present [another essay] & as he is returning by the 3 o'clock boat I hope you will give him the long expected proof if you have not sent it before."[26]

When the galley proof of his article finally arrived, Bonaparte was exasperated that Hays had apparently not corrected his mistakes after all. "I send back the proof which is *shamefully wretched*," he wrote Hays at once, "this astonishes me the more in as much as *I am sure* I had already corrected the horrible blunders. If I was not afraid of abusing your friendship & patience I should request you to read over my corrections & consider the queried ones before you send it to the printer."[27] A month later, his equanimity quite restored, he informed Hays, before leaving from New York City for the northern part of the state, that he started in the morning for Albany and wished Hays well in "the Athens of America, and a quick publication of our journal."[28]

Bonaparte's impatience was at times even directed at Say. The following summer (1825), on his way to see Niagara Falls, he sent a joint letter to him and Hays from Saratoga, explaining that he had not corrected the proof of his article for the *Journal* because it had not arrived and expressing anxiety about some errors it might contain. "My dear doctors," he scolds, "if you are not sure of yourselves, for God sake wait for my return which shall most probably take place in a fortnight."[29] Bonaparte, then only twenty-two, was addressing men highly regarded in their fields and nearly twenty years his senior. But neither Say nor Hays seems to have taken offense at his manner.

Spirited, dashing, mettlesome, and fiery, Bonaparte also sometimes displayed a certain superficiality and a tendency to extravagant gestures and speech, perhaps acquired from the theatrics practiced at home. These volatile traits, puzzlingly combined with his keen intelligence and intense application to study, must have been disconcerting to his sober American peers. Even his own grandmother, Madame Mère, was quoted as saying: "I counsel him to think more and to speak less [*Consigliatelo a pensare di più é a parlare di meno*]."[30] His overexcitability sometimes got him into difficulties. In 1825, a year after being elected a member of the prestigious American Philosophical Society, he stirred up angry feelings in the other members; the "war-whoops" described by Miss Lawson. John Godman, writing to Point Breeze, warned him: "Dr. [Richard] Harlan is '*molto irato*' in relation to your remarks before the A. P. Society, and says he will hereafter when he sees you there, say some fine things etc. The truth is he is vexed and will doubtless seek revenge. I laughed very heartily at his sputtering, as you will do, no doubt, at his threats."[31]

On the other hand, Bonaparte made equally close friends. James DeKay at the Lyceum of Natural History in New York told him he had reexamined some of Bonaparte's "serpents" and had "detected a new species." "I thought of naming it after you but I think you expressed a dislike to such compliments. They seem to me however the most flattering & at the same time the most sincere compliments that can be paid to any naturalist."[32] Bonaparte's apparent humility in this respect exemplifies his complex and contradictory character.

The breadth of his knowledge, his clever conversation, and the depth of his cultivation attracted people, but many were apt to judge him more by his pompous behavior than by the deeper qualities of his heart and mind.[33] Toward his wife, evidently, he was kind and loving. In January 1825 Zenaide wrote her mother (from Philadelphia, where they were again spending the winter), that they were very happy together, and that Charles adored his son. She prays to God that her sister Charlotte will have in Napoleon-Louis as good a husband as Charles. In a note to Charlotte ("Lolotte"), appended to her letter to their mother, she says she has not yet commenced the study of English. Charles is like a "watch dog [*chien du jardinier*]," in that he does not want her to have a teacher, reserving for himself all the "glory" of giving her lessons, but he never finds the time to begin. The only hour he would grant her, she says, is in the late evening when he goes back to the "salon" after his own work is finished for the day, but at that hour she would rather go to bed than be tutored. He is very occupied with his history of birds and writes in his study. It is now ten o'clock at night and she is waiting for him to return from the Academy. Be happy with Napoleon, Zenaide counsels her sister in a postscript, for the true and only happiness is to have a good husband and "to love him with all one's soul."[34]

Charles and Zenaide were indeed content together, but by the summer of 1825 they faced some new difficulties. Charles wrote his father a long letter in which he reports that Zenaide's health is not good. She has had a miscarriage, the second in six months, and little Joseph has been so ill they feared for his life, though he is now recovered. Their most persistent problem, however, is a distressing lack of money, because Lucien has not honored his promise to place a certain amount at their disposal through an agent in New York. Charles accuses his father of not recognizing his obligation to his son and his daughter-in-law and of leaving them devoid of financial support. He says, that in spite of the large dowry Zenaide brought to their marriage—of which she has seen nothing—she is forced to undergo disagreeable privations of all kinds. Only because Joseph has given her a gift of a hundred dollars are they able to pay their servants and partially support themselves. Does his father want him to bury himself, as so many others have done, in the forests of Indiana, or Missouri, to live by the toil of his hands cultivating the "wilderness [*terres sauvages*]" on land "bought at a paltry price"? Or does he want him to accept a professorship in one of the universities of the United States?[35] (This last would probably have been impossible at the time. There were few universities, and the ones that existed did not have departments in natural science, certainly not in ornithology.)

Charles's allusion to "the forests of Indiana" was not random. Some of his colleagues were forming a plan to leave Philadelphia and establish themselves in New Harmony, Indiana, a small frontier town bought by Robert Owen, a Welsh visionary and philanthropist, as an experiment in utopian living. A German religious group had built New Harmony some ten years earlier (1815), but the "Harmonists" had found the climate damp and unhealthy from the often-flooding Wabash River, sold the town to Owen, and started a new settlement near Pittsburgh, Pennsylvania. Owen, with the help of others, asked William Maclure to join him in his venture; and Maclure agreed because he wanted to establish a "school of industry," where science and the "useful arts" would replace "latin, greek, and lilliputian," as Say put it in a letter to Bonaparte.[36] The patron of both Say and Lesueur, Maclure hoped that they would teach science and art in his purposed school and invited them to accompany him on a "visit" to the experimental town. By late summer of 1825, plans for the move of the entire group involved in the scheme had not yet been finalized, at least as far as Say was concerned, since in October he still expected to accompany Maclure on a "western and southern journey."[37]

That his closest friend and mentor would be leaving the Academy and Philadelphia for the foreseeable future was considerably depressing to Bonaparte, in spite of the recent appearance of the first volume of his *American Ornithology; or, The Natural History of Birds Inhabiting the United States, not given by Wilson*, a handsome folio-sized book with hand-colored illustrations. He told his father, who continued to disapprove of his chosen career, that having published "several small memoirs on natural history," he had at last brought out a more considerable work on ornithology that appeared to be having some success. "Dare I offer you a copy for your library?"[38]

In many ways Bonaparte's financial situation was similar to Say's. Say was totally dependent on Maclure for his livelihood, because he was not able to pursue his calling in any other way: there were no paying positions in entomology, just as there were none in ornithology. Bonaparte needed similar support from his father but was continually disappointed. His uncle Joseph grudgingly came forth with minimal amounts, but Bonaparte disliked taking anything from him. Both Say and Bonaparte were caught in the conundrum facing many scientists of their day: how to make a living in pursuits that did not yet exist as "careers."

In the same letter, Bonaparte suggests that if Lucien cannot give him and Zenaide any money perhaps he would cede them a portion of his land in Canino on which to live and support themselves. He has heard that the business of agriculture has revived in Italy and that wheat is selling well. The young couple cannot continue to live in their present manner so something must be done. "You see, my dear father, we are not happy." To demonstrate his homesickness, he complains that his brother Paul has not answered any of his letters; nor has Père Maurice. Only Charlotte and "Bonne-Maman" (his mother-in-law) keep them informed of all that is going on in Italy, such as the marriage of his sister Jeanne and the death of his aunt Pauline (Borghese). These letters are tender and consoling for "the poor exiles."

Bonaparte must have felt even more disappointed when Say and Lesueur left for New Harmony at the end of November. They went with Maclure and a group of others to Pittsburgh, where they were to board a keelboat—later called "the Boatload of Knowledge" because of all the scientists aboard—that would take them down the Ohio River to Robert Owen's "utopian" town. Bonaparte would never see Say again, and Lesueur only years later in Paris. It must have seemed as though the wilderness had swallowed them. There was always the mail, but letters took a long time to reach their destination.

In January 1826 Bonaparte bolstered his spirits by going to New York. He wrote Hays that he was delighted to find swans selling for four dollars apiece and wild turkeys for two. He had also gotten several interesting gulls in the food market; two were unknown to him, and he would include them in the next volume of his book.[39] He is worried about the illustrations for the second volume, however, and asks Hays to check whether Peale has finished the drawing he was supposed to have ready for Lawson to engrave. "Titian is very leasy [lazy], & though he solemnly promised to have these drawings ready by this time, I doubt whether he has one! Thus does he wait until the last moment, & by hurrying the work spoils it entirely. These remarks are severe but true." Lawson and Peale have quarreled, he says, and refuse to see each other, therefore a "mediator" is necessary. Since Hays is Peale's near neighbor and Bonaparte is so far away, he asks him to intervene.[40] As soon as Peale has finished the drawing, Bonaparte continues, the mediator (Hays) is to try to find fault with it, "which is not at all difficult," and after the corrections have been made, the drawing and the bird specimens must be sent to Lawson. Hays is then to have an interview with "that talking being [Lawson], listen to his complaints, abuses & recollect what is good (and there is always a good deal) & propose to Peale the changes in question." If Peale agrees to them, all is well; if not, "the mediator must return the drawing to Lawson & tell him he has full power of changing & correcting himself! etc. provided he does not employ his little boy, or even his beautiful daughter." He admits that he was afraid Hays would refuse his request, because in the course of it Lawson might "kill a couple of *Homines sapientes*, & lame or otherwise cook a dozen. But for science & arts sake & a little for friendship I hope you will assume these important functions."

A week later, he received an encouraging letter from Hays. "I see by your last that all is proceeding beyond my expectations. Peale must have thrown off his leasy coat! . . . as for Lawson . . . if he has spared you, God knows what will happen to me!" But in spite of Hays's assistance, Peale apparently refused to continue working for Bonaparte around this time, for only the work of Rider is represented in the second and third volumes. Peale's work reappears in the fourth volume: drawings of the birds he brought back from Florida.

Shortly after his note about Peale, Bonaparte wrote again to Hays, in a frantic attempt to correct a mistake in the "Observations" on Wilson's nomenclature, which was about to appear in the *Journal*. Much to his horror, he discovered that he had described a new species as an old one. Hays is to insert a quick notice in the *Journal* correcting his mistake. "I tremble that the reviewer should detect it . . . that devil of Temminck for instance to whom I have long since sent my work will know it at once, & Please to God he does not notice it before us."[41]

In December 1825, shortly after Say left Philadelphia, things began to fall apart at the Academy of Natural Sciences. It was Say who had held the Academy together; his even temper and constant presence created an atmosphere of order and amiability. Chaos followed his departure. He had taken almost sole charge of the *Journal* and there was no one to replace him. The Academy was also on the brink of a real estate purchase that not everyone approved of. Bonaparte wrote Hays with concern: "The public voice frightens me! They say the Academy has ruined themselves by purchasing a lot, and announce the *death* of our Journal of which they say another number will never be published! Is it possible! . . . and if so would it not be better to help by funds the Journal, than the building?"[42] Nevertheless, however much Bonaparte may have protested, the Academy members bought the building, a former Swedenborgian church in Philadelphia, only a few blocks away from the old hall, and moved the collections into it in the winter of 1826. Afterward a period of wrangling ensued for the *Journal*, marked in particular by the rejection of papers—Say's as well as others—for personal, spiteful reasons, a situation that formerly would have been totally alien to Academy members.

In the midst of this ongoing dissension at the Academy, Bonaparte found himself also at odds with Audubon over the first volume of *American*

Ornithology. The artist described the book, in a letter to Reuben Haines, as "handsome" and "scientific." But, he said,

nature has not put *her stamp* upon it—there are great errors in it and yet some valuable parts, but, if it is not Willson [sic] who speaks, it is *Monsieur Say qui n'est qu'un homme d'Esprit*—Bonaparte I think has been abused and misled—it is however a Book that will be seen in Europe with pleasure but I must say I am surprised at the Scarcity both of Subjects and Matter contained in it, and could I see Charles Bonaparte, and he listen to me as he would to his half known [?] friend [Say] I feel satisfied that he would acknowledge, that although I have read but Little I have seen a Great Deal—*in the Woods.*[43]

He would like to write the prince "fully on the subject," but fears to offend him and does not want to be thought "forward" in extending his opinions. "I am sorry that Charles Bonaparte was shy of me when in Philadelphia," Audubon concludes, "had he confided in me, depend on it my dear Mr. Haines he never would have been ungratefully delt with—my heart allways Enclined towards him—I Naturally Loved his great Uncle, Napoleon of France."

Unfortunately, Haines had the "kindness, not to say, simplicity" to relay Audubon's remarks to Bonaparte, as the indignant author fumed to his naturalist friend William Cooper in New York. Bad as it might be, says Bonaparte, his book did not deserve such treatment. Audubon might at least have granted him the honor of making his own errors rather than being "misled" and "betrayed" by Say. One arrogant thrust in particular put Bonaparte in a tailspin: the imputation that if only Bonaparte had placed his confidence in Audubon, instead of having his "pretended work written by Mr. Say (who after all, says he, is but a *man of wit*)," Audubon would "have stamped his hand upon it." Certain that his outrage would be favorably received at the Academy Bonaparte read some of Audubon's unfortunate remarks at the next meeting.[44]

Bonaparte wrote his letter to Cooper on board a steamboat headed from Baltimore to Washington. The purpose for this trip is not known, but it may have been to visit the newly elected president, John Quincy Adams, whom he had met at Point Breeze. In any case, for Bonaparte his distance from Philadelphia apparently allowed him to gain a little distance from his book as well. In concluding the subject of the book's reception, he said he could not help laughing when he realized that people considered a work of "great importance to science" because it was well printed and "well finished outside: thus so many think that my reputation as an orn[ithologist] is to rest on the description of 15! species of birds! . . . but the breakfast bell rings & I must spare you a few more nonsenses."[45] To defuse the situation, Cooper would advise him: "I think you ought rather to laugh at any thing Audubon may say, than take it amiss. From what I have heard of him he seems to be a man very hard to please, and it is of not much consequence whether he is pleased or not."[46]

Bonaparte had dined in Baltimore with Dr. Dewees Patterson and the architect William Strickland before boarding the steamboat *United States* for the capital. Dr. Patterson was the brother of Elizabeth Patterson, the American woman who had married Charles's Uncle Jerome but whose entirely legal marriage was subsequently disallowed by Napoleon, even though Pope Pius VII had considered it valid.[47] The son of that marriage, Jerome-Napoleon Bonaparte, had been considered as a husband for Zenaide's sister Charlotte, but she had not been interested in him. For Charles, meeting the Pattersons gave him an added familial link to America, the country whose principles he found so compatible with his own.

No sooner had Bonaparte arrived in Washington than he received a disturbing letter from Hays saying that at the last Academy meeting Ord had objected to the latest installment of Bonaparte's "Observations on the Nomenclature of Wilson's Ornithology." Ord had apparently been quick to catch the mistake Bonaparte himself had discovered, and a resolution had been taken to delay publication. Hays advised Bonaparte to withdraw the paper. This was too much! He stormed back that the resolution was "unconstitutional" and it would be easy for him to prove it, but it would be better not to have anything more to do with "that body" which had already rejected so many of Say's papers. "I am astonished, my dear Sir, at your proposition . . . to me!" "As chairman of the committee of publication of the Academy of natural sciences of Philadelphia, I have nothing to say to you." "Let them follow what course they will . . . they dare . . . take. I will neither withdraw, nor amend, nor ever speak again of my paper. . . . As my friend I now request you to print as quick as possible for my own account the extra copies of my Observations etc. I shall take care of having them circulated etc."[48]

Two days later he instructed Hays to have a copy of his paper struck off for each *Journal* subscriber and to send it along with the publication. "I shall be at your office Tuesday morning at such an hour as I am sure to find you in bed, & will look for a couple of proof sheets if I have not received them in Washington by that time."[49]

Fierce competition raged among naturalists to be first in naming new species and to be absolutely correct in classification. Say had written a short paper accusing a colleague (John Le Conte) of publishing five new species of insect that he, Say, had already published and there could be no doubt as to his

priority. His paper had been one of the ones rejected by the publishing committee. An even more heated debate flared up when John Godman charged
Richard Harlan (another Academy member) with plagiarism. This battling over
nomenclature was inevitable in the early years of natural history studies in
America. So much was new and taxonomy took precedence over all other
aspects of scientific debate. Bonaparte was not alone in controversy.

On a happier note than the one in which he had addressed Hays,
Bonaparte wrote Zenaide that the first person he met on entering the hotel in
Washington was a cousin of his friend William Cooper: James Fenimore
Cooper. This encounter was delightful; in one hour of conversation with the
novelist, Bonaparte learned all the news of the day.[50] Cooper was by then a
famous author; his reputation already established in the United States by *The
Spy* and *The Pioneers*. *The Last of the Mohicans*, to be published also in England
in that year of 1826, would make him internationally famous. Bonaparte told
William Cooper that he and "Mr. Fenimore"—"to avoid confusion we have
agreed to Decooperize him"[51]—enjoyed themselves immensely in Washington.
They "could not help it being in so good a company (no modesty is required).
But we never thought a moment of natural history being all the time deeply and
boldly engaged in the greatest political questions."[52] Politics, at times, overcame
natural history in Bonaparte's enthusiasms.

A contemporary description of "Mr. Fenimore" makes him sound
remarkably like the prince himself: "Mr. Cooper was in person solid, robust,
athletic: in voice, manly; in manner, earnest, emphatic, almost dictatorial—
with something of self-assertion, bordering on egotism. The first effect was
unpleasant, indeed repulsive, but there shone through all this a heartiness, a
frankness, which excited confidence, respect, and at last affection."[53]

Fenimore Cooper later related that he and Bonaparte had visited Mount
Vernon to pay homage to Washington's grave, and a gardener had given the
prince a bouquet wrapped in old paper from the greenhouse. On examining
this wrapping, they had found it was a page from the "Farming Journal of the
Hero himself, in his own handwriting." Bonaparte had given the treasure to
Cooper, who kept it, he said, not only as a sample of Washington's "hand" but
also "as a fine evidence of his method [discipline], even in the most trifling
things."[54] Two months after Bonaparte's encounter with Cooper, the author
left the United States to spend the next seven years in Europe.[55]

Joseph Bonaparte no doubt told his nephew something of the Cooper
family when Charles first met William Cooper at the Lyceum of Natural History
of New York. Judge William Cooper, Fenimore Cooper's father, a legendary
land speculator and entrepreneur (d. 1809), had been the agent for a large tract
of land in the Black River valley of upper New York state owned by a certain

Count de Chaumont. This wealthy French émigré and financier had planned to establish a French colony there. Joseph Bonaparte bought a portion of Chaumont's land before he fled Europe in 1815 and later built a large hunting lodge on it, as well as a house for his Quaker mistress, Annette Savage, and their illegitimate daughter, born in 1822. In the succeeding four years, he had lost interest in his *amour* as well as in his northern land.[56] But in 1826 an intriguing opportunity presented itself. John Lafarge, a New York merchant, had also purchased a large woodland tract at Black River and had built an enormous house on it, but now found himself ruined financially. When he offered to sell his holdings to Joseph, the count conceived of a plan to help Zenaide and Charles out of their pecuniary difficulties.

"I ask your advice in a private affair that has been in question for the last two days," Zenaide wrote to her mother in the summer of 1826. After telling Julie about Lafarge and his offer to sell, she reports that her father has counseled her and Charles to take the property in exchange for the mortgage on Canino, which Lafarge would assume. (The mortgage was held by Cardinal Fesch, and presumably Joseph could persuade him to exchange it for Lafarge's land.) They would then go live on the Black River estate, to clear and cultivate it. Her father thinks this would be advantageous for them, but for herself, the idea of living in the woods is unpleasant though she would be happy to see an end to all their "infamous affairs" in Rome (their quarrels with Lucien over the dowry).[57] Zenaide had given birth to another child, Alexandrine-Gertrude-Zenaide (in June), and was even more anxious than before to gain some financial security for her growing family. The baby, sadly, was hydrocephalic and would need special care. Julie, taking her cue from Zenaide's own distaste for life in the woods, especially under the new circumstances, and eager to have her daughter back in Rome, did not approve the plan and nothing came of it. Although far away, Julie's moral authority mattered.

No sooner had Charles returned from his trip to Washington in late March than the Academy and its ongoing problems immediately took over his thoughts. He wrote William Cooper in New York:

You have certainly heard of the squabbles in the Academy of Nat[ural] Sc[ience] during my visit to Washington . . . of the second challenge between two members still more harmless than the two Doctors [Harlan and Godman who disagreed violently on their approach to natural history] of the first. The first is however terminated without bloodshed . . . but every Gentleman (I ought to say every honest man) will probably never shew his face (at least for a long time) in that society which is now less scientific than commercial, they having made a stock-jobbing business of it. As for myself, I have thought necessary to withdraw not only my list but even the last part of my observations [on Wilson's nomenclature] which are however printing separately.[58]

He says that all the members of the publishing committee have quit in exasperation; "we shall see in whose hands is the Journal now to fall." He thinks it possible that Zacheus Collins ("one of the most disgusted"), Robert Vaux, Godman, Peale, Jacob Gilliams (one of the founders), and "of course the American Linnaeus [Say] etc etc will never again appear in the Ac[ademy]. (I do not speak of my humble self)." As for Ord, Bonaparte says he has "united with the rabble . . . but after all he is with all his faults probably an honest man."

From New Harmony, Say wrote Hays that he had heard Hays had been left out of the publication committee. He feared there were influential people in the Academy so lacking in principle as to sacrifice its best interests to "private pique," and if those members got the upper hand the society's whole object would inevitably be "frustrated."[59]

Poor Hays had little peace from Bonaparte. In April 1826, repeating his behavior of two years before, Bonaparte wrote Hays angrily from Point Breeze that eight days had passed since he had sent back the proofs of the disputed paper [his "Observations] that were to be printed. "I entreated you no less than your confounded printer to go on as quick as possible. You cannot conceive at what inconvenience these wantonless & *unaccountable for* delays put my author-ship." His uncle's friend, Count Melito, was sailing soon for France, and Bonaparte had wanted to send with him copies of "Observations" for all his friends abroad. He ends his letter "in confounded haste."[60] This was surely the nephew of Napoleon speaking.

By the following month Bonaparte was as distraught as ever about his benighted scientific institution. He exclaimed to Cooper, "Do not speak to me of the Ac[ademy]. I think it is d[amned] . . . forever, though the differences appear to have been made up by the honest men taking again the majority! But I am sure no man that *respects himself* will take Hays, Griffith, Say & even Keating's place! The death blow has been inflicted! . . . My feelings are those of a foreigner [*étrangé*]."[61]

Bonaparte's altercation with Ord, in addition to all the other disagree-ments at the Academy, prompted him and several other disgruntled members, such as Jacob Gilliams, an Academy founder, and Dr. John Sharpless, to set up a rival institution they called the Maclurian Lyceum. The first number of their publication, *Contributions of the Maclurian Lyceum*, states diplomatically that "in consequence of an increasing taste for scientific pursuits, it was thought advisable to form another institution in this city, which should afford addi-tional facilities for the acquisition of knowledge. With this view, a society was established in May 1826."[62] It was named after Maclure—without his knowledge—because of all the aid he had given to the development of American science. Maclure was still president of the Academy, but this irony apparently did not bother the new society's members.

Bonaparte nominated Say as president. When Say heard of it, however, he wrote to Bonaparte that he had told the members of the Lyceum he thought it was against the interests of the institution to have a "chief officer" at such a distance, and that Bonaparte should take the position. But since the nomination had been reiterated, he would accept the honor, as long as it was understood that he would resign the minute the interest of the society required it.[63]

Bonaparte shook off his old affiliation completely. He told Hays, "I do not want even to have my name mentioned in your Ac[ademy] *if I can help it.*" As for his "Observations," he would thank Hays for sending a copy to Say, as Hays had suggested. He has seen Ferrusac's bulletin (a French publication), and all that was "new and interesting" in it was attributable to Say.[64]

In June, when John Godman, writing to congratulate Bonaparte on the birth of his daughter, asked him to check over the sheets of his own book, *American Natural History*, he cautioned that "in looking it over you may observe some very warm republicanism which is of course *American*, and will have to be either modified or left out of an European edition."[65] A week later he wrote again to thank Bonaparte for his patience in reading the book and "the kind spirit" in which his criticisms were made. He would have dedicated the book to him, Godman says, except he thought it might prevent his friend from being totally candid with him, and also because readers might turn against the work if it were not dedicated to an American.[66] It must have been gratifying to Bonaparte to feel that his contributions to American ornithology were appreciated by many colleagues, even if that appreciation could not always be expressed publicly.

Europeans also sought his advice. In a letter to Hays in June 1826 he enumerated the papers he had received from Professor Paolo Savi in Pisa and the "small volume of queries, criticisms etc." from Temminck in Holland. In fact, lately he has "received cases, books, & scientific letters from every part of the civilized world."[67] But increasingly he felt the need to examine the collections of foreign savants at first hand and to compare them with his own, to expand his knowledge of the world's birds by visiting the august scientific institutions of Europe. He also had personal affairs to settle on the other side of the Atlantic. In October 1826 he informed Cooper that he had been thinking for some weeks of making a trip to Italy.[68]

He planned to go first to England to meet with the many naturalists with whom he had been corresponding for some time. Zenaide and the children would remain at Point Breeze. Because Bonaparte would be in London, Joseph, who may have been short of cash, entrusted him to ship over—probably on the same vessel—several of his valuable paintings for auction. Included among these masterpieces were Teniers's *Adoration of the Magi*, Van Dyck's *Christ on the Cross*, Murillo's *Virgin and Infant Jesus*, a village fair by Brueghel, and a Rubens "worth more than all the others."[69] As usual, Bonaparte was swamped with his work of describing and classifying birds and may have felt imposed upon by his uncle for this interruption. At any rate, he handled the business carelessly. Unlike his father, Charles did not give first priority to great art. Joseph, already put off by his nephew's prickly personality, would take a dim view of this thoughtlessness.

4

SORTIES TO
FAMILIAR SHORES

"I have been able to meet with the
principal naturalists of Europe, examine their chief specimens,
rob them of what I wanted & have been desired everywhere
to name & arrange the N[orth] Am[erican] birds
according to my Synopsis."

—Bonaparte to William Cooper,
Point Breeze, 11 September 1827

BONAPARTE LANDED in Liverpool after a rapid crossing of ten and a half days aboard the *Canada*. He was met by William Rathbone, a naturalist friend and patron of Audubon's, and stayed a few days at Green Bank, the Rathbones' family home outside the city. From there he went to London, where a letter from Audubon awaited him announcing the imminent publication of the first number of the artist's *Birds of America*, begun a month before by the Edinburgh publisher William Lizars. Audubon wanted to know the best way to send a copy to Bonaparte's cousin the duke of Reichstadt, "the noble son of your Great Uncle Napoleon of France."[1] It was a futile request, for since his father's downfall the young duke had been living in Vienna with his grandfather, the Austrian emperor Francis II, and any contact with Bonaparte relations was out of the question. Austria had been part of the alliance that defeated Napoleon in 1815.

In London Bonaparte was warmly entertained by his scientific colleagues—in spite of his name, repugnant to most English people—and felt "as though he was in his native land." His four years there as a child had left him with fond and vivid memories. He wrote Hays that he had spent "a fortnight in this wonderful city & indeed I could not give less to London after the most flattering reception of all these naturalists & scientific Ladies. Zoology flourishes more than ever in England." Hays could not imagine, says Bonaparte, what a busy life he is leading, seeing merchants, agents, and booksellers. He spends his days with naturalists and his evenings with "many different people." Much to his dismay, however, everyone complains of the difficulty of getting American books. "No copy of my Orn[ithology] is to be found & a friend of mine the other day gave 6 guineas for one!"[2]

The difficulty of transporting books and the absence of any system for distributing them (the book distributor as such did not yet exist) was an ongoing problem for naturalists. And sometimes scientific books were printed in such small numbers that demand outran supply. For example, two years later William Swainson would write Bonaparte that it was a shame so few copies of his book had been printed. He thought it unfortunate that naturalists did not exchange their works more generally, to keep each other informed of their researches. He badly needed Bonaparte's book, but was unable to find a copy in any of the public libraries. "What therefore am I to do? With every wish of doing justice to our predecessors, it is frequently utterly out of our power to know what they have done."[3]

Bonaparte was nominated for membership in the Linnean Society of London in mid-December, and on 1 May 1827 was elected. The society had been founded in 1788, after Linnaeus's death, by James Edward Smith, who had bought all the great man's collections, manuscripts, and books. Bonaparte was one of fifty foreign members—Say was already among them. At the first meeting, Bonaparte noted with interest that the scientists were divided into Linnaean and anti-Linnaean factions. Linnaeus's system of binomial nomenclature (genus followed by species) provided a unified method for categorizing the numerous discoveries made in natural history in the eighteenth and nineteenth centuries. It established the foundation for the systematic work that underlay all evolutionary enlightenment bursting on the scene in Charles Bonaparte's day.[4] But the system used artificial groupings that took little account of the close relationships between certain faunal families. The anti-Linnaeans used a system based on natural structural affinities. Both sides claimed Bonaparte, since he was perceived as holding a median position. It amused him to think that if Linnaeus returned to the world he would be anti-Linnaean, meaning that he would approve the new system, as did Bonaparte himself.[5]

During the visit Bonaparte examined a number of public and private collections and recorded in minute detail everything he saw. The specimens he canvassed were useful for spotting both changes in species names and variations that occurred between similar specimens in different geographical locations. A year earlier he had written to Cooper: "I believe that some genera pass into each other, though others *do not* . . . I believe that some are strongly marked and well characterized whilst others *are not* . . . and this is my profession of faith!"[6]

In the course of his inspections he made many new friends, including John Edward Gray, soon to head the British Museum, John George Children, appointed that year to the museum's natural history department, the great anatomist Richard Owen, and other important men in the scientific field. He was especially drawn to Nicholas Aylward Vigors, the zealous first secretary of the Zoological Society of London—founded the year before, in 1826. After Vigors got the institution organized, Bonaparte was elected a foreign member, one of only twenty-five. The two men remained friends and correspondents for many years, until Vigors, long after he had abandoned natural science and become a member of Parliament, sank into depression and died by his own hand.[7]

The one negative aspect of Bonaparte's stay in London was a letter from Joseph's agents, Sampson Batard & Co., stating that his uncle's paintings had arrived in a very bad state, "much injured by injudicious packing." They should never have been sent with their frames on: three of them were broken from top to bottom and were "perfectly unsaleable" until repaired. Besides this, the asking prices were "so extremely high" as to hinder the sale.[8] Of course Joseph was notified of the sorry state of his masterpieces, and this would be one more bone of contention between him and his nephew.

After a grand dinner and a lively meeting at the Linnean Society on 19 December 1826, Bonaparte left for Dover, where he embarked the next day for the continent. Temminck met him in Brussels and traveled with him to Leiden, where Bonaparte stayed at his home and visited his famous museum, the Rijksmuseum van Natuurlijke Historie. Though the visit was brief, it meant a great deal to Bonaparte, for it gave him the opportunity to deepen his friendship with the famous Dutchman. He had so much to tell Temminck about his stay in America and his New World discoveries in natural history.

Since he was still forbidden to enter France, he traveled through Germany and visited the new Senckenberg Museum in Frankfurt. The director, Dr. Philip Jacob Cretzschmar, who had served as an army surgeon in the Napoleonic wars, gave him two Black-winged Kites from North Africa, among other specimens. Because the Germans were now freed from the "Napoleonic nightmare," the Senckenberg and other newly opened museums in Berlin, Darmstadt, Munich, Dresden, and Halle had been able to concentrate on building their collections, especially those of exotic birds[9]—a blessing for Napoleon's naturalist nephew. These collections were of great interest to Charles in his study of world ornithology. Cretzschmar later told a colleague that Bonaparte "is unquestionably a very scientific man, as he has demonstrated in his works." He added that the prince had offered to work on all species of American birds and that "this patron of ornithology" would join him and his colleagues in their project of a scientific meeting in Germany as a representative of North America.[10]

Bonaparte's meeting with Cretzschmar was highly significant because it gave him the idea of holding scientific congresses in Italy as well, where again he could represent the United States. Such meetings would point the way to Italian unity by bringing together scientists from all over the peninsula for discussions in various disciplines of science. Bonaparte's mind must have been fermenting with plans after this visit with Cretzschmar.

When at last he reached Italy, Bonaparte was especially flattered with the reception given him by Professors Franco Andrea Bonelli in Turin, Paolo Savi in Pisa, and Carlo Passerini in Florence.[11] With the help of Savi, he published in Pisa, in 1827, his small but interesting work *Specchio comparativo delle ornitologie di Roma e di Filadelfia* (A Comparative Register of the Ornithology of Rome and Philadelphia). In it he says that before leaving Italy in the late spring of 1823 he had laid out a history of the birds of Rome, though he had not published it. His observations in North America during the past four years have put him in a position to add the birds of Philadelphia to the earlier study. He hopes that such a comparison will be useful, if only for the geography of ornithology, because these two cities of the Old and the New Worlds are on the same latitude.[12] For brevity, Bonaparte limits his synonyms—the list of names given to a particular species by different naturalists over the years—to those of Temminck, and cites the common names of birds as well, to help "amateurs, hunters, and museum preparators." He finds that there are 247 different species in Rome as against 281 in Philadelphia, and that plumage colors are at least as beautiful in Rome, but that birds in Philadelphia are distinguished by their sweetness of song [*soavita del lor canto*]."[13]

In Rome Charles stayed with a childhood friend, since his parents were no longer living in the city. Lucien had sold his grand palace in the Bocca di Leone to his brother Jerome in 1823, shortly after Charles and Zenaide left for America—news that was covered in a Baltimore paper a few weeks after his arrival in the United States.[14] That his father was paid "above 800,000 francs" for his palazzo must have been galling to Charles. Lucien could have paid out at least part of Zenaide's dowry from the profits on the sale, but not a cent had found its way to the young Bonapartes.

During his stay in the Eternal City, Bonaparte visited Pope Leo XII and gave him a copy of his *American Ornithology*. Bonaparte noted in his memoirs that the pontiff received the gift with "fatherly affection [*paterno affetto*]"[15]—a poignant observation, since Lucien had given his book such a cold reception. Because he had definitely decided to return with his family to Rome the following year, Charles made preparations to rent the Palazzo Verospi on the Via del Corso. The palace had romantic associations: eight years earlier the poet Shelley had rented a suite of rooms there with his wife Mary and her stepsister Claire Clairmont. Bonaparte also took time to pose for a marble bust of himself by the sculptor Trentanove. The artist depicted him as a citizen of ancient Rome with a toga buttoned on his right shoulder. A curly, well-trimmed beard surrounds his chin like a helmet strap, and his bearing is dignified, if not magisterial (see figure 15).

Bonaparte then visited his parents in Sinigallia on the Adriatic coast, where they were spending the summer, before retracing his arduous route back to America by way of the British Isles.[16] His memoirs say nothing of the visit, but undoubtedly there were some heated discussions about money.

Newly arrived back in London, he was invited on an interesting adventure: an underwater excursion to inspect the tunnel being constructed under the Thames River. In order to see the tunnel from the outside, he and several others descended to the river bottom in a "diving bell [*cloche d'immersion*]," where they stayed for half an hour, as he wrote to his mother-in-law. He suffered no other inconvenience than pressure in his ears, which was relieved by holding his nose and blowing out as hard as possible, "like the whales." Alexander von Humboldt, who had tested the diving bell a few days earlier, "had much exaggerated his sufferings in it," said Charles. But the one who would really have enjoyed the device was his cousin Napoleon-Louis (Charlotte's husband); Charles wished he could have been there to share the experience.[17] This pretender to the Napoleonic succession was a clever, adventuresome young man with a strong interest in aeronautics; he was experimenting with devices to replace balloon flight with mechanical flight by means of revolving propellers.[18]

In the same letter to Julie, after recounting his experience beneath the Thames, Bonaparte turns to an ongoing problem, seemingly unsolvable and deeply upsetting to all parties: the bitter antagonism growing between him and Joseph. Julie had apparently received an angry letter about her son-in-law—no doubt occasioned by the incident of the damaged paintings—and had quoted it to him. "I don't think he has anything to complain of about me," Bonaparte states; "perhaps, however, he would find it quite natural for me to stifle the rage and the torrent of complaints my pride alone makes me hold back. In every way, if he is discontented with me, we are a match for each other!" But this does not matter, because they "will not be condemned to live long together!" He seems to have made up his mind at this point to return to Europe for good.

Bonaparte tells his "chère Maman" that it hurts him to open his heart to her. He is sure to lose her esteem, since she has always seen only the good qualities of her husband—qualities to which no one has rendered more justice than he (Bonaparte). But he admits, with a humility that he rarely displayed elsewhere, "it is the effect of my bad character . . . I am perhaps not *hated* without reason." If forced to recommence his career he would do certain things differently. For example, he would not accede to the "false entreaties" of his uncle to rejoin him in America. But the faults he is accused of he would definitely commit again. Yes, he would again leave her; and he would again leave his own mother at Bologna (in both cases for the sake of independence); and above all, he would leave Madame Lacoste at Point Breeze ("forgive me for putting you in the same sentence"). According to his uncle, these defections are his three mortal sins. "I am far from disavowing them and above all from repenting them . . . but, you say my uncle 'was always so good to his children!'"[19] There seems to have been no secret between Charles and his mother-in-law about Joseph's affair with Madame Lacoste.

Charles's antagonism toward his uncle may have sprung partly from repugnance. As a young man he seems to have been chaste and, if not naive, certainly proper. His own parents, until then at least, had presented a perfect example of conjugal devotion, and he himself was completely loyal to Zenaide. His uncle's blatant flirtations, amorous escapades, and entanglements must have been odious to him, especially since he was so fond of Joseph's wife.

From London Bonaparte crossed to Ireland to visit, in Waterford, his troubled younger sister Letizia and her husband, Thomas Wyse, Bonaparte's "much-loved brother-in-law, a zealous defender of the Catholic religion, of progress and of liberty." An Irish aristocrat, Wyse would be elected to parliament several years later. Letizia, unfortunately, showed signs of unbalance. Bonaparte's older half-sister Christine, married to Lord Dudley Stuart and living in London, said that Letizia "affects to resemble her uncle Napoleon, to whose features hers have no likeness. But she tries to obtain her object by frowns and crossing her arms and adopting his tricks—cutting up tables with a pen-knife and other peculiarities which only render her vacancy and absurdity more apparent."[20]

From Liverpool, at five in the morning, after a twelve-hour journey from Ireland, Bonaparte sent off another letter to his mother-in-law. He thanks her for her previous letter to him and asks her not to lessen her favor toward him and Zenaide, because their return to Europe depends on it. (Julie's good will and moral authority were at all times important to them.) He will only return to Italy if he can be independent and at the same time support Zenaide in a style of life suitable for her. In order to be independent he would even live at New Harmony and persuade himself that it was by choice. It would have to be New Harmony rather than Philadelphia, however, since he has spent so much money on this "agreeable voyage." And God knows when they would return to Italy![21]

Back in London, Bonaparte went to see Audubon, who noted in his journal how "pleased" they were to meet each other on that "distant shore." Bonaparte's "fine head was not altered, his mustachios, his bearded chin, his keen eye, all were the same. He wished to see my drawings, and I, for the first time since I had been in London, had pleasure in showing them. Charles at once subscribed [to his book], and I felt really proud of this."[22]

Audubon's spirits were low at the time. His Edinburgh publisher, Lizars, had informed him that the people who colored his drawings were on strike and the publication of *Birds of America* was at a standstill. It cheered him when Bonaparte asked him to join him and a group of naturalists for dinner at the Royal Society Club, but he nevertheless declined because "great dinners" frightened him. Later in the evening, however, Bonaparte appeared at Audubon's lodgings with Vigors, Children, and several others in tow. "My portfolios were opened before this set of learned men," Audubon recorded, "and they saw many birds they had not dreamed of. Charles offered to name them for me, and I felt happy that he should; and with a pencil he actually christened upwards of fifty, urging me to publish them at once in manuscript at the Zoological Society. These gentlemen dropped off one by one leaving only Charles and Mr. Vigors. Oh that our knowledge could be arranged into a solid mass. I am sure the best ornithological publication of the birds of my beloved country might then be published."[23]

Several days later, in early July, Bonaparte left England aboard the *Manchester* for a grueling fifty-three-day passage to America. When at last in New York, at eleven o'clock at night on 23 August 1827 and suffering from a troublesome fever, he was in such a hurry to see his family after his nine-month absence that instead of waiting until morning he hired a gig, changed horses five times on the road, and arrived at Point Breeze by daybreak.[24]

He wrote Cooper that in spite of the great speed of his return trip across the continent—he traveled from Florence to London in only ten days—he had been able to meet with the principal naturalists of Europe, "examine their chief specimens, rob them of what I wanted & have been desired everywhere to name & arrange the N[orth] Am[erican] birds according to my Synopsis" ("The Genera of North American Birds, and a Synopsis of the Species . . . ," a paper he wrote for the *Annals of the Lyceum of Natural History of New York*)."[25] He tells Cooper too that this paper and the notes for it need to be printed by the end of October. After that he could not attend to it, as he would be preparing for the removal of his family to Italy. He had, it seems, made up his mind to leave the United States.

In his unintentional role of international courier, he had brought with him Audubon's "beautiful first number" (the first copy of *The Birds of America* to arrive in the United States). And he had lent Temminck Godman's *American Natural History*, with which Temminck was "so highly pleased" that he refused to give it back. Bonaparte too must have been pleased with Godman's book, because of the author's glowing tribute in the preface. It was a heart-warming accolade from a close American friend and colleague:

We should act with injustice to our own feelings if we omitted to avow the liberal and valuable assistance we have received from one whose name is sufficient to justify any encomiums on expanded views and zeal in the cause of scientific truth. The prince of Musignano, Charles L. Bonaparte, has at all times thrown open to our use his own rich library and cabinets, and still farther enhanced this kindness by contributing in numerous instances the result of his own scientific observations. Similar liberality in the cause of science has long since secured to him the esteem and respect of those who are devoted to its cultivation, and the warm admiration of all who have the advantage of his acquaintance.[26]

In preparing a box of specimens and books for shipment to Temminck in Amsterdam, after his return from Europe, Bonaparte told Cooper that in matters of classification and nomenclature Temminck had said that he never relied on anyone but himself: "this is his principal merit & he is right in our days."[27] He meant that natural science was still at that time in such a state of confusion that it was risky to take writings of others as gospel.

Bonaparte was completely worn out when he reached Point Breeze, not only from the long grueling ocean voyage but also from the intense and voluminous work he had done in England. Benjamin Leadbeater, a London taxidermist and dealer in bird specimens, thought the prince must have been greatly "confined" during his visit or he could not have written so much. "It would take some of our English Gentlemen as many years to write as much," he said. "It seems too great a trouble for them, which makes us always behind in describing Birds, otherwise many New Birds [unexamined specimens] in London that has been waiting 4 or 5 years to be describ'd [would have to wait] until Mr. Temminck or some other Person describes them [but] it is then too late."[28]

Nor did Bonaparte's pace relax much now that he was back in the United States. His decision to return to Europe for good, and as soon as possible, threw him into a flurry of activity in order to fulfill various scientific and literary obligations before his departure. For weeks, he only left his desk for two or three hours of sleep each night and a half-hour for meals. Even a year earlier a visitor had described Bonaparte's parlor, across the hall from his study, as having a canopy bed and a "vessel, its usual accompaniment, not grateful to my eyes occupied a corner without disguise! I wondered indeed if it was an accident!"[29] This punishing regimen caused his health to deteriorate, and he began to spit blood. He ignored this symptom, and eventually it disappeared, but certainly it had been a sign that he was pushing his body too far. In a few months, he finished two volumes of *American Ornithology* and his long article on the genera of American birds.[30]

His normal tactlessness was aggravated by exhaustion, and he wrote to Cooper in a tone of asperity about the printing of his article. He had received the proof but was "deeply *afflicted* with it . . . for the careless way in which it is printed shows that you have hardly been at the trouble to read the Mms. as I find often the two versions of which I submitted to your choice printed together. You must know that I rely on you alone in this country for advice & by you again to *improve*, or stop the printing."[31]

A few days later, after leaving his desk long enough to go hunting, Bonaparte wrote Cooper excitedly, "I have been very busy & successful these days with my gun! I have even shot a beautiful specimen of the almost lost S[ylvio] Wilsonii . . . Peale has not been less successful in Philadelphia & is himself astonished *at his crop!*" He says his taxidermist has mounted an average of twelve birds every day, and Peale, who in an hour shot enough for two days' work, has some valuable specimens. "What a treat it is to be watching amongst the leaves these rare & sometimes unknown feathered little beings!"[32] He seems by then to have reestablished his friendship with Peale.

Toward the end of October he traveled to New York to confer with Cooper about his manuscript. On his return, he wrote his long-suffering friend: "Are your printers asleep, or has the indigestion of Ornithology you must have had during my stay in N.Y. prevented you from pushing on with the Synopsis? As for myself overpowered by work I am quite sick with science & would willingly never muddle with authorship again!"[33]

In struggling with the manuscript for his book, he sought Cooper's advice for the English of certain hawks: "Circus, Elanus, & Astur," and could he use "Goshawk" for the latter? Also, could he say "the Goshawks" as he would say "*Les Autours*" in French? Had any English name been applied to them, and if not how could he "baptize them"? Cooper thought Bonaparte was likely to be confounded if he tried to find English names for all the subgenera of *Falco*. "*Hawks* is very good for *Astures*, but I hardly think *Harrier* will do for *Circus*. *Harrier* is the name for the kind of hound used in England for hunting hares." "Why not call E[lanus] Dissar *whitetailed? Uneventailed* is better than *Irregulartailed*."[34] In addition to Cooper, Bonaparte had also been consulting Godman about his problems with language. Godman suggested that if any passage of his work was too difficult to express in English he should underline it, "or append your intended expression as may be most satisfactory to you in Latin, French or Italian." He wants to help as much as possible but is terribly busy himself.[35]

To honor his friend, Bonaparte named a hawk he had shot near Bordentown toward the end of September, *Falco cooperii*, or Cooper's Hawk (today *Accipiter cooperii*). In *American Ornithology* he says he named the bird after Cooper because of his "sound judgement, and liberality in communicating useful advice," adding that Cooper is the only one to whom the author "on the eve of his departure for Europe, would have been willing to entrust the ultimate revision and superintendence of his work."[36]

Flattered to have a bird of prey named after him, Cooper replied: "It is not I presume from any *congeniality of character* you may have observed between us [himself and the hawk], though it might be said our *pursuits* are similar. I am sorry my name Latinises so awkwardly. My ancestors must have been Barbarian saxans [sic]."[37]

Since Cooper had shot another example of his namesake on Long Island, Bonaparte was anxious to compare it with his own bird: "For God sake let me know every particular about your specimen. Please to draw at leisure hours a minute description that I might compare it with mine . . . do not neglect the dimensions etc. What had it in its stomach . . . who shot it . . . How? & please to mention every little circumstance even not connected with Nat. Hist. Is that asking too much? Excuse my indiscretion on account of my zeal for Science."[38]

A week later he wrote that he had been working regularly for fifteen hours a day, sometimes eighteen. "I do not even answer my business letters. All this is because I have been foolish enough to take up as business things that ought to be nothing but amusement."[39] He here adopts (sardonically) the nineteenth-century attitude that natural science was a genteel pursuit, not a profession. So many people at the time assembled cabinets of natural curiosities that it was almost a fad.

In the same letter he informs Cooper that he has finished the account of the Bohemian Waxwing and sent it to the publisher. "If I had known of Bohemian Silk-tail I might have adopted it . . . though this truly mysterious bird is not more common in Bohemia than *anywhere else.*"[40]

In early December Bonaparte asked a serious favor of Cooper, which "though very great," he hoped Cooper would not refuse, because otherwise he would not know what to do. "My departure from America is finally decided & fixed at about Christmas! . . . How I can manage my Ornithology I am at a loss to conceive & there is no living man but yourself to [whom] I could confide its publication." He says he has finished the scientific part of the manuscript but not the literary part, which would take him more time than he has between now and his departure even if he worked night and day on it. If only Cooper would be willing to take his "rough notes," refine and publish them, then together they could continue the third and fourth volumes, with Cooper taking the title of editor or (Bonaparte's preference) joint author. If Cooper needed to spend time in Philadelphia for the project, Bonaparte would of course cover his expenses.[41] For the present, his chief concern is that Cooper take over the publication of the second volume, one-third of which is already complete and the rest roughly sketched out. If Cooper agrees, he will come to New York the following week to put everything in his hands, "settle doubts," then work until the last day before he sails in an attempt to finish the whole. "I hope that neither your modesty nor anything else will make you refuse me this true mark of friendship of which I shall be grateful as long as I live."[42]

Cooper's answer must have come by return mail, because less than a week later Bonaparte wrote him:

I do not know how to find terms to express to you the pleasure, the gratitude & all the different sentiments I experienced at the reading of your letter which has been a salutary balm to my anxiety & state of irritation: the mere acceptance of *the job* by you would have delighted me even without the kind sentiments with which you have been pleased to season it. Yes, my Dear Sir, not only do not I know of any *better qualified person* but without excepting my friend Say I know of no man in America I might safely state in the whole world to whom I would have intrusted even the printing of my Catalogue.[43]

He adds that anyone else who undertook this project would undoubtedly change the meaning of Bonaparte's text and make him say the opposite of what

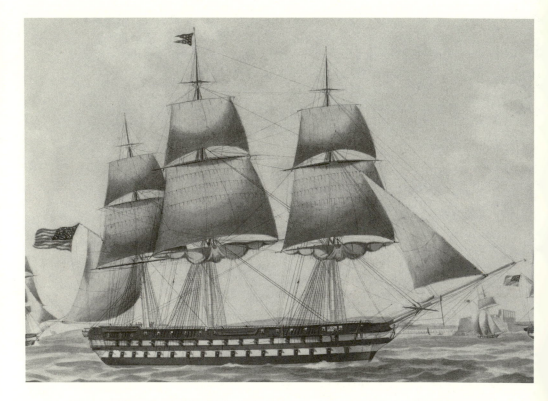

Figure 21. Two views of the *U.S.S. Delaware*, 1828. Courtesy of the Mariners' Museum, Newport News, Virginia.

he meant to say, and make him "elegantly speak nonsense!" This he has no fear of "in the hands of one who combines the enlarged mind of a Theoretical Naturalist to the greatest accuracy & knowledge in the practical details." Cooper knows only too well Bonaparte's deficiency in English, that he could not pretend to publish "any work in any degree litterary in that language without what Temminck calls a dyer [*teinturier*]." Even if he had time to "concoct" his writing, much would have to be done to make it "elegant." So, "what will it be now that time hard pressing upon me I have been obliged to sacrifice entirely elegance & diction to the accurate collection of facts, synon[yms], descrip[tions], & all scientific matters which is as complete as possible"? He will be in New York in a week for a "last visit" when he will put into Cooper's hands all his "papers, illustrations, plates etc."[44] Cooper writes back to assure him that he will take a "fraternal interest" in his *Ornithology*.[45]

Before leaving, Bonaparte turned over his collections of birds to Lawson,

so he could engrave the plates with the specimens before him. All the drawings were to be kept in Lawson's hands.[46] At the same time, he cautioned Cooper that "too much modesty will not do with Lawson who is a character of antiquity & would exclaim with Horace: 'I am the first of Poets.'"[47]

The arrangements for Bonaparte and his family were to sail to Leghorn, Italy, aboard the *Delaware*—a warship carrying more than one hundred cannons and the largest ship that at the time had ever crossed the Atlantic. The arrangements were made by no less a person than President John Quincy Adams. Charles and Zenaide once enjoyed a delightful evening with Adams and his wife at Point Breeze, and the president was now only too glad to help them. By mid-December, the secretary of the navy notified Bonaparte that the *Delaware* was due to sail on 5 January from Norfolk, Virginia. The prince decided to leave Bordentown on Christmas Day, spend a few days in Philadelphia, and then move on to Baltimore, where he would leave his wife, two children, and servants while he himself traveled to Washington for a leave-taking with President Adams. He told Cooper to address his letters to Stephen Girard, or Dr. Hays at Eighth and Sansom Streets, either of whom would send them on to Italy. Learning that a shipment had arrived in New York from Temminck, he asked his agent to join it to the other boxes—thirty-two in number—that he is sending to Italy.[48] A letter from Reuben Haines, addressed to Bonaparte at the Pennsylvania Hotel on Chestnut Street in Philadelphia, encloses Mrs. Haines's receipts for cakes and muffins and expresses the hope that "beneath the bright sky of Italy, your far distant friends may not be forgotten."[49]

Bonaparte wrote Cooper from Washington: "You will easily see in what confusion must have been my head after the busy three days I have spent in Philadelphia not only settling about my Nat[ural] Hist[ory] but money matters, visits & other concerns, having besides reviewed my sketch of a Synopsis for Godman & written my *animadversions* & a quantity of letters." With little thought of the demand on his friend's time, he then gives him a long list of people and institutions, both domestic and foreign, to whom Cooper is "to present" extra copies of his *Genera of Birds*. These include Godman, Peale, Hays, Ord, Say, Lawson, Audubon, Gray, Vigors, Temminck, and the "Count of Survilliers (my Uncle please don't forget, though I had almost forgotten him myself)." Also, Cooper is to send copies to the American Philosophical Society, the Maclurian Lyceum, the Academy of Baltimore, the Linnean Society of London, and others. The Academy of Natural Sciences is conspicuously absent from the list. "If I have forgotten any *matador* please to make up for it," he says, and asks Cooper to pardon his "abrupt conclusion," but he has run out of space on the page.[50] He does manage, however, to squeeze under his signature, in minuscule writing, "Prince of Musignano." In spite of his professed republicanism, Bonaparte had difficulty letting go of his title, even in the New World.

A week later, however, having given some thought to how his name should appear in print, he wrote Cooper, "for God sake do not forget to drop each & every title of every description (not excepting Prince etc.) in that of the third [volume]." (Perhaps Ord had made his point about the use of "Mr." in the United States.) Cooper was also not to forget, when writing the dedication of the new hawk, to "clearly & elegantly say" that Cooper is the only living man to whom Bonaparte would entrust the "*ultimate* revision" of his works. "This," he says with characteristic candor, "I do not mention so much as a compliment to you as a justification for my leaving such a task *to any body at all.*"[51]

He told John Edward Gray at the British Museum that he was busy preparing his "final return home" and asked him to notify the taxidermist Leadbeater that he had delivered to Stephen Girard, "the most careful man in the U.S.," "a wellpacked can"—was he still smarting from the affair of the paintings?—to be shipped to Leadbeater containing the birds he had lent him, together with an American turkey and a few other interesting specimens. He explains that, because Leadbeater wants only "very rare, highly beautiful, or things *ugly in the extreme,*" he has been limited in his choice, but he has included a few skins of small quadrupeds and some turtle shells that Leadbeater could give to the Zoological Society or to any friend or institution he "thinks proper." He tells Gray he has finally received "the celebrated box of Mr. Audubon" (a box Audubon had apparently told Bonaparte he would send him), but it would have been better for both of them if it had been lost: "no drawing! no new species!! 3 bad skins of the young Scarlet Ibis, not in 'most brilliant plumage' but in their fall brown dress, 2 Wood Pelicans & a bale of unpicked cotton formed its whole content!"[52]

Bonaparte's desire to be back in Italy had intensified in the late fall when he learned of a family tragedy: his eighteen-year-old brother Paul had died. Paul, a self-styled freedom fighter for Greek independence from Turkey, had obtained a false passport and, without the knowledge of his parents, had boarded an English ship for Greece. On the very day Bonaparte left Point Breeze, he received a letter from his Boston friend Edward Everett, giving him an eyewitness account of his brother's death, published in a Boston paper. The letter, dated 13 September 1827 and written from Poros, stated that Paul Bonaparte had died a few days earlier in his cabin on board the *Hellas* from a wound inflicted by the accidental firing of his pistol. A Dr. Howe, who attended him, reported that "Paul Bonaparte met death like one worthy of the name he bore." Howe was a skillful young Boston surgeon, Everett told Bonaparte, and must have done everything possible for his "unfortunate brother."[53] Paul at one time had thought of coming to America with Charles and Zenaide, but had changed his mind. Charles must have reflected with sorrow that this tragedy would never have happened had he been successful in persuading his brother to join them. His remorse must have been particularly acute when a rumor surfaced that Paul had deliberately shot himself, over an unhappy love affair.[54]

When Bonaparte returned to Baltimore for his wife and children, he wrote Cooper of another sad turn of events: the illness of their mutual friend Godman. Not long before, they had both heard from the poor young doctor that he had attempted suicide. Godman, married to Titian Peale's niece, Angelica Peale, had been suffering for some time from tuberculosis, which would kill him two years later, in 1830.[55] Bonaparte had lost Say and Lesueur to the wilderness. Soon he would lose Godman, another close American friend, to death.

There were many reasons for Bonaparte's returning to Italy. The Academy of Natural Sciences, which had once been the center of his activities, was in disarray and closed to him, if only by his own disgust with the institution. His relations with his uncle were decidedly hostile, and Zenaide was intensely homesick for her mother. It is entirely possible that, like her husband, the somewhat straightlaced, sober-minded Zenaide did not share or sympathize with her father's life of a *bon-vivant*. Then, too, there was the pressing question of finances. Bonaparte refused to accept charity from his uncle, preferring to return to Italy and confront his father about his obligations to him and his wife. And last there was the dream of establishing scientific congresses in Italy, an idea that had taken firm hold of Bonaparte ever since his inspiring visit with Dr. Cretzschmar in Frankfurt.

The return was delayed for nearly a month when the *Delaware* caught fire in Norfolk harbor. Bonaparte and his family waited many weeks at Old Point, Virginia while repairs were made.[56] But at last he was able to write Cooper from shipboard, as the *Delaware* prepared to depart: "Farewell, my dear sir, Farewell . . . & let me hear from you . . . at Gibraltar & at all events at Leghorn. May we carry together safely into port the American Orn[ithology] & communicate to each other accurately the results of our favourite studies on our representative sides of the Atlantic." Cooper must visit him in Italy for a "protracted time," for, "my house will be your house." And, he concludes sweepingly, "your plants will adorn my garden, your birds my Museum & we do not know that it will not be one of Reference to the Am[erican] Naturalist."[57]

5

INTERNATIONAL

CORRESPONDENTS

"[Audubon] kills me with his letters,
I have received upwards of a dozen since I returned from Rome."

Bonaparte to William Cooper,
Florence, 3 July 1828

FOR THE FIRST TEN DAYS of the journey, the wind blew so violently that "the heavy *Delaware* was pitching her lofty masts into the deep & though close reefed" the ship was going faster than anyone wished. "I really do not think that all vessels would have stood it," Bonaparte wrote Cooper. Nevertheless, alarming and uncomfortable as it was, the wind carried them to the Azores. Five more days would have brought them to Europe, but the gale turned easterly. "We were between calm and head winds more than a week in making St. Mary the Southern of the Az[ores], though we had been that length of time in sight of the Islands, then we were pushed back, & finally beating every inch of our way, when the wind came fair we were (owing to our unlucky management) too much to the South, & for one night sailed in some danger to the coast of Mogadore [Mogador, present Essaouira, Morocco] where of every other coast in the world a shipwreck is the less to be desired."[1] In his memoirs he added that the passengers were afraid of being murdered by "barbarous" Arabs.[2]

It was a harrowing trip in many ways. One night, during a storm, the head carpenter startled the sleeping captain with news that the hold was full of water and taking on more at the rate of two inches a minute. This alarm was false, and the ill-informed carpenter was put in irons for his disturbance. Bonaparte was appalled at the harshness with which American seamen were treated; he was a frequent witness to their humiliation and cruel beatings.[3]

But the trip was not all bad, as he recounted to Hays, for he had been "very fortunate in the Ornithology way." Off the coast of Africa and in the Mediterranean the ship had been "daily visited by numbers of little winged strangers, some very rare & interesting." He had even secured specimens of two species undescribed in Europe, and at least one that was "entirely new" (unseen and undescribed). Little Joseph benefited from the sea air, as did the "poor baby."[4]

When at last they reached the Straits of Gibraltar, the wind and current rushed the ship along at sixteen miles an hour to Algeciras, Spain, where the *Delaware* dropped anchor. They stayed for two days, then sailed for Leghorn (Livorno) with "a cracking breeze," covering over 260 miles in twenty-four hours. But the wind again turned "cruel" and they were four or five days getting near the Balearic Islands, to be "jammed between them" for three more days. Finally, losing sight of Minorca and "beating along inch by inch," the great ship slowly made its way past the "snowy hills of Corsica" and then Elba to the tiny island of Gorgona, off the Italian coast. "Night was coming on," Bonaparte told Cooper, "& the wind leaving us still faster."

Then was seen an almost unprecedented sight! . . . Our captain, mad as possible, finding himself in a situation w[h]ere no sloop of war even would have ventured through choice, ordered every bit of canvas to be set. The little air (hardly enough to move a light) that we had being right aft: shoulder-sails were placed on both sides, thus exhibiting the greatest spread of canvass ever known. But all this was of no avail, we hardly moved two knots through the water, the sun was setting, a thick fog covered the light house . . . & here we were left in the most awkward predicament, [when] a threat[en]ing breeze springing up, which an hour before would have been salvation, & now was almost d[amnation]. . . . Shortening sails at once & progressing in the dark by slow steps & handing the lead at every step as soon as we found bottom the anchor was dropped without knowing w[h]ere or how, the 10th of April. You may imagine with what relief the dawn of day was watched . . . when we discovered we were only 12 or 14 miles from Leghorn.[5]

After landing at Leghorn in mid-April 1828, the passengers were immediately quarantined in the lazaretto, a precaution taken with vessels from foreign ports. Such was the "absurdity" of sanitary regulations in the Grand Duchy of Tuscany, Bonaparte complained, that he and his family were "condemned" to spend fifteen days in "this kind of prison. . . . Patience . . . Patience!"[6]

By then he was feeling nostalgic about his colleagues in America, and asked Hays, in a letter written while still aboard the *Delaware*, to remember him to all their mutual friends, especially Reuben Haines. He wants to hear all about Say, Maclure, Godman, Lawson, New Harmony, and natural history journals. He hopes to get a great many things from Philadelphia when his carriage arrives—apparently by a different ship—but he is not sanguine about that, since Peale, who had been asked to send various articles with the carriage, was so "forgetful" and "procrastination itself." Also, one of his boxes, scheduled for shipment from Baltimore, had been stolen: "This package contained the tin case with Audubon's Ornithology plates & a dozen books *& nothing else fortunately. The plates of Audubon being the only copy of the splendid performance* in the U.S. may lead to the discovery of the thief."[7]

From his "prison," Bonaparte told Cooper that Audubon had sent him, back in the United States, five numbers [installments] of his *Birds of America*, which remained unclaimed in the "accursed N.Y. customs house." "He [Audubon] is a fool not to have accompanied one [of the numbers] with a letter. He writes to me from London (by America) that he is delighted of the success of his *vast enterprise*. I am delighted that your birds to which I can put up a small claim, should all be as largely represented." (He means specimens that Cooper had given Audubon and several that Bonaparte had given him.) He adds that "few will patronize poor Audubon in America . . . but if with the Giraffe [a great new novelty in the London zoo] & [a] thousand other things he has got into the London view of fashion . . . he can do without his adopted countrymen."[8]

Audubon was indeed making his mark in England. He was also perhaps up
to his old trick of fabricating a glamorous history for himself. Mary Swainson,
wife of the ornithologist/artist William Swainson, wrote a friend in early June
that Audubon had just visited them. She described him as a "guileless simple
character," who had been "very much brought up by Dr. [Erasmus] Darwin."
In a literal sense, this was impossible, since Audubon grew up in France; but
perhaps she was speaking of the doctor's philosophical influence. She said too
that Audubon had given them an interesting account of Charles Bonaparte,
who was "immensely rich, between two or three hundred thousand pounds a
year and only twenty eight." Charles was in fact twenty-five and had essentially no means of his own, although somehow he found the wherewithal to travel
and to buy specimens. She had also evidently been told that Bonaparte was educated at Cambridge, when in fact he had left England at the age of eleven. The
fabrication that would have infuriated him the most, however, was Audubon's
absurd assertion that "[Bonaparte's] wife writes most of his letterpress and
papers."9

Not knowing any of this, the prince was pleased to receive Audubon's
complimentary letter from London in response to his from Leghorn. Audubon
writes: "The only hope I have that you will live happy in Europe deters me from
saying that I regret your having left America—so much remains to be done in
our Science there that it is now with a sore heart that I must relinquish the
ardent wish I had to see before my death, the natural history of that fine country *fairly* investigated! No one now remains on whom *I* can depend—and mon-
strosities only will appear."10 In writing his wife, Lucy, back home in the United
States, to tell her that Bonaparte had left America for good, Audubon said that,
"in him I had there the only Scientific Friend I care about."11

When finally freed from the lazaretto of Leghorn, Bonaparte and his fam-
ily proceeded to Florence to stay a short time with Zenaide's mother and sister
Charlotte, who had left America in early 1824 to marry Napoleon-Louis, son of
Louis Bonaparte and older brother of the future emperor of France, Louis-
Napoleon. Afterward Charles and his family took up residence at the Palazzo
Verospi, in Rome, where they stayed until 1836, the year of Madame Mère's
death, after which they moved into the immense Palazzo Bonaparte on the
Piazza Venezia. The warmer months would be spent at the Villa Paolina on the
outskirts of the city, left to Charlotte's husband by Pauline Borghese (aunt to
both Charles and Napoleon-Louis), who died in 1826. Zenaide was pregnant
again, and two-year-old Alexandrine, the hydrocephalic child born in America,
was ill.12

In July 1828 Bonaparte informed Cooper that a museum was "building in

Figure 22. *Villa Paolina* by Charlotte Bonaparte. Engraving. Courtesy of Historic Wyck. Charles-Lucien sent this lithograph of his house in Rome to his friends in the United States such as Reuben Haines and Thomas Say.

[his] Villa & all goes on nicely. Come and help me in arranging every thing." He has spent a month in Rome and is now in Florence with his family visiting his mother-in-law, then they will go on to Bologna to visit his parents and siblings, and then to the Adriatic—that is, to Sinigallia, his parents' summer home— then back to Rome by the end of September, "never, I hope, to move again!" He adds that Audubon "kills me with his letters, I have received upwards of a dozen since I returned from Rome!"[13] (The same complaint would later be made of him. In 1830, Swainson told Audubon that Bonaparte wrote him "very long letters," but he could not answer them "so rapidly" as the prince expected.[14])

In one of Audubon's letters to Bonaparte, he said it was no wonder Bonaparte never saw in the United States a copy of *Birds of America* other than the one he himself possessed, because Audubon had only one subscriber besides the prince, a woman in New York. And though he had written to different institutions, to the president, and to Henry Clay, he had received no replies. It would be his lot, he believed, to spend his life for the "benefit of Science in a very humble way," "unknown" and "neglected." Bonaparte was by now losing patience with Audubon's woefulness and fulsome praise, yet Audubon was no doubt sincere when he said, "I have been always very proud to be able to say that you have used me as a friend and to follow Science in your wake is an honour worthy the attention of every man." And he was correct in saying that he could not have managed the naming of American birds without Bonaparte's "valuable observations" on the nomenclature of Wilson's *Ornithology*.[15]

Audubon believed that Leadbeater, the London taxidermist and dealer in specimens, did not like him, since he refused him "the pleasure" of making the drawings Bonaparte asked for.[16] Leadbeater told him he had orders from Bonaparte to find another artist.[17] Yet less than a month after this rejection, Audubon wrote again to Bonaparte, persisting in his offer: "if you want any drawings made, pray say so—I will lose not a day in finishing them for you."[18] In another letter, he says he is sending seven numbers of *Birds of America* containing thirty-five plates plus a full set of uncolored proofs, which he begs Bonaparte to accept "from a Man who never will cease to admire your talents or forget your kind attentions." He says that Temminck, whom he has seen in London, said it would have been a good thing if Bonaparte had joined him in the publication of his "Great Work." "How gratified I should have felt at such an event no one but myself can well conceive, but I have no doubt that the same feeling & wish to be guided by a Superior Man although always at heart never will be realized. I remember well when I offered my joining Mr. A. Wilson in *1808* and also the remark he made me then—'I must *trudge* by myself!'" In response to Bonaparte's annoyance at finding his name placed far down in the list of subscribers to *Birds of America*, when he had been one of the first to sign up, Audubon says: "I am sorry very sorry that you should have felt vexed at the situation of your name on my list, when it is reprinted I will alter it but I really did not think you cared a fig about that as the name of Bonaparte speaks in defiance of the world."[19]

At the end of August, from "beautiful but unknown mountains," which, as Bonaparte wrote Cooper jubilantly, "combine every thing good & fine," he was enjoying "fresh air, high mountains, beautiful scenery (from a [single] spot you discover Pisa, Leghorn, Corsica, & La Spezia near Genoa!!!)." He has had good trout fishing and excellent shooting, and has seen many interesting insects and alpine plants, olive trees, and grapevines growing right down to the seashore. He will travel for a few more weeks, then shut himself up for good in Rome. Turning to his enthusiasm for America, he says, "nothing can give me more pleasure than seeing your nation already the finest & happiest on earth raise herself to enlightened & liberal views for the good of science." Cooper had told him about the United States Exploring Expedition to the South Seas, for which many of their friends were being considered, including Peale. "The South Seas is an excellent choice, he responds, "but Columbia River & the N. W. coast would be still more valuable to the U.S., why look elsewhere when you don't see at home?"[20]

In regard to the expedition, he says—in a statement anticipating Darwin's voyage on the *Beagle* and his subsequent years at Down House working out his theories of evolution—that "to collect as many species & *as many individuals* as possible, make as many observations & *reasonable facts* must be the object of every traveler & naturalist & they must wait *to be at home* to build wild theory or even establish species, genera etc." Since the New York Lyceum is to provide scientists for the journey, Bonaparte suggests James DeKay, but if DeKay won't go, why not Say? "He would not refuse & after all he is still *The* American Zoologist. The Lyceum putting aside all awkward feeling [Say was not a Lyceum member] would cover themselves with honor by proposing & getting him agreed. As to myself . . . I shall feel proud to suggest him & will think I have by that alone rendered a service to Science & America."

He thinks Cooper's "private choice" to make a trip to Santa Fe is an excellent one. "I know of none better & only one equal . . . my darling Columbia River! . . . but Audubon is making up his mind to go there before losing by age his energy and *ironness* & I have been encouraging him to go. *I think he shall & shortly.* With your expedition almost all N[orth] Am[erica] will then be tolerably explored." But he has been so short of money lately that he will not be able to contribute as much as he would have liked to Cooper's "admirable plan." If fifty dollars will help, then Cooper may draw that sum for the journey, or "if convenient, twice that value in copies of Am[erican] Orn[ithology]—to which your expedition will surely furnish an additional volume." He ends this letter with the curious self-deprecation he sometimes exhibited to those close to him, "I have said pretty nearly all I had to say & at all events enough to annoy you beyond measure. Eight of my pages are a good dose to swallow, & generally take more time to read than to write. I will not give up hope of seeing you in our delicious clime."

Shortly afterward he heard from Isaac Lea, his friend at the Academy of Natural Sciences and publisher of his book, thanking him for some shells he had sent. Lea said he had met and liked Cooper and that Cooper had "left [Philadelphia] about two weeks earlier for the Western Country in his little travelling chaise in search of objects of Natural History."[21]

He also heard from his friend Edward Everett in Boston, who as editor of the *North American Review* was trying to get someone to review Bonaparte's book. On a personal note, Everett mentioned that, when he had returned from visiting Bonaparte at Point Breeze for the last time and had given his little girls the bon-bons "little Joseph" had sent for them, he could not make his children "fully comprehend the near relationship of the bon-bons to the most distinguished man of the Age [Napoleon], but they agreed that they tasted very nicely—which was perhaps all that could be expected from the infants."[22]

In October Bonaparte received from Audubon, in London, a set of "beautiful drawings" with which he was "highly pleased." Since he had not known what to expect from the drawings, "surprise was added to all other enjoyments." Seeing Audubon's breathtaking depictions stirred up the old regrets he had in regard to the illustrations for his own book on American birds. He tells him:

I should have been very happy to join you or have you to join me to complete the Am[erican] Orn[ithology], we might have given all your drawings & begun by those "not given by Wilson" thus combining our two places in one & I might have made use of your valuable observations as I have so freely done for the Turkey! . . . you might have employed the little knowledge I had about classification and the philosophy of the science, as well as the experience I had of American and European birds which I studied & compared from childhood, & thus we might have produced if not a great, at least a *true* book. We talked of it you recollect in Philadelphia . . . but *men* interfered . . . & besides you had not kept the skins of your birds [these were essential for exact scientific descriptions]. Had you had them, with your drawings & your valuable observations, no power on earth could have separated us, & I should have been the editor (if nothing else) of your work! . . . but you have nothing to regret for the benefice [sic] of science, the only thing we must think of.[23]

In reference to the proposal that Audubon collaborate with William Swainson on a book of English birds, Bonaparte remarks, "who like Mr. W[ilson] 'wants to *trudge* by himself'?" He describes Swainson, whom he had met in 1827, as "one of the best living Ornithologists" and predicts that his help will be "highly valuable to you & the scientific world." However, he cautions Audubon not to rely entirely on Swainson, "but add him to your long walks, extensive correspondence & *self observations* [your own observations]."

In the same letter he asks about Temminck's recent visit to London, for it seems curious to him that Temminck had not mentioned Audubon: "Did you not meet? Did he not admire your drawings? Did you not deliver my old letter?" He has seen in the papers that Cuvier spoke favorably about Audubon's work at the French Academy: "Such flattering an account from so high an authority cannot fail to be highly profitable to you & at all accounts very pleasing to your friends." For his own part, he has "spread all over Italy" Swainson's favorable review of *Birds of America*. But he is afraid Audubon "will not find great patronage in this classical land, where men of science are all positively poor & where the rich prefer pictures, statues & antiquities to books on Nat[ural] Hist[ory]." Undoubtedly he was thinking of his father.

In November Audubon wrote back, saying that he had been to Paris and while at Baron Cuvier's "had the pleasure" of hearing many "savants" speak of Bonaparte as he "deserved." As for Audubon's reception by Temminck in London, "He came in in a great apparent bustle, would not even look at one of my Drawings or engravings, mistook my work for that of Selby's [John Prideaux Selby, an English naturalist and artist] and probably *I* for that Gentleman—I felt anxious to see him again and talk but in vain—that is all of him." Audubon asks Bonaparte to send him a good portrait of Napoleon, since he had tried to no avail to find one in Paris. "Paris abounds in bad copies which I would not have as I hate to see the *first specimen of nature* caricatured at random."[24]

In March 1829 Bonaparte informed Audubon, then about to return to America, that a case of his drawings had arrived by ship at Leghorn and was about to be sent on to Bonaparte at Rome. "I expect every moment to be gratified with the sight of your new wonders, which are every day more *enrapturing* to me." When Audubon goes to New York, he wants him to call on his "excellent & beloved friend" William Cooper and to "compel him" to give his opinion of each plate. "It will be exceedingly well done to bring your skins with you!" he insists. "Would to God you had done so before!!!" Waxing eloquent, and happily assuming the position of mentor, he adds, "Every step you shall make towards the perfection of Am[erican] Orn[ithology], every new species, every interesting *fact* with which you will enrich your valuable store, I shall consider as something done *for me*."[25]

He wants to know what the adult plumage of his *Falco Cooperii* looks like. He agrees that Audubon probably will not get much encouragement in the United States ("Your work is too expensive for republicans"), but suggests a call on a Mr. George Harrison, who might become a subscriber ("Do it in my name if you like"). He ends the letter, "God bless you my dear Sir, & help you in all you may undertake."

Although he was only in his middle twenties, Bonaparte seems to have been tired out from all his frenzied endeavors in America, and for the first few years after his return to Italy he spent relatively little time on natural history.

Perhaps, in addition, he was distracted by the formidable task of arranging his affairs in Italy. He was still receiving warm letters from his friends in the United States, but may have felt somewhat lost without the tremendous stimulation to study natural science he had experienced in the New World. On 6 January 1828, the day the prince was to board the *Delaware*, Say had written him from New Orleans: "I cannot leave this place without addressing a few lines to you. I am here with Mr. Maclure on our way to Mexico for the winter & we have to regret that your multifarious labors prevent you from participating in our excursion as we have no doubt that we shall find much novelty in that interesting region."[26] Without question, Bonaparte much regretted the opportunity to work with his much-admired friend gathering specimens of Mexican birds, many of which were sure to be new to Euro-American science. Say mentioned that he had sent the manuscript of the third volume of *American Entomology*— his pioneering study of indigenous insects—to Philadelphia to be published. Jacob Gilliams had offered to oversee it, but, not knowing Bonaparte had already left Philadelphia for good, Say had "taken the liberty of stating that in case of any difficulty, you would have the kindness to give able counsel." Say felt the kind of confidence in Bonaparte that Bonaparte felt in him.

A year later Say was still living in the frontier town of New Harmony, Indiana. "In this remote region we have not even a loophole through which to peep at the scientific world," he tells his friend. He upbraids Bonaparte for neglecting him: "How could you depart from our shores without bestowing upon me a parting farewell or the legacy of a single line! I do not even know how long you intend to remain in Europe, or indeed whether or not you propose ever to return." He is at least glad to hear "that a portion of your mantle has descended upon one of the naturalists [Cooper] of 'Gotham [New York],' who has proved himself worthy of the trust, for I have heard that your second vol. is published." Say wants to know what "scientific labours" are occupying Bonaparte; he has "a hundred questions to ask," but will conclude by assuring him of the "undiminished attachment with which I have the honour to be your most obedient servant and friend."[27]

Reuben Haines told Bonaparte a year later that Robert Owen had disappointed his associates: "After all his high promises of the reform that was to emanate from New Harmony, [he] has suffered his community to make entire shipwreck." Scarcely any of the former inhabitants of New Harmony were left, except Lesueur, Say, and Say's wife Lucy, and both of the latter had been "very ill with the Harmony fever." Haines and his colleagues had been hoping for a long time that Say and Lesueur would return to Philadelphia. Haines had written them both to urge it, but without effect, though he thought it was only their desire "to gratify Maclure" that kept them in Indiana.[28]

By this time Bonaparte must have felt immensely relieved that he had not gone to New Harmony himself, even if Say was there. Nevertheless, the idea of that "utopian" town, tied up with his feelings about America in general, had once been a powerful draw. A year after Say's departure in 1825, and before Bonaparte's disillusionment with New Harmony, Bonaparte wrote to Hays, "My admiration for your country and institutions is too well known to require me to make here again my political *credo* etc. What is the best of it is that you have no restraint to prevent you from quotidian perfectibility and that if you do not attain the highest degree of happiness to which man may aim with reason, it must be entirely your own fault . . . and so God bless you and may you soon get need [sic] of your spirit of individuality; may you all be convinced of the necessity of introducing the cooperative system . . . may you sign the declaration of mental independence . . . "[29] These were Robert Owen's ideas, to which Say too subscribed at the time. The arch-republican Say, in addition to his scientific expertise, represented for Bonaparte all the American ideals he cared for so deeply. In his memoirs he wrote that Say was his most treasured friend in America.[30]

At the beginning of 1829 Bonaparte confided to Cooper that he had been plagued by a certain idleness: "I have been three months in Rome, & my collections, nay my books are not yet arranged, not yet safe . . . not yet looked into. I have had 'tis true, other cares, establishing, settling, arranging etc etc & even an addition to my family [Louis-Lucien-Joseph, born 15 November 1828] . . . & all this may be an excuse." "Other cares" may refer to the attempted suicide of his sister Letizia, who had tried to drown herself in the Serpentine in Hyde Park, London. A passerby had saved her,[31] fortunately, because she went on to live a full life. She eventually separated from her husband, however, which must have been disappointing for Bonaparte, who was so fond of Thomas Wyse.

Bonaparte told Cooper he now had sixty of Audubon's plates, some of which were excellent, especially the rendition of the Cooper's Hawk, which he thought was superior to the one Lawson had executed for *American Ornithology*, "thanks, it is true, to that scoundrel of Rider" (meaning that Rider had drawn a bad picture of the Cooper's Hawk for Bonaparte's book). Before he had seen Audubon's plate, Audubon had written him "that his *Astur* [hawk] was not my *F[alco]. cooperii*, that he had compared them & that of my bird he had the male, female & young! I was therefore the more astonished in finding them the same. Never trust but your own eyes."[32] Audubon, thinking his bird was different from Bonaparte's, had named his hawk after Lord Stanley, the Earl of Derby, but would be forced to retract the name when it became clear that his and Bonaparte's were the same bird and Bonaparte's name had priority.

That winter of 1829 was a difficult one. Charles came close to death from pneumonia and spent a long time convalescing. His little daughter Alexandrine died; Zenaide had been devastated by the ordeal, so he took her to Canino for a few weeks to rest. Then the death of Pope Leo XII and the question of his successor threw the entire local scene into confusion. Bonaparte felt nearly besieged by the constant "tiresome knocking at the door" and looked forward to the time when he could at last devote himself again to science and his scientific friends.[33]

He was pleased with the way Cooper edited volume 2 of *American Ornithology* and thought his friend had greatly improved it. He complained only that Cooper was too self-effacing and had not sufficiently acknowledged his own contribution: "you have certainly done more than you make me confess & that is not right." His publishers, Carey and Lea, were anxious to go on with volume 4, he tells Cooper, but if he did continue it, the text would be minimal, except for the description of the condor, which he would have to leave almost entirely in Cooper's hands. Would Cooper also continue with volume 5? Peale would help him, especially with the drawings, which cost twelve dollars apiece. He (Bonaparte) is making up a package of birds for Cooper that are common to both continents, and exclaims, "you know what I want from you . . . everything; for my collections are fast decaying!!!" His ex-secretary, Riccioli, is the best collector, who can furnish Cooper with everything he could wish, "being *our Cozzens*" (Cozzens was their collector in America). Soon he himself will be leaving with several friends on a scientific expedition to La Spezia (on the Tyrrhenian Sea, below Genoa): "by sea & land we shall ransack all from the tip top of the Apennines to the bottom of the Mediterranean."[34]

At the end of August, Bonaparte received volume 3 of his *Ornithology* and was "delighted to find it so correct and *reading so well.*" In reference to the entry on the Cock of the Plains (today called the Sage Grouse, *Centrocercus urophasianus*), he thanked Cooper for the "excellent & splendid additions you have brought into my composition from Lewis & Clark which would have been unpardonable not to quote in grouse matters; some of the quotations were entirely new to me & the author learned something new by reading his own book!"[35] Cooper had written that Lewis and Clark found the bird "near the fountain of the Missouri, in the heart of the Rocky Mountains," and that it was also "found on the plains of the Columbia [River] in great abundance."[36]

In this same volume Bonaparte discusses the "Dusky Grous" (today called the Blue Grouse, *Dendragapus obscurus*). He acknowledges that the figure in the plate was taken from the specimen on which Say established the species (the type specimen) and then cites his own qualifications for describing this bird. "Perhaps no other naturalist has personally inspected all the known species of this genus of both continents, and having examined numerous specimens even of some of the rarest, and possessing all but one in my own collection, my advantages are peculiar for giving a monograph of this interesting genus." He adds that he hopes to publish such a work some day.[37] Such self-commendation comes off as pretentious, but his claims were not in fact exaggerated: his expertise at that point was indeed unrivaled on either side of the Atlantic.

In comparing specimens of different species, Bonaparte sought to resolve scientific questions concerning the why and the how of variations. This was getting at the heart of evolutionary conjecture, a necessary element of modern classification. In essence, he was asking why was one species different from another, and how did it get that way?

That summer Swainson wrote that he was anxious "to profit" by Bonaparte's valuable work on North American birds, for he was disgusted with the "existing pompousness" and the "lack of philosophical conjecture" among naturalists. So many were apparently stuck in the theory of spontaneous creation; the idea that God created each species separately. "I see so many others committing the most incredulous [sic] blunders, and writing so *authoritatively* about affinities, that one would suppose *they*, instead of *nature* were the creators. No bird—however strange, is discovered, but its place in the scale of being is instantly known; nothing is strange, nothing is perplexing, nothing requires doubt, hesitation, or deliberation. I confess all this folly has kept me back from writing anything beyond the definition of groups, or the characters of species. But my silence will not last much longer." He plans to do "something else" in *Northern Zoology* (*Fauna Boreali-Americana, or the Zoology of the Northern Part of British America: part second, The Birds* [1832]). This book, funded by the British Government, covered the avian discoveries made by Dr. John Richardson on his two expeditions to the Arctic with Sir John Franklin. Swainson was given the birds to describe and classify.

Swainson was glad to hear that Bonaparte was forming a general collection of birds: "The beauties of the science are lost without one, but *it is absolutely necessary to study the variations that occur.*"[38] The following June, writing to Bonaparte about two new gulls he was describing for the *Northern Zoology*, Swainson said he had had the "great pleasure" of naming one *Larus Bonapartii* and the other *Larus Franklinii*.[39] As a scientific name, this compliment to his friend would not endure: the gull had previously been named *Larus philadelphia* by none other than George Ord. But Bonaparte's Gull is still the common name for this petite, ternlike bird, as Franklin's Gull is the common name for *Larus pipixcan.*

That year of 1829 was in many ways one of trial for Bonaparte. In addition to the crisis with which the year had begun, on 22 September his beloved younger sister Jeanne died of pneumonia. She was only twenty-two and the mother of a little girl by her husband, the Marchese Honoratio Honorati. And Charles again had a serious falling out with his father over money.[40] On the other hand, he was finally shaken out of the writing lethargy he had described to Cooper by the publication of Baron Georges Cuvier's second edition of *The Animal Kingdom* (*Règne animal*). Perhaps he was inspired on learning that John Le Conte, a colleague at the New York Lyceum, had sent the French savant information on American birds but that Le Conte was displeased with quotations attributed to him.[41] In an article Bonaparte published in the *Annals of Natural History of Bologne* for 1830, he said that politics had distracted Baron Cuvier from his studies. Perhaps it was just as hard to revise a great work as to write an altogether new one, Bonaparte said, but in either case Cuvier's edition disappointed expectation and did not correspond to the actual science of the time. In the section on vertebrate animals, Bonaparte had noticed many omissions and imprecise descriptions, in particular among the birds of Europe and America, his own area of expertise. He had made corrective notes on the book for his own interest, but after much thought had decided to publish them. This he owed to science.[42]

It was Say who had informed him in the fall about Cuvier's book and the part played in it by their American colleague Le Conte, whom Say considered a traitor to American science. "It seems to me that Cuvier surrendered his judgement to Le Conte pretty much as John Bull [England] has done to Audubon, or is it possible after all that Cuvier can be so sublimely ignorant as not to know that the name *carolina* was given before Le Conte was born. The young *picta* [woodpecker] has sometimes the 2 large neck spots like [one of Say's insects] and of course, according to Le Conte, it must be the same species, that is to say, a whale has two eyes and so has the horse, of course they are one species." Say concludes that if Cuvier's treatment of the *picta* is an sample of the improvements in his new edition, then it would have been better to have had the old one and "to have believed the Grouse & Pheasant the same thing etc etc."[43]

Of Cuvier himself Say exclaims bitterly: "But what business have such poor miserables in intellect as we are, to judge of the handiwork, the condescending dispensations of a minister of a king [Charles X]!! and so great, good and learned a king too!! No! we must humbly receive what may be thus graciously vouchsafed to us and thank god for the favour." Say's politics had become increasingly liberal, if not radical, during his stay in New Harmony. Owen and Maclure had left their mark on him.

In the preface to the 1830 edition of *The Animal Kingdom*, Baron Cuvier

Figure 23. *Portrait of Georges Cuvier* by Rembrandt Peale, 1808. Courtesy of the Mütter Museum, College of Physicians, Philadelphia. Peale painted this portrait in Paris for his father's portrait collection of famous people, housed in his museum in Philadelphia.

had acknowledged his indebtedness to "the new views and facts contained in the numerous and learned writings" of many naturalists, including Wilson, Vigors, Ord, Harlan, Say, and Bonaparte, but he had misapplied some of their information.[44] For both Say and Bonaparte, however, Cuvier's unpardonable sin was in serving the repressive Bourbon king Charles X, who succeeded his brother Louis XVIII on the throne of France in 1824 and abandoned the principles of the French revolution. The connection between science and politics was keenly felt by many progressives of the day. Bonaparte wrote in his memoirs that in America he had been totally absorbed in natural history because it reaffirmed the doctrines of "progress, philanthropy, and Christian equality" by which he aspired to live. He had been impressed by the abolition of slavery (in the north), and the general enlightenment of the educated classes.[45] He strongly espoused the ideals of the French Revolution, to which his father also had been so devoted.

Bonaparte approved wholeheartedly the July Revolution of 1830 that put Louis-Philippe on the throne of France as a constitutional monarch. But he was not yet personally involved in European politics, as he would be later; his interests were still centered in the United States, where his book was being published. He was particularly concerned with the illustrations, and told Cooper that since Rider had "behaved" so badly (too often drunk), perhaps Cooper might induce the publishers to give Lawson's daughters the job of coloring the plates—if Cooper thought that, working "under their father's eye," they could do better than Rider. But he cautioned Cooper to be careful about the "tinges," and to consult Peale about the quality of the colors, so that they would not change as those of Rider had "shamefully done." Bonaparte must have seen proofs of his illustrations (the drawings before the color was added), because he asked that Lawson add a crest that Lawson had mistakenly omitted from Peale's Egret Heron (*Ardea pealii*, today the Reddish Egret, *Dichromanassa rufescens*).

He told Cooper he was assembling a museum and making an aviary and would like to have a few "strong birds" from America. Cardinals especially would cross the ocean with success and were often available, since they were "trapped by the boys" and sold in the market. Also, Cooper is to think seriously of the "subsequent & concluding volumes" of his book, which can only be written under joint authorship.[46] Almost simultaneously, Cooper had written Bonaparte asking him to instruct Carey & Lea that from now on Cooper was to appear as co-author of *American Ornithology*: "You will perceive the necessity of replying by the first opportunity."[47]

Bonaparte replied that he rejoiced to hear that Cooper would be one of the "*answerable* authors," since he would then feel more at liberty to make additions and corrections. Thus *American Ornithology* would become "always more perfect" which was his "sole & major object in continuing Wilson."[48] But the prince's letter to the publisher must have been lost, because Cooper's name never appeared as joint author.

Bonaparte's correspondence with Audubon, too, was always directed at the perfection of American ornithology. It must have rankled when he learned from the artist that he had been elected a Fellow of the Royal Society of London, since Bonaparte himself, the leading expert in the field, was not a member. Audubon had been candid: "now the query is do I deserve all those honours?"[49]

A year later, Audubon would open his heart to Bonaparte about his shortcomings in the science of ornithology:

To no one on Earth have I spoken so openly as I now do to you . . . yourself knows better than any Man [,] being the best judge [,] that I am not a Learned Naturalist—I am only, and that not to a very great extent a *Practical* one . . . I am no Scholar of any kind and I have no Pretensions. . . . Some *one thing* in the work [*Birds of America*] may be useful hereafter, this being the case it is to you that I look to find advice and it is from yourself alone that I wish to receive them—in errors of nomenclature I will doubtless be much reprimanded, because the short notices in your Sinopsis puzzle my poor brains when reading names & words all new to me as the skins of *two Hawks* now on my table just received from America—I wish I could be near you for a year or so to study the new alphabet [ornithological terms] of such matters, I would try to improve although I am fast getting old—I have shown your letter to Mr. Havel [Havell, the engraver] and he has begun the amending the plates of which you complain.[50]

To Havell, Audubon wrote that Bonaparte's letter had pointed out to him numerous mistakes in his pictures. He believed that his friend had his best interests at heart and was as anxious as he was for a faultless execution. He had examined all the plates as they hung about him on the walls of his room and was surprised to see how many errors he had carelessly passed over.[51]

Bonaparte's answer to Audubon's letter was warm and reassuring:

Believe me, you are too modest and do not value enough that which you call your slender practice; many scholars, many student naturalists occupy themselves in building the systems, & in turning & returning in every sense the few facts (of which some are unfortunately even false) that others have brought to their notice: compilations on compilations, some well done, some as they are (& God knows how one does it in our day [i.e., it has all become so complicated]) only serve to perplex science. It is the facts, the observations, made with judgement & especially with confidence which increase the scope of science & he who being within reach of doing so, neglects them, is culpable towards nature & towards men, as well as he who having done them, keeps them for himself or does not draw from them all that he can.[52]

He sees few mistakes of nomenclature on Audubon's plates and does not mention the birds he thinks Audubon has misnamed, nor that he has "always & perhaps a little too much so" followed his (Bonaparte's) writings. He is sorry that his *Synopsis* is difficult to understand. "I have used in it the fewest possible technical words, and meant it for persons much less versed in ornithology than you; but perhaps they are my errors (and I discover them myself every day) which makes you dissatisfied with my book."

The following July Bonaparte, still working on his *American Ornithology*, makes no apology to Cooper for the condition in which he sends off the manuscript pages for volume 4, apparently riddled with cross-outs and changes: "you are used to see my dirty linen." He has been in Florence for three months and is going with his family to the Gulf of Spezia for six weeks in search of "shells & health," then to Florence for September and back to Rome by October. He is sending specimens of Italian birds for Cooper and Peale.[53]

By September, however, Cooper still had not received the manuscript for Bonaparte's fourth volume, and the plates remained uncolored in Philadelphia. Lawson, he informed Bonaparte, had told him Rider was so "diseased and dissipated" he could not do them, and Lawson's daughters would have to be given the job; they had been doing this kind of work for two or three years. Audubon had set out on a collecting voyage to Florida, Cooper writes, from whence he planned to cross over to the Gulf of Mexico and eventually to the Pacific. Audubon had visited him, and he thought the artist showed "some jealousy" of his collection and appeared "much altered in some respects. But his work is going on and I suspect is very profitable. He has been made a member of the Royal Society, and seems to be looked upon by the Scotch and English as a great naturalist, which he himself says he is not. *You*, he says, are a naturalist."[54]

According to the historian Robert V. Bruce, by the mid-1830s "the Royal Society, unsupported by government, had come under the control of nonscientific members and was sinking to little more than a London club for titled dilettantes."[55] William Swainson would have agreed with him; as he told Bonaparte, he was cynical about being named a fellow of any society in his country.

If science has declined *in Italy* since the days of the Medici, it has, and is, declining very perceptibly *in England*. Fashionable and aristocratic societies, when 40 or 50 pounds must be paid on admission of their members banish all but the wealthy: so that every one who can *pay* for having F.R.S. [Fellow of the Royal Society] or F.L.S. [Fellow of the Linnean Society] or F.Z.S. [Fellow of the Zoological Society] or every letter in the alphabet tacked to their names, pass off as *Savans* and learned men! Not the least encouragement being given to works truly profound. The History of the Wild Beasts, published under the auspices of the zoological society! in shilling numbers, being the only book which pleases the childish understandings of the age, or is at all patronized by "learned members."[56]

Swainson was actually quite off the mark about the Zoological Society's publications. A few months later, Bonaparte was pleased to hear from Nicholas Vigors, the society's director, about two new and very important books that were being published under the auspices of his organization and which he would exchange for Bonaparte's *American Ornithology*. One book, on parrots, was by a young artist named Edward Lear, "of much talent and deserving of encouragement," who executes the drawings under Vigors's "inspection." Vigors has subscribed in Bonaparte's name for this work as well as another— by John Gould—entitled *A Century of Birds Hitherto Unfigured from the Himalaya Mountains.*[57] Lear would come to be considered one of the finest bird artists of the nineteenth century, and Gould's publications presented original material on numerous previously unknown birds and thus were also a major contribution to the field of ornithology.

But the disgruntled Swainson would have nothing to do with Vigors because of the way he had been treated at the Zoological Society of London. He told Bonaparte that the birds were "guarded in boxes out of sight with the most watchful jealousy," and as an example of the "*liberality* of the Institution," he was once requested "*not to take notes*" on some well-known specimens he had been looking at.

As for other European colleagues, Bonaparte found that every day his esteem for the French ornithologist Louis Pierre Viellot was growing; he thought Viellot one of the best ornithologists who ever lived.[58] Bonaparte's admiration for this aged but indefatigable man was almost unique at the time; Viellot was virtually unrecognized and lived in a state near poverty. Bonaparte may have identified with him because the older man had devoted his life to studying birds, first in Santo Domingo and later in the United States. On his return to Paris, he had described a considerable number of exotic bird specimens brought back by others from various expeditions and had attempted to reform existing ornithological systematics. He died at the beginning of 1831.[59]

In early October 1831 Bonaparte finally explained to Cooper why he had not sent the manuscript for volume four of *American Ornithology*. "The fact is that during my six weeks stay in Porto Venere where I intended copying it off etc I was on a sudden taken violently in love *with the Fishes* to which I devoted all my time. (I hope not without success.)" Catching, studying, and classifying them had totally occupied him, and it was only by working night and day since his return to Florence, where his family was staying with Zenaide's mother, that he managed to have the enclosed sheets ready to be sent by a ship the next day from Leghorn. His friend, the Marquis Rovadies has sent word that he delivered the drawings (proofs) to Cooper's hands. He commends this young Roman noble to Cooper: "he is a very useful & attentive man." Bonaparte asks Cooper if he could give the Marquis, "should he be willing to take charge of them," some living turtles of different species, "especially some big terrestrial fellow that you could purchase for me & of some cardinals for my aviary I should be delighted."[60]

Furthermore, he wants all the "scientific intelligence" possible and especially wants Cooper to send him fishes, about which he is "so crazy." He regrets not having collected or studied them while in America. "What a beautiful Class! I can already send you 300 hundred [sic] species of Italian some of which are rare. Shall I?" In two weeks he will be back in the midst of his collections and in the silence of his library. He will write again from Rome "*even* if you have been wicked enough not to drop me a line before that."

While his relations with Cooper were always on an even keel, just as they had been with Say, those with Audubon constantly shifted. He told Cooper that he had just seen Audubon's *Ornithological Biography*, the text to accompany his magnificent plates. He had expected Audubon to say more about the habits of birds, but most of all he resents the way Audubon speaks of him in the preface and he solicits Cooper's support. He had never thought that the leading feature of his character as a naturalist had been "running after new species" (seeking to divide and subdivide the existing categories of birds). On the contrary, grouping them together had always been, and still was, his "hobby," and Audubon should have known that. As to Audubon's implication that he had robbed him of some new discoveries (publishing them first), he can only say that, even if Audubon had asked him to name and describe some of his birds, he has too little faith in Audubon's truthfulness to depend on his statements. (He means that he would not trust Audubon to reproduce accurately what he, Bonaparte, told him.) "What in fact must we think of a man who prints he is born an American, after he has for years repeated to every body he was a Frenchman by birth though an American *by heart*."

"I cannot help mentioning another anecdote as to his veracity," Bonaparte continues, "so that I must give up the good opinion of one whom I defended against my best friends (Say etc) until lately. Audubon has strenuously maintained to me that Strix noevia & Strix Asio [owls] *were two species*, that he had bred them, found their nests & had every possible proof." He did his best to convince Audubon they were the same species; they discussed the subject at length, and when he saw Audubon's drawing, he complimented him on his "conversion." Yet in Audubon's published text, he acts as though he and everyone else had known for years that the two species were the same! "What must we suppose by such misrepresentation?"[61]

Audubon was apparently oblivious to the offense he had given. A year earlier he had told the prince of his plan to write a text to accompany his drawings. "I think I see a smile on your lips at the Idea of my presumption [of writing about birds], but I could not well help writing *something* and as I am fully convinced that the book will be composed of nothing but plain truths I hope that your smile will continue to the last word." He said he had wanted the help of a learned naturalist and had asked Swainson, but the latter demanded an exorbitant fee and wanted his name on the title page, so employing him for the task was out of the question. Instead of the two hundred pounds per volume Swainson would have charged, he was paying (William) MacGillivray a little more than sixty pounds to put his ideas into good English.[62]

About the same time, Swainson told Bonaparte that Audubon had mentioned to him "something about editing his book," but Swainson thought "there would be so much trouble in ascertaining species & synonyms" he could not make up his mind to accept the job. "I hate such drudgery, and never investigated species unless for studying & explaining affinities."[63] Swainson was especially interested in the philosophical theories behind the similarities and differences between birds, not just in categorizing them and listing all the names other naturalists had given them in the past.

In his reply to Swainson Bonaparte said that he had heard of his doubts about Audubon's project and understood "how difficult it would be to speak or even *admit* species on the mere authority of his drawings. Would to God he had kept at least the skins of his birds! This was the reason I refused taking for my Am[erican] Orn[ithology] his drawings when he first showed them to me in the United States."[64] Bonaparte does not mention the other obstacle: that Lawson refused to engrave them.

Swainson was equally negative about Audubon's ability as a naturalist. He told Bonaparte he quite agreed with his remarks about Audubon's designation of species. "Many are too obscure to be admitted on the mere authority of drawings which do not point out their specific characters; while others are clearly young birds, his Sylvecola Swainsonii is one of the description, and as you say, in all probability a female bird. In truth, I am much disappointed in finding our friend is very loose and incorrect, on occasions where I thought he would have been an authority, but few men can transcendently excel in more than one branch."[65] He himself had for a long time been devoted "to the investigation of very abstruse questions on the law of creation and on the natural families' value of the groups in ornithology."

When the first volume of Audubon's *Ornithological Biography* appeared, Swainson wrote critically to Bonaparte that "the errors in nomenclature, as you may suppose, are numerous; and two thirds of his *new* species are known even to *me* as *old* ones. So far as technical science is concerned, it is, in short, a complete failure. He wanted me to assist him, but to my utter astonishment, he did not wish *my name to appear.* This foolish vanity of his, of course put a stop to the plan altogether."[66]

Audubon's lithographs of his drawings were something else, however, and Bonaparte was always delighted to receive them, though he often had reason to correct Audubon's nomenclature (in spite of once denying this to Audubon). In April he wrote the artist to say he had just opened the package of ten of his plates that had been missing in the mail. Among these was the "Petit Corporal," which Audubon had named in honor of Napoleon. Bonaparte says this bird is none other than the adult of the *Falco columbarius* (Pigeon Hawk), known from the time of Catesby. As for the illustrations themselves, he cautions Audubon to be more careful in overseeing their production. The Columbian Jay (Magpie Jay) is "most shamefully" splotched by the colorer . . . it is by no means a good plate . . . compare it with the amazingly fine plate of the Kingfishers & nobody will think they form part of the same work! You must not fall asleep, or at least allow your friends to awake you." He will be happy to examine Audubon's "Washington Eagle," but he is sure it is none other than a young Bald Eagle.[67]

By December 1831 Bonaparte could announce to Cooper that he was working hard on his *Iconografia della fauna italica* (Iconography of Italian fauna), "both on paper & in collecting." This was the beginning of his great work on the mammals, birds, amphibians, reptiles, and fishes of Italy. He described for his friend the extensive collections he possessed in Rome, which helped so much to make his classifications accurate: "One of European birds nearly *complete*; one of North American very rich & a third general, counting nearly 2000 species. Considering that I am exceedingly poor in South American & New Holland [Australian] birds it may be called one of the best for the remaining."[68] It was essential for his work on Italian birds to know which species were endemic to Italy, something he could only ascertain by amassing a comprehensive collection of birds from all over the world.

This new endeavor absorbed him so completely that he was eager to be done with *American Ornithology* once and for all and exasperatedly reprimanded Cooper for not getting it out with more dispatch: "For God's sake do not think of consulting me any more about vol. 4 too long delayed already *under any account.* Believe me it is necessary to *lay it down* & I wish to hear of it only when printed." He sent his patient friend a long list of the birds of which he wanted specimens and reiterated his request for living turtles. "I will endeavor to send you shells, but *fishes* being my new hobby I could supply you better with those than with anything else. Could you not send me a complete collection of the New-Yorkers? I should reciprocate with *all* those of our Mediterranean."[69] Fish, too, had to be compared with those from other parts of the world, and no request struck him as outrageous to make, so long as he offered to reciprocate in kind.

Bonaparte's natural history collections were unique in the Eternal City. He had written Swainson in 1830 that he would find in Rome hardly anyone but himself who knew "a bird from a bat," and that the public collections were "wretched." More collections could be found at Florence and Bologna, though the establishments there, once great, were now barely worth visiting. The museum at Turin was one of the richest in the world, but it was superintended by "the learned Bonelli" whose health was "rapidly carrying him off from science & Italy." He told Swainson he always preferred to exchange specimens rather than purchase them, "having to devote the little money I can spare to the acquisition of books, my own publications & scientific expeditions."[70] Swainson in return said he had to turn his talent "to pecuniary advantage" if he aimed, as he did, at having the finest library of zoology and the "most valuable systematic museum in England. You tell me you did not recollect that I wished Italian birds, when you were sending so many to America!" he complained. He also mentioned that he had thoughts of sending a collector "to investigate Central So[uth] America or Western Africa." "This should be done by Princes, Kings and Governments and not left to impoverished men of science like myself," he said, adding that he believed "*true science* [was] rapidly declining in every part of Europe."[71]

A month later, Swainson wrote again to thank Bonaparte for having him as illustrator, but said he could not afford to work at a rate lower than 3.3 shillings for each plate that contained one or two subjects. Also, it would be "utterly impossible" to comply with Bonaparte's "stipulation" to have the "*birds themselves*" sent for his inspection, because they belonged to either the British or the Edinburgh Museums. However, he was "very much pleased" at Bonaparte's endorsement of the idea that "*definite groups*" really existed in nature, since this was one of the "first sound principles of zoological science upon which the whole fabric of [his] system (or rather of Nature's)" rested. He had decided, he said, not to adopt any genus or subgenus until he had tested and proved it to be a natural one: "With so many *genus makers* rising up, it is quite time to check shallow pretensions." He was sorry to hear Bonaparte was "wandering among the *fish*, be assured that you and I have much to learn in ornithology without distracting our attention to other branches."[72]

But if Bonaparte planned to write about the fauna of Italy, he certainly needed to include fish, amphibians, and mammals, as well as birds.

6

THE NATURALIST

IN ITALY

"Since I left Rome I have been rambling all over Italy.
Leghorn, Lucca, Bologna & all the coasts
of the Adriatic have been ransacked."

Charles Lucien Bonaparte to William Cooper,
Florence, 9 September 1833

BONAPARTE WAS NOW FASCINATED by the fauna of Italy, the land in which he was raised and in which he was to spend the majority of his remaining years. Although always thought of as a "closet" naturalist, he now became an explorer, traveling the length and breadth of the peninsula in search of specimens, especially fish. In 1832, he started publishing his *Iconografia della fauna italica per le quattro classi degli animali vertebrati* (Iconography of the Fauna of Italy in Four Classes of Vertebrate Animals), the four divisions representing mammals, birds, amphibians, and fish. Brought out in parts with unnumbered pages, the work, which took nine years to complete, could be arranged and bound by purchasers according to individual tastes and interests. To illustrate his text Bonaparte employed three excellent Italian artists: Carlo Ruspi, who had made exquisite drawings of Etruscan artifacts for Lucien Bonaparte's book of 1829, *Muséum étrusque*, Petrus Quattrocchi, and Alexander Capalti. The beautiful watercolor depictions of animals, birds, bats, turtles, lizards, snakes, and fish were then lithographed and hand colored. Cooper advised him that lithography had been so perfected that copper plates could no longer compete with it; Gould's *Birds of the Himalaya Mountains* and *Birds of Europe* could never have been executed on copper as well for twice as much. "If you have good artists in Italy, I advise you to employ lithography for your future works."[1]

In addition to detailed scientific descriptions, Bonaparte enriched his text with poetic quotations from Homer, Dante, Boccaccio, and others. This part of the work was pure pleasure for him; seeking subscribers for his expensive enterprise was another matter. The list he would eventually publish in 1841, when the work was finished, included illustrious names from science—Agassiz in Switzerland; Gould, Jardine, and Selby in London; Schlegel in Leiden; Ranzani, professor of natural history in Bologna; Paolo Savi of Pisa—as well as Roman aristocrats such as Prince Filippo Doria Pamphili and Prince Alessandro Ruspoli; great collectors, like Lord Derby of Liverpool and Baron C. M. Rothschild of Frankfurt; members of Bonaparte's own family, such as his in-laws the count and countess de Survilliers (Joseph and Julie), the count of St. Leu (his uncle Louis Bonaparte), and his sister Princess Charlotte Gabrielli. Libraries in Dresden, Berlin, Vienna, Stockholm, and Paris also subscribed, as did libraries in a great many Italian cities: Rome, Parma, Florence, Pisa, Lucca, Bologna, Padua, Venice, Milan, and Turin. Oxford University, the Zoological Society of London, and the American Philosophical Society are also named.

In March 1833 Bonaparte wrote to Swainson seeking his advice on the best way to distribute his *Fauna italica* in England. Two numbers (installments) had already been published, and a third was in press. The total work, in folio, would comprise twenty parts, or *livraisons*, each one containing six plates with the cor-

Figure 24. *1. Bufo vulgaris 2. Bufo calamita* by Petrus Quattrocchi, 1838. From Charles-Lucien Bonaparte, *Iconografia della fauna italica per le quattro classi degli animali verte-brati,* vol. 2, *amfibi,* unpaged. Author's collection. Photo credit: Lisa Tyson Ennis.

responding Italian text. Bonaparte thought this last circumstance would prevent many an "English amateur" from subscribing to his book, and he had arranged for a total of only three hundred copies, of which he would consider himself lucky to sell fifty in the British Isles. He asks Swainson to be his agent, because he hates booksellers and is "not able to risk any loss upon a work of which three hundred copies are published and sold at mere cost."[2] The great expense of the book had caused him a year earlier to ask his mother-in-law for a loan of fifty thousand francs at 5 percent interest, "to secure the future" of his family and that of his "great project."[3]

In June he wrote to Cooper to tell him that he was sending him five copies of the first four numbers of the *Fauna*. He asks him to distribute the publication through Carey & Lea; however, since the work is in Italian, he is afraid that not many Americans will be interested. At the same time he issues a tall order to Cooper—typical in its exaggeration but also a bit tongue-in-cheek—to spread the fifty prospectuses he is sending "from Canada to New Orleans & also South America." He adds that he is including a tin box containing bird skins— "many of which are rare"—fishes, reptiles, and shells, and asks Cooper to send him in return birds, fishes, reptiles and "small Quadrupeds." He is particularly anxious to get Bald Eagles and rattlesnakes.[4]

It was important for Bonaparte to have creatures from the New World in order to compare and contrast them with those of Europe. Only in this way could he classify each species appropriately. Through studying the minute differences between species, he hoped to develop a system of classification that truly matched the order of nature. To this end he missed an opportunity to collect specimens. The previous year, a German colleague, Prince Maximilian of Wied, Neuwied (in Germany), to whom Swainson had introduced him, had asked him for "letters and directions" for his planned expedition to the far western territories of the United States. Bonaparte gave Maximilian a letter of introduction to Cooper and then urged Cooper to "counsel" the prince and suggest "some good fellow" to accompany him as collector, such as Cozzens, "who will think of us and about science."[5] He also advised Maximilian to visit Say in New Harmony.

Aside from Cooper, Bonaparte often thought of his other American friends and was shocked to hear that Reuben Haines had died in the fall of 1831. "No death could affect me more than that of my excellent friend Reuben!" he writes Cooper. "I had heard nothing of it previous to your letter nor since though we have here some of his relations!" More than likely Haines's relatives were reluctant to speak of his death to Bonaparte, since Haines had committed suicide. Haines's mental problems seem to have been known to some of his colleagues. Richard Harlan once wrote Swainson that Haines often neglected his duties as secretary of the Academy of Natural Sciences because he was "afflict-ed with hereditary monomania."[6]

There had also been an unexpected death in Bonaparte's own family, that of Charlotte's husband, Napoleon-Louis, at Pesaro on 17 March 1831. He and his younger brother Louis-Napoleon had joined rebel forces in Italy to fight the hated Austrians, who at the time occupied a large portion of northern Italy. Napoleon-Louis contracted measles while involved in a guerrilla campaign and rapidly succumbed to the disease. He was only twenty-eight, a year younger than Bonaparte, and it was of course a shock for Charlotte. But her marriage had not been a happy one. In spite of his intelligence she had thought Napoleon-Louis too immature and had often had occasion to reproach him for his "despotism," jealousy, and perpetual recriminations. His appearance reminded her of their common cousin Achille Murat,[7] an unflattering compar-ison, since Zenaide had once described Achille as having "the face of a monkey and the manners of a pig [*la figure d'un singe, et les manières d'un cochon*]."[8] After her husband's death Charlotte remained in Florence, living with her mother at the large Serristori Palace that Julie rented on the bank of the Arno.

A year and a half later, on 22 July 1832, the duke of Reichstadt died of tuberculosis at Schonbrunn Palace outside Vienna. The death of this nineteen-year-old, unmarried pretender to the imperial throne of the Bonapartes—at the time the succession was a political reality—meant that Charles's father-in-law Joseph was next in line. Joseph had been besieged for years with requests to return to Europe and take up the cause of the Bonapartists. Disillusionment with Louis-Philippe had set in soon after he ascended the throne of France in July 1830, and it was hoped by many that Napoleon's son could replace the unsatisfactory "Citizen King." When he embarked for England in the summer of 1832, Joseph did not know the young duke was terminally ill and only learned of his nephew's death on landing at Liverpool on 16 August. At the age of sixty-four, the count de Survilliers was reluctant to enter the political fray. He had never been ambitious for political power in any case and had been against Napoleon's empire from the start. His friend Victor Hugo wrote him, "in truth we are marching more toward a republic than [a new empire] . . . but to a sage like you, the exterior form of the government is of little importance."[9] (Was Hugo being facetious in calling Joseph a sage?)

Bonaparte apparently planned to visit his uncle that summer, because he wrote Cooper at the end of June that he was contemplating a trip to London in a few days.[10] But there is no evidence that he actually went. In September he informed Cooper from Florence that he had spent the summer collecting nat-ural history specimens from many locales in Italy, particularly along the Adriatic coast. He plans to return permanently to Rome in December, when he will send another "envoy" to America with subsequent numbers of his *Fauna italica*. Although he is working constantly on this book, he now wants to continue the *American Ornithology* as well, and if Carey & Lea will not undertake the fifth volume, he will publish it without them, either in America, England, or Italy. "I hope you will not abandon me in this useful enterprise for which I have new immense materials," he says with his usual enthusiasm.[11] Bonaparte may have obtained these new American specimens through James DeKay, who four years earlier, in the winter of 1829, had outlined to him an expedition to be undertaken by a "Dr. H. Gates" to the Arkansas Territory. Gates would collect plants, roots, seeds, and animals of all kinds including birds and insects, and also shells. He would need six hundred dollars for the journey, so shares were being sold for ten dollars apiece. The specimens gathered would be divided in lots and drawn for.[12]

Cooper had already told him that Carey had no interest in publishing a fifth volume. "When one considered the disadvantages of having one person concerned with the work in Italy, another in New York, and a third in Philadelphia," Cooper explained, "one could see that a 'driving man of business' like Carey would not agree to it."[13] The book was not a money-maker. As Godman had once written to Bonaparte, "the services he had rendered to natural history in America" would be "highly estimated in the future," but at present there were too few who could "correctly" appreciate what he had done.[14] When Cooper received the box containing the *Fauna italica*, he told Bonaparte that it was "well executed in all respects" and he would circulate the prospectus, but acknowledged that Italian was hardly known in America, except by a few literati and opera amateurs in large cities.[15] If Bonaparte thought it worthwhile to employ a collector in the United States, he could recommend one of the best for birds, insects, and mammals, and could also teach this person to collect fishes and reptiles, "which nobody here will buy of him."[16] Later, he sent Bonaparte two live turtles someone had sent him from Surinam and suggested that even if they were dead on arrival, he hoped Bonaparte would at least find the shells of interest.[17]

The prince and his family left Florence for Rome in early January 1834. "I assure you I should rather go to America alone than to Rome with five children & the necessary company," he confided to Cooper. In addition to their two sons Joseph and Lucien, he and Zenaide had three living daughters: Letizia-Julie, born in 1830; Charlotte-Honorine, 1832; and Léonie-Stephania, 1833. Undoubtedly the journey from Florence to Rome, a distance of over two hundred miles, with five young children, a number of servants, and mountains of luggage, all to be transported in horse-drawn carriages over rough and uneven roads, and without satisfactory inns in which to stop, must have been a nightmare. But he and Zenaide often made this journey to visit her mother.

Before he left, Bonaparte complained to Cooper that he still had not received a printed copy of the fourth volume of his *American Ornithology*. He thinks the publisher's conduct is "outrageous," because he keeps his money without paying interest on it. Also, he is shocked to hear that Say has been in New York without visiting Cooper: "Such things I cannot understand even taking in account your American coolness. I should myself *walk* [a] hundred miles to see either of you!"[18] Neither Cooper nor Bonaparte knew that Say was very ill and only came to New York because his wife's family lived there. His other mission in the East was a visit to the Academy of Natural Sciences in Philadelphia, to see his scientific colleagues again for what he must have known was the last time.

In the winter of 1832–33 Prince Maximilian, on Bonaparte's advice, had stopped in New Harmony to meet Say, whom he had liked immensely. He stayed in that frontier town longer than he had planned, because he had been ill for several months with "Harmony fever," but Say made the time pass by visiting him daily and bringing him books on natural history from the vast library Maclure had sent him from Paris. Not knowing that Maximilian had been laid up in New Harmony and thinking he was much further west, Cooper wrote Bonaparte in February that nothing had been heard from the traveler and he suspected he might be "in great danger in the western country." A hunter who lived for some time in the Rocky Mountains had told him that the Blackfoot Indians would attack any whites that came near them.[19]

Prince Maximilian, safely returned to Europe in the late summer of 1834, recounted to Bonaparte some of his adventures. He said he and his party had arrived a short distance from the falls of the Missouri when the Assiniboins attacked their "allies the Blackfeet and stirred up all the northern savages in our vicinity." This situation had caused the cancellation of his project to visit the Rockies, but in spite of not reaching that interesting part of the country he hoped there were objects in his collections "worthy to be received" in Bonaparte's work "following the Ornithology of Wilson." In speaking of his own enterprise, he mentioned that his atlas (collection of drawings) was considerable, because he had had with him a clever young painter, Charles Bodmer of Zurich, Switzerland, who had skillfully rendered both the landscapes traversed and the portraits and costumes of the Indians. Perhaps some day he would be able to publish "something on this material, principally on these remarkable tribes, who speak of the cruelty and avarice of the whites and respond by withdrawing more and more to the Rocky Mountains."[20] (Today Maximilian's atlas is extremely valuable, because Bodmer is considered "the most able of the early artist/explorers" who painted the Rockies.[21])

On their return trip in June, Maximilian again stopped in New Harmony for a second, and final, visit with Say. Say died of dysentery and liver failure the following fall, on 10 October 1834. Some years later, Bonaparte would record in his memoirs: "more than any other my heart was wrung by my dearest friend Say, whose death was so sudden."[22]

For the next several years Bonaparte's life was taken up with his growing family and his *Fauna italica*, particularly the division that dealt with fish. In the winter of 1834, when his interest in studying fishes intensified, he began a correspondence with the brilliant young—he was twenty-seven—Swiss scientist Louis Agassiz. "I see that it is necessary to compare the species of Italy with those of northern Europe and I will only publish mine after you have reviewed them," he writes. He is sending Agassiz fifty specimens, largely in response to Agassiz's questions but also in the hope that some of them will "help you to clear up my ignorance." He thinks Agassiz's "*genera piscium*" will be a work of great importance and will do for the fishes what [Johann Carl Wilhelm] Illiger has done for mammals and birds and [Johann] Wagler for reptiles. He will do everything he can to make this work known and to procure subscriptions for him in England and America, but he will probably be the only one in Italy to subscribe. He can furnish Agassiz with many of the bird specimens he wants, and asks in return for certain specimens of freshwater fish and rare reptiles.[23]

A year later, when he told Agassiz how highly he valued his correspondence, he added that he would appreciate it greatly if Agassiz could get subscriptions for his *Fauna italica* in Switzerland; if recommended by Professor Agassiz, his work in ichthyology would not be overlooked.[24] Bonaparte was apparently au courant with the changing enthusiasms of Europeans in natural science: Audubon wrote him from London about the "failure of ornithology in Europe," how the "taste" in individuals who had till recently been "warm advocates" was now shifting to insects and fishes. He was sorry to hear that Bonaparte had "put aside the feathers for the fins of the animal kingdom."[25] Bonaparte had written him of his great desire to be in London, where so many of his colleagues were located. Audubon replied that Charles was so different from himself: "you wish to be in London and I wish ever to be out of it."[26] Although Audubon wanted to be gone from England and did not consider himself the scientist Bonaparte was, ironically it was he, not the prince, who had made a strong impression on the English. Charlotte Brontë, giving suggestions for informative reading to a friend in 1834, suggested Audubon for natural history.[27]

From Ariccia, in September 1835, Bonaparte lamented to Cooper that his *Fauna* needed subscribers badly. He thinks it is "impossible" that his publishers, Carey & Lea, from whom he has not heard for two years, will not take a few copies to sell for him. Concerning the *Ornithology*, he says: "You speak of being

Figure 25. *Louis Agassiz* (1807–1873) by F. T. Stuart, 1828. From *Louis Agassiz: His Life and Correspondence*, edited by Elizabeth Cabot Carey Agassiz, vol. 1 (Boston: Houghton Mifflin, 1886), frontispiece. Photo credit: Lisa Tyson Ennis.

in my debt! . . . & what shall I say of me towards you?—for the handsome manner in which you have conducted vol. 4 of the ornithology—shall we not complete that work? Do not stay so long without writing . . . let us sometimes recollect of our mutual promise of writing once every month & be ashamed of ourselves."[28] He did not hear from Cooper for a long time, however, because of upheavals in Cooper's life: his wife and youngest child died, and a year later he married his wife's sister and moved to a farm in New Jersey.

When Bonaparte spoke of completing the *Ornithology* and having "new immense materials" for it, he may have been thinking of the collections Prince Maximilian had brought back from the American West. But this hope was dashed the following month, October, when he heard from the prince that seven cases of his specimens, including the most interesting, had been destroyed in a steamboat fire. Maximilian said how disappointed he was not to have anything more to contribute to Bonaparte's book. It hurt him to recall the "beautiful figures" Bonaparte had published of the "Cock of the Plains" (today the Sage Grouse, *Centrocereus urophasianus*) and the Sharp-tailed Grouse (*Pedioecetes phasianellus*) because these were among the specimens that had been lost. He noted that he had seen many beautiful birds used as ornaments on the heads of Assiniboin and Blackfoot Indians, birds such as the *Fringilla (Passerina) amoena* (the Lazuli Bunting first brought back from the West by Say). Maximilian ended his letter with the hope that Bonaparte's proposed trip to England would take him through Germany, because he would "find much of interest" at Neuwied.[29]

At the beginning of 1836 Audubon wrote that he was sailing for America in the spring and wanted to know if Bonaparte planned to continue his *American Ornithology*. If not, he would like to obtain from Cooper several rare bird specimens that would be useful to him in his own work.[30] Bonaparte answered that he was not proceeding further with *American Ornithology*, but nevertheless would not allow Cooper to surrender the specimens. Audubon was distressed: "I even sigh as I write this, but never mind for these are, after all, American specimens"; he would find them for himself. And Bonaparte must have misunderstood him, he says, about the sale of his bird skins, since he never intended to get rid of his collection, but only thousands of duplicates he has for sale at Havell's shop. As for having any influence with people likely to subscribe to the *Fauna italica*, Bonaparte is "completely mistaken" about that, for he rarely sees anyone but intimate friends and his own family and he never visits scientific societies. Audubon was not about to render favors when he had just been refused one. He asks, finally, why Bonaparte sealed his letter with black wax.[31]

The answer was that Madame Mère had recently died. For many years she had lived in a large palace on the Piazza Venetia, in the heart of Rome. This palace she left to her oldest son, Joseph, who would in turn leave it to Zenaide. In due course she and Charles would make it their winter home, while continuing to spend spring and fall at the Villa Paolina.

Figure 26. *Letizia Ramolino Bonaparte* (Madame Mère) by Baron François Gérard. Oil. Musée du Château de Versailles et Trianon.

As occupied as he was with natural history and his voluminous correspondence with Audubon and others, Charles thought it time he took a serious interest in his children's education. Since he did not want them to attend school, which he himself had disliked so much, he hired Luigi Masi from Perugia, a young man in whom "an elevated mind was combined with a pure and sentimental heart," to tutor them at home.[32] Masi would be with the Bonapartes for years, not just as the children's instructor but also, later, as Charles's secretary. He became a personal friend, and at all times accompanied the family on their travels. Bonaparte often took his entire retinue to Florence to visit Zenaide's mother and to Bologna and Sinigallia on the Adriatic to see his own parents, Lucien and Alexandrine. To escape the heat of Rome, he and Zenaide built their own summer retreat, a modest house in Ariccia near Castel Gondolfo, the pope's summer home, two hours by carriage from Rome. It would serve them as a refuge when cholera struck the city in 1837.

Several more years would pass before Bonaparte visited England again, but he was in touch with his affairs in London through Audubon, who wrote to him regularly. The artist had accidentally met at Havell's a Count Metaxa who was anxiously trying to settle some of Bonaparte's accounts with booksellers. He reported that the count showed him a bill from Bingham & Hilliard in which Bonaparte was charged with eight copies of the *Fauna* supposedly delivered to Audubon. But since the latter had "not had the pleasure of seeing even a single number or plate" of Bonaparte's work, he gave the count a note to that effect. The count told him many sets had been destroyed or rendered useless by their having been sold at random as single numbers. (He meant that many installments of the *Fauna* had been taken apart and the plates sold singly.) Audubon protests that all this is painful to him, since, if asked, he would have strongly advised his friend to have nothing to do with booksellers. Besides, he has frequently offered Bonaparte his personal services. And though "not a man of much importance in any way, I possess the feelings of friendship to a degree of which I am proud, and to have served one whose esteem I shall ever value, would to me have been a pleasure."[33] The friendship was not entirely one-sided. In a letter of July 1836, Bonaparte wrote Lawson, his Philadelphia engraver, that though Audubon's work was not faultless, Lawson underrated him. Bonaparte expressed regret over Audubon's poor reception in the United States and pointed out that he himself had managed to secure him several subscribers in Europe. "I cannot take your wicked commission [?] to Temminck," he adds, "for I have scolded him severely for not subscribing to the work [*Birds of America*] at my recommendations. Some of Audubon's plates are superior to Temminck's who vilifies them."[34]

Audubon's next letter to Bonaparte was delivered personally by the artist's adult sons, Victor and John Woodhouse Audubon, who came to Rome "to see as many great pictures as possible." Their father's trip to America had been postponed because of a fire in New York that burned up his guns: by the time new ones were made the best season for hunting would be past. Audubon sent with his sons a case for Bonaparte containing the first fifty-eight numbers of *Birds of America* and an accompanying letter in which he expressed the hope that Bonaparte would come to England before he himself sailed for America in August.[35]

It was impossible for Bonaparte to leave Italy during 1836, however. Among other things, his younger brother Pierre, the family black sheep, had gotten himself into serious trouble. An irresponsible would-be revolutionary, he had conspired against the pope, and when tracked down in Canino, fatally shot the papal policeman sent to arrest him. Taken into custody and imprisoned in Rome's Castel St. Angelo for many months, Pierre was condemned to death by a tribunal of eight judges. The pope finally commuted his sentence to exile, after receiving a barrage of pleading letters from his mother, Alexandrine, and Lord Stuart de Rothsay, former ambassador to France and uncle by marriage to Pierre's half-sister Christine. Lord de Rothsay even came to Rome to implore his pardon.[36] Pierre had a choleric Corsican temperament and led a chaotic life. In later years he would be popularly known as "the Corsican Wild Boar."[37]

It was not until early September 1837 that Bonaparte went to England, taking his son Luciano with him. As Bonapartes were still barred from entering France, father and son traveled through Switzerland and Germany. From Mannheim he wrote Zenaide: "We are at last at the end of our fatigues . . . the Rhine offered us a delicious rest. Loulou [Luciano] has never been so happy . . . you must have received our letter from St. Gothard. We have crossed Switzerland in the most interesting part and have seen the most remarkable sights. I am now *high-spirited*."[38]

In England, he stayed with Joseph at his London house in Park Crescent and then at his rented estate in Suffolk. For political reasons, notably the increasing dissatisfaction with Louis-Philippe, the count de Survilliers had again found it necessary to situate himself nearer to France and had been living in England since August 1836. He also had to settle his mother's estate. There had been much squabbling over her sizable legacy, particularly by his sister Caroline Murat, who instigated a lawsuit in Paris against her siblings.[39] Bonaparte's own father, Lucien, had come to England to visit his brother, whom he had not seen in many years, and to discuss their common financial problems. The mortgage on Canino was an ongoing source of serious contention, because Lucien had still not lived up to his obligation to pay Zenaide the interest earned by investing her dowry, and Charles instituted a lawsuit against his own father at this time. An extant document, written for Joseph, presumably by a lawyer, states: "The Count of Survilliers is profoundly tormented by the proceedings against all the laws of nature and of civilized society that exist between his brother Lucien and his son-in-law and nephew, because of the dowry of his daughter Zenaide, which was by the contract of marriage put on the mortgage of the principality of Canino at 4%."[40] However, the suit may have been settled by October, when Bonaparte again wrote to Cooper, because his handwriting, often scrawling when he was in an agitated frame of mind, was neat and legible, and he reported that he was more than ever engaged in natural history and postponed his studies for nothing except "domestic happiness the most important thing after all." God had blessed him with seven children, two boys and five girls. (Marie-Désirée-Eugénie-Joséphine-Philomène had been born in 1835 and Augusta-Amélie-Maximilienne-Jacqueline in 1836.) Even so, he may have been feeling somewhat alone in the aftermath of so much family discord, for he entreated his friend, "do not drop me entirely I beseech you."[41]

While in England, he traveled to Liverpool to visit the menagerie and vast natural history collections of the earl of Derby at Knowsley Hall, where the artist Edward Lear had been working for four years drawing the animal residents. Back in London, he saw friends and colleagues and visited various scientific societies, the British Museum, and the Zoological Gardens. He made a point of visiting Audubon, who wrote his friend John Bachman in South Carolina that Bonaparte was "a most amiable good Man, and I Know that you would enjoy his society much. —He Kissed me as if a Brother, and I really believe that he is My Friend."[42] After two days in the city, Bonaparte went to Suffolk to hunt with his father-in-law. The nine-year-old Luciano wrote his mother proudly that he had often been hunting with his grandfather Joseph without holding his ears when the guns went off, and, much to his delight, his grandfather Lucien had given him a gold repeating watch.[43]

After Bonaparte returned to London he went again to see Audubon. The hour was late; in fact, the artist had already gone to bed. "But there he came," Audubon complained to Bachman, "sat by my side and talked about birds for upwards of an hour, the consequences of which were that I scarcely closed my eyes afterwards that Night." The next morning he came again, and Audubon, with his son Victor, accompanied him to look for lodgings. "He did not want it known except to naturalists that he was in London," Audubon explained, "and because he dislikes the Humbug of the Nobles that are ever and anon at his Father in law, Joseph Bonaparte. He is now therefore in humble street [inexpensive lodgings]." Bonaparte later went to Audubon's rooms to shave and dress, and brought him pheasants, hares, and partridges that he had shot, but aside from these encounters he was "almost always" with John Gould, Audubon said.[44]

By the end of December 1837, relations between the two colleagues had changed dramatically. Audubon was thoroughly disgusted with Bonaparte's attempts to wrest ornithological material from him and wrote a long tirade to Bachman:

I feel dispose[d] to give you my now real view of Charley! When he first came to London, he began by going the rounds, and trying to pump each, and every one, of those from whom he thought he might acquire Knowledge, and of Course as far as the Birds of North America are concerned, I was the very first on his list. Days after days he has visited us, pumped me as far as I was willing to be, Made list[s] of all our new species, examined each bird in the Skin, coresponded [coordinated?] his systematical arrangements, after asking me thousands of questions, and after all is still desirous that I should give him my Ideas or in fact Knowledge of their Habitats, Migrations etc! . . . The beauty of his manouvers is that whil[s]t doing all this for his own fame and benefit, he pretends that he is acting for my sake! Capital is it not? When I am as confident that he *positively speaking* Knows very little indeed of our Birds! Otherwise he is a mild, pleasant speaking personage, not at all the Prince about him whil[s]t with us at least, but so very fond of praise, that I doubt of his sincerity, (I am sorry to say this) as it has become rather too clear to me, that he never possessed one half the credit which I have been wont heretofor to grant to him, blinded as I have been by the apparent friendly manners which he never ceases for a moment to assume. —Yesterday he even carried off the whole of the list which he has made at our House, including among them one in Victor's hand writing. —he has Kept me at Home waiting for him, for hours and whole days, without attending to his appointments, and has made his appearance, sometimes early, at others late, and in fact only when he has found this to be most convenient to himself. —I now greatly regret my not having paid more attention to the strong language of Harlan respecting Charley, for if I had been more prudently guarded, he would at this moment Know still less than he does.[45]

Audubon's ire at Bonaparte is a perfect example of the field naturalist resenting the cabinet naturalist, or, in a broader context, of the old way of pursuing natural science resenting that it was slowly but inexorably being replaced by the new. The discipline of ornithology became more and more scientific as the number of specimens increased and the need to organize and classify them more urgent. As the days of exploration and the search for new species drew to a close (because most of the world's birds had been found), the romantic explorers and artists such as Wilson and Audubon became obsolete and the classifiers and more purely scientific workers, who spent their time poring over books and specimens, took over. Bonaparte's time in England was limited, and he was clearly frantic to gather all the information he could from Audubon. His aim was not necessarily to announce new species to the world; more likely he sought information that would help him to classify specimens correctly. That he was selfish and thoughtless in his use of Audubon was typical of the arrogance that was part of his character, in spite of his pleasant manners.

Audubon was to have even more cause for resentment, however. While in London, the prince, in the course of classifying Audubon's and John Gould's works, had drawn up a comparative list of the birds of Europe and North America and published the result—*A Geographical and Comparative List of the Birds of Europe and North America*—in January 1838. In his preface, Bonaparte states that his list is the most complete yet to appear on the birds of these two regions and presents them "arranged under their respective Genera and Tribes according to the present state of Ornithology." The specific name is always the one given by Linnaeus, or the first describer after the establishment of Linnaeus's binomial nomenclature. Throughout the book he used as type specimens the plates in Gould's book for Europe and in Audubon's for America, "as they must be considered the standard works on the subject."[46] At that time, when there were few museums to house the type specimens themselves—the actual birds from which the descriptions were taken—well-executed plates in books had to serve the purpose. That he published in his book some of the species Audubon had discovered was bad enough, but there was something even more annoying to Audubon: Bonaparte said in his preface: "the merit of M. Audubon's work yields only to the size of his book; while Mr. Gould's work on the Birds of Europe, inferior in size to that of M. Audubon's, is the most beautiful work on Ornithology that has ever appeared in this or any other country."[47]

Bonaparte might have anticipated Audubon's reaction. Not only did he feel that his species had been "stolen," but his vanity was wounded. "Charles Bonaparte has treated me most shockingly," he exploded to Bachman, "he has published the whole of *our* Secrets, which I foolishly communicated to him after his giving me his word of honour that he would not do so, and now I have *cut him*, and he never will have from me the remaining unpublished Numbers of my Work. —(which by the by he calls a poor thing) and the latter simply because I at last refused to give him my Knowledge of the Migratory or Geographical distribution of our Birds—So much for *a Prince!*"[48]

Although Audubon was disillusioned with Bonaparte as a scientist— "Charley" never merited "one half the credit" Audubon had given him—others were impressed. One of the highlights of Bonaparte's stay in London was in reading his paper, "Systema Vertebratorum," at a meeting of the Linnean

Society. Some time later this essay was given to the anatomist Richard Owen to review. Owen wrote the society's secretary that it would be presumptuous of him to offer an opinion on the paper, since it related to the "systematic" rather than the "anatomical" branch of zoology, with which he was more familiar. But he believed the merits of those sections of Bonaparte's "Systema" that included "the subdivisions of the wider groups" were of a "high order." Owen said Bonaparte's views were "indicative of a highly philosophical appreciation of natural affinities," and that he Owen "would be influenced more by the established scientific character of the Author" than judging by the paper alone.[49] Through the encouragement of Owen and Agassiz, Bonaparte's essay systematizing vertebrate animals would be published several years later in the *Transactions* of the society.[50] It was a triumph for him to be accepted and recognized in this way in England, particularly since he was not welcome in France. As a Bonaparte, he was still not allowed to enter the city of his birth.

When, in mid-December, John Edward Gray at the British Museum learned that Bonaparte had been refused permission to visit Paris, he sent an angry letter to a prominent Parisian scientist, Henri de Blainville:

I am quite disgusted with the conduct of your government. Prince Charles Bonaparte, a Naturalist of whom France should be proud, for I don't know any living man who has such an excellent knowledge of European & American Zoology and who has such just views respecting Natural History and has shown such independence in the study of it and justice to its professors, having expressed a desire to visit for one week the Jardin des Plantes, the Austrian Ambassador said that he did not see that any body could object but I understand that your Ambassador has refused to sign his passport! What a state you must be in with your boasted liberty. To fear the presence of the nephew of one of the men who was an honour to your country and the highest star of military glory in modern times and that man a peaceful man of science who has endeared himself to all the scientific men of the country by his manners and the extent of his information. I do say that France is degraded by such conduct.[51]

This letter from the director of England's largest and most prestigious museum paved the way for Bonaparte's return to France. He left England for the continent at the end of December, and after crossing to Antwerp traveled by railroad to Brussels to see his old friend Professor Drapiez. In Brussels he took time to call on an old family friend, General Henri-Gratien Bertrand. Bertrand and his wife had faithfully accompanied Napoleon to Saint Helena and had stayed to bury him on that forbidding island. Bonaparte had known the general intimately in America, where he had emigrated after Napoleon's death, and was especially pleased that Bertrand, hearing of Bonaparte's efforts on behalf of natural science, had dubbed him "the Napoleon of Peace." Bonaparte must have told him how much he yearned to go to Paris and visit the museum there and his French colleagues, because, the general, an admirer of Louis-Philippe and his constitutional monarchy, advised Bonaparte to go and pay his respects to the French king. Thus, armed with a copy of Gray's letter and General Bertrand's blessing, Bonaparte set out for the French capital.[52]

Not surprisingly, Louis-Philippe himself agreed to receive this "peaceful man of science": he wanted to appease the Bonapartist faction. At the time he was vehemently opposed by the two extreme ends of the political scale, the legitimists and the liberals, and badly needed support of the middle. At the meeting, the two men discussed such subjects as Italy and the pope, of whom Bonaparte assured the king he was a "most faithful son." They also discussed his father, Lucien, his uncle Napoleon, and the law of exile. When the king's oldest son, the duke of Orléans, appeared, he kissed Bonaparte warmly on both cheeks and later in the prince's visit, took him to see the seat of the *ancien régime*, Versailles, which ironically, much impressed the ex-emperor's fervently republican nephew. But most important, the duke promised he would ratify Bonaparte's nomination to the French Academy of Sciences.[53]

Little did Bonaparte suspect, as he sat opposite Louis-Philippe discussing his family, that in roughly twelve years his own cousin, Louis-Napoleon, would be sitting in the king's place as the prince president of France, to become three years after that Emperor Napoleon III.

But was Louis-Napoleon really his cousin? Was he in fact a Bonaparte? This question has been asked ever since Louis-Napoleon's birth, because of the intense dislike his parents bore for each other and the fact that he was conceived at a time when his mother, Hortense, was having an affair with another man.[54] It was an ironic twist of fate that Charles, a true Bonaparte with an uncanny resemblance to Napoleon, should have been shut out from the succession, while Louis-Napoleon, of dubious paternity and Charles's junior by five years, should become the next emperor of France.

After paying his respects to the king, Bonaparte sent a note to the venerable old scientist Etienne Geoffroy Saint-Hilaire, who as a young man had been to Egypt with Napoleon. The note requested permission to visit the Jardin des Plantes. "I salute you with a sentiment of admiration as a member of a race of heroes," Etienne Geoffroy answered him, "and with the respect that I have as a naturalist for your powers [*puissance*]."[55] He added facetiously: "we await you without weapons [*sans les armes*]." It was very moving to Bonaparte to meet one of the most important savants from the expedition that had set out in 1798 to a secret destination, known at the time only to the emperor. Etienne Geoffroy brought back numerous exotic specimens for the Jardin des Plantes, one of which, a fish called "le Polystère bichir," caused him to philosophize on the unity of plan and organization of living beings.[56]

In spite of a bad attack of gout brought on by the cold weather, Bonaparte made his way to the great French museum and was escorted through the halls by various professors, including Etienne Geoffroy's son Isadore, who took him through the mammal section. Others showed him the reptiles, fish, mollusks, insects, and gardens. And the birds—"great God, the birds I had to visit myself," he wrote in his memoirs. He thought they surpassed even those of the English collections. And he was thrilled with the ornithology collection of the duke of Rivoli, as well as the beetle collections of General Dejean, and the butterflies of Boisduval.[57]

After several pleasant months in Paris, Bonaparte took his leave of the king, of various friends, and of Zenaide's cousins, Joachim and Juliette Clary, with whom he had stayed. It had all gone well except for his visit to the Chamber of Deputies, to which he had been invited by the president, Jean-Marie Dupin (there were some in the chamber who thought the presence of a Bonaparte was an insult and made their feelings known by shouts of disapproval). But as he left Paris the two postilions who rode beside his carriage warmed his heart when they gave him "votes of confidence" and wished him well "in the energetic language of the people."[58]

By March he and Luciano were back in Rome, though the rest of the family was still in Florence with Zenaide's mother. Charles wrote his mother-in-law, Julie, that he planned to be at the Serristori Palace by 7 April, but one thing might detain him, concerning which he sought her help. Again, it was his old enemy Cardinal Fesch, who had spoken against him with "his filthy, contemptible mouth [*sa sale et méprisable bouche*]." It seemed his great-uncle, the cardinal, had read before ten people, "composing a veritable family council," an alleged letter from Joseph that was deeply injurious to Charles. It concerned Madame Mère's will. Charles told Julie that the expressions in this letter guaranteed that it was "fabricated by his Eminence," and if he would not willingly retract it Charles would attack him for lying. "I will make the world see that in Rome even Cardinals cannot injure with impunity those who have the courage to pursue them," he declares to his mother-in-law, "and in punishing a coward I will perhaps render a great service to the cause of civilization and of humanity."[59]

Bonaparte unfolds his plan to invite for dinner all the attorneys of Madame Mère's heirs, those heirs who have been "treated" to this letter. He will then demand from each of them a declaration that they had actually heard (other than the letter) all the allegations from the cardinal himself. Secured by these testimonials, he will summon his great-uncle to produce the letter, and if

Figure 27. *The Garden of the Palazzo Serristori at Florence* by Luigi B. Napoleone. Watercolor. Courtesy of the Museo Napoleonico, Rome.

he pretends to have burnt it, then his "lies and falsifications" will be manifest. But, his mother-in-law could prevent all this by writing the cardinal and getting him to confess his fault; this would save Charles much expense and precious time. Cardinal Fesch is the most "infamous calumniator" he has in all the world, but he might have overlooked this if the cardinal had not used his father-in-law to "strike him." Those who wish to console him have said that Joseph could not have considered the consequences of what he wrote, and in any case he would certainly be the first to blame Cardinal Fesch for a breach of confidence. Charles asks Julie to forgive his rambling letter. He has nearly decided to return to England and forget the whole thing, but he must think of Zenaide and the children. He asks her to embrace them all for him, and to believe him always her devoted son-in-law, who will never cease to have great affection for her. Whether or not Julie intervened and Cardinal Fesch produced the letter, the fact remained that Charles hated his great uncle with a passion. His relationship with his father-in-law was more complicated, since Zenaide and Julie still loved and respected Joseph (though the latter had not seen him for nearly twenty-five years).

At all events, Bonaparte was in Florence by 14 April. It is with "high spirits" he has taken up his pen, he writes Cooper, "hoping always that *la reprise* of our correspondence shall be kept up as it ought always to have been in our common interest & I dare to say it in the interest of Science." Since writing last, he has visited London and Paris and "undertaken much more than I could accomplish in a life much longer than I expect mine to be!" He thinks his *Fauna* will be completed this year and he plans to print his "Systema Vertebratorum" and his "Manual of Italian Ichthyology," though he does not mention "minor works," of which he has sent Cooper several. Also, he has bound himself in three years to "begin *in french* a General History of Birds of which I already know 8000!! species, in 25! volumes! . . . I am sure you will pity me."[60]

While in Paris he had seen his old friend Charles-Alexandre Lesueur. The artist/naturalist, who had stayed on in New Harmony after Say's death, had recently returned to France and was living near the Jardin des Plantes working on his manuscripts and sketches and earning a marginal living as a drawing teacher. He had shown Bonaparte a paper of Cooper's on bats which, the prince assured Cooper, he would have "given anything to possess" a bit earlier, because he had himself gone deeply into the subject in the twentieth and twenty-first numbers of his *Fauna*. There he had described and figured no less than eighteen Italian species. But he had advised Lesueur to give Cooper's essay instead to their colleague de Blainville, who was then writing on bats.[61]

After his return from England, he heard from Prince Maximilian, who was disappointed not to have met him on his journey across Europe. Maximilian wants him to know, however, that his *Geographical Distribution of the Birds of Europe and America* is of much interest to him. He thinks that "a complete synopsis" of birds has been needed for a long time and this could be arranged so supplements of new discoveries could be included from time to time. "It is thus a most agreeable enterprise that you have taken on and all zoologists must assist as best they can! If my feeble observations would be of any interest to you, I would be delighted to send you whatever you want." For information on the birds of Brazil, he suggests Jean Natterer of Vienna. Also, he explains that Bonaparte's "grand and beautiful Fauna Italica" is not in his collection of books, because he has had so many works to buy on American and "exotic" zoology that he has had to delay purchasing it. "Perhaps you will exchange it for my voyage in America which is being published right now?" Since Bonaparte knows German, he would be able to read this edition, of which two numbers are ready.[62]

In fact Bonaparte did not know German. Three years later he would write to Hermann Schlegel, concerning a book Schlegel had sent him, that he was thwarted by not understanding his language and awaited with impatience the French works he had promised him.[63] It was Zenaide who knew German, having lived in Frankfurt as a girl and having translated much of Schiller's poetry. Because many of Bonaparte's letters are written in her neat legible handwriting, it is safe to assume she helped him in other ways as well, and may have translated German letters and articles.

Maximilian thanks Bonaparte for his description of a certain bird and adds: "I give you sincere thanks my Prince, for the goodness with which you have been pleased to think of me, who does not merit the honor to be considered by a naturalist as distinguished as you are. You, who have also been a long time in the United States and know the nature of the country and its fauna. You judge, I hope, with indulgence, the humble descriptions of my voyage! The only merit you will find there is exactitude in the observations, the only merit to which my work could pretend; but you could imagine yourself in my place better than any other person and for that I hope that my essay will be of interest to you."

Before he left Rome for England, Bonaparte had also received a letter from another German zoologist, Eduard Rüppell, an explorer and cartographer some ten years older than himself. "Altesse [Your Highness]! I am delighted to receive your letter from Mr. Cretzschmar. And I am flattered that you want to exchange your *Fauna italica* and the 4th no. of *Ameri[can] Ornith[ology]* for my *animaux vertebres abysiniens.* But the disproportion respecting the commercial value of these works is too much for me to be able to accept this generous offer." (Moreover, he had already bought parts 1 through 19 of the *Fauna.*) He planned, he said, to spend the next winter in Italy, and looked forward to consultation with Bonaparte near the sea, to study fish. Meanwhile, he would send his book on Abyssinia (*Neue Wirbelthiere zu der Fauna von Abyssinien gehörig* (New Vertebrate Fauna of Abyssinia, 1835–40) in the next case shipped to the library of the grand duke of Tuscany.[64] Several months later Rüppell wrote again to praise Bonaparte's principal work: "The energy, the talent, and the great sacrifices, with which you have laboured and published your superb *Fauna italica* is a scientific monument as precious as it is rare."[65]

In June 1838 Bonaparte spent a month with his family at the famous spa of Montecatini in the mountains near Lucca, to take the saline waters. The family spent July and August outside Leghorn, near Montenero, the little town where Byron wrote his tragic poem "The Cenci" in 1818. By the sea at Leghorn, Bonaparte was totally absorbed in ichthyology. The paper he wrote there, on a type of fish called "selachi," would later in the year be published in Neuchâtel, Switzerland, under Agassiz's direction and be reproduced in various journals— an anticipation of his *Manual of Fishes* of 1840. But he had by no means abandoned ornithology. From Leghorn, he informed Swainson in England of his plans and goals, which included the big book of birds he had mentioned to Cooper. The first volume of this work (not yet begun) was due at the printer's in two years, he said. He wondered if it should be published in English as well as in French, and if so, would Swainson consider joint authorship? "It would be welcome I am sure by the learned & may be made very profitable," he assures him. "You told me you would like to spend some time in Rome & I offerd you a comfortable lodging in my Villa within the city. I now reiterate the offer which I shall be delighted if you profit by it. Should you come with your family you could have room enough to make your *ménage*, kitchen etc."[66]

Swainson answered the following month, setting forth his terms for coauthoring a comprehensive natural history of birds. If he settled his affairs in England and came for three years, or perhaps five, to "inhabit the Villa your Excellency proposes (which I should think is a house distinct from your Palace in Rome)," he would bring his two little boys, his only daughter, "a young lady" (his wife had died three years earlier), and one woman servant. During this time he would devote himself "almost entirely" to producing their common work. He anticipated completing two, if not three, volumes every year, for which he would be paid 175 pounds sterling, to be considered as the purchase of the copyright. He would draw all the drawings for the plates. He hoped to receive the prince's answer as soon as possible, because a "Mr. Hodgson of Nepaul" was negotiating with him to undertake the publication of his "grand folio work on Indian Zoology."[67]

At that time Bonaparte had no leisure to consider Swainson's proposal—which he would eventually turn down, since Swainson also wanted to sell him his entire bird collection, at a price Bonaparte considered exorbitant. He was busy planning a trip to Freiburg, in Breslau, southern Germany, to attend a scientific congress in October. The celebrated Rüppell wrote that he would have the honor of presenting Bonaparte to his colleagues[68]—the best introduction he could possibly have. He had found over the years that the wonderful network of European scientists was an invaluable resource, facilitating the interchange of ideas and allowing each researcher to know what the others were attempting and accomplishing. He had met Cretzschmar through Temminck and Rüppell through Cretzschmar—only two of many fruitful contacts brought about through the international community of natural historians. Because of his plan to initiate scientific congresses in Italy, this trip to Freiburg was of extraordinary importance to him. He looked forward to meeting the celebrated naturalist Lorenz Oken (1779–1851), among other notables who would be present. Above all, he wanted to meet Louis Agassiz, with whom he had been corresponding for several years.

7

THE NAPOLEON

OF PEACE?

"Yes my go[od] friend, I have succeeded
(and you cannot imagine again[st] how many difficulties)
in founding an Institution which will in a very short time
change the face of this fair peninsula."

Bonaparte to Edward Everett,
Rome, 15 December 1840

BONAPARTE TRAVELED NORTH to Freiburg with his secretary, Luigi Masi, and made a stopover in Genoa to see his great friend the Marchese Carlo Durazzo, whom he described as one of the most zealous ornithologists of Europe. He then went to Turin to see Giuseppe Genè, the new director of the Turin Royal Zoological Museum, and to acquaint him with his reasons for attending the German congress and his plans for Italy. Genè was destined to play a significant part in the Italian scientific congresses.[1] From Turin he continued northwest across Mount Cenis, in a blinding snowstorm, to Geneva, where he was welcomed by the eminent botanist Augustus Pyramus de Candolle. The great man had first visited him in Rome—an honor, Bonaparte noted proudly in his memoirs, that many foreign scientists had accorded him. In Basel he renewed his acquaintance with the banker and magistrate Jean Passavant, "a friend of science and of scientists," who accompanied him to the congress.[2]

In Freiburg he was heartily welcomed by Eduard Rüpell and at once struck up a friendship with him, as well as with the celebrated Lorenz Oken, with the son of de Candolle, and of course with Louis Agassiz. He was also delighted to see Richard Owen, who had come over from London. Aside from the official meetings, Bonaparte spent many pleasant hours in scientific ramblings with his colleagues on the lovely hills surrounding Freiburg and at a number of banquets. When the conference ended, he accompanied Agassiz and a Dr. Heule to Basel, to "experience again the splendid hospitality of Passavant." He then spent time with Agassiz at Neuchâtel (where von Humboldt had secured Agassiz a position as professor of natural history some years earlier), conferring on their favorite subjects in science. It was there too that Bonaparte published his *Selachorum tabula analitica*, a small work, written in Latin, that preceded his *Manuel d'ichthyologie italienne* of 1840.[3]

At this time the Swiss were at the boiling point over the possibility of war between France and Switzerland. The French had demanded that the Swiss expel Bonaparte's cousin Louis-Napoleon, who a year earlier had staged a coup d'état at Strasbourg, France, in an attempt to overthrow King Louis-Philippe. The coup was a fiasco, and Louis-Napoleon was tried and exiled to the United States. After some time in America and in England, he had recently returned to his home in Arenenberg, Switzerland, to be with his dying mother. The authorities of the canton of Thurgau, of which he was a naturalized citizen, refused to comply with the French demand to expel him, and the Swiss Diet, composed of all the cantons, concurred. Thus war appeared imminent.

Bonaparte noted in his memoirs that he had not hesitated to denounce his cousin in public and in private, for the "crazy and guilty conduct [*pazza e colpevole condotta*]" of his Strasbourg caper. He was not the only one in the family who thought Louis-Napoleon foolhardy: Joseph too was disgusted with his nephew for sullying the Bonaparte name in such a misguided endeavor. But Charles himself was acquiring a different reputation, at least in some quarters. Crossing Lake Neuchâtel by steamboat on his return journey, he overheard a conversation among the passengers in which he was contrasted—favorably—with his cousin.[4] Apparently others agreed with General Bertrand that Charles Bonaparte was the "Napoleon of peace."

The day he spent in Geneva, he was so distracted by the turmoil of impending war that it was impossible to work. So he abandoned his studies and attended a performance of Rossini's *William Tell*, an opera that tells the story of a legendary fourteenth-century Swiss hero who fought against Austrian oppression—staged, Bonaparte noted, as an obvious strategy to stir up republican ardor against the French. The next day, as he left Geneva, he passed long lines of French soldiers positioned to attack the city. How sad, he thought, to see the physical and moral degeneration of this militia: small, unimpressive men who drew from his postilion, once a soldier under Napoleon, the disgusted observation that these men were no longer French but "Frenchish."[5] At Lyon he boarded a steamboat on the Rhône for Marseilles, where he had a prearranged meeting with the secretary of the French Chamber of Deputies. The secretary informed him that England had at last granted permission to bring Napoleon's remains back to France from Saint Helena—welcome news for the entire Bonaparte clan, even though it would be several years yet before the former emperor was finally laid to rest in the Hôtel des Invalides.

After a brief reunion with his family in Florence, Bonaparte went at once to see the grand duke of Tuscany at Poggio a Caiano, a nearby resort. He was eager to describe the Freiburg congress to him, knowing that Leopold could be immensely helpful in organizing similar congresses in Italy. To his satisfaction, the duke was enthusiastic and suggested holding the first gathering at Pisa. Bonaparte later acknowledged that without the duke's help this initial congress would have been impossible, because Leopold made sure that other powerful people disregarded the "dark slanders" often leveled against the congresses by those afraid of their potential political impact.

Such apprehensions were not in fact entirely groundless, for the object of the Italian congresses was twofold, one overt and the other a subtle undercurrent. Scientists from all over the peninsula would be brought together to share their knowledge, and at the same time the need for a united Italy would be emphasized. A modern historian has written that, "while the role of these *Congressi* in encouraging scientific activity and in disseminating scientific information is not to be minimized, they are remembered today especially for their political import; for they were the first concrete expression of Italian national unity."[6]

Bonaparte had hoped to bolster his prestige within the congresses by his election to the French Academy of Sciences, after the ratification promised him by Louis-Philippe's son. But on his return from Freiburg he learned from Isadore Geoffroy Saint-Hilaire that he had not been elected, even though Geoffroy knew that the majority of academy members were "full of esteem for a life so useful and so important to science." The ostensible reason was that the division of zoology already included three foreign members (which the committee seemed to think was sufficient), though Geoffroy himself thought it made no sense to consider Bonaparte a foreigner since he was a member of "la grande famille française." "Thus it is that a man with your name must be able to carry with dignity the burden of such celebrity," he said, "ennobled by the unhappiness of undeserved exile and the pain that this last news prolongs even further." To soften the blow, Geoffroy mentioned an extract from an American article, reprinted in a French newspaper, that compared Bonaparte and his cousin Louis-Napoleon with respect to their opinions and goals. "It is not necessary to tell you that they speak of you with admiration."[7]

Geoffroy reported also that he had accepted a post in Bordeaux.

I must tell you that a career in science in France is still so full of difficulties. So little is in the interests of savants. The honor of my admission to the academy at 27 years (an honor much greater than I had asked or hoped for) has left me today at 33 years still at the point I was at nineteen! Yet with two children and a modest income I need to advance and improve my position, so that [accepting the job in Bordeaux, that of organizing a science faculty] was only a means to carry me for now. But what I hate, along with so many others, is to do the scientific trifles, the manuals, the resumes [abstracts], the newspaper articles etc. The other alternative is to acquire a position in a university.[8]

In this last statement Bonaparte must have heard an echo of his own impassioned letter to his father written from America a decade earlier.

Geoffroy's account of how little his election to the French academy had benefited his career was of no consolation to Bonaparte. Deeply disappointed, he turned instead to England in search of the recognition that would enhance his stature as a scientist. Writing to Richard Owen on 26 February 1839 to congratulate him on his election to the French academy and his "triumph upon the first luminaries of Germany," he hinted rather broadly that he himself would prefer membership in the Royal Society of London (to which Owen already belonged). It would be so helpful in forwarding his "favorite plan, the periodical meetings of the Scientific men in Italy."9 He also wrote John Edward Gray at the British Museum on the same subject, saying that the grand duke of Tuscany was a member of the Royal Society and that it would "produce a good effect" if he too were elected. "What must be done to obtain such an honour?" he asked.10

In his letter to Owen, Bonaparte advises him of the Italian congress to be held the following October (1839) in Pisa and expresses the hope that he and "other English eminent men" will attend. He asks Owen for scientific news, although he has none to offer in return from Italy, "which has no information to give, but so much to receive." He must be excused for not writing because he has been otherwise occupied and unable to answer his letters.

Perhaps he was distracted by the dramatic events taking place within his own family. His sister-in-law Charlotte, who had been staying with them at the Villa Paolina for some months, had just departed under tense circumstances. As far as anyone in Florence knew, she had simply been in Rome to visit her sister, but actually she had been in hiding. Charlotte, though a widow for eight years, was pregnant. After the death of her husband there had been several unhappy events surrounding this charming, artistic woman, who had become the center of a lively group of writers, poets, and painters in Florence and had been much admired. In Rome she had had a brief affair with a Swiss artist, Louis-Leopold Robert, whose studio in the Via Sistina she and her husband had often visited in the past for instruction in drawing, painting, and lithography. During the course of painting Charlotte many times, Leopold fell in love with her. In an oil portrait he showed her sitting demurely, her hands in her lap, looking out at the viewer with large, rather sad eyes. She did not return Leopold's love, which perhaps accounts for her expression. Tragically, it may have been from this unrequited passion that in 1835 Leopold committed suicide. Later a group of exiled Polish aristocrats replaced the artists at Charlotte's salon, and she fell deeply in love with one of them. Count Potocki was married, but his wife was far away in Poland. He was apparently the father of Charlotte's unborn child.11

Zenaide pleaded with her sister to return to Florence and confide in their mother, but she refused. Not wanting to give birth where she was known, she left Rome in mid-February for Genoa, traveling by sea with her private physician, Dr. Allertz. Soon after leaving the port at Civitavecchia, a sudden fierce storm forced the captain to put in at Leghorn, from which Charlotte and her doctor proceeded overland. The cruel bumping and shaking of the carriage brought on a dangerous hemorrhage, and they had to stop for a time at Lucca. By February they had gotten as far as Sarzana, about halfway from Leghorn to

Figure 28. *Charlotte Bonaparte* by Leopold Robert. Oil. Collection of Giuseppe Primoli. Courtesy of the Museo Napoleonico, Rome.

Genoa, when Charlotte was too ill to continue. Another doctor was called in for consultation. The case was too complicated for him and the patient too critical, so he sent to Pisa for a famous gynecologist. The baby was safely delivered by caesarian section, but it did not live long, and Charlotte, who had lost such a quantity of blood, could not be saved either. She died on 3 March 1839.[12]

When news of Charlotte's death reached Charles in Rome, it was at first necessary to keep any mention of it from Zenaide, as she had only just given birth to her son Napoléon-Charles-Grégoire-Jacques-Philippe. It was terribly difficult to tell his wife of this dear sister's death. From their first meeting, Charles had been charmed by his sister-in-law. In his memoirs he described her as a woman with "wonderful spirit and energy," a second mother to his children, the "joy and delight of his house."[13] From America he had written her mother that "the more one knew her the more one loved her."[14] After she returned to Europe he had written to her often and sent her packages containing his works. Because he shared her love of music, he once wrote her from New York, where he had attended an opera featuring the famous Italian singer Manuel del Popolo García, that "America as you see *marche à grande* toward refinement of civilization since she has taste in Italian opera."[15]

Charlotte had considerable artistic ability, which her studies with David in Brussels had enhanced. On several occasions she had shown her paintings at the Pennsylvania Academy of the Fine Arts in Philadelphia and may be credited as one of the first in the New World to use lithography. Alexander Lawson's daughter, calling Charlotte "quite an artist," said that while she lived with Joseph in Bordentown she painted several "views" of the Delaware River and afterward engraved all the drawings on stone, of which Charles Bonaparte had given her father some impressions.[16] Bonaparte may have introduced her to Lesueur, who was himself experimenting with lithography in Philadelphia at the time, and shown her Lesueur's lithographs, which he began publishing in the *Journal* of the Academy of Natural Sciences in 1822.[17]

Charles took Zenaide to Florence as soon as possible to be with her mother, and from there he wrote Joseph at Point Breeze: "Bad news has wings! . . . and you will have known for some time of that which has plunged us into the most terrible depression [*le plus terrible anéantissement*]." From now on, he said, their family reunions would lack the person who was the "soul" of them. The grief of Zenaide and the children was equaled only by his own and Joseph's, but was perhaps itself surpassed by the "prostration [*abattement*]" of "the most sensitive of mothers." He consoled himself nevertheless with the thought that nothing had been neglected that might have forestalled or prevented the "fatal catastrophe."[18] Perhaps this pragmatic attitude was his way of putting tragedy behind him so that he could continue his work. He sent Joseph a copy of Charlotte's will and went into detail over the estate she had left, which was principally distributed to his own children. He asks Joseph's help in clarifying various parts of the document, then ends with an attempt at consolation. "Think that nine children (because I do not intend to count myself) remain for you to cherish, to enjoy your goodness; and that their great pleasure will be to embellish your old age with their caresses."

Charlotte bequeathed to Zenaide the Villa Paolina on the outskirts of Rome that their aunt, Pauline Borghese, had left to Charlotte's husband at her death. Charles and Zenaide had been living there for some years, as well as at the Palazzo Bonaparte in the center of Rome. Because the expense of maintaining two homes and raising eight children was formidable, Zenaide followed up Charles's letter to her father with one of her own several months later. She says it is only by "privations" that they are able to manage. She knows well enough that her children will inherit all Joseph's money at his death, but it is now that she and Charles need some of the income from his capital. She appeals to his generosity and goodness with this "request not a demand."[19]

The spring of 1839 was gloomy, for Charlotte's death, though by far the most keenly felt, was not the only one in the family. Caroline Bonaparte Murat, aunt to both Charles and Zenaide, died in Florence several weeks later. She was Napoleon's youngest sister and the widow of one of his generals, Joachim Murat, who had succeeded Joseph as king of Naples when Napoleon made the latter king of Spain in 1808. In the following month the hated Cardinal Fesch died, or as Charles put it in his memoirs, "ended his less than luminous career." The cardinal's soul was clean, Charles added facetiously, because all he had was a body.[20]

In April Bonaparte heard further from Geoffroy Saint-Hilaire about his proposed membership in the French Academy of Sciences. "I have insisted above all and I believe it was an important point, on the universality of your knowledge; a person who is opposed to you responded that you are a great scholar [*fort savant*] but only in Ornithology, and that the academy cannot accept a savant so specialized." Geoffroy had cut short this detractor in his "perfidious insinuations." Monsieur [François] Arago (a famous physicist and permanent secretary of the academy) had said a few supportive words concerning Bonaparte's special position: a French scientist held outside the country for political reasons. Geoffroy then spoke again in Bonaparte's favor, "As a friend and as a zoologist full of esteem for your work . . . but also from our conversations and above all by the visits we have made to collections; visits by which you have shown me knowledge so profound and precise that I was astonished, even after the idea that I already had from your works." Geoffroy's father Etienne had said a few words in support of Bonaparte, and Constant Duméril testified to the importance of his work on reptiles. Only one person spoke to diminish the high idea that they had given of Bonaparte; Monsieur Arago stopped him, explaining that "Monsieur Duméril on reptiles and Geoffroy on ornithology qualified as excellent judges in these matters."[21] But even after all these encomiums from distinguished scientists, Bonaparte's election gave way to Agassiz's. Geoffroy avowed that he had as much affection as esteem for Bonaparte and he had only met Agassiz once, but "the geological consequences of his work are of such importance" that when the other members gave him "first rank" he had had to agree.[22]

It was clear that political circumstances weighed against Bonaparte. And in a way his being a *fort savant* in ornithology told against him too, for at that time it was still more important to know a certain amount in every field than to be an expert in only one, and he was apparently perceived as proficient only in the study of birds. At the end of May Geoffroy wrote again to say that he had voted for Agassiz, and that if some people were determined to oppose Bonaparte's election from political motives then it was a shame to them. He himself saw it as regrettable that his friend has been isolated from the country under three successive dynasties (Louis XVIII, Charles X, and Louis-Philippe).[23]

Political considerations also determined how Bonaparte signed his works. Several months later Geoffroy wrote that he had seen one of Bonaparte's papers attributed not to Prince Charles Bonaparte of Musignano, his "imperial and papal titles," but simply to M. Charles Bonaparte. "I know the value you attach to a title, and besides, the name that you carry combines two of the most honored of titles one could wish for and a title anyone would be honored with. It is petty and ridiculous if, as I think, a political consideration has dictated this suppression."[24]

By summer Bonaparte's mind was again fully occupied with the first Italian scientific congress. He went to Pisa in July to plan the event with the grand duke and to write an announcement and description of it, but much to his surprise there was great debate in the planning committee over the use of the name Bonaparte. Because of its implications of tyranny, the name was considered a serious obstacle to attracting the liberal élite of the Italian scientific community, and many felt it should be omitted from any advertisement of the congress. In the end, however, "Principe Carlo L. Bonaparte" appeared on the announcement circular, at the top of a list of six coordinators of the congress.

The others were Cavalieri (Knights) Vincenzio Antinori, director of the Museum of Physics and Natural History at Florence; Giovanni Battista Amici, astronomer to the grand duke; Gaetano Giorgini, head of the University of Pisa; and Doctors Paolo Savi, professor of natural history at the University of Pisa, and Maurizio Bufalini, professor of clinical medicine at the principal hospital in Florence.

The circular stated that the meeting would be held in Pisa because "this city, in the center of our peninsula, flourishes in every branch of study." Pisa was rich in music, religion, philosophy, and science, exemplified by its lofty tower, where one could explore the wonders of the sky. The congress would be held on 15 October 1839 and bring together Italian professors and practitioners of physical science, including medicine and agriculture, "so useful to humanity." Professors of science at various universities in Italy, directors of botanical gardens and museums (natural history and fine arts), and members of the institutes and academies of Milan, Turin, Modena, Bologna, Naples, Rome, Florence, and all other Italian cities—all were invited to attend. "Most Enlightened Gentlemen [*Chiarissimo Signore*]," the brochure concludes, "this is one of the most efficacious means to spread useful knowledge, and to obtain our noble aim [*a conseguire si nobile scopo*]."[25] The last phrase is interesting in its veiled allusion to Italian political unity.

Bonaparte sent Richard Owen a batch of these circulars and asked him to distribute them to his friends and otherwise to make the meeting known by all possible means. He told Owen he had had great difficulties to conquer in establishing these congresses, but the idea of a series of meetings had been hailed as the "dawn of scientific regeneration throughout Italy," and he was sure the congress in Pisa would be "as brilliant as useful."[26] He also sent word of the *congresso degli scienziati italiani* to the American Philosophical Society in Philadelphia, asking for any support the society would be willing to give and, especially, to name him their delegate. The idea was indeed a clever one, because in representing an American institution Bonaparte could call into play American ideals of unity, liberty, and freedom—the very concepts the congress organizers surreptitiously promoted. Bonaparte might also have been motivated by the hope that as a delegate of the society he could express—and with impunity—ideas purportedly transmitted from America.[27] His request was speedily granted.

After some time spent in Florence, in early August he returned with his family to Rome, traveling by boat from Leghorn to Civitavecchia. It was so hot on the ride from the port to the city that one of the carriage horses dropped dead from heat prostration—a bad omen. From Rome the family left shortly for their house in Ariccia, where a tragedy equal to the loss of Charlotte awaited them. With almost no warning, little Léonie, age five, died of a heart ailment. Charles said she was "the wittiest and perhaps the most beloved of my daughters [*la piu spiritosa, e forse la piu amata delle mie figlie*]." The importance he attached to the child's death was manifest in his request that the pope conduct her burial service. She was laid to rest with her sister, Alexandrine, in the small chapel of the Villa Paolina.

It was just as well that Edward Lear, the superb young English painter of birds and author of the popular *Nonsense Rhymes*, did not come to Ariccia for a visit after all. Lear, originally introduced to Bonaparte through a letter from Nicholas Vigors, had several times in the past visited the Bonaparte family. But this time he wrote that there were too many of his friends in the neighborhood to allow him to study "as one so backward in so difficult a profession ought to do." Therefore, he had determined "to go to the farther mountains." He enclosed for Bonaparte's children—his "young friends"—some drawings "to fill up a corner of some little Album." Two of them were for "Don Luciano," whom he had "kept waiting so long for his Papagallo [a character from the *commedia dell'arte*]." The modest Lear adds diffidently: "they are (as is easily perceived) worth nothing in themselves, but I wished to shew you in the only way I am able that although I have not been to l'Ariccia I had not forgotten your kindness." He concludes that the friend he wrote to about the *Fauna italica* would like to subscribe.[28]

After leaving Ariccia, Bonaparte took his family to live in the enormous palazzo on the Piazza Venezia, at the very heart of ancient Rome, which Joseph inherited from Madame Mère. Straight ahead rose the Capitoline Hill, with the Roman forum stretching out beyond it, and Trajan's market a short way to the left. When Charles and Zenaide learned that her father intended to sell the palace, they had hurriedly negotiated with him to lease and eventually buy it. Zenaide was now his only child and would undoubtedly inherit the Palazzo Bonaparte, so the purchase must have been strictly a formality. Nevertheless, Joseph, writing his daughter from England to say that he was glad she had settled in his mother's house, noted that he had informed his agent of her intention to buy it for "30 million piastres," with the furniture that was left in it. Perhaps to explain his temporary need of funds, he said he had left his "immense establishment in America" without having sold anything, and although his investments were not saleable at the time they were secure and paying good interest.[29]

In early October, Bonaparte took his son Luciano and Luigi Masi with him to Pisa for the congress. As president of the section of zoology, he presided over the meetings, one each day for seven days. He also delivered a paper on the distribution of European amphibians and the method of describing them,

"Amphibia europea, ad systema nostrum ordinata," which would be published in the memoirs of the Academy of Sciences at Turin the following year. "One knows in what chaos the history of European Reptiles has been plunged for some years," he said, "and the volumes already published on general herpetology relative to these groups [European] have numbered few representatives from our country." He himself had almost entirely revised the classification of European serpents. In this paper as in his *Fauna italica*, he said, he had attempted to shed light on questions relative to these animals and had overlooked nothing in determining their genus and species, or in verifying the original name of each, along with its synonym.[30]

Much to Bonaparte's gratification, two distinguished guests had answered his invitation and come to the congress: Jean-Victor Audouin, a disciple of Cuvier, member of the Institute of France and administrator of the Jardin des Plantes; and Professor Lorenz Oken, founder of the scientific congresses in Germany, who would speak on the philosophical principles of classification in the animal kingdom. Although Richard Owen could not attend, Bonaparte read a letter from him announcing the birth of a giraffe at the Zoological Garden in London after a fifteen-month gestation. The event had created much excitement, as it was the first giraffe born in captivity; unfortunately, the mother lacked enough milk and the newborn died after nine days.

Bonaparte recounted in his memoirs that he had been enormously pleased to be elected president of the zoology section, but had to admit that he had made entirely too much of this honor and only later realized his mistake. How could he have restrained his enthusiasm, however, when so many important men in the field had been bypassed in his favor?[31] This kind of self- aggrandizement and pomposity would be Bonaparte's bête noir throughout his life. He could not resist the self-glorification that was bound to irritate his colleagues, so that at the peak of some success he would immediately destroy the respect he had just achieved. His uncle, the emperor, with his supreme self-confidence, cleverness, and subtlety, had managed to get away with stupendous egotism, but his look-alike outspoken nephew could not. Always a controversial person, Bonaparte unfortunately, and possibly unwittingly, made many enemies. Because of his name and national origin, there were those on the political scene who suspected that, under the guise of an Italian liberal, he was fighting for personal interests. Typical of the misunderstandings he attracted, the Sardinian minister at Florence noted that "in spite of the little sympathy Napoleon's brothers [Charles's father and uncles] give him in public, the Prince of Musignano dreams of elevating the Bonaparte family and seeks to make a name for himself. This in order to acquire the influence to carry out the ambitious aims of his relatives."[32] Little did they realize he shared none of the aims of his self-seeking relatives such as Louis-Napoleon. Geoffroy had recently expressed admiration for him in just this regard: "You have rejected illusions that are so difficult to renounce and have wanted nothing for yourself."[33] Bonaparte had no personal political aspirations (though he certainly had scientific ones). His political aims were disinterested and magnanimous, and chief among them was the unification and independence of Italy.

An anonymous pamphlet circulated by nationalistic zealots during the conference demanded, in regard to the Bonapartes, and specifically Charles: "What in God's name have these people to do with Italy [*In nome di Dio, che hanno a fare costoro con l'Italia*]?" Napoleon had not shed a tear over their country while he was on Saint Helena. And where were the Bonapartes in 1815, when Italy fell under the Austrian yoke? They had escaped to Rome or to Tuscany, where they had laid aside vast riches for themselves.[34] This last salvo was aimed directly at Lucien's plunder of Etruscan artifacts from his land around Canino and his subsequent sale of them for large sums of money. In defiance of animosity such as this, Bonaparte wrote in his memoirs that at that point in his life he would not have stopped in his endeavors "even if all the guns of Tuscany" had been pointing at him.[35]

That winter, 1840, much to his annoyance, he had to spend a good deal of time disposing of Cardinal Fesch's gallery of paintings. The job had been left to Joseph in Fesch's will, but since Joseph was not in Italy his son-in-law had to take it on. He sold some of the works, disregarding the cardinal's "exaggerated idea of their worth," while others, including books, a superb collection of drawings, and various artifacts, were handed over to Louis-Philippe and the French government in accordance with the cardinal's will. These collections were later transferred to Corsica, where a public gallery was established at Ajaccio in Cardinal Fesch's name.[36]

By spring, Bonaparte was at last able to return to his studies, which included finishing the *Fauna italica*. He was most interested to hear from George Robert Gray at the British Museum that the last part of Charles Darwin's zoological collections from his four-year expedition aboard the *Beagle* was shortly to be published; it was the section that dealt with the birds. John Gould had been given the task of describing and illustrating them. Gray also told Bonaparte that Swainson had sold his collection of bird specimens preparatory to emigrating to New Zealand, and would have left already except for unfinished "literary engagements."[37] Swainson's proposed move was not surprising to those who knew him. Ten years earlier he had written Audubon: "I am sick of the world and of mankind and but for my family would end my days in the primeval forests of my beloved Brazil."[38]

Bonaparte spent most of that spring in the Villa Paolina, except for short trips to the seashore, where Pope Gregory XVI allowed him to use his own apartment at Civitavecchia. Toward the end of June, however, all his occupations were brought to a total standstill by the news that his father was gravely ill. Lucien had first fallen sick in England and when partially recovered had returned to Canino. Finding the weather there too hot and humid, he had gone north to Siena but only got as far as Viterbo. Bonaparte left at once to join him there; he feared that he might not reach his father in time, for he had been told that Lucien was in the throes of "violent black vomiting."[39] Zenaide later told Joseph that Charles had had the "consolation to be called to his father in the last days and to be able to give him all the care imaginable." She said he had passed five days and five nights at his father's bedside without undressing and "witnessed the longest and most painful agony that one could see" (apparently stomach cancer, the same disease believed to have killed Napoleon and Caroline Murat). "Supported by heroic courage and soothed by a pious resignation," as Zenaide described him in his last hour, Lucien died in Charles's arms. It was 29 June—the anniversary of his own wedding, as Charles noted—and in his father's final moments Charles was there to give him the proper blessing.[40] After all Charles's battles with Lucien over titles and money, in the end he proved himself a devoted son. Bonaparte may have been feisty, strong-willed, and possessed of a fiery personality, but his sense of family was in the true line of his clan-oriented Corsican ancestry.

The issue of the mortgage on Canino, paid for with Zenaide's dowry, was still an ongoing concern. In the same letter to her father that announced Lucien's death, Zenaide explained that she had not spoken of the mortgage since Joseph had become the "proprietor" of it (by Cardinal Fesch's will), in the belief that this was "too delicate a subject" to put to him and would make him choose between a daughter and a brother who were equally dear. "Today, alas! Because that brother exists no more, I take courage to present to you the wrong that has resulted from the dowry you gave me that has been put on this mortgage." Because her mother-in-law was Lucien's sole heir and would inherit Canino, the mortgage would go with it, to the detriment of Zenaide's children. She asks "dear Papa" to render her a great service by giving her and Charles the administration of "the famous mortgage [*la célèbre hypothèque*]." At one time Lucien had promised her own mother (Julie) to cancel it (but he had not done so). Zenaide says that she and Charles had even asked Cardinal Fesch to give it to them, but he had refused, not wishing to put his nephew (Lucien) "in their hands." She adds that the cardinal, in his animosity toward Charles, had believed that such an act would bring ruin on Lucien. (Undoubtedly Cardinal Fesch's stance on this issue accounted in large part for Charles's hatred of him.)

Zenaide concludes her letter by saying that her mother-in-law

(Alexandrine) will have a considerable inheritance from Lucien's estate, and it would not be surprising to anyone if Joseph preferred his daughter by giving her the mortgage on Canino instead of canceling it for Alexandrine. She needs his answer as soon as possible so that they can act accordingly. It is quite clear that Zenaide had no faith in her mother-in-law's beneficence. She herself, however, was a generous and big-hearted woman, for after Lucien's burial she and Charles took Alexandrine and her two youngest children back to Rome, where they spent several months at the Palazzo Bonaparte in the Piazza Venezia.

The death of Napoleon's brother was a matter of international interest. Bonaparte's friend Edward Everett, then living abroad, read about it in the newspapers of Paris. "I believe it is the general opinion that his talents, at least for civil life, were in no degree inferior to those of Napoleon," he wrote, "and though circumstances did not long favor their brilliant development, you have the consolation that your father's retirement from the most eminent political career was a sacrifice to principle, and that what he lost in the splendors of rank & power, he gained in the tranquility of his existence & the happiness of his family."[41]

Everett then expressed his pleasure in seeing Bonaparte's name in certain journals connected with the scientific meeting at Pisa. "I rejoice that you continue to find your happiness in the peaceful pursuits of science, and in the acquisition of literary reputation," he said. "As I advance in years, my own inclinations are reverting to the same quiet channel." Little did Everett suspect the deluge fast building up in that quiet channel.

8

PRINCE OF

CANINO

"Votre maison illustre ne perda sûrement rien
de sa glorie en vous, monsieur le prince."

George Ord to Bonaparte,
Philadelphia, September 1841

A T LAST, having inherited the legitimate title of prince of Canino at his father's death, Bonaparte acquired the prestige he thought he would need to promote the Italian scientific congresses. He was devoted to these meetings; he saw that they were signs of an awakening national conscience. The revolution in France had given the Italian people aspirations to liberty and civil progress that had been difficult to relinquish after Napoleon's downfall in 1815, when repressive monarchies were restored to Italy's various principalities. Even those who had acclaimed the return of the sovereigns now opposed the resulting suffocation of individual thought and action. Discontent was spreading, not only among political radicals of all classes, but also with the intelligent, though more conservative, middle class, who were increasingly cognizant of the values they had lost and the freedoms other countries had that Italy lacked. This class, the new leaders in the army and the bureaucracy, were at odds with absolute rule.[1]

Nevertheless, those who dreamed of a free and united country were divided by traditional rivalries—between Genoa and Turin, between Sicily and Naples, even among cities of the same state. Still, these visionaries of unity were tireless. Some followed a path of gradual reform; others, more aggressive, formed secret societies. Political liberty had to be pursued under the cover of intellectual progress, legal, economic, or scientific, and always against the distrust and opposition of the various governments, particularly the Papal States, which at the time extended from Rome to Venice. Helpful to the insurgents was the first railroad, built in 1839, since it facilitated closer ties among members from different states and quicker and safer communication.[2]

It was in this climate that Bonaparte evolved his important idea of convening scientific scholars from all across Italy; it was no surprise therefore that, from the first congress (Pisa, 1839) to the last (Venice, 1847), the Italian government and police officials, especially those of the Vatican, reacted with suspicion. It was well known that the scientific congresses affirmed nationalistic ideals. Alarmed at the foreseeable political consequences of these periodical meetings of highly qualified, cultivated, and influential men, governments of the various states put the congresses under constant surveillance. The Holy See, under Pope Gregory XVI, made serious attempts to obstruct the first meeting at Pisa, since the Church was convinced that the purpose of the congress was "to establish secret intelligence among the members to work out the ungodliness of a so-called philosophy of Italian liberty." The court of Naples, frightened at the precautions taken by the pontifical government, even went so far as to refuse passports to scientists who wished to attend the meetings.[3]

Bonaparte felt strongly that the congress at Turin, held in the fall of 1840, was the kingpin upon which the destiny of the entire enterprise depended. "God knows the finesse [*sollecitudine*] I adopted and maintained to make it a success with the king and the Saluzzo family," he wrote in his memoirs.[4] Turin, in the northernmost Italian province of Piedmont, was ruled by Charles Albert, a trying man who had to be handled with tact and diplomacy. According to his contemporaries, this absolute monarch lacked the strength of character to reach firm decisions or to live up to those he did make. It was said he spent his time cutting out paper images of saints and playing with toy soldiers. Dominated by the Jesuits and ready to repress by force anything he regarded as subversive, he was regarded with suspicion by all progressives.[5] But Bonaparte had to keep on the king's good side; he therefore accepted Charles Albert's invitation to dine with him and his queen and presented him with a copy of *American Ornithology*.[6] Bonaparte's friendship with Alessandro Saluzzo di Menusiglio, president of the congress as well as of the Academy of Turin, was another matter; he would have been drawn to Saluzzo, if for nothing else, because of his connection with America. It was Saluzzo's ancestor, Giuseppe Angelo Conte di Saluzzo di Menusiglio, who had opened the initial correspondence between the Turin academy and the American Philosophical Society many years before, in 1773.[7] Bonaparte sought a similar interchange between the American institution and the Italian congresses.

Unanimously reelected president of the division of zoology and comparative anatomy, Bonaparte delivered a paper on the shrews of Italy and another on the *Falco Eleonorae*, a bird of prey named by his friend Professor Genè. All went well during the week of the congress, and at the farewell dinner, he recorded in his memoirs, he was greeted with "an uproar of applause" on entering the dining room.[8] Bonaparte must have been proud of his paper on shrews, for he sent a copy of it to Edward Everett, now living in Florence for reasons of health. He hoped Everett would translate and organize the paper and have it published in both England and America, though Bonaparte had doubts about its reception in these countries. He added, "you will easily perceive it has been written as you say at Washington '*for home consumption!*'" He says the next meeting, in Florence, will be "*grand* & we want some *Americans*." He will write at once to the future president of the congress, Marchese Cosimo Ridolfi, and propose Everett as their "transatlantic Apostle." He asks Everett to attend the planning meetings in Florence, to "advise our friends in their work of emancipation & you will do good to science, Italy, & human kind at large." Everett will soon feel at ease with his Italian friends, he says, and should Everett answer his letter as he hopes, Bonaparte will continue to trouble him with his schemes and ask his "active cooperation in a great many things which will probably please your noble & elevated mind." With characteristic warmth, he ends: "But why select Florence rather than Rome, where lives one of your most devoted and enthusiastic friends?"[9] By then Everett must have understood that these Italian congresses had a much broader implication than he originally suspected. Some months earlier he had written: "It seems to me that in bringing about this scientific organization, you confer upon Italy many of the advantages of that unity, for which some political theorists sigh; of which the benefits would probably be counterbalanced by some serious evils."[10]

The previous December, in 1840, Bonaparte had also urged President Jean-Marie Dupin of the French Chamber of Deputies to attend the next meeting of Italian scientists, to be held in Florence the following year. At the same time, he requested a favor of Dupin that would certainly have political implications for himself. Because of Louis-Philippe's kind reception of him in 1838, he thought the king might not be against a Bonapartist rally at the ceremony for the interment of Napoleon's remains in Paris. Charles asked permission to assist at the services as an envoy from the "microscopic but bountiful republic" of San Marino, of which he was a colonel and from which it would be entirely possible to obtain such a commission.[11] To represent the one truly independent and republican state of Italy at a rally for Napoleon, where he could expect a large, sympathetic crowd, was an opportunity not to be missed.

He did miss it, however. In January 1841 Dupin responded that Bonaparte's letter had been received too late to accomplish what he requested, though he assured the prince that his majesty "could only see with pleasure the desire you express for a rally with his government."[12] Charles's request would have fitted well with Louis-Philippe's plan to court the Bonapartists, since the two extremist parties in France were dead against him. The king had already, in 1833, had the statue of Napoleon replaced on the column in the Place Vendôme. It would definitely have suited Charles's republican hopes for Italy to strengthen the Bonapartists in France. But his letter was dated only one week before Napoleon's body was to be placed in Les Invalides, so even if the reply had been favorable there was no way he could have received it in time. Was his suggestion only a gratuitous gesture to assure himself a place of continued favor with the French king? Or was he in such turmoil, with all his activities, that he neglected to note the date? More than likely, both factors were in play. Perhaps too, his suggestion that he wear the uniform of a colonel from independent San Marino may have implied too much republicanism to suit a monarch.

Geoffroy Saint-Hilaire was present at the interment and wrote: "We deplored the absence at the head of the cortège of the French family who should have walked first. What a grand and beautiful occasion [at which] to see the deplorable traces of civil decrees, that is, the exile from the country of the family who had given it such brilliance." He spoke of Napoleon as "no less a legislator and administrator than a warrior," and recounted how French soldiers had stolen many souvenirs from Saint Helena and sold them to various admirers—French and above all, English. His father Etienne had been given one as a gift by a sailor from Toulon who had helped to bring back the obelisk (now in the Place de la Concorde) from Egypt. Etienne was eager to revisit the monument that he had seen in another time and place.[13]

Americans, too, sought Napoleonic souvenirs. Bonaparte's supplier of bird specimens, Forrester, had once asked him for a button from Napoleon's coat. And no less a person than Edward Everett, ambassador to Great Britain at the time (1841–45) and future president of Harvard University, would ask Bonaparte to favor him with "a minute portion of your uncle Napoleon's hair." If this were not possible, he asked for his autograph, or "some trifling article" that had belonged to him.[14] When Bonaparte responded that he would send the hair, along with a book once owned by his uncle, Everett was ecstatic and said Bonaparte's generosity was "a piece of good fortune far exceeding" his expectations. "To receive them from you—a member of the Emperor's family who without compliment possess most of his talent and character—and as a token of your kind regard, adds immeasurably to the favor. I beg you to believe that I consider these relics as a sacred deposit, and . . . when I am gone they will pass into the possession of those who will feel their value."[15]

Among all the scientists and dignitaries that Bonaparte encouraged to attend the scientific meeting at Florence, there were none he pressed more strongly than Agassiz: "nothing would then be lacking if [he] would enrich it with his presence." At the same time, he expressed the hope that this year Agassiz would shift his attention from the north of Europe (where Agassiz was currently studying the movements and effects of Swiss glaciers) to the middle, since Bonaparte wanted him to favor zoology over geology. (He was thinking, no doubt, of Agassiz's valuable work in ichthyology, *History of the Fresh Water Fishes of Central Europe*, printed in parts between 1839 and 1842.) He also asked Agassiz to comment on the last parts of his *Fauna*.[16]

Completed the following year, 1842, Bonaparte would dedicate his magnum opus, the *Iconografia della fauna italica per le quattro classi degli animali vertebrati* (Iconography of the Fauna of Italy Through the Four Classes of Vertebrate Animals), to "His Imperial Highness, the Grand Duke of Tuscany, Leopold II." The sole reason he offers this work to the grand duke, he explains in the dedication, is "the desire to pay homage to a savant who worthily occupies the seat of Lorenzo the Magnificent." The real reason, of course, was Leopold's support of the congresses. In the preface, Bonaparte writes of his adopted country's classical past: "the scattered remains of Italy's greatness in science, in letters, and in art are extant in the works that reveal them." He says that, "under a pure sky, in the beauty of a countryside bathed by two seas, and closed in and divided by mountains, Nature has favored this land with the abundance and variety of her gifts."[17]

Until the appearance of Bonaparte's work, Italy had lacked a comprehensive study of its animal life. But the prince possessed the position in society, the connections, the resources, and the leisure to assemble what was considered one of the most beautiful and complete studies of its time.[18] The book, when all the *livraisons* are bound, consists of three folio volumes: the first on mammals and birds, the second on reptiles and amphibians, and the third on fish. In all, there are 260 pages of text, describing 320 species, and 180 hand-colored plates. According to a French contemporary, the work made him as famous in the "Latin" countries as he was in America and England, and "before the publication was finished, Prince Charles Bonaparte was included among the members of the principal scholarly societies of two hemispheres."[19]

In the section devoted to birds, thirty-five species are illustrated and discussed. They include examples of all the orders then found in Italy, minus the pigeons, which the author believes are already known. It is particularly in this portion of the *Fauna italica* that the relationship between science and politics is evident: Bonaparte shows how different names are attached to the same bird in various parts of Italy and then makes a case for standardization (unification). The European Nuthatch (*Sitta europa*, Linn.) has one name in Rome, another in Florence, another in Volterra and Pisa, yet another in Venice and Genoa.[20] It is necessary, he believes, to standardize the name of this particular bird, and all others whose nomenclature is equally confused, so that wherever one is in Italy one will recognize what bird is being discussed. Certainly the unification of Italy is inherent in this concern for improving the country's scientific classification. If the congresses he so earnestly promoted could only bring some order into the confusion of Italian natural science, they would have played their part in the regeneration of Italy.

Because of the prevailing disorder, certain animals have remained totally unclassified, he notes. Of the small rodent *Mus tectorum*, he says, "this little quadruped, which is common in all southern and central Italy, has remained unknown in zoological science because it was confused with all the other species. It has been the same with a certain wolf, *Canis Melanogaster*." Bonaparte credits the "discovery" of this animal to the eminent Professor Paolo Savi of Pisa.[21] Savi had named a bat after Bonaparte—*Vespertilio bonapartii*—"this precious honor coming from a person so learned and such a dear friend."[22]

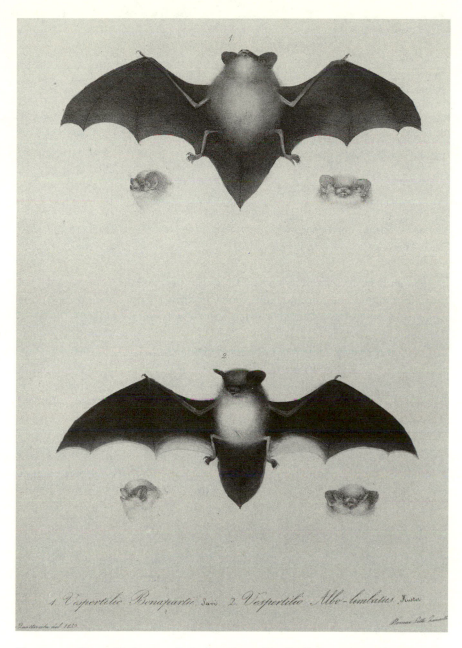

Figure 29. 1. *Vespertilio bonapartii, Savi;* 2. *Vespertilio albo limbatus,* Kuster by Petrus Quattrocchi, 1839. From Bonaparte, *Iconografia della fauna italica per le quattro classi degli animali vertebrati*, vol. 1, *mammiferi e uccelli*, unpaged. Author's collection. Photo credit: Lisa Tyson Ennis.

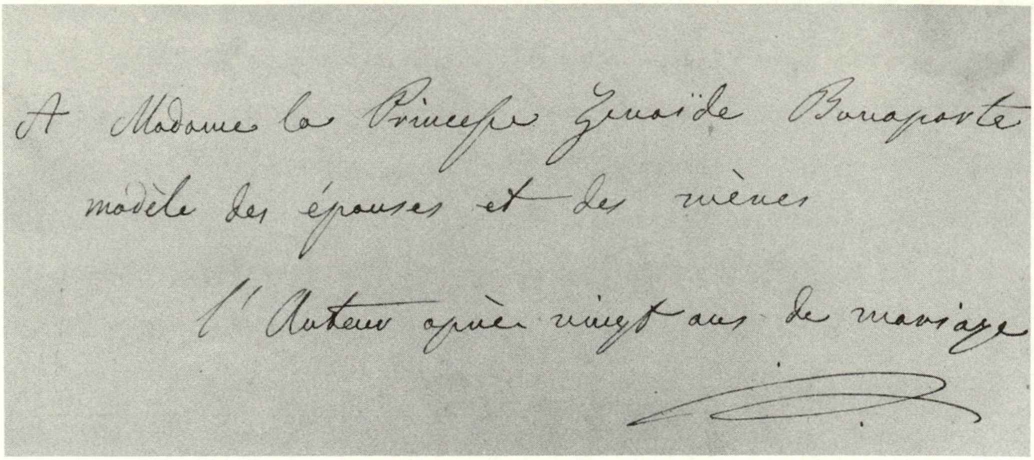
A Madame la Princesse Zenaïde Bonaparte
modèle des épouses et des mères
l'Auteur après vingt ans de mariage

Figure 30. Presentation copy of *Iconografia della fauna italica per le quattro classi degli animali vertebrati* from Bonaparte to Zenaide. Author's collection. Photo credit: Lisa Tyson Ennis.

Some time in 1842, Bonaparte had all the parts of the *Fauna* assembled into three volumes and bound handsomely in brown leather, with gold tooling richly embossing the spines. He inscribed the set: "A Madame la Princesse Zénaïde Bonaparte, modèle des épouses et des mères, l'Auteur, après vingt ans de mariage (To Madame the Princess Zenaide Bonaparte, model wife and mother, the Author, after twenty years of marriage)."[23] He was devoted to her in his way, though his own interests invariably took priority over hers, and his increasing political radicalism was at odds with her devout conservatism. Perhaps she was a "model wife" because she always gave in to him.

As the publication date drew nearer, Bonaparte accelerated his scientific investigations. He chastised John Edward Gray, then head of the British Museum of Natural History, for not sending a paper on bats: "A pretty fellow certainly you are, my dear friend, to have dropped me so completely as you have. I am afraid your high standing at the head of the first scientific establishment of our age has turned your liberal head still more than your numerous duties have occupied it. How can you think (or rather not think) of neglecting a friend and a fellow labourer in that way? Are you not ashamed of not helping me with the lights [insights] you collect from my quarter of the lake? Are you not ashamed of not having sent your papers on Bats so often applied for and to deprive of it a man who is working hard in that department . . . ?" Furthermore, he would have liked to learn about Gray's promotion to head the British Museum from Gray himself, rather than from others, considering the friendship Gray has always professed for him.[24] Bonaparte was at all times a demanding friend but one who invariably gave back as much as he received.

A friend who never disappointed him was Geoffroy. Bonaparte sent him a recent picture of himself—a lithograph of a pencil drawing—to which friend

Figure 31. *Charles-Lucien Bonaparte* by C. E. Liverati. Lithograph. Bibliothèque Centrale du Muséum National d'Histoire Naturelle, Paris.

responded, "Your precious portrait will be in my study beside that of my father, M. Latrielle . . . and three other naturalists whom I love and admire."[25] In his next letter, Geoffroy again mentions the picture: it "strongly resembles one I love and honor (a rare thing in this period)—the man and the scientist are the character and the talent."[26] The drawing depicts a handsome, youthful looking man (Bonaparte was then thirty-eight) with a serious but kindly expression. The hooded lids of his intelligent eyes, the curly, dark hair somewhat askew and receding from his high forehead, and the exaggerated sideburns typical of the period suggest a sensuous, romantic personality. He is fashionably dressed, with a high collar that holds in his somewhat ample chin. Deep in thought, he looks beyond the paper held in his left hand, as though he has paused for a moment to contemplate something profound suggested by this document. His signature appears at the bottom: "Carlo L. Bonaparte, P[rinci]pe di Canino."

During the late winter of 1841 it became clear that Bonaparte would have to travel to England to bring his father-in-law back to Italy for his last years. Joseph had suffered a stroke, and his attendants had written repeatedly that they could no longer handle his care. Since his doctor urged him to seek a warmer climate, Italy was the natural choice, and he asked his son-in-law to write the king of Piedmont for a passport that would permit him to land at Genoa. This concession the king made at once, accompanying his decree with a gracious letter describing Joseph as a great man of many accomplishments. Bonaparte noted in his memoirs that some said Charles Albert could do nothing on his own, but after this personal kindness he was inclined not to agree.[27]

As he had done on his previous trip to England, Bonaparte took along his son, Luciano, and the boy's tutor, Luigi Masi. They set off from Civitavecchia in the middle of April aboard the *Mentor,* stopping at Leghorn and then, for an entire day, Marseilles, where Bonaparte visited the museum and saw some Algerian birds that were new to him. From Marseilles, the party traveled by carriage to Lyon, then by boat up the Seine to Chalon. A twenty-four-hour carriage ride brought them to Paris, where Bonaparte took time to visit the Jardin des Plantes and to see some of his colleagues and mentors, including Isadore and Etienne Geoffroy Saint-Hilaire. Then it was on to Rouen and by steamboat down the Seine to Le Havre and the sea, after which another full day brought them to the Tower of London, amid a "forest of masts," ships arriving and leaving for all parts of the world. After meeting with his father-in-law in a hotel in Cavendish Square, Charles went to confer with Joseph's doctor, who advised chartering a steamboat for the return voyage—the most secure and comfortable way to take his patient to Genoa. But for the moment he could not endure the journey at all; it would be necessary to wait three weeks for Joseph's health to stabilize.

In the meantime, Bonaparte met with his scientific friends Richard Owen, Benjamin Waterhouse, and the brothers John Edward and George Robert Gray, and visited the Zoological Society. At a private club, he met Daniel O'Connell, the great Irish statesman known as the "Liberator," and Joseph Hume, a reformer tireless in his efforts to stop the impressing of English sailors and in other noble causes. Charles also dined with his favorite brother-in-law, Thomas Wyse, and other "eloquent members of Parliament." Invited to many dinner parties, he attended one grand affair at the Linnean Society celebrating the anniversary of the institution's founding, and he sat in on three sessions of Parliament. But the highlight of his stay in London was his presentation to the twenty-two-year-old Queen Victoria, at which he at last had occasion to wear his colonel's uniform from San Marino.[28] Toward the end of his English visit he received a note from the young naturalist Hugh Edwin Strickland, saying that he and his father "would esteem it a great honor" if the prince would visit their country house before leaving England.[29] Bonaparte was pleased and accepted. It must have seemed to him that to be sought out in this manner was surely a sign that he had attained an international reputation. From his brief encounter with Strickland, he struck up a correspondence that lasted for many years, until this talented naturalist was tragically killed by a train in 1853, as he was examining exposed rock strata between the tracks.

The day of departure finally arrived, and the chartered steamship *Hibernia* weighed anchor. The new fuel being tested by the captain produced such a large amount of steam that the vessel arrived at Falmouth in an unusually short time. Bonaparte went ashore to investigate the markets, where he discovered some beautiful fish, unknown, he thought, to the ichthyologists of London. The ship took on coal and on 1 June reached Rotterdam, where he was able to spend some time the next day with his friend Hermann Schlegel of the museum in Leiden. In a few days of "serene skies and peaceful sea," the ship reached Gibraltar, where he and Masi disembarked for a few hours. During this time, Masi collected a number of plants and Bonaparte observed some unusual birds, but he was disappointed not to see the rare and "celebrated" monkeys—the last of their kind in Europe—so well protected by English laws (Gibraltar being, then as now, under the jurisdiction of Great Britain). On 6 June the boat docked at Genoa. As Charles Albert had waived the requirement for quarantine in the lazaretto, Bonaparte was able to settle his father-in-law at once in reasonable comfort. He then left his son and Masi with Joseph and proceeded to Florence by himself to obtain permission from the grand duke for Joseph to enter Tuscany. Much to his annoyance, on his arrival he found that Leopold would not grant this petition without the consent of his brother-in-law, Ferdinand II, king of Naples. In the meantime, Joseph was not to leave Genoa. Bonaparte was obliged to return to Genoa to report this, instead of going on to Rome as he had planned.

After accomplishing his mission in Genoa, he embarked for Rome in mid-July aboard the *Mongibello*, a beautiful ship of the Neopolitan line, in which he had a small financial interest. According to the captain, with whom he conferred, all was in order, except for a slight alteration in the compass caused by a tiny metal fragment that would be removed in Naples.[30] The night was clear and filled with stars, and Bonaparte would have stayed on deck to enjoy the beauty of it all, but he was tired and instead went below to his small, spare cabin. He was just removing his coat and cravat in preparation for bed when he was suddenly thrown across the room by a tremendous crash. Pulling himself to his feet, he rushed up to the bridge, thinking the defect in the compass had caused the ship to be dashed against the coast. There was chaos on deck, but above the mêlée Bonaparte heard the strong voice of the captain giving orders to stop the ship. At the same time, he heard a sailor screaming that they had been rammed and were lost. It was an hour before midnight, and Bonaparte figured they were roughly three or four miles from Porto Longano on the island of Elba, in the strait between Elba and the mainland. Only two lights were burning on the *Mongibello*, but they clearly illuminated the tragic plight of the ship with which they had collided, the *Pollux*. It was a heart-stopping sight: the *Pollux* was nearly cut in half, and flames were bursting from its interior. According to an article in the *Courrier de Lyon*, both ships had been traveling at full speed, about twelve knots, when the *Mongibello* struck the *Pollux* on its starboard side, behind the paddle-box, knocking off its chimney.[31]

Bonaparte helped the sailors on the prow to hitch the two boats together with ropes so that they would not drift apart and to pull aboard the passengers of the *Pollux*, who by this time were up to their necks in water. Dressed only in nightclothes, some showed great courage, while others were close to hysterics. Bonaparte later recalled that the forty-five travelers represented most of the nations of Europe. There were Spaniards, Portuguese, English, French, Russians, Poles, Germans, Swiss, and Italians, and he noted that no group, as a whole, had shown either more or less courage than another. The captain of the *Mongibello* was particularly calm and authoritative; he kept the two ships in contact until all the passengers of the *Pollux* were safely removed and then, since so many bewailed the loss of their possessions, he ordered a rope tied to the stern for towing the wreck. But before the rope could be secured, the *Pollux* began its slow descent to the bottom of the sea, first the prow, then the stern. In twelve minutes, it was gone. When it disappeared, cries went up in fear that a similar fate was in store for the *Mongibello* (although badly damaged it did not sink), because in spite of the pumps it was filling with water. The terrified passengers clambered into the first available lifeboat, but it began to go under from the excess weight. With the help of several sailors, Bonaparte got some of them into another boat, all the while attempting to comfort the women and children. During this turmoil, which lasted several hours, four people drowned, among them the good Dr. Allertz who had been Charlotte's physician. After Bonaparte had done all he could for the survivors and the lifeboats were completely full, he took hold of a floating piece of wreckage and set out to swim to shore, a distance of roughly three miles.[32] Those long ago days when he had developed his swimming skills in the thermal pool at Canino now served him well.

The passengers of the *Pollux* considered him a hero. In a strange coincidence, the English naturalist Charles Waterton was on board the ship with his three children, and wrote to his friend George Ord of Bonaparte's bravery. Ord replied to Waterton that he lacked words to express what he felt "in regard to

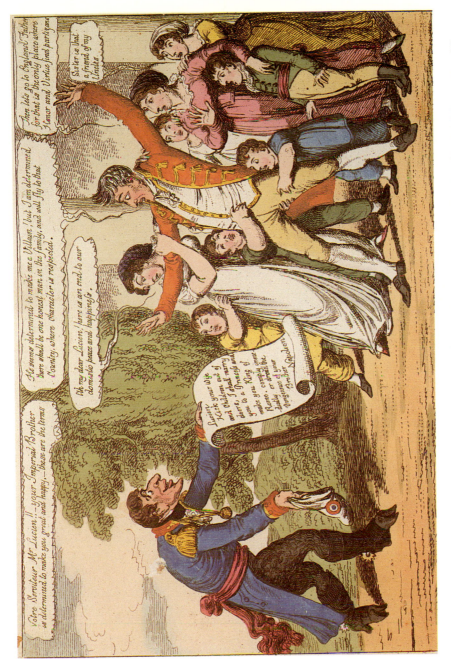

1. *Universal Murderer of Domestic Happiness, or the Fraternal Tyrant,"* 24 December 1810. Published by S. W. Forts, Piccadilly. Courtesy of the Houghton Library, Harvard University.

2. *Lucien Bonaparte* by F. X. Fabre, 1808. Oil. Collection Gabrielli, and Giuseppe Primoli. Courtesy of the Museo Napoleonico, Rome.

3. *Portrait of Alexandrine de Bleschamps Bonaparte* by Carlo Maria Viganoni, 1815. Oil. Inv. No. LM74767, neg. CO3129. Courtesy of the Swiss National Museum, Zurich.

4. *Charles-Lucien Bonaparte* by Charles de Châtillon. Miniature. Courtesy of the Museo Napoleonico, Rome.

5. *Charles-Lucien Bonaparte with Zenaide at the Harp* by Charles de Châtillon. Pencil drawing. Courtesy of the Museo Napoleonico, Rome.

6. *Point Breeze on the Delaware* by Thomas Birch, 1818. Oil. Private collection.

7. *The Sisters Zenaide and Charlotte Bonaparte,* 1820. Oil. The J. Paul Getty Museum, Los Angeles. Zenaide holds a letter from her father, Joseph, in her left hand with "Philadelphie" visible in the right corner.

Wild Turkey. Male and Female.

Meleagris Gallopavo.

9. 1. *Swallow tailed Flycatcher, Muscicapa forficata* 2. *Arkansaw Flycatcher, Muscicapa verticalis* 3. *Say's Flycatcher, Muscicapa saya* [known today as Say's Phoebe, *Sayornis saya*] 4. *Female Golden crested Wren, Regulus cristata* by Titian R. Peale, 1825. From Bonaparte, *American Ornithology; or the Birds of North America not given by Wilson*, plate II, vol.1. Photo credit Lisa: Tyson Ennis.

Facing 8. *Wild Turkey, Meleagris Gallopavo, male and female* by Titian R. Peale, 1825. From Bonaparte, *American Ornithology; or the Birds of North America not given by Wilson*, plate IX, vol.1, 1825. Photo credit: Lisa Tyson Ennis.

10. *Atrium of the Villa Paolina* by J. S. van den Abeele, 1836. Watercolor. Courtesy of the Museo Napoleonico, Rome.

12. *1. Hyla viridis 2. Rana esculenta 3. Rana temporaria* by Petrus Quattrocchi. 1837.
From Charles-Lucien Bonaparte, *Iconografia della fauna italica per le quattro classi
degli animali vertebrati*, vol. 2, *amfibi*, unpaged. Author's collection. Photo credit: Lisa
Tyson Ennis.

13. *Acridotheres roseus 1. Adult 2. First year juvenile 3. Second year juvenile* by Petrus
Quattrocchi. From Bonaparte, *Iconografia della fauna italica per le quattro classi degli
animali vertebrati*, vol. 1, *mammiferi e uccelli*, unpaged. Author's collection. Photo
credit: Lisa Tyson Ennis.

14. *1. Serranus hepatus 2. Anthias sacer 3. Anthias buphthalmus* by Carolus Ruspi, 1832. From Bonaparte, *Iconografia della fauna italica per le quattro classi degli animali vertebrati*, vol. 3, *pesci*, unpaged. Author's collection. Photo credit: Lisa Tyson Ennis.

15. 1. *Aulopus filamentosus* 2. *Chlorophthalmus agassizi* 3. *Sternoptyx mediterranea* by Petrus Quattrocchi, 1839. From Bonaparte, *Icongrafia della fauna italica per le quattro classi degli animali vertebrati*, vol. 3, *pesci*, unpaged. Author's collection. Photo credit: Lisa Tyson Ennis.

16. *Bonaparte's Gull* by John James Audubon. From Audubon, *Birds of America*, Academy of Natural Sciences of Philadelphia. The academy's copy of the *Birds of America* was subscribed for directly from Audubon. No other natural history museum in America can make that claim.

the noble conduct of Charles Bonaparte." "There is just cause to believe that you owe your preservation to his timely exertions; had he not been on board of the Mongibello, it is probable that, in the confusion arising from the collision, the separation of the vessels would have been inevitable." In the same letter, Ord quoted to Waterton parts of the letter he had written to Bonaparte commending his actions. "Your illustrious house will surely lose nothing of its glory in you, *monsieur le prince*, who combine the clear mind of a savant with the amiable virtues of a benefactor of humanity [*Votre maison illustre ne perdra sûrement rien de sa gloire en vous, monsieur le prince, qui savez allier l'esprit éclaire du savant avec les vertus aimables du bienfacteur de l'humanité*]." He told Waterton he had once taken offense at something the prince had criticized him for and had written him a letter "chiding him for his discourteous" behavior, a rebuke that had ended their correspondence. But now, "my heart reproaches me for sentiments which sprang from my ignorance of his amiable character."[33] Ord may have been acerbic at times, but as Bonaparte once observed, he was "with all his faults probably an honest man."[34]

After much confusion, red tape, and angry words with the port authorities who were "rude, difficult, and unsympathetic," Bonaparte boarded another ship and returned with "doubled pleasure" to Rome and the embrace of his anxious wife and children.[35] There were now, again, eight: Bathilde-Elise-Léonie had been born on 25 November 1840. Among the letters awaiting him was one from Geoffroy Saint-Hilaire, who was in a rush but had to send a few lines praising his "philanthropic and courageous conduct" in the accident at sea. "You have saved and contributed to saving many people," he said.[36]

There was also a letter from John Gould, recently arrived back in England after nearly two years in the wilds of Australia and a circuit of the globe. Gould wrote that his journey was highly prosperous and the time spent away from his native shore one of the happiest of his life. Although exposed to every type of climate and living roughly in the woods for months at a time, he never suffered in the least, and "Mrs. Gould greatly benefited by the excursions," for all of which he is "duly grateful to a divine providence." He believes the results of his journey will be of great advantage to science, for he has returned "loaded with novelties in every department of Zoology." The first part of his book on the birds of Australia has been published, and he has already forwarded a copy to Bonaparte: "If you can procure me any supporters for this, the finest and most perfect work I have yet attempted, you will be doing me a real kindness." He asks Bonaparte to give him advice on certain birds, to give a notice of the work to any of the Italian journals he subscribes to, and to show it to his "excellent friend Mr. Lear."[37]

Bonaparte would not remain in Rome long enough to attend to any of

Gould's requests, however. After an absence of fourteen years, Zenaide was eager to see her father. With only a few days at home to catch his breath, Charles hired a spacious carriage and nine horses to convey his large family to the harbor at Civitavecchia, where they boarded the chartered *Maria Cristina*. After an uneventful journey of twenty-eight hours, they docked in Genoa, and Zenaide had a joyous reunion with her "dear Papa." Luciano, of course, had much to tell his siblings about his trip to England.

Because it was necessary to thank Charles Albert of Piedmont formally for his generosity in allowing Joseph to enter his domain, Bonaparte set out at once for Turin. As was typical of the conflicting elements in his character, his republican sentiments did not prevent him from enjoying himself immensely at court. He visited the king's magnificent park, hunting grounds, and other properties and accepted a handsome medal from Charles Albert at his departure. But much to his surprise and annoyance, when he arrived back in Genoa his father-in-law upbraided him for his long absence. Word had arrived from Florence granting Joseph his passport, and he was anxious to be off. Charles Albert offered his handsome private steamboat for the journey to Leghorn, from which Joseph and his retinue traveled by land to Florence, to be reunited with the wife he had not seen since the disastrous year of 1815.[38]

Because it was August and the weather was lovely, Zenaide and the children wanted to stay on in Genoa and swim in the sea. So Bonaparte spent a month with his family enjoying the beautiful Riviera, while at the same time studying the fish and bird life and gathering information for the papers he would read at future scientific congresses. They traveled home in fine weather, by a route of which their contemporary Charles Dickens had said, "nothing in Italy, more beautiful to me, than the coast road between Genoa and Spezzia."[39] At Lucca, Bonaparte left Zenaide and the children briefly to take the baths— probably at Montecatini, for he also conferred at the same time with Duke Leopold about the congresses. This meeting had an unfortunate side effect, however, for it resulted in a game of faro at which he lost heavily. It was the first time Bonaparte had gambled to such an extent, but it would not be the last. His assets had once been so meager that he could not have indulged in such a dangerous pastime, but the inheritance from Lucien had altered the picture. In the small hours of the morning, he rejoined Zenaide, and they proceeded to Florence.[40] No sooner was his family ensconced with Zenaide's reunited parents than Bonaparte was off again, this time to a scientific congress in Lyon, France. He had hoped that Agassiz also would attend this meeting (September 1841) in order to discuss the upcoming congress at Florence, but to his disappointment Agassiz was not able to leave Neuchâtel.

In Lyon Bonaparte found that the political currents in France were flow-ing in the opposite direction from those of Italy. Science and "all the rest" were centered in one place, Paris, and a strong movement of decentralization was afoot. The scientific congress at Lyon was in the hands of this majority decentralization party, sanctioned by the king but not endorsed by the masses. The members of this party saw Bonaparte as a republican (a radical), so he was not welcomed with the enthusiasm he automatically expected in France because of his legendary uncle. In fact, his request to attend the congress had been refused, by none other than François Guizot, Louis-Philippe's recently appointed minister of foreign affairs, but the letter informing him of this had not reached him, either in Rome or in Florence. In spite of Monsieur Guizot, Bonaparte was elected general president of the congress—a short-lived triumph because the legitimist directors (directors of the party sanctioned by the king) declared they would close the conference at once if Bonaparte's election were confirmed. "On the advice of his friends," he withdrew his name.[41]

The next day a similar situation came up: he was chosen to head the natural history section and again had to resign his seat to a Frenchman. Nevertheless, with the tremendous enthusiasm for promoting his goals that rarely deserted him, at the meeting's close he hosted a large dinner party for the French naturalists and invited them all to the congress in Florence. In a toast, he said he considered himself French *and* Italian, since he had been born by the Seine and had grown up in Italy. Because of this, he was happy whenever he could serve as a "bond of love and esteem" between the "two brother nations."[42]

This bond was reenforced on 10 September when several hundred members of the congress, festively dressed, boarded a steamboat for a short trip down the Rhône to the city of Vienne. There they disembarked to the rousing sounds of a welcoming band. Later, at a sumptuous banquet, a group aroused by Bonaparte's strong resemblance to his famous uncle clamored for him to make a speech. With his glass held high, he responded that "the Great Emperor belongs not to an island, not to a family, but to France!" Warming to his subject, he would have continued at some length, but military music drowned out his voice. The legitimists were still in charge of the congress. However, when the clergyman who had been named president of the natural history section rose to thank the members for his election, a great shout smothered his words: "Vive Napoléon, Vive l'empereur, Vive le prince Bonaparte, Vive le neveu de l'empereur!"[43] When at last he departed Vienne, the townspeople embraced him and entreated him to stay on. He wrote in his memoirs, with the honesty that was such an integral part of his character, that this tremendous outpouring of feeling was all in memory of his father and his uncle and had nothing to do with science or with him personally.[44] From Vienne, he descended the Rhône, stopping at Avignon, Arles, and finally Marseilles, where he boarded a French boat for Florence, accompanied by several other scientists also planning to attend the Italian meeting, including Count Saluzzo from Turin.

The third Congresso Scientifico Italiano was inaugurated with a mass in the magnificent church of Santa Croce, where Ghiberti, Michelangelo, Machiavelli, and Galileo were buried, and of which several chapels had been painted by Giotto. Santa Croce also housed Canova's monument to the great Italian poet Count Vittorio Alfieri (1749–1803), and that fact also may have played a part in the choice of site. Alfieri, who wrote plays centered on the struggle against tyranny and odes on American independence, had helped revive the national spirit of Italy, and he is thus considered a forerunner of the Risorgimento. Bonaparte may have felt a special affinity to Alfieri, who died in 1803, the year Charles was born. Perhaps he saw himself as carrying on the battle, albeit in a different field.

Amid the splendid monuments of art and science for which Florence is world-famous, the *reunione* began on 15 September and continued for two weeks. The president, Marchese Cosimo Ridolfi, opened the ceremonies with a ringing speech. "Your Royal Highness [Leopold II], illustrious scientists, honored guests, when I consider this immense hall, where the voices of many great citizens have sounded; this hall, celebrated in the country's memory and sumptuous with great art, I feel such profound respect, one would almost call it religious." Ridolfi's oration took a pragmatic turn when he said that a great benefit awaited Italy from these scientific congresses, since the peninsula, divided into little states with ancient political boundaries, had no national center for science comparable to London or Paris. Education was too elementary, there was crass ignorance and everywhere civilization was being held back. The great institutions lacked scientific teaching. While all loved the country of Italy, they had not made it a common country.[45]

Although these words decidedly echoed Bonaparte's sentiments, the event as a whole disappointed him. The grand duke and the directors of the congress acted toward him in a manner he found very disturbing, and to his outrage neither he nor Count Saluzzo was given a prominent seat in the church. Bonaparte took this as a personal affront to each of them. The count, after all, was a diplomat and a member of the Piedmontese court, while he, the prince of Canino, was the principal organizer of the meetings.[46] (Undeniably, the original idea of inviting men in many disciplines of science from all over Italy, as well as from foreign countries, to meet at regular intervals was indeed his.)

Bonaparte was ambitious and eager to lead, devoted to the popular cause, and ready to sacrifice himself for the people. But everywhere he went his personality was against him; he was so full of contradictions that it was difficult to take him seriously as a political figure. As intelligent as he was, he could so often be thoughtless and superficial; his oratory especially, though at times inspired, was apt to be ruined by inconclusive nonsense. He was capable of noble and elevated sentiments, yet his pompous attitudes were continually subject to criticism. Of a less than prepossessing figure, he nonetheless drew people's attention with his theatrical gestures and copious loquacity. Though he irritated many, it could not be denied that he was imbued with a profound humanity and concern for his fellow man; attributes for the most part overlooked by his contemporaries. His credo, taken from the published *Atti* (Acts) of the congresses, attests to this: "I have always been in favor of the oppressed and prayed to heaven that my strength and my moral power would be equal to my good wishes. Holding sacred the principle of equality among men, I approve of all those who preserve this and disapprove of all those who turn away from it. I am sure of the rapid and progressive development of the human species and I rejoice at the anticipation of what will be in a few years. I look forward to the regeneration of enlightenment and to the diffusion of education among all classes of society."[47]

Bonaparte was careful at this time not to succumb, in Italy at least, to the dangerous fascination of the Napoleonic myth and the temptation to exploit the famous name of his uncle, since the moderates suspected there were Bonapartist intrigues afoot even at the very first scientific congress. He wanted to disassociate himself from partisanship. It was rumored that he was a member of Guiseppe Mazzini's Giovane Italia (Young Italy), an underground organization promoting Italian nationalism, but this has never been proved, and Bonaparte himself denied it. He had friends who belonged, however—Enrico Mayer of Leghorn, for example, whom Bonaparte helped to free from the dungeons of Castel St. Angelo in Rome.[48]

The Catholic Church was especially suspicious of the congresses, since it was totally opposed to the idea of Italian nationalism, having no desire to give up the temporal power of its extensive states in order to be incorporated into a unified kingdom. The choice of Santa Croce, with its monuments to great Italians in the arts and sciences, as the site of the Florentine congress was viewed by the church as the "deception [*mistificazione*]" of mixing the sacred with the profane. To add insult to injury, the scientists called the church "the Pantheon" (a pagan term).[49] It followed that the Papal States would be strongly against its subjects' participation in these meetings. Two professors from the University of Bologna (located within the Papal States) arrived at Florence planning to attend the congress and tried to divert the police by saying that they only came because one wanted to verify several manuscript letters of Galileo, while the other wished to examine some exotic plants. But they were shortly recalled to Bologna, with the threat of losing their teaching posts if they did not comply.[50]

At the gathering were a few political refugees who, being particularly outspoken, alarmed the Austrian government. Although Florence was not part of Austrian territory, the meeting for the following year was to be held in Padua, which was. Strict surveillance was therefore placed on the men who were expected to attend the Padua congress, and the Austrian police reserved the right to admit or exclude delegates, and even to prevent future meetings from taking place if these suspected troublemakers dared too much.[51] The prince of Canino was at the top of their list.

More important to Bonaparte than any of his political enthusiasms, however, was his intense and continuing interest in natural science. At the congress, he reported on a certain duck (*Querquedula agustirostris*), a teal with an elegant "*ciuffetto* [little tuft]" not noticed by Temminck, that had been discovered on the Caspian Sea by one person, killed in Sardinia by another, then found by a French expedition in Algeria. Bonaparte also reported that, from observations he had made on Lake Trasimeno near Perugia, a certain duck described as a new species was none other than a cross between two other species already known. He read a paper on two new birds of Europe: a Crested Coot he called *Fulica cristata*, which he noted was figured in the tapestries of China and therefore could be assumed to exist there; and a Slavonian grebe he named *Podiceps longirostris*. He also described several fish, comparing characteristics of the families *Percides* and *Scombrides*. Of a certain ray (*Dasybates fullonica*), he said that, native to the Mediterranean, the creature had heretofore been entirely omitted from the ichthyological systems and that in this paper he was giving it its rightful place. In another paper, he compared the brains of lampreys with those of rays, and by noting the considerable differences confirmed the views on ichthyological classification of a certain professor.[52]

As early as 1800 a few ornithologists believed that comparative anatomy was the key to a natural classification based on empirically discovered relations. But as a modern historian has written, "although the use of comparative anatomy was suggestive and in its more general conclusions in classification widely accepted, it did not completely dominate avian systematics until after mid-century."[53] Bonaparte was on the cutting edge of his science in this regard, for he used comparative anatomy in his classification of birds from the very start.

At one of the zoology sessions, he read a letter sent to him from Isadore Geoffroy Saint-Hilaire in which Geoffroy spoke of his strong interest, and that of his father Etienne as well, in the scientific congresses of Italy. Since he was unable to send a work detailing his principles of zoological philosophy, he was including an outline of them in this letter to the prince of Canino. He began by dividing the different sciences into four groups: mathematics, physics, natural and biological science, and social science. The "light and truth" of these disciplines was subsumed by one of a superior order, philosophy. Geoffroy compared mathematical with biological science and stated that before long this combination would open an important epoch of progress. One of the corollaries of this mode of thinking was the classification of animals in parallel series, rather than in a single, continuous series.[54] That is, species branched out and developed along separate lines.

Toward the end of the conference, Bonaparte read a long paper on the state of zoology in Europe in regard to the vertebrates. He said he had been able to put together a number of observations (consistent with Geoffroy's ideas) from books, journals, and correspondence with zoologists in different parts of the world, as well as from various museum visits and journeys since the previous October, including his recent attendance at the congress in Lyon. He noted that in England ornithology was flourishing more than ever, because of the work of Gould, MacGillivray, Yarrell, Jardine, and Selby. He mentioned Darwin's *Zoology of the Voyage of the Beagle*, for which Gould had illustrated and described the new species of birds, Owen had described the fossil mammalia and Waterhouse "the existing ones." In an extraordinarily comprehensive survey for one who was so involved with his own studies, Bonaparte reported on the work of scientists in Sweden, Denmark, Russia, Germany, Switzerland, Holland, Belgium, France, Spain, Portugal, and many different cities of Italy. In particular he cited Prince Maximilian of Weid for naming two new North American bird species; Johann Natterer of Vienna, recently returned from sixteen years in Brazil, where he collected more than a thousand bird species; and Agassiz of Neuchâtel, "who in the morning of his life, launched into such reputation, that the Academies of Rome, of Paris, of London, of Petersburg, of America, strove to enroll him among their members."[55]

Bonaparte spoke of his stay in Zurich, "where the Saxon, Oken, has his peaceful abode, and continues to edit the *Isis*, perhaps the most scientific journal of natural history, not in Germany merely, but in the whole world." He also mentioned Temminck, but with some harsh criticism for his old mentor when he recounted the disagreements he had had with him over the study of bats. Temminck had apparently taken exception to some of Bonaparte's remarks in his paper on Cuvier. Bonaparte stated with candor that "to correct the errors of eminent writers is the most effectual means to advance science, while the great veneration which is entertained for Temminck, and his *ex cathedra* tone, may in some cases prove fatal to truth."[56] He proposed to read on another occasion a catalogue he had been compiling for some years of all the genera of mammals. Then, shifting to another plane entirely, the naturalist turned to religion and told his assembled colleagues with the deepest sincerity: "Man, the older he grows, by the wisdom which he acquires, approaches always more and more to God."[57]

The significance of all this work Bonaparte was doing has been summed up by the eminent ornithologist Erwin Stresemann (1889–1972). "Bonaparte, as an evolutionist, revised the work of the pre-Darwin period and set up the dividing lines between orders and families with delicate discretion in systematics; by separating them into 'parallel rows' according to the natural data, he took into account a greater number of factors than his predecessors had done."[58]

9

THE NETWORK

"La cooperazione essendo secondo me l'anima del mondo!"

Bonaparte, "Cenni Autobiografici"

WHEN THE CONGRESS in Florence was over on 1 October 1841, Bonaparte made plans to return to Rome with Zenaide and the children. It was always difficult to organize such a large household, but finally they were ready to depart. But at the last minute, as he was helping Zenaide into the carriage, Joseph, no longer able to contain his feelings, asked his son-in-law to leave her and the children with him for the winter because he was old and sick and needed them. For some reason, he was especially anxious that Zenaide, three months pregnant, should deliver her child in his house. If by spring he was still alive and his health permitted, he would bring them all back to Rome. The worldly Joseph, who had seen so little of his family for so many years, was totally dependent on them now that his life was ending.

Of course there was no denying the old man's request. Bonaparte conceded and set out alone for Rome, where he had pressing affairs to settle. He planned to be away for only eight days before rejoining his family in Florence, but the time stretched out to as many weeks. In the city he had commitments to a number of friends that had to be met, and he needed to visit his mother at Canino, in order to make plans for her future. He also had to finish the last article for the *Fauna italica*, on raylike creatures called *Torpedine*, and see the book's introduction and preface through the press. The exquisite drawings for the *Torpedine* had already been completed by Carlo Ruspi and would be hand-colored after the plates were lithographed. At last, by the beginning of 1842, *Fauna italica*, an enormous project, would be finished.[1]

In a letter to Richard Owen he used the essay on the *Torpedine* as a possible entrée to the Royal Society. He asked Owen to present his paper to the organization; "perhaps this favourite subject of theirs may induce them to admit me as a candidate for the first available place among their foreign members." He adds that, as "the happy founder of Italian Sci[entific] meetings, my zele [sic] in the cause of Science & my connection with English *savants* may help me in this noble ambition of mine. I rely on your friendship."[2] Unfortunately, friendship was not enough in this instance; Owen did not fulfill Bonaparte's request.

Agassiz wrote in December that he was flattered by the honor Bonaparte had paid him in his remarks at the congress in Florence: "It is for me a new mark of your benevolent friendship and I find traces of that on nearly every page of your Fauna. Don't the zoologists understand, as you show them, that to advance the science [of ornithology], we must not have dry diagnoses, but comparative descriptions between miscellaneous (*mêlées*) discussions of principles. This is also the only way to read it [the *Fauna italica*]."[3] The following month Agassiz came to Rome with his son to visit Bonaparte; on his return to

Neuchâtel he wrote that in order to understand the *Fauna* he had been studying Italian and was spending an hour daily in reading and contemplating Bonaparte's "learned researches." "I understand thus better every day how to appreciate the luminous ideas which distinguish your comparisons, the wisdom of your distinctions, and the clarity of your descriptions, which are all little masterpieces, all expressed in a harmonious diction. I must tell you to my shame, that until the present, ignorant of your language, I was incapable of appreciating the value of your work."[4]

That fall Bonaparte had to resolve a serious financial issue with his mother: would she stay in Canino and pay its expenses? From Florence, the perceptive Zenaide wrote him a letter of caution.

I hope you will have seen your mother if she has come to Rome, or if you have gone to Canino, that you have listened well. In one hour of good amicable conversation you can advance your affairs with her better than with any number of letters or consultations with lawyers. Don't forget that one day you and I will find ourselves in the same situation [*en relation d'affaires*] with our children and we would love to find them well disposed toward us and confident as your mother of the desire to reach an agreement with her oldest son. I am persuaded, besides, that she has good intentions toward us and feels that although richer than your brothers, you are also poorer than they, because you have a wife, a number of children, and a position to sustain.[5]

As Zenaide implies, Alexandrine was not an easy person to deal with, and her relations with her eldest son were invariably emotional. As it turned out, the meeting between them resolved nothing.

While in Rome Bonaparte learned that John Gould's talented artist/wife Elizabeth had died in London. Bonaparte sent him a letter of condolence, of which Gould said, in his reply, that it breathed sentiments of the greatest tenderness and would be preserved for the perusal of his children. He mentioned the beautiful cameo brooch Bonaparte had earlier sent to Elizabeth Gould by way of Duke Charles Torlonia. Had his wife lived to receive it, she would have valued it most highly, "not only for its extreme beauty, but also for the sake of its highly talented donor. I did not like to return it to your highness as I have a particular desire to preserve every thing that is indicative of respect for my late wife."[6] In an earlier letter, to Gould's secretary, Edward Prince, Bonaparte had said of his gift—a cameo of Napoleon—that it was "a remarkably fine one, worthy of Mrs. Gould on any account." It had been in his family for many years and was selected because of a "strong likeness," which he hoped she would perceive as he did.[7]

Gould also thanked him for obtaining a subscription to his *Birds of*

Australia from "His Majesty the King of Sardinia [Charles Albert]," and for getting him elected to the Royal Academy of Turin. He had sent the academy fifty-two species of Australian birds as a donation, and now reminded Bonaparte of his offer to obtain a subscription from the library of the pope that he thought might lead to other subscriptions, both in Europe and in Australia.[8]

Bonaparte was back in Florence in time for the birth of his ninth child, Albertine-Marie-Thérèse, in early March. She was baptized by the archbishop of Florence, and her godparents were none other than King Charles Albert and his wife, the queen. Bonaparte observed in his memoirs that such a move by "the firstborn branch of the Bonaparte family" was obviously a compliment to the king and undoubtedly would redound to his descendants.[9]

Throughout March he worked on his introduction to the third section of the *Fauna*, the section dealing with fish. He told Agassiz he had worked many "white nights" over it and was exhausted, but mentioned too the pleasure he took in thinking of the voyage to America that he and Agassiz had agreed to make together: "What diversion [*délassement*]! and at the same time what useful work!!"[10] The United States had been the scene of Bonaparte's greatest successes; there he had been everywhere sought after and introduced as a brilliant and fascinating man. The most prominent scientists of Philadelphia and New York had been among his friends and promoters, and he had easily gained membership in the learned societies to which they belonged. By stepping into the role of classifier for a large collection of undescribed birds from the American West and publishing them in an elegant format, he had established himself instantly as an authority on avian fauna, though only in his early twenties. On the other hand, here in Florence, almost a second home to him because of the time he and Zenaide had spent there with her mother, he had not even been elected president of the zoology section at the congress he and the grand duke of Tuscany had arranged, let alone president of the congress itself. No wonder he thought of America with nostalgia. And just as significant to Bonaparte as his personal triumph, the United States enjoyed the freedom and independence so lacking in Italy and in which he so earnestly and passionately believed. It was a place, he told Agassiz, where "man could develop without shackles [*sans entraves*]."[11] (No doubt Bonaparte was referring to the constraints imposed by the papacy and the various Italian monarchies and not recalling the slavery issue in the New World.) In a letter to Edward Everett he called America "Freedonia."[12]

On the first of April, accompanied by his son Luciano and daughter Julia, Bonaparte went to Canino to see his mother, who had been impatiently awaiting them for some time. Much to his surprise and delight, the townspeople had prepared an elaborate welcome for their illustrious prince: an arch of laurel, a lively band with players dressed in full regalia, and a small cannon fired at regular intervals. The enthusiastic folk insisted on unhitching the carriage horses and pulling the vehicle in which Luciano and Julia were seated, while Bonaparte rode on horseback beside them. In this way, they proceeded from the town itself to the villa of Musignano, three miles beyond.[13] Situated amid cultivated fields and high above a valley threaded with a meandering stream, the large, ancient house was fronted by a meadow planted with orange, mimosa, and eucalyptus trees. A former convent, it was built around an interior brick courtyard, in the center of which stood a beautiful well. All was serenity and quiet in this lovely, isolated spot. Bonaparte and his children spent six weeks there, enjoying the beauty of gentle hills, acres and acres of olive trees, and fields stretching off to the distant sea.

Bonaparte left the children with his mother and returned to Rome by himself, where he lived at his usual dizzying pace and from which he soon departed for a whirlwind journey to the north. He left Rome on Sunday, arrived in Genoa on Tuesday, reached Florence by early Wednesday, and returned to Genoa the same evening. Stopping in Florence to pick up his eldest son, Joseph, and three saddle horses, he then embarked by boat for Civitavecchia. In a sad accident, the horses perished while they were being unloaded from the ship, but he was able to hire others at the port and in three-and-a-half hours he was back at Musignano.[14]

He passed several pleasant days surveying the estate, livestock and crops, and even took time to excavate several Etruscan vases. Archaeology had been his parents' passionate enterprise for many years. Together Alexandrine and Lucien had unearthed a number of magnificent and valuable artifacts, beginning in 1828, after several Etruscan vases had initially been found by poachers in a subterranean grotto.[15] Alexandrine, aware of the current interest in Etruscan art throughout Europe and the British Isles and eager to recoup the couple's fast-disappearing resources, had encouraged her husband to sell many of these pieces. But before doing so, Lucien published in 1829 a beautifully illustrated book on his discoveries (*Muséum étrusque de Lucien Bonaparte, Prince de Canino*). Much later, the English writer D. H. Lawrence painted a dour picture of the Bonapartes' excavations, claiming that basketfuls of rough, black, ancient Etruscan shards were smashed as they were dug up, in order not to cheapen the market, and that an overseer with a gun on his knees watched over the workmen to see that nothing was taken away. Even so, according to Lawrence, the Bonapartes took more than two thousand Etruscan objects out of tombs occupying a few acres of ground.[16]

Lucien, often in financial difficulties because of his all-absorbing passion

for fine art, had most likely arranged Charles's marriage in 1822 in order to
secure Zenaide's substantial dowry, since it was in that year that his banker,
Torlonia, threatened to appropriate the property of Canino to retrieve his loans.
In 1826, when Charles was in America and writing his father pleading letters
about the privations he and Zenaide were enduring for want of interest on the
dowry, Lucien was facing bankruptcy and had to apply to Cardinal Fesch and
Joseph for help. Apparently having spent the dowry, Lucien then mortgaged
Canino with Cardinal Fesch holding the mortgage deed. The discovery of precious Etruscan artifacts buried on their own property was a windfall that
enabled Lucien and Alexandrine to retain Canino by paying the interest on the
loan, and eventually to pass it on to their eldest son. Alexandrine as a widow
continued to sell various pieces. Charles would write her several years later that
his brother-in-law, Valentini, had sent him "the famous Etruscan chariot [prob-
ably a bronze statuette] of which all the world speaks," and that he hoped to sell
it at a good price.[17] Not surprisingly, in later years the local people of Canino
would bitterly resent what they considered the pillage of their collective inheritance.[18]

On the day in early June that Bonaparte returned to Florence with Joseph,
Lucien, and Julie, the new baby, who had been asthmatic from the start, died
suddenly in a violent fit of coughing. She was buried with her Aunt Charlotte
in a chapel of Santa Croce. The death was much more devastating for Zenaide
than for Charles: he scarcely knew the child, as he had been away traveling
throughout most of her short life.[19]

At that time he again wrote Agassiz about the proposed trip to America,
reiterating that the main reason he wants to go is to show his eldest son, Joseph,
the country where he was born. But the prospect of the voyage also pleases him
immensely because he would have the happiness of having Agassiz as a companion, and therefore he is sure it will make an "epoch in science."[20] He also
notified the secretary of the American Philosophical Society of the proposed
journey: "Our plans are vast, & we are come to find sympathy in your noble
land."[21]

In his letter to Agassiz he speaks of his work in classifying fish and says he
believes that the comparison of scales nearly always reveals the fishes' true and
natural relations to each other. He notes that he has transferred species from
one class to another on the basis of these affinities and adds: "in the name of
heaven let me know without delay what other transpositions to make in the
other classes, because you know that I am occupied incessantly in perfecting my
system." Also, he wants to know why Agassiz has not written an "Ichthyology
following Buffon," as he offered to do, since he, Bonaparte, had taken the liberty to "conjure up" this book idea publicly at the congress in his review of the

progress of zoology. He is sending the last four *livraisons* of his Italian fauna, which Agassiz can now have bound into three volumes. In future, he counts on sending everything that comes from his pen, in order to receive everything that comes from Agassiz's. He thinks that they should make each other's books known, that is, not the little brochures without importance, but the large, expensive works that are of commercial value. If Agassiz doesn't have his *American Ornithology*, he will gladly send him a copy.[22]

In an entirely different tone, Bonaparte speaks candidly to Agassiz about a circumstance that had disturbed him. It seems that someone had told Bonaparte that Agassiz was not pleased with his works and Agassiz had denied the rumor. Bonaparte answers that "those persons who said my works did not please you are not at all fools, they are your best friends at the Institute of Paris and they have even made this argument in the discussion of our candidacies, where my friends, led by my dear Isadore, gave you their votes." Bonaparte is without rancor, though he clearly suspects Agassiz of duplicity, for he adds, "no one better than you could organize an animal kingdom and I will always be proud to enroll myself under your banner." Agassiz answered him at once: he did not know who could have been "so stupid" as to say that he did not "show in public the highest opinion" of Bonaparte's works. However, he does not often have occasion to cite Bonaparte's publications because their researches are not in the same fields.[23] One cannot help wondering whether the professional alliance of Bonaparte and Agassiz would have endured had Bonaparte lived to see the publication of Darwin's *Origin of Species* in 1859.

Agassiz to the end of his life opposed the theory of evolution and maintained that each species of plant and animal was a distinct thought of God. He failed to recognize the importance of distribution and segregation in the development of new specific forms, a concept Bonaparte was intensely interested in and was exploring through his study of the geographical distribution of birds. Bonaparte, at the recommendation of Isadore Geoffroy Saint-Hilaire, arranged the families of birds within their orders, and the genera within their families, not in continuous lines but in parallel columns, and thus "foreshadowed the theory of evolution."[24]

Agassiz sent Bonaparte a proof of his own paper on birds, which the latter corrected and returned in early July. He added a postscript: if Agassiz could come to Florence in the first days of September, he would take him to Sinigallia to see the magnificent collection of fossils belonging to Prince Ricci. From there they could embark for Venice and go on to Padua for the congress.[25]

Because Agassiz was spending the entire summer high in the Swiss mountains studying the stratification of fields of snow on the Glacier of the Aar, he did not answer until September. "I thank you most sincerely for the pains you have so kindly taken with my proof, and for pointing out the faults and omissions you have noticed in my roster of birds. I made the corrections at once, and have taken the liberty of mentioning on the cover of this number the share you have consented to take in my Nomenclator." (He is referring to *nomenclator zoologicus*, a catalog of all the names applied to the genera of animals since the beginning of scientific nomenclature, about 1758.) He tells Bonaparte of the exciting discoveries he has made about the glacier and asks him to announce his findings in the geological section at Padua. "I wish I could accept your kind invitation," he adds, "but until I have gone to the bottom of the glacier question and completed my 'Fossil Fishes' [*Recherches sur les poissons fossiles*, 1833–44], I do not venture to move. It is no light task to finish all this before our long journey [to America], to which I look forward, as it draws nearer, with a constantly increasing interest. It would have been a great pleasure for me to visit the collections of northern Italy in your company."[26]

Agassiz says that on his return to Neuchâtel he will write an article on Bonaparte's "*Fauna italique*" for the *Bibliothèque universelle*, which he thinks is the most widely distributed of the scientific and literary journals and the one in which one can hold forth more than in a zoological journal. He says it is now snowing (though it is only the first of September) and is so cold in his tent that he can barely hold his pen. But his greatest privation is the lack of fruit or vegetables; every day, morning and night, for two months, it is mutton, "*l'éternel mouton.*" At this point Bonaparte and Agassiz seem to represent the two extreme types of naturalists: Agassiz pursuing his studies in the harshness of the field and Bonaparte almost entirely in the comfort of his study. Bonaparte's type was more typical of the emerging state of scientific inquiry in the mid-nineteenth century, since so much had already been discovered in the field and the need to arrange and classify these ever-expanding collections was paramount. Of course Agassiz's research into ice floes and the remains of ancient seas could only be done in the field.

At a meeting of the British Association for the Advancement of Science in that year of 1842, a committee issued a report on the rules by which a "uniform and permanent basis" for zoological nomenclature could be established. The "vagueness and uncertainty" by which all fauna were currently named was said to be a "great detriment" to the state of zoological science. The committee acknowledged that their colleagues often differed in their opinions as to the natural affinities of animals, which would of course affect their ideas on classification, but it was necessary to allow systematists perfect freedom in this regard, in order to arrive eventually at a "true system of nature." But before the theoretical debates concerning this system could be settled, nomenclature must be standardized. The "international character of the emerging zoological disciplines made it a practical necessity."[27] Bonaparte must have rejoiced at the political metaphor used by the committee in their report:

The world of science is no longer a monarchy, obedient to the ordinances, however just, of an Aristotle or a Linnaeus. She has now assumed the form of a republic, and although this revolution may have increased the vigour and zeal of her followers, yet it has destroyed much of her former order and regularity of government. The latter can only be restored by framing such laws as shall be based in reason and sanctioned by the approval of men of science.[28]

The formal code was compiled by a committee that included Charles Darwin, Professor John Henslow, Dr. John Richardson, and Bonaparte's friend and correspondent Hugh Strickland. It was later known as the Stricklandian Code because Strickland had drawn up and promoted it.[29] Also published in this British Association meeting report of 1842 was Owen's naming of enormous extinct reptiles as "Dinosauria" (from the Greek for "terrible lizards"), the first time this term was used. Owen intended the name as a powerful argument against the idea of evolutionary progressivism gaining ground in the 1840s: because these early, gigantic creatures were more complex than present-day lizards, the latter could not have "evolved" from them.[30] Bonaparte most likely would have disagreed with his friend.

Bonaparte's ambitious plan to prepare a general synopsis of all the known birds of the world was becoming more and more a necessity for the science of ornithology. Prince Maximilian counseled him to issue this synopsis in unnumbered pages so that new discoveries could always be inserted. Bonaparte had already seen this method used in Say's *American Entomology* and had used it himself in *Fauna italica*. "The work [a general synopsis] would not be easy, I agree," Maximilian said, "because the discoveries are without number and the synonyms infinitely confused [*embrouillés*]. For myself, I am no longer able to keep up with the new ornithology, since it has begun to take nearly every species for a genus. Ornithology disgusts me at present by the innumerable numbers of generic names, and if that goes on the cart will soon be overthrown."[31] Several years later Bonaparte himself would be guilty of the same sort of thing in another branch of natural history. "I am proud of the interest you have taken in my Amphibia Europea," he would write to Schlegel, "in spite of the scandalous multiplication of genera."[32]

Maximilian was at all times an interesting correspondent, because, despite his claim that he was not kept au courant with ornithology, he knew everything concerning the latest findings in the various sciences. Three years earlier, in May

1839, he had told Bonaparte that he already possessed "the zoological observations of the voyage on the ship Beagle," which is most likely where Bonaparte got the information he relayed to the congress in Florence. Maximilian also told him about McKenney and Hall's *History of the Indian Tribes of America*, which he wanted to buy in order to compare the plates with Bodmer's work (but "like all the works of the Americans" it was very expensive.) It was also he who told Bonaparte of Titian Peale's leaving on a "great voyage to the South Seas" (the Wilkes Expedition of 1838–42).[33]

Perhaps in anticipation of his trip to America, Bonaparte was delighted to renew his old friendship—if one could call it that—with George Ord, who had written to him so glowingly after the *Pollux* disaster. In early September he wrote Ord that only a few days before he had learned, with a "lamentable certainty" (perhaps from the loss of a ship), that his answer to Ord's "kind letter" had been lost along with the letters of many other people. Because "few things in the world could have been more acceptable to me than the renewal of our scientific and friendly intercourse, I take a safe opportunity to write again, hoping that for a single moment you have not accused me of neglect or carelessness. No, Sir, I shall be indebted to our common friend Waterton, much more than he is to me for procuring me your friendly opening of last year."[34]

Well aware of Ord's aversion to Audubon, Bonaparte cannot resist complaining of his old colleague and erstwhile friend. "You know the trick played to me by Mr. Audubon, who leaves my copy of his big work incomplete, after it cost me so much money, having taken my name out of his list of subscribers. What redress can I have for the first, since for the second I care nothing?" Ord comments skeptically to Waterton: "There is room for conjecture here, but the prince must not have advanced money for the numbers, otherwise the publisher, it would seem, would be glad to complete the copy at the subscription price. In my answer [to him], I take the occasion to remind the kind-hearted prince of the effective part which he performed in bolstering up a vagabond [Audubon], who I had assured him was unworthy of his regard." Ord, in his inimitable manner, continues with Waterton an account of what he had told Bonaparte about Audubon: "Unhappy is he who has anything to do with him. The charlatan however knows how to play his role; and in a country where imposters are honored, he can cajole the world and laugh up his sleeve. For his calumny touching the *Musicapas minuta* of Wilson, I have taken him by the nose (see the Bulletin of the Philosophical Society, No. 13). . . . His Ornithology Biography is the most enormous collection of stupidities and lies that has ever appeared. It is the thousand and one nights of natural history."

Bonaparte's book does not entirely escape Ord's censure either. He mentions that Joseph Bonaparte has sent a copy of his son-in-law's "costly work" (the *Fauna italica*) to the American Philosophical Society. Because Ord does not read Italian, he cannot "judge of its literary merits." However, he finds the illustrations unequal: some of the quadrupeds and birds are "ill done," although the amphibians and fishes are beautiful.

Ord had also written Bonaparte in early September (their letters must have crossed each other on the high seas). "What wonders is steam producing in the world!" he enthuses: it is now possible to write to England and get an answer in the short space of five weeks. A royal mail steamer leaves Liverpool for Boston on the 4th and 19th of every month, so Bonaparte can communicate with America by means of an English agent whenever "dispatch is an object of importance." Ord is now treasurer and librarian of the American Philosophical Society and reports that unfortunately the *Acts* from the meeting at Florence have never been received.[35] A later historian has surmised that the police in each city where the congresses took place deliberately intervened to prevent these reports from circulating; "One must conclude that in all likelihood the American Philosophical Society would today have on its shelves a complete set of the rare and valuable *Atti* of the Congressi degli Scienziati Italiani had they not been intercepted and confiscated as a part of the effort to control the subversive activities of those reunions!"[36]

To Bonaparte's query about the sale of his *Fauna italica* in America, Ord answered that there was little probability that it would sell in "this inauspicious period." The book trade, as well as every other branch of commerce, was in a "deplorable state": "The rage for speculating, fostered by our infamous banking system, has spread desolation and misery every where." Only a few nights before, a well-bound copy of Bonaparte's "Continuation of Wilson" sold at auction for only $4.62 per volume. Ord informs him of the return of "our national Exploring Squadron" after a three-year cruise in the South Seas. "Titian Peale was one of the scientific gentlemen who accompanied it; but he had the misfortune to lose a large part of his most valuable specimens by the shipwreck of the Peacock sloop-of-war, in which he was stationed, at the mouth of the Columbia river."[37] In a later letter, Ord described how Peale's collections were "seized by the government," and only Dr. Pickering, another naturalist on the expedition, had been retained to arrange, describe, and publish the material. "The country is in a mess," he exclaims, "at Philadelphia everything is going to the devil [*toute y s'en va au diable*]."[38]

As the summer progressed, Bonaparte received two unexpected honors that pleased him immensely. One was his election to the Academy of Brussels— he felt there were those who deserved the honor more than he did—and the other was a flattering letter from the general president of the congress to be held in Padua that September, inviting him to speak. After the meeting he planned to take his family back to Rome for good—they had been in Florence with Joseph and Julie for a year—and to devote himself to his children's education and his own studies. His scientific projects included finishing and publishing various zoological-geographical tables to complement the *Fauna italica*, the *Systema vertebratorum*, the *Manual of Ichthyology*, and of course, his great work on the birds of the world. He had also thought of a general fauna of Italy, and perhaps, if heaven permitted ("si ciel mi da vita") a comprehensive "Animal Kingdom."[39]

By this time naturalists from many countries recognized Bonaparte's scientific expertise and consulted with him to ensure that their works were accurate and used cutting edge methods and theories of classification. He confided to his memoirs that it was immensely gratifying to him that "a Gould, a Strickland, and a Gray [George Robert]" had proposed that he collaborate with them in their study of birds; that "a Titzinger" wanted his help with reptiles; and that "an Agassiz" had asked him to look over his major undertaking. His limited time would always be at the disposal of his learned friends, and he would never refuse to cooperate in useful scientific work. "For me, cooperation is the soul [*anima*] of the world," he wrote.[40]

Bonaparte himself benefited from this *anima*, for Maximilian among others was ever ready to help him. Earlier in the year, he had asked Natterer of Vienna to compose a list of South American birds for Bonaparte. Natterer, he said, had a magnificent cabinet and library and a knowledge of all the collections of the day.[41]

For the most part the congress in Padua went well, perhaps because the president had initially cautioned the participants to confine themselves to scientific topics and to bear in mind the danger of expressing political aspirations. The Paduans themselves welcomed the scientists with a warmth that surprised everyone. They opened the famous Café Pedrocchi for them, struck a medal in their honor, arranged a horse race, and staged a Meyerbeer opera (in German, of course) at the theater. Private libraries were put at their disposal, and various literary and scientific works were sent to them from Italian, as well as foreign, cities. The convention ended with a grand reception, attended by the governor, who assured them of the good will of the sovereign.[42] But of the eight or nine hundred participants expected, only about five hundred showed up. Three hundred were scientists, mostly young; the rest were auditors.[43]

For Bonaparte, this meeting was very different from the one in Florence that had left him feeling so unappreciated. Even the Florentines, however, could not have denied his contributions to science at these congresses. It was recognized by the participants that he had proposed a new system of classification for vertebrates, a new nomenclature spanning botany and zoology, and a new non-Latin terminology. He was the first to introduce these ideas into Italy, having acquired them from his trips to England, France, and Germany. The use of a vernacular terminology accorded with his stated aim to lower science to the level of the masses in anticipation of raising the masses to the level of science.[44]

At every opportunity (in disregard of the caution against expressing political views), he tried to express his opinions about liberty, fraternity, and equality. During the course of the meetings, he accused England of having bought its industrial power with blood. He called the blacks his brothers and earnestly hoped that poverty would one day disappear from the face of the earth. For him the congresses represented the first step in the fight for Italian liberty and the chance to put Italy on a par with the other nations of Europe. Although his strategy was not deliberately revolutionary, still, he was aware that Italian scientists meeting together would talk subtly about national unity by inserting the subject in between the description of a fish, or the presentation of a new bird. And the convening of these scientists would set an example that would foreshadow unification. It was not surprising that he was considered a dangerous man by the police and secret agents of the principalities where the congresses were held. The governor of Pisa was recorded as saying: "Not for a moment do I let the prince of Musignano out of my sight [*Non perdo un momento di vista il principe di Musignano*]."[45]

Geoffroy, in Paris, saw only the scientific advantages of the meetings. "The news you give me of the congress at Padua gives me true pleasure," he writes, "since it makes me realize that this beautiful institution perhaps may now be considered as solidly and definitely established." By contrast, he attaches little importance to provincial congresses in France, because all the French scientists are in Paris and communicate their discoveries and opinions at the academy, "our perpetual congress." Some day it will be the same in Italy, he predicts, and no longer will men of merit who are neighbors but separated by artificial barriers called frontiers be unable to exchange their ideas.[46]

Bonaparte and his wife spent the fall and winter of 1842–43 in Rome, where another child, Charles-Albert, was born to them in March. Zenaide's convalescence was short and happy, and the baby, "a prodigy of strength and beauty," took avidly to the breast of the young Roman nurse they hired for him. "Is it necessary to have new proof that the bad and the good things intermingle in this life?" Charles philosophized to his mother-in-law. "Young and old, sickness and death pursue us in all ways ... the wisest one is he who, though weeping and honoring the memory of the departed, seeks to console the living and occupies himself with the happiness of those dearest to him ... after all we have the sweet certitude of the ineffable approbation of the dead who repose with the Father."[47] There was a depth of feeling in Bonaparte not always visible to his friends and colleagues, but often shown to Zenaide's mother, whom he seems to have loved and respected. It is in his letters to her that we have a glimpse into his heart. Though he often disagreed with the Catholic clergy for their repressive tactics, his religious faith was strong and secure.

A week after penning this letter, in the midst of his own joy over the healthy new baby and deep into his studies, Bonaparte received a letter from a less than happy Agassiz, who was entangled in obligations and financial problems arising from his geological and zoological research. Agassiz says that, if his financial position doesn't change, his job (as professor of natural history at the University of Neuchâtel) will become untenable and he will be obliged to seek other means of support: "Meanwhile, costly projects present themselves, which is apt to be the case when one is in difficulties. That of accompanying you to the United States was so tempting, that I am bitterly disappointed to think that its execution has become impossible in my present circumstances." He mentions how little interest the government of France has in anyone situated outside of Paris and the indifference to natural science publications in Russia. His friends have been unable to obtain subscriptions for his work on fossil fishes in either country. "Do you think any position would be open to me in the United States," he asks, "where I might earn enough to enable me to continue the publication of my unhappy books, which never pay their way because they do not meet the wants of the world?"[48] Bonaparte must certainly have been sympathetic to this complaint, since his own *Fauna italica* had had such limited sales, but his financial situation was, of course, very different.

Agassiz says he has profited by Bonaparte's criticisms of his avian and mammalian nomenclature and has joined Bonaparte's synonyms to the part of his work that is about to be published. "If you wish me to make known in detail your remarks on mammals and birds, I will publish a supplement of these classes at the end of the work." But he declines to accept Bonaparte's gift of his *American Ornithology*. "If I could have been able to push forward the publications that I planned and that I could send you in exchange, I would have accepted your proposition with gratitude, but without that you will, I hope, understand my sentiment."[49]

A few months later Bonaparte wrote back to encourage Agassiz in his work, for he thought his friend would definitely produce great things—and he himself might, too, if he did not have nine children. In the same letter Bonaparte says he also must postpone his trip to the United States, though it has already been announced to the world. But postponing it does not mean abandoning it, and perhaps they can go in 1845. He assures Agassiz that, "with me, you will always have the title, not of helper-naturalist, but of master in science, for we are friends of the heart and of the mind [*amis du coeur et de l'esprit*]." He says that perhaps Agassiz's work will bring him some money to cover the cost of the voyage, but if not, "accept the offer that I make to you from the bottom of my heart."[50]

From Strickland, Bonaparte had good news about his own endeavor. Strickland had exhibited a copy of the *Fauna italica* at a meeting in Ireland, where it was much admired and was purchased for the library of Trinity College, Dublin. He is delighted to hear that "the Italian Committee" has adopted almost word for word the same rules for zoological nomenclature as those laid down "by us in England." He hopes this will prove that the rules themselves are "framed according to truth and reason and that the naturalists both of Italy and England are aiming at the same object, namely the true interests of science—and of science alone. And there is every reason to hope that the naturalists of all the other countries in Europe will exhibit the same unanimity!"[51]

This networking among naturalists—promoting uniform rules for nomenclature, exchanging and furthering each other's books, sharing information, and procuring specimens—was for the most part amazingly altruistic and enormously useful in advancing the development of science. As an example of this interaction, John Edward Gray informed Bonaparte in August that a friend of his would be in Florence and Rome for a few days en route to his plantation in Ceylon (Sri Lanka) and would be happy to send him a collection of birds from that part of the world.[52]

There were of course disagreements as well. Audubon wrote that he understood Bonaparte had been after his agent to send the missing plates of *Birds of America*, but they had not been sent because Bonaparte had not paid for them. Payment having now been received, the plates will be shipped. "That I was disappointed with your conduct toward me when in London, is the truth and I acknowledge that I said to some of *your remarkable* friends, then, that I would not deliver you any more n[umber]s or plates of my Work, unless you did pay me the balance then standing due." In order to prove that he feels no enmity toward Bonaparte, he says he is sending him the first number of his new work on quadrupeds of North America. He is publishing this book with his friend the Reverend John Bachman of Charleston, whom Bonaparte had met when Bachman was in Europe some four years before. Audubon informs him that he starts for the Rocky Mountains on 10 March (1843): "I cannot tell how long I may be absent, but hope to return loaded with new knowledge and [an] abundance of drawings from those I shot and not from stuffed museums' moth-eaten remains."[53] He cannot resist this jab at Bonaparte, the cabinet naturalist.

Audubon continues that, "being poor," he has left New York and built a house nine miles north of the city on the Hudson River (he can see William Cooper's house on the opposite side). "Under this humble roof" he draws night and day, writes the histories of quadrupeds, and wouldn't change his life for anyone else's in the world. "I received a few pages of your Work" (the *Fauna*), he says, "but being no scholar, and not understanding a word of its contents, I simply retain it as a memento from one, who some 20 years ago *I did love as a Brother* . . . . To forgive and to forbear is a rule which cannot well be too highly recommended to every one in our poor world, and therefore I have written to you, as of old and to prove to you that I have no bad feelings toward you, and that on the contrary I remain with sincerity your poor old Friend and Servant."[54] This was the last letter Bonaparte would receive from Audubon, who by then was gradually slipping into senility.

That September of 1843 the congress of Italian scientists was held at Lucca, in Tuscany. The poet Giuseppe Giusti, a promoter of the cause of unification, wrote that it was "small but good [*piccino ma bonino*]." There were fewer than five hundred participants, including scientists from other European countries, but there was more frequent and open discourse on the theme of a united Italy than in previous sessions. Because Lucca was a suspected center of revolutionary operations, the police kept a close eye on things, but the congress went off without incident. Bonaparte, ever somewhat defensive, was not pleased with his initial reception and threatened to leave, but when he was elected president of the zoology section, he changed his mind.

The scientific congresses always exacerbated suspicions about the Bonapartes and their involvement with revolutionary causes. In the secret archives of the Vatican is a letter from a clerical spy at the congress of Lucca reporting to his cardinal that, "it is known in Paris and among us" that the brothers Charles and Louis Bonaparte have a plan to procure the escape of their cousin Louis-Napoleon and to land him on the coast of Italy."[55] Louis-Napoleon had been imprisoned since 1840 in the medieval fortress of Ham, in France, for his second attempted coup, at Boulogne in Normandy—another fiasco. This rumor was apocryphal. Bonaparte did not approve of his cousin's actions, and his brother Louis-Lucien had little interest in politics at the time; he was a scholar, who would go on to become a noted philologist, specializing in Basque and English dialects, on which subjects he published numerous books.[56] However, it was undoubtedly true, as the informant also told the cardinal, that "the Prince of Canino did not omit the words *independence* and *Italian glory* from his discourse to the zoology session."[57] Others might have been arrested for such inflammatory language, but Bonaparte, invariably outspoken anyway, was probably in this case taking advantage of the protection his papal title afforded him.

A month later, he was laid up in bed for some weeks after a nasty hunting accident. He told his mother that neither he nor his mount, "an excellent English horse," was at fault. Fox hunting nine miles from Rome with several Englishmen and the "three Borghese princes," his horse at a full gallop over rough terrain, had plunged with both front feet into a grass-covered hole. "The horse fell over his nose with such violence," Charles recounted to his mother, "that we finished in a somersault; happily mine was to the left of his so that he did not fall on me. And though I landed on my head, my hat deadened the blow considerably, and after being unconscious for a short time I was able to remount unassisted and ride back to Rome." He ached badly and had some difficulty in breathing but was essentially unhurt and making a steady recovery.[58]

In the next part of his letter he moves on to what he terms "the grand affair," that is, the question of Canino. He can only afford to keep the large property if his mother lives there and pays all the expenses of it; if she leaves, he will be burdened with more than he can handle. He says it is sad for him to have "to choose between two plans of which one deprives you of Canino, *or rather Canino of you,* and the other reduces my family to misery. I do not know if it is true that Canino can only give me twelve thousand piastres per year, but if that is so, I can only curse the day when, carried along by family pride, and in spite of the counsels of those as interested as I am in the future of my children, I allowed myself to buy this land on conditions that were only tolerable by the security I had that you would *never* abandon it." Taking over Canino from his mother would cost more than half his income, but if she insists on leaving, he will send her an agreement to take to her lawyer. "Here is what I ask you, such as it is, and in despair of the situation I do not look forward to your next letter which will be to entirely pillage the future of my family."

A week later, he writes again, having heard from Alexandrine in the interim. He does not mince his words but speaks "with a frankness" that she "will always find" in him. Although she affects to think he is a millionaire, she knows very well what his fortune is based on. But she can count on it that he will declare bankruptcy rather than compromise a single cent of his wife's money or his children's. He wants her to continue the administration of Canino and to be the proprietor. If she too wants to stay there, for her own benefit and not just for his, fine. On the other hand, if she really wants to retire from Canino, in spite of the harm it will do him, then she must tell him so sincerely. But he will not hide from her two things that are very displeasing to him: one is that the price he must pay is much too high, and the other is that the land she has sold off, which he always believed to be the least valuable, she now tells him was the only worthwhile piece.[59] Alexandrine, a strong-minded, highly cultured woman, was tired of her lonely, isolated life at Canino. It was Lucien, not she, who had enjoyed its peaceful retirement, and now that he was gone and she could follow her own preferences, she longed for a cosmopolitan life. At this point, she was definitely planning to move to Paris and to let her son take over the administration of Canino.

If Bonaparte seems to have spent a great deal of time worrying and wrangling over inheritances, it should be borne in mind that inherited money was the only sure means of livelihood for men and women of the upper classes. All forms of employment, "trade," even professional work such as medicine or law, were considered unsuitable and demeaning for aristocrats, and in Italy there was no army, as such, to join. Only the priesthood was an acceptable career for a nobleman at the time, and that meant celibacy. In light of his increasing animosity to the Church and its repressive measures toward the scientific congresses, Charles certainly did not envision his sons as clerics and felt that he had to provide for their future in some other way. Inherited money was equally important for his daughters, since having a substantial dowry would secure them husbands of rank equal to their own. Bonaparte himself had worked all his life as hard as any professional but without remuneration, except the pittance he got from his publications. However, these usually cost him more to produce and distribute than he made from them in sales and certainly did not yield enough income to support his family. He had had to rely entirely on family money, his inheritance from his father and the anticipation of Zenaide's from Joseph. This explains what might otherwise look like avaricious squabbling: he was simply trying to support himself and his dependents.

IO

LEGACIES OF
TROUBLE

"Le Dieu me faisait un Job sans me donner la patience!"

Bonaparte to Alexandrine Bonaparte,
Rome, 4 November 1844

I N JANUARY Agassiz wrote Bonaparte from Neuchâtel that he was sending a young painter to see him in Rome, in the hope that Bonaparte would sit for his portrait. This portrait Agassiz would place in his study, he says, next to those of Cuvier and von Humboldt. In spite of the pleasure he has gotten from the lithograph Bonaparte sent—perhaps the drawing by Liverati— he would rather have him "more animated, more himself." He thinks that in the lithograph "the Napoleon eclipses the naturalist too much." "I wish to see the great forehead of the philosophical observer handsomely portrayed in the noble face."[1]

A month later Agassiz addressed a letter to Bonaparte in Milan, where he had gone to arrange for the next scientific congress. He expresses his immense appreciation for the interest Bonaparte takes in him despite his own unsociability (*sauvagerie*) in not having written. He has received several of Bonaparte's brochures, but not the *Acts* from the congresses (the same complaint Ord had made). Again, he speaks of their upcoming trip: "I am ready to go with you to the United States. I know that with you I would be truly myself and that you prefer serious work and are against the distractions of the world."[2]

The "distractions of the world" had actually made considerable inroads on Bonaparte's life at that point, especially his anxiety over his election to the Academy of Sciences of the Institute of France. But finally, in March 1844, he had word from Geoffroy that he had received ten votes more than his nearest rival and was elected a corresponding member. He had at last reached one of his most cherished goals as a scientist, and it was with a proud heart that he set out for Naples in early spring to arrange for the Italian congress the following year. He boarded a steamship at Civitavecchia but neglected to obtain a passport for the short journey; when he disembarked on the Neapolitan quay without it, the authorities were much annoyed. This was typical behavior for the prince of Canino: he habitually neglected to obtain official documents, in the belief that his rank and name entitled him to eschew such rigmarole. Now that he was a member of the French Academy of Sciences, he must have felt particularly exempt from bureaucratic regulation.

It was not his intellectual stature, however, that impressed the police on this occasion but his costume: he was splendidly dressed in his colonel's uniform from San Marino, sparkling with medals.[3] Clearly, this elegant man was someone to be reckoned with, and he was taken at once before Ferdinand II, the Spanish Bourbon ruler of the kingdom of Naples. Ferdinand had long ago sought unsuccessfully to marry Charles's half-sister Charlotte, and then Zenaide, in order to be connected to the family of Napoleon. Under the circumstances, he could not turn down a request from Napoleon's nephew couched as it was in such earnest rhetoric, to grant permission for the congress to be held in his domain.[4] Afterward, Bonaparte wrote his mother that he had had an excellent reception at the court in Naples and that the meeting with the king would redound to the benefit of the congresses, the cause so dear to his heart and never far from his thoughts.[5]

At the same time, his thirst for knowledge remained undiminished, and he was still communicating almost daily with his scientific friends. Prince Maximilian wrote that he had been attempting to read Temminck's book on India—Dutch being somewhat similar to German he felt he might be able to understand it—but was having difficulty with Bonaparte's "great and beautiful work on Italian zoology" because of the language barrier. He says the English are doing much valuable work in natural history at the present, though he wishes Gould would not make a genus of every species—"and the barbaric names!"[6] John Edward Gray wrote to report that Gould was "wife-hunting," but so far had been unsuccessful though he had "asked at least fifty." "He is not likely to get so good and useful a wife as his first in a hurry," Gray observed, "and has made himself rather ridiculous by his proceeding."[7]

Probably Gray more than anyone else kept Bonaparte in touch with the naturalists of England, with whom all along he had had so much in common. Bonaparte responded to Gray that a letter from him was such a valuable treasure that he would always answer it at once in the hope of getting another. He asked him to please send all possible information and to bear with the fact that his correspondent is situated in Rome, where "nothing scientific takes place," and therefore cannot reciprocate in kind.[8] In this, he is echoing a phrase used by his lost friend Say, though one could hardly call Rome "a backwater," as Say had called New Harmony. Rome did boast the ancient Accademia Nazionale dei Lincei, founded in 1603, though it had fallen on hard times after the death in 1840 of its *restaurateur*, Feliciano Scarpellini.[9]

In Florence, at the Serristori Palace, Joseph's health was failing rapidly. The stroke he had suffered in 1840 left him partially paralyzed on one side and he was losing feeling in his limbs. He died in his sleep on 28 July 1844, with Zenaide and the children by his bedside, along with his wife and Louis Mailliard, his faithful secretary.[10] Charles was in Rome at the Palazzo Bonaparte, where Masi wrote him that "the king died in the morning, after little agony."[11] Before leaving for Florence, he received a note from Edward Lear asking him to forward to the princess of Canino some sketches he had made of Musignano the year before.[12]

Joseph was interred in the Church of Santa Croce in Florence on 3 August. Two companies of the grand duke of Tuscany's grenadiers escorted his funeral carriage along a route lined with thousands gathered to pay their respects to the brother of Napoleon, once king of Naples and then of Spain. Joseph's obituary in the Paris newspaper *Le Siècle* described him as "a friend of study, of repose, and of quiet pleasures" and recounted a vignette from his childhood to illustrate that he had never been a leader.[13] According to the story, Joseph's and Napoleon's uncle, the archdeacon Luciano Buonaparte, had called the boys to his deathbed and said: "You are the oldest Joseph, but Napoleon is the head of the family, never forget it." The article concluded that Louis Bonaparte (the fourth brother, an invalid living in Florence) was next in the line of succession and that he was the father of Prince Louis-Napoleon, presently detained in the Château of Ham. In his will, Joseph charged his daughter and her children with finding him a resting-place in France when it was again a free country. Joseph's secretary, Mailliard, would later write persistently to Charles begging him to carry out this request, but it was not accomplished until 1862, some five years after Charles's own death, that Joseph's remains would be placed in Les Invalides, near those of his more famous brother.

Julie, herself frail and weak, would not long survive her husband. Her "stubbornness" in refusing to leave Florence was deeply annoying to her son-in-law. Charles confided to his own mother that by remaining there it was clear Julie would be "plundered [*dépouillée*]" by his uncle Jerome (Napoleon's youngest brother, who was perpetually in debt due to his lavish lifestyle), "whom she loves more every day."[14] Also, she would not "inventory" a dia-

mond necklace worth 100,000 francs that Napoleon had given Joseph, and Charles thinks this is a bad sign as regards her intentions toward his children. What most offends him in Joseph's will is the belief, "breathed into every line," that his wife and daughter are at odds. This, he insists, is simply not true. Also, Cardinal Fesch's gallery of paintings still has to be disposed of, and he wishes this assignment had been left to his mother-in-law instead of to himself.

Bonaparte had no time to attend to this matter, however, because he had to leave Rome in early September for the congress in Milan. For the second time, Austria had agreed to allow the meeting in its domain, and the viceroy of the duchy, the archduke, the governor, and the archbishop were all present at the opening ceremony. For fifteen days balls and concerts were interspersed with visits to the gallery and library of the great seventeenth-century Palazzo di Brera, where the meetings were held. As usual, the president of the congress, conscious that the Austrian police were watching closely, in his opening remarks, asked the participants to attend strictly to scientific business and not to veer into political issues.[15] In accordance, Bonaparte delivered a paper in which he cataloged the mammals of Europe, enumerating all the known European species as well as several new ones, with synonyms and descriptions. Among these was the "Isard of the Pyrennees," a kind of chamois or goat, which he called *Rupicapra pyrenaica.* He also spoke on birds and gave an account of the state of ornithology in Europe. Last, he read several essays on fish and reptiles, which included accounts of his painstaking attempts, after many

Figure 32. *Sketch of Musignano* by Edward Lear, 1839. Courtesy of the Houghton Library, Harvard University.

dissections, to classify these creatures according to certain organs in the former and teeth in the latter. His papers would subsequently be published in the *Acts of the congress*.[16]

After Bonaparte left Milan, Eduard Rüppell, an attendee, wrote to him that he wanted a copy of his new "System of Ichthyology," presented at the congress, as he had no doubt Bonaparte would publish it immediately. Milan was then deserted; everyone had gone to the country, and "the sadness that results contrasts singularly with the familiar gaiety that reigned at the time of the congress."[17]

After Milan Bonaparte had a rare and special treat when he visited Alexander von Humboldt at his château on the Iles d'Hyères off the southeast coast of France. He wrote to his mother, now in Paris, that "the sweetest satisfaction" he had had from his trip to the north (of Italy) was in the intimacy he had enjoyed with the learned von Humboldt. Charles had spoken much of her with "this great and truly excellent man" and his niece, wife of the Prussian minister of foreign affairs. On returning to Rome he heard from von Humboldt, and the great man's approbation filled him with pride. "I have been touched by your *admirable* letter. After you left here the impression lived on of your profound simplicity of character, of an erudition as solid as varied, of an ardor of talent and of action worthy of the great name you carry. Hurry again to visit us another summer in Hyères, at the far end of beautiful Italy."[18]

In his letter to Alexandrine, Bonaparte then turns to the subject of Canino, still much on his mind. He does not want to take charge of the property until his return from America. Can she not give him a year's respite, during which she will still take charge of it? After all, he says, thinking to play his trump card, Canino is the site of his father's grave (and therefore, presumably, must have tender associations for her). As for the administration of the estate, he does not have the "courage" to live there, or the means to keep it up. If she has been a little surprised at what the papers have said about the fortune of his father-in-law (the exaggerated accounts of it), she knows well enough how little he left in reality.[19] "God wanted to make of me a Job without giving me the patience!" he exclaims in his next letter.[20]

While he was away, Zenaide, still in Florence with her mother, also wrote Alexandrine but on an entirely different subject. Her father has made her a most unusual bequest: the Bonaparte house in Ajaccio where he, her Uncle Lucien, and the emperor all were born. But this "monument" requires repairs and upkeep that will be very expensive. "If my pecuniary means corresponded with the impulse of my heart," she says, "I would think to make of it a Temple,

Figure 33. *Princess Zenaide Bonaparte* by Charlotte Bonaparte. Signed and dated "Charlotte Napoleon 1835." Watercolor. Collection of Giuseppe Primoli. Courtesy of the Museo Napoleonico, Rome.

guarded by a veteran of the Empire, and open for the numerous pilgrimages that, without doubt, would continually be made there."[21] However, no one knows better than her *chère Maman* the impossibility of doing this, since she has nine children and only a "very modest inheritance [*fortune bien modique*]" from her father, in spite of the absurd reports in the newspapers. She thinks, and Charles agrees with her, that the best way to conserve the property and to make the repairs necessary to keep it from falling into ruins, is to sell it. Prince Demidoff (Anatole, the wealthy Russian of a dubious title married to her cousin Mathilde) has offered to buy it, but to tell the truth she and Charles are loath to turn over their rights to this house to a Russian. Therefore, they have decided to sell it to the one person who would be able to care for it in the best way, King Louis-Philippe; or else, to his son the prince de Joinville, who at one time expressed a wish to acquire it. "It would be satisfying to me to know that the cradle of our family was in the hands of the same Prince who paid homage to the remains of the Emperor, and it seems to me that the care he would take of the paternal house in Ajaccio would be in line with his voyage to Saint Helena." (In 1840 the prince de Joinville had gone to that lonely island in the Atlantic off Africa to bring Napoleon's remains back to France.) She has never doubted her mother-in-law's friendship, and since she has often told them to count on her, Zenaide now feels she can request this favor, that Alexandrine should broach the matter to Louis-Philippe. Charles says no one but his mother could succeed so well in this mission of approaching the king—but all must be kept secret until the transaction is completed.

She has had good news from Charles: he was elected president of the zoology section at the congress in Milan. She adds, "he seems content with the success he has obtained." Apparently she was relieved he has not made a fuss, or had any occasion to storm out because he was not duly honored, as he had not been in Florence. Zenaide was a dignified, patient woman. Since Charles was so continually traveling, either for scientific or political reasons, or both, she had to shoulder all the responsibility of the house and children. Moreover, her own intellectual gifts were by no means insignificant: she had, for example, translated all the works of Schiller from German into French.

In November Agassiz responded to Bonaparte's suggestion that they collaborate on an illustrated *American Ichthyology* while visiting the United States. This is an excellent idea, says Agassiz, but it will be necessary to take along an illustrator "clever enough to paint live fish on the spot." He also believes "there is justice to render Rafinesque." This eccentric naturalist had written extensively on American fishes but had been disregarded by his colleagues because of his species-splitting (tendency to proliferate species in his classifications) and his exotic ideas on a number of subjects. Agassiz says he is not the first since

Rafinesque to see the necessity of multiplying species in ichthyology, and for the older naturalist "the thing was more difficult [then] than in our day" because the science was so new. Many of Rafinesque's species have priority over those that are now accepted, Agassiz says, and in the United States it will be easier to find the papers on which he worked. And they must not neglect to ask the Americans for specimens with which to make their work truly comprehensive of the North American continent. "If you consent to accept me as your collaborator," he concludes, "I will put together notes and objects of nature and write to some friends in the United States."[22]

Rafinesque was a brilliant but peculiar naturalist of French and German origin. Born in Constantinople, in 1773, he had spent many years in America studying the flora and fauna and publishing at his own expense innumerable pamphlets, covering a wide range of observation and speculation. He died a spurned pauper in a Philadelphia attic in 1840, but though reviled by his contemporaries for rushing into print too many of his findings without thorough investigation of their priorities—that is, who had published first on the subject—in later years he was recognized as a genius who anticipated the theory of evolution. He had tried to befriend Bonaparte during the latter's stay in America. Once, while visiting Reuben Haines, he had written formally to Bonaparte at Point Breeze: "Professor Rafinesque wishes to show his work to Mr. Charles Bonaparte, and to show him a number of sketches on the subject of the sciences. He has the honor of informing him that he is currently at a friend's house in Germantown (after a 1200 mile trip to Ohio, over Lake Erie into Canada, following the great canals) . . . when can we get together we great observers of nature?"[23] Bonaparte seems not to have responded to this opening, probably to his later regret.

A year before he died, Rafinesque sent Bonaparte a long list of his publications. They covered such disparate subjects as "Celestial Wonder and Philosophy of the Visible Heavens," "Genius and Spirit of the Hebrew Bible," "American Nations Before Columbus," "Grape Vines of North America and the Art of Making Wine," and "The Art of Curing Consumption." He had also published a collection of twenty poems and "100 notes on worldly mutations" entitled, "Instability of the World, or Philosophy of Mutations." In his accompanying letter, he says that, since Bonaparte had made use of his researches in ichthyology, he takes the liberty to let him know that he is still working in all branches of natural history. He has commenced, and hopes to publish the following year, a work that will be indispensable, *The fishes & fisheries of North America*.[24] This idea may have inspired Bonaparte's suggestion to Agassiz.

In his next letter to Bonaparte, several weeks later, Agassiz made a mistake that was fatal to their friendship. Bemoaning his many debts, he asks Bonaparte for a loan of ten thousand francs. He dares to hope that Bonaparte will send all, or part, of this sum, "so that if one day these projects of which I conceive are realized, I will never forget that it is you I owe for them." He concludes with a fervent complement: "Be persuaded that you do not have in the scientific world a more sincere admirer of your zeal and of your perseverance for natural history, nor an appreciator more aware of your beautiful works [than myself]."[25] Bonaparte did not answer, so Agassiz wrote again in early February of 1845 to say that the king of Prussia would give him fifteen thousand francs for his journey to America, and he wants to know if Bonaparte definitely plans to go the following summer. He still needs the ten thousand francs he had earlier requested and promises to pay Bonaparte back when they return from their journey. "I dare to hope you will not refuse a service to me that will give me the peace of mind that a man in my position must have to honorably pursue a career totally devoted to science."[26]

Bonaparte was now unwilling to lend him the money, and told him as much. Although it seems he had once hinted that he would pay for his friend's journey if he could find no other means of financing it. Agassiz wrote back, clearly piqued, that it would have been more acceptable to him "if in refusing the service I had asked of you, you had understood my position, or rather, you had extended faith to the details that I gave you on the subject. Perhaps someday you will regret it, when you know me better."[27] Perhaps Agassiz too had read the erroneous accounts of Joseph's legacy in the newspapers and thought his friend better off than he actually was.

The previous fall, Bonaparte had also broached to Gould the subject of a transatlantic voyage. Gould replied that he was contemplating it and mentioned also that he had heard Bonaparte planned to visit England the following spring. Gould hoped to see him at the meeting of the British Association for the Advancement of Science at Cambridge in June. "Not only many private friends but all naturalists will be most happy to be joined by so distinguished a person as yourself." Gould added that he had sent the first part of his *Odontophorinae* (a study of the grouse family), which he dedicated to Bonaparte as a "slight token of the value I entertain for your friendship and a just tribute of respect for your talents as a Scientific Naturalist."[28] In April, he wrote again to say that he felt greatly obliged to Bonaparte for his kind invitation to join him and Agassiz on a trip to the United States. "It is a country I have long contemplated visiting and if nothing occurs to prevent it I shall be most happy to accompany you to the States."[29] Bonaparte obviously had not informed him that he probably would not be going with Agassiz after all.

For some time, he had kept George Ord abreast of his actions and plans, and Ord wrote in regard to the purposed journey that if the Gould Bonaparte mentioned as likely to accompany him was the famous author of "some magnificent works on ornithology," he would "rejoice" to see him. He was also excited by the idea of a congress at Naples: "What a country for the researches of the Antiquary and the Geologist! It is entirely unique in the remains of that glorious nation [the Roman Empire], whose impress is still visible throughout the civilized world." He thinks the learned men of Europe, who will flock to the meeting, may even "suggest some means of which the buried City [Pompeii], with its inestimable riches, may yet arise from the tomb of ages."[30]

Ord's enthusiasm fell on deaf ears, however, because Bonaparte's plans of all kinds had already been seriously thwarted. The main reason for his American journey had been to show his eldest son the land of his birth. But in February the twenty-one-year-old Joseph, who much to Bonaparte's annoyance had inherited the estate of Point Breeze from his grandfather, left abruptly for America to inspect his legacy on his own and without his father's permission. The first signs of a rift between Charles and Zenaide appear at this time, for she apparently knew and approved of her son's plans. This was a "big issue [*grand événement*]" in the house, according to their daughter Julie.[31]

Zenaide mentioned nothing of this controversy when writing to Alexandrine at the end of April. She said only that Joseph had left from Leghorn, that she had had a letter from him in early March from Gibraltar, and that he planned to return the following September.[32] However, some time after young Joseph's arrival in the United States, the ever-vigilant Ord cast more light on the subject. He told Bonaparte that there was a "strange story" going the rounds of the newspapers about his son's departure from Europe. The substance of it was this: that because of his youth his family had taken legal steps to prevent his departure; but through the agency of young Mailliard [Louis Mailliard's son Adolphe] he was smuggled, in female attire, on board a Swedish vessel at Leghorn, which brought him to New York. Ord noted that he had no means of ascertaining the truth of this story and that probably it was only newspaper gossip. But, he adds, "should I be enabled to learn anything of an authentic and interesting character in relation to your beloved son, depend upon it I shall not fail to inform you thereof."[33] Ord dearly loved a scandal.

In May Zenaide received a letter from Louis Mailliard, who was still living at Point Breeze. "I am sorry that the Prince of Musignano punished my son for aiding the voyage of his, which he could never have refused [to do]," he said. "[But] it is necessary that men acquire experience and knowledge."[34] Once Bonaparte would have agreed with Mailliard—when Bonaparte himself was twenty and went to America in defiance of his father's wishes.

Zenaide had written to Alexandrine about Joseph from Florence, where she, Charles, and their other children had gone to attend her ailing mother. Julie died on 7 April 1845. After the burial Charles returned to Rome alone, while Zenaide stayed on to pay her respects to one she would "always mourn," before undertaking the tiresome journey home with her children and servants. After six days of traveling, when she finally reached the city, she was cruelly surprised to be met by their groom Baccano, on horseback, instead of by Charles as planned. But she soon saw that, in a closed carriage a little beyond, Charles sat huddled with his head wrapped in bandages. For several days he had had a high fever caused by a large abscess that Zenaide described as a beehive (*ruche*). She later told Alexandrine that the doctors had lanced this swelling and that Charles was now much better and at last able to sleep. The faithful Padre Maurizio (Charles's old tutor), came every day to visit him, and it touched Zenaide to see the eagerness with which he was willing to do anything he could for Charles. Charles was, she said, pressing her for an answer about Lucien's telescope, which he hoped his mother would give him.[35] This was the large instrument his father had bought in England during the family's exile, from the great astronomer John Frederick Herschel, and which Lucien and Padre Maurizio had set up in Sinigallia to assiduously study the heavens. Perhaps Padre Maurizio was behind Charles's request for the telescope. In any case, astronomy may have been the one scientific interest Bonaparte had shared with his parent.

In June Bonaparte wrote again to Agassiz, this time laying bare his heart and explaining fully his emotional and financial situations as well as the poor state of his health. Agassiz responded at once with a letter that was contrite and apologetic:

> Today I put aside all traces of disagreement to write you, my dear and noble friend; you have anticipated me, but only by a few days . . . an irresistible voice told me that I was deceived in my impression of your refusal. If you could have witnessed the emotion I felt at reading your letter. . . . Am I then to leave without you? Is it irrevocable? The king of Prussia has given me 1000 louis for a prolonged visit to the United States. Tell me again, if deferring my departure until February would make it possible for you to leave Rome. It would be wonderful if we could make the voyage together. Give me again, positively, your latest word on this subject.[36]

Unquestionably by this time Bonaparte had lost his enthusiasm for the journey. His infection was slow to heal, and he was having trouble again with gout. And perhaps more than anything else, by then he was so enmeshed in politics that it was no longer possible to absent himself from Italy for any extended period.

By the end of May he was still convalescing from an operation at the site of the infection, for the incision had not entirely closed. Even so, as Zenaide wrote Alexandrine, he went for long walks, insisted on horseback riding, and was fully occupied with other activities. He had nearly finished selling Cardinal Fesch's gallery—a financial disaster for Fesch's estate because the cardinal's legacies amounted to more than three times the proceeds realized from the sale of the paintings, in spite of all Charles's efforts. They had had no news from Joseph since the letter from Gibraltar, but they hoped every day to hear of his arrival in New York.[37]

By July Charles was still attempting to sell the remaining paintings from the gallery. He wrote—with Zenaide as his usual amanuensis—to his friend and colleague Hermann Schlegel to say that Schlegel would render him a great service if he could sell some of the masterpieces to the royal Dutch museum. These included a *Crucifixion* by Raphael that Bonaparte could offer for 85,000 francs; *The Preaching of John the Baptist* by Rembrandt, 100,000; a *Crown of Thorns* on copper by Teniers, 35,000; *The Madeleine* by Van Dyck, 20,000; and a small *Holy Family* by Jules Romain, of which the figure of the Virgin had been attributed "to Raphael himself," 10,000.

Bonaparte hurried through this list in order to turn to what really interested him: the ornithological manual Schlegel had sent him to critique. In a long and detailed list he answers questions Schlegel had put to him. But he has many questions as well: "You have made two varieties of my two species of wild vultures. Are you quite sure that the *F. auricularise* [?] is found in Greece?"; "the subdivision of the Chouettes [owls] into *Otus* and *Strix* is bad. I do not know the difference between *Athene noctur* of the north and of the *midi*." He wants to lure Schlegel to the next scientific congress, but Schlegel, like Bonaparte, has apparently been ill, so he says, "don't you think a little journey to Naples would entirely restore your health? With *your* mind you will doubly enjoy our beautiful Italy."[38]

Ord wrote again, still excited about the congress in Naples because of its location. "Above all when you shall have witnessed the excavations at Pompeii, record everything, I beseech you, for the happiness of one who takes an extraordinary interest in every thing relative to the illustrious people whose remains have left an indelible impression upon European civilization."[39] It was significant that this congress would take place in Naples, for it was the early Roman Republic—and Pompeii had existed centuries before its destruction by the eruption of Vesuvius in A.D. 79—that had all along been the inspiration behind the Risorgimento, a word meaning renascence, or revival. The forward-thinking intellectuals of Bonaparte's own time wished to reintroduce to the peninsula the blessings of that earlier period: freedom from oppressive rulers, equality, and independence. Ord, as an American, felt a special affinity with those long-ago republicans. "If you could be permitted to retain some little memorial," he entreats Bonaparte, "dug from the grave of ages, some precious trifle, which had been seen by Roman eyes, which had been touched by Roman hands, to be preserved among the jewels of your transatlantic correspondent! But I forbear; pardon the impertinent suggestion!"

The congress at Naples was held from 20 September to 5 October 1845, and well over two thousand Italian and foreign scientists attended, including the illustrious Richard Owen. Before the meetings started, Owen wrote Bonaparte, already in Naples, that he had exhausted himself mountain climbing in Italy. But he was "dedicating his confinement [recuperation?]" to preparing his paper on the anatomy of the *Brachiopoda* (marine invertebrates), which he planned to deliver at the zoology session of the congress on the following Saturday morning.

Ferdinand II attended the inaugural ceremonies with his family and entire court. He appeared to be wholly in favor of the congress, but, apparently moved by information given him by the minister of police, his attitude changed abruptly, and he prohibited all the festivities proposed in the savants' honor by the city of Naples. Consequently, the meetings themselves were troubled and confused; something ominous hung in the air. In hindsight, the congress at Naples was seen as the precursor of the revolution.[40]

In his talks to the zoology section, Bonaparte stuck to natural science, particularly fish. He spoke of his manual of Italian ichthyology, which included the dictionary of common names he had given at the Congress of Turin in 1840. In addition, he gave a detailed catalog of European fishes, the fruit of considerable research, in which he united for the first time in one work all the marine and freshwater fish of Europe.[41] A few years earlier, in his introduction to part 4 of the *Fauna italica*, he had elaborated on his pursuit of ichthyology. He said he had spent a great deal of time on one of the most beautiful gulfs of Italy, that of Spezia, visited the two seas—the Tyrrhenian and the Adriatic—many times, and frequented many fisheries in the principal cities of Italy. He had procured specimens, and all sorts of other help, from correspondents. The writings of Rafinesque had been most valuable to him and he regretted the recent loss in America of that distinguished naturalist, who had contributed so much to the science of ichthyology with his accurate list of the fishes of Sicily. He himself had tried hard to give accurate comparisons of the common names of fishes for each part of the Italian peninsula.[42]

After the congress, he was delighted to have Richard Owen visit him and his family in Rome, though the timing was less than perfect: Zenaide was ill from a premature delivery in October. (The baby girl had lived only a few hours.) But life went on as usual at the Villa Paolina and Bonaparte, assisted by his fifteen-year-old daughter Julie as hostess, entertained at dinner a large group of savants from the congress.[43] On his way home, Owen wrote warmly from Milan. He said that among the many pleasing recollections which would "furnish the subjects of our fire-side chats in England, none will recur more frequently than those of the scenes at Rome associated with the remembrance of your kindness and hospitality, and the amiable and interesting members of your family, with whom to have been domesticated I shall ever esteem a pleasure and an honour." He said that while in Florence, the grand duke had asked to see him, and he had spent "a most rewarding hour" with him. During the visit, Leopold had asked what pleased him most in Florence and Owen had answered, "to witness the happiness that reigned throughout." In Florence the poor did not appear "*too poor*," nor the rich "*too rich*," as in England, where the contrast was "fearfully great," and where it was "very rare" to see a cheerful and contented expression on the face of an English agricultural laborer. In Tuscany, he had found this expression "constant and characteristic" of the equivalent class. His health and strength were much improved from his trip to Italy, and he "never contemplated any of the wonderful memorials of [Italy's] great men without feeling the determination *to energize in my own science* stir strongly within me." He hoped to send Bonaparte the "fruits of this determination."[44]

The following May, Owen made good on his promise with a copy of his work on British fossil mammalia, the completion of which he "owed to the stimulus and improved health" resulting from his Italian sojourn. In the book, he says, he has proposed and, he hopes, established the theory of the geographical distribution of the pliocene, or "the last extinct races of the Mammalian Class." Owen says he is preparing his ideas on comparative osteology (bone structure) for the press, and as soon as his article is published he "will have great pleasure in submitting [his] views" to Bonaparte, whose knowledge embraces "so wide a range of Zoological Philosophy."[45]

The prince wrote back at the end of June that he was really ashamed of himself for not having answered "such a friend and master!" In his typically enthusiastic manner he adds: "but you are as busy a man as myself (I can't say more!) and you well know how time passes off with us! . . . In how many things do we not sympathize? Your deep attachment to your family! The philanthropys [sic] I would like to imitate! the footsteps I should be so proud to follow!!! Italy you *must* visit again, and visit it with your wife and your dearest child." His own wife is at last well again, "but I cannot say so of my poor legs which are as bad as ever, and have prevented me from walking as I should have wished to do."[46]

Bonaparte particularly needed to be up and about, because of his political commitments. For him and for all his compatriots, it was a time rich with possibility, when enormous changes might be in the offing. In the middle of June 1846, the repressive and authoritarian Pope Gregory XVI had died, and the hastily elected new pope, Pius IX, was being hailed as a great liberator.

II

THE PRINCE AND
THE POPE

"Oh, absolute power, when wilt thou cease to crush our Italy?"

Stendhal, The Charterhouse of Parma

WHEN GREGORY XVI died on 1 June 1846, the liberals in Italy were relieved. He had been one of the Church's most reactionary popes, employing Austrian troops on several occasions to put down uprisings in the Papal States and opposing Italian nationalism, freedom of conscience and of the press, and the separation of church and state.[1] The subsequent election of Pius IX (Giovanni Maria Mastai-Ferretti), son of a count, resulted from a deadlock between the conservative and the liberal cardinals and was at first disappointing. But when the new pope chose the liberals' candidate, Cardinal Gizzi, as his secretary of state, the mood of progressives all over Europe began to change.[2]

One of his first acts, along with dispensing alms, stopping inquisitions, and relaxing censorship of the press, was to declare a general amnesty for exiles and political prisoners. This alone sent the populace of Rome into a joyous frenzy. In anticipation of his procession, they decorated the entire length of the Corso, the main thoroughfare in Rome and covered the walls with his picture. The joy and enthusiasm were overwhelming. Poets sang of his magnanimity, and in the Bonaparte household Luigi Masi composed a hymn in his honor.[3] He was portrayed by the people of Rome as "an apostle of liberty and an angel sent to regenerate the country of Caesar."[4] Because Pio Nono (Italian for Pius IX) gave indications that he was in sympathy with Italian nationalism, Bonaparte too was excited over his election and requested a private audience as soon as possible. At this meeting the pope assured him that the congresses of Italian scientists would enjoy his protection and favor. But he cautioned Bonaparte to make his colleagues understand that they could not convene in the Papal States. This was unfortunate, since Bologna had been chosen as the site for the following year's meeting. But Pio Nono, whatever his personal views, did not want to be seen as going too quickly, or too visibly, against the policies of his absolutist predecessor.

The Austrian chancellor Prince Klemens von Metternich, a strong supporter of Gregory XVI, looked on the demonstrations in Rome with increasing concern, for they were distinctly patriotic and anti-Austrian. It was ominous that cries of "Long live Pius!" were often coupled with "Death to the Germans [Austrians]!" and "A free Italy!" Intellectuals hailed Pio Nono as the liberator long ago predicted by the poet Vincenzo Gioberti. Giuseppe Garibaldi, destined ultimately to lead his countrymen to victory in the struggle for a united peninsula, called him "the Messiah of Italy."[5] Pio Nono, unaware that he had let a genie out of a bottle, had created expectations he could not possibly meet. The dichotomy of his position as head of the Catholic Church and temporal ruler of the Papal States, both of which he believed in wholeheartedly, put him at cross-purposes. He had never intended to crusade for the liberation and unification of Italy.[6] But this was not clear at the beginning of his papacy.

In July Bonaparte received letters from Edward Everett authorizing him to represent both the American Antiquarian Society and the American Academy of Arts and Sciences at the upcoming Congress of Genoa. (Everett's letters were mailed from Cambridge, Massachusetts, where he was about to assume his duties as president of Harvard University.[7]) At the same time, Bonaparte heard from Ord that the American Philosophical Society had also named him their representative at the congress. Ord again asked about the missing Acts from the second congress; only the first and third accounts had reached the society's library.[8] The fact was that after the congress in Florence, the police, believing the publication inflammatory, had made every effort to prevent further issues from leaving the country.

The following month Bonaparte heard from Isadore Geoffroy Saint-Hilaire concerning a proposed statue of his father, Etienne, in Etampes, where he was born. The sculptor Pierre-Jean David of Angers had agreed to do it without charge, but there would be many other expenses involved, and Geoffroy had sent a copy of the circular outlining the project to the congress at Genoa. It was the number of subscribers, not the size of the subscriptions, that mattered, he said. "I count on your good offices as a scholar, as a Frenchman so influential in all the scientific world, as a corresponding member of the Institute, and as a friend of my father. You would do this not only for me but for all the friends of science in France." Etienne Geoffroy Saint-Hilaire had been one of the most influential naturalists of Europe. Isadore once told Bonaparte that Goethe had expressed preferences for his father's doctrines over those of Cuvier.[9] He had founded the menagerie at the Jardin des Plantes in 1794 and served as its first director, and, with six others, had founded the Institute of Cairo during the 1798 expedition to Egypt. Napoleon had named him to the Institute of France in 1807. Erecting a statue in his honor was a project Bonaparte would embrace wholeheartedly, for his friend as well as for the glory of science.

That summer young Joseph returned from America, and Bonaparte was on the dock at Civitavecchia to meet him. He had come by way of England and France and had much to tell of his journey, which perhaps overcame his father's anger at his having left Italy without his permission. The family spent the summer at Ariccia and returned to Rome at the end of September.

Bonaparte was already in Genoa by the 15th for the opening of the congress. It was an exciting place to be. The Genoese atmosphere was charged with enthusiasm for the liberal new pope, and King Charles Albert was having diplomatic problems with Austria. Both factors augured well for the cause of Italian independence. At the opening meeting, after remarks by the president, Bonaparte stood to tell the assembly he had been empowered by His Holiness to say that he was not opposed to their gatherings, that he offered his protection, and that he would regenerate the ancient Accademia dei Lincei. A papal attendee reported that it was impossible to convey the sensation produced by the prince of Canino's words, which were constantly interrupted by applause and acclaimed at the end with a general "Evviva!" Rome was proclaimed the site of the next congress, but Bonaparte had to discourage the idea, knowing that the pope would not allow it.[10]

During the meetings the Piedmontese government let various members, Bonaparte foremost among them, make a series of patriotic pronouncements, in essence proclaiming Charles Albert and Pio Nono joint leaders of the nationalist movement. The king even permitted his subjects to celebrate the expulsion of the Austrians a hundred years earlier. Austria, of course, watched all these proceedings with a sense of alarm.[11]

At the last general meeting, Bonaparte reported on the work of his colleagues in natural history. He praised Rüppell for raising zoology to ever higher levels with his studies of the fauna of Abyssinia; he lauded the Prussian Schmid for his work in entomology and his friend Durazzo for bringing "luster" to the ornithology of Liguria (the small Italian province that includes Genoa). Scarcely a single Italian naturalist was left out of his encomiums to those studying mammals, birds, mollusks, reptiles, and fishes. He credited his co-workers with many discoveries, and did not neglect to mention that a fish had been named after him, *Cybium bonapartii*. He had been honored, he said, with correspondence from the first zoologists of Asia, America, and Europe, including letters from Müller, Heckel, Strickland, Owen, Geoffroy St. Hilaire, and above all (because of the great respect he bore for him), from Oken. In his tributes, Bonaparte was careful to include Charles Albert for allowing the conference to take place in his domain. And he honored in general the discoveries of Americans in natural science.[12] He also spoke of the poet Gioberti, "the champion of Italian civilization." During the course of this congress, more political than any of the others, Bonaparte waxed increasingly zealous. He and Masi sang patriotic songs, gave speeches extolling unity, fraternity, and independence, and attended numerous dinner parties and receptions to promote their cause of a unified Italy, freed from Austrian domination.

He was so involved with the swelling pressures of Italian politics that he felt no disappointment at not being with them when he heard from Ord in October that Agassiz had been in Philadelphia with the botanist Asa Gray. Still, he must have pictured himself, with a touch of regret, traveling with these two naturalists to various American cities, meeting colleagues, and examining diverse collections. Ord mentioned that Agassiz was to deliver a course of lectures on geology at the Lowell Institute and that America was indeed a "noble field for Geologists."[13]

At the end of January Bonaparte entertained the celebrated English economist Richard Cobden and his wife, who were visiting Rome. He, Masi, and other liberals organized a grand banquet in Cobden's honor to celebrate his ideas on reform. A week later Massimo d'Azeglio, the Piedmontese writer and champion of the regeneration of Italy, called at the Palazzo Bonaparte for a private conference with the prince of Canino.[14] Rome may not have been a center for natural science, but politically it was a beehive of activity.

Hugh Strickland wrote in March to thank him for the report of Strickland's "valuable labours" that Bonaparte had delivered to the zoology section at Genoa and said he was glad to hear that Bonaparte would be visiting England in the late spring on his way to America.[15] Apparently the prince had not informed his English friends that he had canceled plans for a transatlantic journey, perhaps because he still intended to go to the meeting of the British Association for the Advancement of Science at Oxford and would have the opportunity to tell them then. In England he would have the chance to see new American specimens that might not be obtainable in their native land. George Robert Gray had written that "young Audubon" (John Wodehouse) was "obliged to come to London to draw the Quadrupeds of America," as more than eighty species were missing from his work that could only be obtained in Europe.[16] Some years before, Bonaparte himself had had to borrow American specimens from the London taxidermist Leadbeater in order to write his continuation of Wilson's *American Ornithology*.

June found him in Paris, where he came down with chills and fever after undergoing a suite of cold baths followed by an intense regimen at a spa. The popular water cure of the mid-nineteenth century was not the rendezvous of card players and ballroom dancers it had been in the eighteenth, but a serious medical affair consisting of daily cold showers, wrappings in cold, wet sheets, long, vigorous walks, and a regulated diet.[17] The cure had been too much for him. But he soon recovered and plunged again into his multitudinous scientific affairs, attended the theater frequently, and dined with Victor Hugo at Alexander Dumas's home, Monte Cristo. Both men were political liberals and sympathetic to republican causes. He told his mother, who had known Hugo for years, that the great writer had said (with typical continental exaggeration) to tell her she was "the person in the world he most respects and loves [*la personne du monde qu'il respecte et aime le plus*]." Bonaparte attended meetings of the French Institute and was present at the Chamber of Peers to hear Victor

Hugo give a discourse on the family (an interesting choice of topic for Hugo, a known adulterer).[18]

While in Paris he heard again from Strickland, who hoped Bonaparte's illness would not prevent him from coming to the meeting at Oxford after all. He himself, he says, is to deliver a lecture on the "history and affinities" of the dodo—the enormous flightless pigeon from Mauritius last seen in 1662—on which new light has been shed by the recent dissection of both the foot and the head. Strickland says these two Oxford fossils will be exhibited at the meeting, but he wants the alleged dodo bones at the Paris museum brought over for comparison. Cuvier briefly described the bones in 1830 and de Blainville somewhat later, but no exact descriptions or pictures of them had been published. "Now if you have any influence with M. de Blainville, in whose custody I believe these bones now are, you oblige the naturalists of all countries very greatly if you could persuade M. de Blainville to bring these bones himself, or to allow them (or at least casts or drawings of them) to be brought to the Oxford meeting." Plaster casts had been made of "our own Dodo's head and foot to be given to public museums," Strickland wrote, and they would be pleased to receive similar ones of the Paris bones.[19] Bonaparte must have been successful in borrowing the Parisian dodo relics and carrying them across the channel himself, because Strickland gratefully sent him, via Sir William Jardine, a cast of the Oxford dodo's leg.[20]

Bonaparte arrived at Oxford at the end of the month, having traveled from London by train at a thrilling forty-five miles per hour. He wrote to Zenaide of his excitement at the speed, adding that he wished he could have gone even faster.[21] After the congress, he tells her, he plans to return to London for four days before traveling to Scotland, and then on to Copenhagen for the meeting of the Scandinavian Association of Scientists. In London and Paris, he is finding the stimulation in his field that he could not find in Rome. He concludes: "Certainly one of the most perfect benefits of civilization is, *Knowledge is Power*."

No doubt the Oxford meeting was exciting, because the scientific community three years earlier had been set on its ears by an anonymous publication, *Vestiges of the Natural History of Creation* (1844). The book put forth the idea of the transmutation of living things and described the progress of the animal world from the lowest form of living matter to human beings. It unquestionably stirred up all manner of evolutionary conjecture, which would continue for years to come. Bonaparte found himself in the thick of one of the most important scientific debates of all time, and his own contributions to it, through his ornithological studies, were undoubtedly significant. Most of the important naturalists of the day attended the meeting, and he must have been especially pleased to see Agassiz, who had returned to Europe to settle his affairs before beginning his course of lectures at Harvard. Agassiz gave a speech that much impressed Charles Darwin and sped him onward in his study of barnacles, a line of research that ultimately led to his theory of the origin of species.[22] (There is a certain irony in this, since Agassiz never accepted Darwin's theory.) It was all immensely stimulating, and Bonaparte was obviously in jubilant spirits when he ended his letter to Zenaide, "I embrace you with all my heart," and signed himself "Zig," the nickname she had used for him since the beginning of their marriage.[23] At this period, all seemed well between them. If there was any trouble brewing, he evidently chose to ignore it.

Before leaving Oxford, he attended a grand farewell dinner at which he was given "one of the most beautiful tributes" he had ever received. This included complimentary references to Pius IX, the Italian people, and Italy itself. All his friends were there, he said, and there was "much applause." The geologist Sir Roderick Murchison "flattered" him the most.[24] Strickland later sent him copies of the *Oxford Herald* quoting Bonaparte's presentation at the meeting. He said Bonaparte could not confer a greater benefit on science than by bringing numerous Mexican birds, described much earlier, within "the pale" of the modern classification system.[25] Bonaparte had already published an article on Mexican birds for the Zoological Society of London and another, on quezalts (quetzals), for a French magazine.[26]

After leaving Oxford, he traveled to Scotland with John Gould. Gould's granddaughter later recorded in her scrapbook an amusing anecdote about him, quite typical of his headstrong personality. The two naturalists visited a public bath one Sunday afternoon but were told by the woman in charge that they could not bathe on Sunday. The prince pretended not to understand and kept saying "nice water," while taking off his coat. "But you can't bathe today," said the woman. He only answered, "nice water," and took off his waistcoat. The woman repeated her protests. "Nice water," said Bonaparte and began to take off other garments. At this the woman fled, and he and Gould had their bath in peace.[27]

The next leg of his journey took him to Copenhagen, where he wrote Zenaide: "I send you the petal of a Rose more interesting than that of Mortfontaine [Joseph Bonaparte's estate outside Paris, which he was forced to abandon after Napoleon's downfall]. This petal is from a variety called Victor Hugo, and it was the Queen of Denmark who gathered it and gave it to me yesterday, when I had the honor to dine and pass some time in the park and at the château of the royal family." He had been at the dinner table for four hours and then had gone to Tivoli, the city's famous amusement park. He cannot resist quoting for Zenaide his introduction at the queen's dinner. "*Messieurs*, we have here at our table a foreign naturalist, who, I know, would interest you greatly, as much for his family, by which modern Europe is now formed, as for his father, the great Lucien Bonaparte, the Academician, who even in the most violent times of the French Revolution cultivated and patronized the sciences [actually, the arts]. But principally we honor [Charles Bonaparte], who applied to the natural sciences all the genius he inherited from his ancestors. This eminent zoologist honors our gathering with his presence: *Vive* Charles Bonaparte, prince of Canino!" Bonaparte adds that everyone thought he resembled the emperor, "under the beard [*sous barbe*]."[28] Concluding his letter, he tells Zenaide to stay in Ariccia at least through August and that he anticipates with joy the marriage (apparently to take place at Ariccia) of their oldest daughter, Julie. (Julie's fiancé, Alexander del Gallo Roccagiovine, was a young nobleman from an ancient Roman family whom Charles had known since Alexander was a child.) He adds that for a week in the middle of August he will be in Vienna, "where *we must go together*."[29]

One brief note to Zenaide was written on the back of a concert program dated 11 July 1847, probably from a performance he attended in Copenhagen. The program lists five selections from Giuseppe Verdi's operas: the finale from the first act of *Nabucco*, two arias from *I Due Foscari*, one from *Attila*, another from *I Lombardi*, and a duet from *Ernani*.[30] All these operas are revolutionary in tendency and with them, it has been said, the spirited Verdi "forged weapons of his own."[31] The music must have moved Bonaparte deeply. Zenaide probably understood this and disapproved of the underlying implications in Verdi's work, because she recognized that the story lines and the incendiary words in the arias posed an indirect threat to the Vatican and the Papal States. A devout Catholic with a deep reverence for the pope, she was definitely not sympathetic with the revolutionary cause in which her husband was becoming ever more involved. A deep-seated rift was slowly opening up between her and Charles.

From Denmark Bonaparte crossed to Sweden, where, much to his delight, a crowd on the beach greeted him with "Vive Napoléon!" By this time he must have been exhausted from all the excitement of the trip and his numerous encounters, for he wrote Zenaide wistfully that on his return to Rome he hoped to find "absolutely all in peaceful order at last [*tout absolument en règle tranquille enfin*]." He even tells her he thinks this phrase should be his epitaph. (He meant, perhaps, that to have all in "peaceful order" in the science of ornithology and in his personal life, was his ultimate goal.[32]) From Stockholm he writes that the dowager queen (Zenaide's aunt, Désirée Clary, the widow of Bernadotte), has given him all possible attentions; he is even writing from her boudoir which she has lent him for the purpose.[33] The queen had shown him other kindnesses in the past, one of which—her gift of the small white porcelain cup and saucer that had belonged to Linnaeus—was particularly treasured and occupied a special place on the mantelpiece of his study at the Villa Paolina.[34]

After spending a day and two nights on a train, Bonaparte arrived in Berlin and had the great pleasure of sinking into a bath and reading his letters. He spent an evening at Potsdam with the king of Prussia, during which he was seated on the king's right at dinner, the queen being absent. Best of all, he had a three-hour conversation with von Humboldt in which he had been very touched by the great scientist's "bienviellance" and affectionate manner toward him.[35]

Perhaps he was growing somewhat addicted to adulation, so it galled him that his own wife did not mention in her letter an event of which he was inordinately proud. "How is it that you do not speak to me of my nomination to the presidency of the Academy of Lincei [the venerable academy at Rome] of which the newspapers are full and which they speak of here? Are you hiding this according to your lovable habit? That would be too bad!" Hoping for a little sympathy at least, he adds that his legs are always in pain: another serious attack of gout. Finally, he changes his tone and says that for three out of every four days he has wanted to fly to her arms. And how much he has looked forward to her letters! And he thanks the children for theirs: one from Julie, who was seventeen, another from Napoleon, eight, and a scribble from four-year-old Albert. "I embrace you all while waiting the opportunity to do it in reality."[36] He could not appreciate the full poignancy of that communication from little Albert, who would be dead before the year was out.

From Vienna, he wrote John Edward Gray that he had been "too busy travelling, studying, discussing and visiting kings and queens at Copenhagen, Stockholm, Berlin etc" to thank him and all his other English friends for his "too short stay" in their "fabulous metropolis." "The events of my country and the confidence placed in me by his Holiness in consequence of them hurry my return back in Rome where I shall be a fortnight at most, not without having however given a *peep* into the scientific meeting of the Hungarians . . . so in one year I shall have been present at four sc[ientific] meetings!" He also mentioned that he hoped the British Museum would buy from him a "superior" Murillo for which his father-in-law had refused 2000 guineas and which he would sell for 1200, and a "classical Giulio-Romano," worthy of Raphael, who "even painted the Virgin's head," for 1000.[37] All this traveling and the support of a large family were undoubtedly draining his finances.

He was back home in time to celebrate Julie's marriage on 30 August and to see her off on her wedding trip to Paris, where she and her new husband planned to stay with her cousin, Princess Mathilde, daughter of her great-uncle

Figure 34. *Julie Bonaparte, marchesa del Gallo di Roccagiovine* (Charles-Lucien's daughter) by Andrea Belloli, 1850. Watercolor. Courtesy of the Museo Napoleonico, Rome.

Figure 35. *Alessandro, marchese del Gallo di Roccagiovine* (Charles-Lucien's son-in-law) by Andrea Belloli, 1852. Watercolor. Courtesy of the Museo Napoleonico, Rome.

Jerome.[38] Soon after the wedding, Bonaparte made plans for his trip to Venice for the congress. There a series of dramatic events would begin that eerily paralleled those of his childhood.

By 1847 Charles-Lucien Bonaparte had established himself in the eyes of the authorities as a rabble rouser. It behooved Pio Nono to get such an unruly person out of Rome, and he therefore facilitated in every way the prince of Canino's journey to Venice by arranging passports and other necessary papers. But before leaving, Bonaparte, thinking to capitalize on the general agitation of the populace, decided to do something "memorable." Dressed in a uniform of the Roman Civil Guard, which bespoke secular rule, he staged a massive protest before the Tuscan and Piedmontese consulates and forced the reluctant diplomats onto the balconies of their respective palazzos. The next evening, supported by the same crowd, whose tone had become decidedly more menacing, he approached the Austrian embassy and the Jesuit monastery, both emblematic of repressive, autocratic rule and natural targets for popular resentment. This demonstration was too much for the secretary of state. Already beset by worries about the rising tide of republicanism and fearing the reaction of other European diplomats to the incident, he ordered strong disciplinary measures, including the arrest of the leader of the demonstrations.[39]

Bonaparte, accompanied by the faithful Masi, was then already on his way to Venice. He traveled in stages to Leghorn, Pisa, Florence, Bologna, and Ferrara, organizing protests in each of these cities and pledging oaths, with crossed swords, to defend the country of Italy. Often his horses were unhitched and his carriage dragged by the crowd, an enthusiasm caused by the first sight the people had of this Roman Civil Guard uniform (*uniformi civiche romane*). Exalted by this outpouring, he lost all prudence in his demeanor and in his speeches, and after he crossed the Po River he deliberately ignored the fact that he had arrived in Austrian territory and that the atmosphere had changed. Nor did he realize how different in character the congress in Venice was from the one in Genoa. At times, in his overweening and inappropriate ardor, he would shout, "This is our land and we will revenge it with our blood!" On a police document asking for his reason for staying in Venice, he wrote, "Italian national civilization."[40]

While there, he received a letter from Zenaide telling him of an audience she had just had with the pope. She had gone to see the Holy Father to protest the clamor raised by her husband's actions in Rome and to assure Pio Nono that Charles had not intended any disrespect. The pope had replied that, there, in that very room, at the same hour of the day, he had begged her husband and

Masi to use all their influence to pacify the multitude, and they had both promised to suppress all tumult and demonstration. He flattered himself that they understood all his concerns and shared them. But, the very next day he had received both written and verbal protests from foreign ministers whose embassies had been invaded by Italian dissidents. The prince, leading the demonstrators through the streets and shouting "Evviva!" had appeared on the balcony of each embassy, forcing the resident minister to stand beside him while he made a speech. It was one thing to voice liberal ideas in the cafés and other public places, but to take over the homes and offices of foreign ambassadors was something else. He told Zenaide frankly that Masi's actions could be attributed to his youth and impressionability, but he was astonished at the hotheadedness (*chaleur*) of the prince: a man of his mature years and high rank, the father of a family and one with a considerable fortune, who had done so much valuable work in science and had been lauded by savants from many countries. Besides, the pope had added (with a smile?), her husband had just returned from a voyage of many months, in which he traversed most of Europe—one would have thought he needed a rest![41]

At this point in their meeting, Pio Nono had launched into his strongly negative views on the idea of Italian unification, which he believed would destroy individual fortunes and breed revolution and massacres. He assured Zenaide that unity was strictly a utopian idea because, even if the Italians themselves achieved it, the Austrians, the French, and even the English would set themselves against the new nation and destroy it. Since the time of the Caesars it had not been possible to achieve unity, so how could we hope to achieve it now, surrounded as we are by all these jealous powers? It was thus necessary to be content with making each individual state better. The pope concluded by saying that all the speeches Charles and Masi had given since their departure from Rome—and he knew all the details of their voyage and of their "triumphs" against the Austrians—would not forward the cause. "Whether you return here immediately, or remain at the congress in Venice," Zenaide tells her husband, "His Holiness has recommended that I use all my influence to calm you and to make you understand that the greatest moderation is indispensable at the moment."[42]

Bonaparte was not to be deterred by Pio Nono or Zenaide, however. And the Austrian authorities did not move in time to stop his election to the presidency of the section of zoology and comparative anatomy, a position that gave him a pulpit. "I will avow," he said, "that the desire I have always had to contribute to the progress and the state of Italian science, has become even greater when I see how the nation has grown greater in the opinion of the world since the advent of Pius IX. It is above all France and England that I have visited in the interval between the congresses of Genoa and Venice, and I assisted with great interest at the British Association held this year in the university city of Oxford. In effect, I saw there the religious spirit continually supporting and stimulating the scientific spirit. You will agree with me that all human enterprise motivated by this double power can only succeed." He went on about the "supreme pontiff" and his liberalism, the "great national glory and prosperity" of Italy, and "not stopping the drive of the Italian Risorgimento." He said that it was with joy that he found himself in Venice in the midst of the most illustrious representatives of Italian science. "But why must this joy be troubled by the absence of a great number of our colleagues from Rome, Turin, and Florence, who have not come to this meeting, in spite of the gracious invitation sent to them? They are held back by a lack of confidence in the irresistible force of things which henceforth irrevocably will carry along princes and ordinary people on the road of progress."[43] Bonaparte was not careful with his words, either in the hall of the congress or at the Café Florian in the Piazza San Marco, "the drawing room of Venice," where he wore his provocative uniform. He had dared to appear this way also at the congress and even at the residence of the governor. Inevitably, the following day at five o'clock in the morning, several police agents forced their way into his lodging. Scarcely allowing him time to dress—while he muttered that Italians certainly had much to fear from Germans—they escorted him and Masi to the border. More than a punishment, it was a warning to the other scientists. The congress continued, but the atmosphere was decidedly heavy.[44] Bonaparte, on the other hand, exulted in being judged a revolutionary. A contemporary wrote from Venice that "the prince of Canino came and has gone. It seems, in fact, that he came on purpose to go away, because he used such language in public and in Italian [rather than German?] that the government had reasons to send him on his way."[45]

Back in Rome, he continued to agitate, totally disregarding the pope's attempt to dissuade him. He wrote John Edward Gray at the British Museum that he expected Gray had seen the speech that got him "so *gloriously* sent off from Venice by the Austrian tyrants of that fair city!" He also hoped Gray had seen his daughter "Julia, Marchioness of Roccagiovine," to whom he been unable to give letters of introduction for her trip to England, as she was to have met him in Venice where would have given them to her. He signs his letter "with the warmest hopes of a real regeneration of this fair land."[46]

Geoffroy, just returned to Paris after a long voyage, informed him that the French newspapers mentioned him every day: "The discussions speak little of the Italian cause . . . they say you have been blamed and are out of favor [*disgracié*] with the pope. But they speak of you in a manner totally deserving [*digne*], and I was delighted to read of your election to the presidency of the zoology section at the congress of Venice. Let me know your news that is in contrast to that of the newspapers [let me know what really happened]."[47]

In response to a scathing Austrian article that claimed what he had said at the congress in Venice had nothing to do with science, Bonaparte responded that the spirit of liberty and independence had already been breathed into the congresses' first program in 1838. "Did you not find it at Pisa, at Florence, at Turin, at Lucca, at Milan—a place dominated by Austria—also at Naples, at Genoa, and even Padua, a city so close to Venice? All the world knows that for a long time the scientific congresses have been the only way by which Italy could achieve national power to the high degree that she merits and can no longer wait to attain."[48]

Shortly after his return to Rome, he was arrested for his revolutionary activities and brought before the commandant of the Civil Guard (in some histories called the National Guard). Bonaparte protested that he had been arrested by an officer of the Civil Guard's ninth battalion, of which he was a member. Also, it had been said that he was in good health, which was a lie, because he was suffering from an attack of gout and was even now limping and suffering greatly. Nevertheless, he was "free to respond to your questions and to confound the calumniators of Italy."

To the question whether he possessed a uniform of the Civil Guard and, if so, how many times he had worn it, Bonaparte answered that indeed he owned one, and in his enthusiasm he had been one of the first [citizens] to wear it. He had worn it the afternoon of 7 September at his audience with the pope and had slept in it that night. Two days later, he had put it on again when he left for Venice and did not cease to wear it until his return to Rome on the 20th. The commandant asked whether he had worn it on the streets of Rome the night after his audience with the pope. "I had been with a group of Romans," he answered, "and after dismissing my carriage I returned to my house on foot by way of the Corso, where I saw a large crowd assembled before the beaux-arts café. In their curiosity to see my uniform, they opened a passage for me into the café. I was joined by two others in the same uniform, and when we left we were soon followed by a large crowd which was doubled by another in the Piazza de Populo." The uniform had undoubtedly aroused revolutionary ardor in the populace, because of its implication of secular rule.

After the questioning ceased in mid-October, since Bonaparte had to appear more than once, his case was pending for five months. Then, in March 1848, he was summoned before the tribunal of the papal court and charged with wearing the costume of the Civil Guard, insulting the authorities, abusing the name of the Roman people, and shouting seditious threats in the Piazza Venetia, which included "Death to the Jesuits!" This last he hotly denied, saying he did not wish death to anyone.[49] Because of his lawyer's eloquent defense, denouncing the arrest of a Roman prince in the heart of the Villa Borghese (his aunt had been Pauline Borghese, so this was family property) Bonaparte was acquitted, but the ordeal left him more radicalized than ever and even more convinced that the clergy should be stripped of their temporal power.

Bonaparte was not alone in his heightened sense of crisis. All across Europe, revolutionary ferment was building. In France, there was general and deep dissatisfaction with Louis-Philippe's rule because he had not enacted the reforms anticipated when he ascended the throne in 1830. Every one of the German states was seeking a constitution, and a popular movement was pushing Prussia and Austria to join in a united Germany, either a republic or an empire. In Hungary, a strong movement for national independence was gaining ground.

In Italy, the organization Giovine Italia (Young Italy), inaugurated in 1834 by Giuseppe Mazzini, the Italian patriot and prophet of the Risorgimento, kept hatred of Austrian rule alive while advocating a free and united country. Mazzini would have welcomed either a king or a pope. He wrote Pius IX in early September of 1847, urging him to unite Italy under papal leadership and said that unification would come in any case because it was part of God's plan, but papal patronage would be an immense blessing. "With you at our head our struggle will take on a religious aspect and liberate us from many risks of reaction and civil war."[50]

The pope did not accept Mazzini's proposal. To unite Italy, it was necessary to drive the Austrians out of the northern part of the peninsula. This he would not do, for he was the spiritual leader of the church universal and could not declare war on a Catholic country, especially one that had been his strongest supporter. A contemporary historian and statesman, Luigi Carlo Farini, wrote of Pio Nono that "in the secret struggles of his mind, pontifical and priestly conference [soliloquy] always outweighed the conscience of the prince and citizen."[51] In actuality, the pope was in an impossible position.

In mid-July the Austrians sent eight hundred Croats in full war regalia to occupy Ferrara, part of the Papal States. Although a champion of peace, Pio Nono recognized his responsibility to preserve the independence and integrity of the church's province and sent troops to keep watch over the situation, though not to fight, while awaiting the outcome of diplomatic initiatives.[52] Prince Metternich called on France and England to maintain the territorial divisions of the Italian peninsula resolved on at Vienna in 1815. Louis-Philippe's powerful minister Guizot seconded Metternich's request, approved Austria's occupation of Ferrara, and instructed the French ambassador to Rome,

Pellegrino Rossi, to attempt to prevent the pope from taking actions displeasing to Austria. On the other hand, Lord Palmerston, the liberal British prime minister, opposed Austria's interference in the internal affairs of the Italian states.

Meanwhile, in Piedmont, the enigmatic and vacillating Charles Albert supported Pio Nono in words but did nothing to resist the Austrian aggression. It was suspected by the Vatican, as well as by Lombardy, that Charles Albert sought to expand his state at the expense of the lesser duchies of north central Italy.[53]

In this same year of 1847, Mazzini had inaugurated in London, where it was completely acceptable, a People's International League, "to embody and manifest an efficient public opinion in favour of the right of every people to self-government and the maintenance of their own nationality." Charles Dickens, who was engaged in his own crusade to expose the dark side of England's industrial revolution, served on the league's regulating committee. The league would not survive, but Mazzini's visions of nationhood and international community were far ahead of his time. Bonaparte must have approved of Mazzini's collected writings, published in Lugano in the same year, which subsequently forced Charles Albert and Leopold of Tuscany to grant political reforms, because of the popular demands embedded in Mazzini writings that they could no longer resist.[54] While in London, Mazzini had met Verdi, by then an idol of Italian revolutionaries. The choruses of *Nabucco* and *I Lombardi* gave their movement a voice, and the association of Pius IX and the chorus from *Ernani*—based on Victor Hugo's subversive play *Hernani*, with its glorification of the bandit Hernani and its attack on authority—had roused Milanese audiences to demonstrate, at a time when this was forbidden. *Attila*, also, championed patriotism in emotion-laden lines.[55] *Nabucco*, performed in April in Milan, had set off a near-riot—the baritone had been arrested and the conductor threatened with jail.[56]

Bonaparte probably met Verdi in Rome, at a banquet given in his honor by Prince Alessandro Torlonia to celebrate the premiere of *I Due Foscari* on 3 November 1844. Set in Venice, the libretto is based on an historical drama by Byron, popular not only for his poetry but also for his devotion to the cause of Greek independence from Turkey. Like Mazzini, Verdi became a prophet of the people. Bonaparte, with his revolutionary sympathies, rich cultural heritage, and lifelong love of opera, was a strong supporter of both men.

Great masterpieces of literature also addressed the struggle for Italian independence. *I promessi sposi* (*The Betrothed*), Alessandro Manzoni's brilliant novel of seventeenth-century Lombardy under the repressive administration of

Spain, published in its first version in 1825–27, was a barely concealed protest against the Austrian subjugation of Manzoni's own day. Stendhal's *The Charterhouse of Parma* (1839) satirized the autocratic rule of an absolute monarchy over a small principality during the 1830s and 1840s.

For Bonaparte and others who shared his views, recent political events on the other side of the Atlantic had also fired their imaginations. Europeans could there witness an example of national determination, or "manifest destiny," in the American war against Mexico. By 1846, American troops had driven the Mexicans out of the southwestern part of the continent and added to the United States the vast region that would become the states of California and New Mexico. Though the United States was extending rather than unifying its territory, its actions were perceived as nation building and encouraged Bonaparte and like-minded patriots in their struggle to consolidate the peninsula and free it from Austrian and papal domination. In referring to the courage and resourcefulness of Americans to establish a free, unified, and independent state, Bonaparte had written his mother in 1823: "Oh, happy country, which possesses that which Italy is so far from possessing."[57]

By December, Mazzini, in London, was prepared with a forged American passport to enter Italy the moment revolution broke out. He had also raised money to charter a ship for the return from South America of the freedom fighter Garibaldi and his "Italian legion."[58] In Rome, at the center of growing disillusionment with the pope's inadequate concessions and his intransigence in transferring his temporal power to a civil authority, Bonaparte put aside natural science as politics overwhelmed him.

12

A PRINCE IN
POLITICAL
TRENCHES

"Posterity must find the true history of
revolutions in our era more in the
extemporaneous speeches of men who took
an active part than in the laborious
accounts of those who were actors or
witnesses."

—*Discours, allocutions et opinions de
Charles-Lucien Bonaparte* (preface).

THE YEAR 1848 was a fateful one for the European continent, and certainly for Charles Bonaparte. In early January a revolt in Sicily against the tyrant Ferdinand II, the Hapsburg ruler of the kingdom of Naples, set the ground rumbling with revolution in the rest of Italy and in France and Germany. By the end of the month Ferdinand was forced to grant constitutions to both Sicily and Naples. Because his uncle and father-in-law Joseph had been king of Naples from 1806 to 1808, Bonaparte took a keen personal interest in the city-state's affairs and of course applauded its move toward republicanism.

In Piedmont and Tuscany, Charles Albert and his brother-in-law, the grand duke Leopold, also had no choice but to grant constitutions to their subjects. And Pius IX felt so threatened by the news from Sicily and Naples that he issued a proclamation announcing the enlargement of his army and the appointment of more laymen to his Council of Ministers. At the announcement of this last concession, an immense crowd gathered in the Piazza del Populo. In the midst of it, of course, was the prince of Canino. With banners held high, the great throng marched to the Vatican. The pope, appearing on his balcony, warned them against making requests that were incompatible with the sanctity of the Church, for he could not grant them. In Austria Metternich was decidedly alarmed when word reached him that the pope had allowed such demonstrations to happen at all. Subsequently, the Austrian field marshal Johann Joseph Radetzky declared Venice to be in a state of siege and threw the revolutionary leader Daniele Manin in jail.

With the earth shaking around and beneath him, Bonaparte heard reassuring words from Geoffroy in Paris: "Do not forget that in these very difficult times you have *true friends* here."[1] Several weeks later Geoffroy's own city erupted in violence. On 24 February, barricades were thrown across the streets and cries of "Down with Guizot!" echoed through Paris. Louis-Philippe, who had totally lost his people's confidence and had been too late in dismissing his authoritarian ministers, including Guizot, was forced to abdicate and flee to England. In his absence, a provisional government declared a republic, knowing the other powers of Europe were helpless to intervene, because every monarch was occupied with preserving his own kingdom. "A new '89 is in preparation!" shouts a character in *A Sentimental Education*, Flaubert's fictional account of the 1848 revolution. "People are tired of constitutions, charters, subtleties, lies!"

Shortly afterward bloody street fighting in Berlin compelled the Prussian king, Frederick William IV, to grant a constitution, and in mid-March a revolt, unexpected and much welcomed by liberals, broke out in Vienna. Metternich, the high priest of repression and enemy of Italian unification, his grand house in flames, was forced to escape the city in a washerwoman's cart. Blaming the Vatican for unleashing the liberal ideas that brought about his downfall, he is supposed to have said: "We were prepared for everything except a democratic pope."[2]

In the great piazza before St. Mark's Cathedral, Manin, who had been released from jail, declared Venice a republic. News of the Venetian revolt caused unbounded excitement among the masses in Rome. Bonaparte would have heard guns going off and every bell in the Eternal City ringing. He would have seen flowers strewn everywhere and flags mounted on balconies and towers. And from his palace in the Piazza Venezia he could have witnessed the Austrian flag with its double-headed eagle stripped from the Palazzo Venezia, as shouts of "Italia! Italia!" filled the air.

In Austria-dominated Milan, the reaction to the revolt in Venice was more violent. The populace—mostly workmen and artisans—attacked the Austrian garrison and expelled its soldiers after five days of vicious fighting, the famous "cinque giornate." Encouraged by the Milanese, the people in the duchies of Parma and Modena ousted their princes and forced them to flee.

Charles Albert, king of Piedmont, taking the lead in the fight against Austria—as it was believed, more for his own aggrandizement than for nationalistic reasons—called for volunteers from all over Italy to join him in his war to win Lombardy and unite it to his own kingdom. Only a small number showed up, however. All the Italian states together contributed less than a quarter of the men that Piedmont sent into battle. Pope Pius reluctantly sent a small force under General Giovanni Durando, but when the general led his troops across the Po River—the Austrian border—the pope recalled him. General Durando, however, taking the situation into his own hands, continued northward with his depleted force to join the Piedmontese. Ferdinand of Naples, against his will but under much pressure, sent his regular army under General Pepe to aid the Piedmontese. The people of Lombardy, themselves caught up in internal squabbles, were of negligible assistance in this first Italian war of independence. They were particularly suspicious of Charles Albert's ambition—with good reason, for he annexed Parma and Modena in May, Lombardy in June, and Venetia in July.

On 29 April Pope Pius gave a speech in which he said he would not prevent his subjects from volunteering, as individuals, to fight in the war for Italian independence, but he could not declare war on Austria. In the Papal States this decree sowed profound seeds of distrust. Turbulence broke out in Rome because it was widely believed that the pope had delivered a fatal blow to the Italian cause. To restore order, on 4 May the pope allowed the ministry of Count Terenzio Mamiani della Rovere, a liberal, to assume leadership of the Roman parliament. Mamiani appointed Charles Bonaparte deputy from Viterbo.

The Roman parliament had been in session for only a few weeks when, in mid-June, the president, Mamiani, announced the capitulation of General Durando's troops at Vicenza. With the fervor and theatricality that were so much a part of his nature, Bonaparte leapt to his feet and shouted: "To arms, Italians! To arms! The moment has come to wage war to the death. If your ancestors had not been defeated many times by Hannibal, republican Rome would not have been the greatest nation in the world." With these words, he touched the very heart of the Risorgimento mystique: the recovery of an idealized past. "Italians, after so many lost years in the debasements and corruption of despotism, we must not wait to be vanquished by our enemies [the Austrians] at the first encounter." He suggested that the Roman troops be put at once under the leadership of Charles Albert, "that truly Italian king." "*Signori*," he said, "you know that I have never had a weakness for kings, not even those of my family. But I swear to you, Charles Albert, after having embraced me, declared his intentions to deliver and advance our country."[3]

A week later Bonaparte proposed that the Italian insurgents accept help from France. He said he hated the thought of foreign intervention, "of which even the idea should not come to a good Italian today." But in a desperate situation surely it is permissible to accept outside help, especially since that help is "no longer from France under the princes of the degenerate house of Bourbon [Louis-Philippe had fled to England], but from France which, in proclaiming a republic, has reestablished its rights in full. We will not call upon the French with joy, with enthusiasm, as our adversaries call upon the Austrians, but with regret we will call upon them out of necessity." (After all, though he did not say so, his own brother Pierre and two of his cousins, Prince Napoleon, or "Plon-Plon," and Lucien Murat, son of Bonaparte's late aunt Caroline, were all deputies in the French assembly, elected in April.[4]) Bonaparte added that the Romans must be prepared for financial sacrifices; taxes on luxuries and on the rich especially must be imposed, for heretofore the burden of the government has weighed almost exclusively on the classes least able to support it.[5]

Bonaparte's social conscience and his ideas on government were enlightened and progressive for his time, and the Council of Deputies provided him with the forum he had been waiting for all his life. At last he could express his ideas on social justice where it was appropriate to do so. In his speeches before the scientific congresses he had always risked arrest by expressing his radical political views; even so, he had certainly never been reticent to encourage independence from Austria and the unification of Italy. At the council, however, he could also put forward those demands for social reform to which he and other liberal thinkers of his day were equally devoted: women's rights, prison reform, an end to anti-semitism, a rectification of the inequities of the death penalty, a stop to economic exploitation of the poor, and freedom of religion. An idealist, too emotional and too conflicted to be a leader, he was unable to effect change in the repressive period and milieu in which he lived. But by his impassioned oratory, often enriched with quotes from the classics of Roman literature, he must have encouraged social reform in the minds of his scientific and political colleagues.

He addressed the parliament in late June, saying that all government should come from the people; history, political science, and religion all teach us that maxim. "Liberty comes to us from God," he said, "and the most noble attribute of man is to use this divine gift in all that he does." Only to pronounce this magic name of liberty moves him in all the fibers of his being. "*Signori*, it is the renewal of a whole society that we undertake today . . . to open up all the sources of public good for the diverse members of Italian society and to at last leave that state of atrophy in which it has languished for so long. The task is immense." He stated that the civil and criminal codes—was he thinking of the Napoleonic Code his uncle had initiated in France and which had been copied in much of Europe?—needed revision since they were based on "the barbarity of the Middle Ages." Women should have legal rights, especially the right to make contracts; the laws of primogeniture should be abolished and the age of majority reduced; and prisons should be constructed on a totally different model, allowing them to "become schools of moral instruction instead of, as today, schools of perversity." A uniform system of weights and measures and of monetary values should be established throughout Italy, in order to facilitate exchange and restrain fraud. Better public education was needed, above all, better primary schools. He also proposed that admission to the museums of Rome should be free for its citizens, who had such a lively interest in letters and in fine arts. "It seems right to me that the Vatican museum and all the masterpieces of which it is full should at last be declared national property." Bonaparte finished on the note of optimism that was so much a part of his personality: "*Signori*, keep always present in your minds the marvelous destiny reserved by Providence for the city of Rome. Ancient Rome believed, and modern Rome would not deny, that a truly prophetic spirit animated the poet [Virgil] who said:

Roman, remember by your strength to rule
Earth's peoples—for your arts are to be these:
To pacify, to impose the rule of law,

To spare the conquered, battle down the proud.

[Tu regere imperio populos, Romane, memento;
Hae tibi erunt artes, pacisque imponere morem,
Parcere subiectis et debellare superbos.][6]

"Is it not true, he continued, "that the rude Calabrian on his mountains, the ingenuous Tuscan on the banks of the Arno, the Venetian living happily in the lagoons, and other Italians from the greatest to the smallest, all different in character and in spirit but united by sentiments and language, form in their happy assemblage a nation worthy to hold the first rank among the most powerful of Europe?"[7]

When an amendment was proposed to urge the pope to continue the war and thus erase the dishonor of the Treaty of Campo Formio—Napoleon's treaty of 1797 giving the Venetian Republic to Austria, whom he had defeated—Bonaparte quickly rose to defend the honor of his family. "What is your intention here?" he snapped. "We all agree not to leave Austria one inch of Italian territory. Mentioning the Treaty of Campo Formio does nothing to confirm the patriotic determination we all have." Thinking that perhaps he had been too hasty, he added, "but perhaps this observation would be better placed in another mouth than mine . . . [still], the glory of a hero is not the heritage of a family, nor of a nation; it is the patrimony of the entire world. I cannot understand the fitness of this accusation against a great man who honored his modest Italian birth in living gloriously French." He was interrupted by shouts that the treaty of Campo Formio was "an iniquity!" "It was a bad treaty, I do not deny it," he agreed, "but is it the only memory that evokes the epoch of Napoleon? And since you are silent on other acts that do him honor, why can't you also be silent on one that was a stain on his life? Is it the time to call as a criminal before your tribunal the shade of a great man who, if he still lived, would, with a flash of his valiant sword, rout the Austrians who disgrace Italy by their presence?" He added that not only the generosity of the Italian nation but also the spirit of equity should suppress the malevolent allusion to a man who was one of the glories of France as well as of Italy.[8] In the fevered flush of his defense, Bonaparte, true to his Corsican ancestry of closing ranks around his family, had completely forgotten the long-ago menace of the ambitious tiger that overshadowed his childhood.

On the last day of June he again addressed the issue of legal reform, so crucial to the new government. This time he tackled the death penalty: "Today I wish to look at judicial reform from the point of view of a principle that I often expounded in the scientific congresses, which were the cradle of Italian liberty."

He said that the wrongdoer who has fallen into the hands of justice does not lose any of the rights of a member of society. On the contrary, he acquires a new one: the right to be set on a good path. Thus the right of society to punish the culpable is subsumed with, and lost in, the duty of working toward their amelioration. It was the glory of Leopold II of Tuscany that he abolished the death penalty from his state. And it was not long ago that Rome removed from its codes the punishment of quartering—one of the infernal inventions of the legislators of the Middle Ages, who believed that only excess of terror [for those witnessing the quartering] could restrain crime. Pope Gregory XVI substituted death by firing squad. Moreover, the death penalty was inequitably meted out. "I have never understood," Bonaparte declared, "how the more elevated a rank in society a citizen holds, the more extenuating circumstances are cited for his offense in order to soften it in his favor." He pointed out that in certain countries serious criminals of the nobility have the right to be beheaded while for the same offense the commoner must be hanged. "It is never the people who demand exceptions in their favor; generous by nature, they submit without opposition to the common law." He particularly demanded the abolition of the death penalty for political offenses.[9]

The next day he held forth on the lottery, which he said, "only ignites the most ignoble passions by the unequal contest it establishes between deceitful government agents and the incredulous public." Government swindling dishonors honest men. "The kings of England and Prussia have abolished the lottery—is it not astonishing that an ecclesiastical government such as Rome's, which should be an example of morality, has not taken the initiative in this matter?" Bonaparte added, perhaps with a slight smile: "One would be astonished if it refused to follow the good example set by heretical princes." His proposition was rejected, however.[10]

At the same session, he continued his attacks on the violation of human rights in Rome, this time speaking out on behalf of the Jews, who were confined in the ghetto and denied their proper rights. "Do you not recall that in this past year an Israelite, Lionel Rothschild, was elected, after much opposition, to the parliament of Great Britain? I had the good fortune, being in London at the time, to contribute in a small way to this victory of reason and the public interest over deplorable prejudices. [He had apparently spoken in Rothschild's favor when he visited parliament in 1847.] Is there no one today to support my supposition that a cause as just will soon triumph here as it has triumphed in France and England?"[11] Unfortunately, because Bonaparte was way ahead of his colleagues in his humanitarian ideas, many of his suggestions for equity and justice were bypassed without further discussion, as was this one.

On 17 July the minister of the interior announced to the Chamber of

Deputies that five thousand Austrian troops had crossed the Po River and established themselves in the territory of Ferrara. When informed of this incursion, the pope had been indignant but had taken no action. The next day, as the deputies became immersed in petty debates over procedures, Bonaparte interrupted to urge that everything of little importance be put aside so that they could occupy themselves totally with the war. "Do not imitate the last councils of the decadent Greek empire," he cautioned, "who, while the barbarians besieged the city, lost time in scholastic disputes, until the assailants forced the door of their meeting room and massacred them all." He asked the chamber to declare the country [all of Italy not under Austrian rule—the Austrians held Veneto and Lombardy] in danger and called for a special meeting to conserve the menaced northern provinces of the Papal States. One of the deputies stated emphatically that the pope would never make war on Austria. Bonaparte replied that this was a question of a defensive not an offensive, war, and that all military actions taken so far had been defensive, because fought on Italian soil. Italians had never attacked; they had always been attacked. "The offensive will begin," he said, "the day we cross the Tyrol mountains and take the war into Germany [including Austria]. If we ask the Germans to respect our nationality, it is because we have decided to respect theirs." A commission was then organized to speak to the pope about the Roman army joining the Piedmontese army to fight for the cause of Italian independence. Bonaparte was one of five deputies selected for this mission.[12] His assignment had the support of the people. Outside in the courtyard of the Palazzo della Cancelleria [Chancellery], a large crowd had gathered and was shouting, "To arms! To arms!"

But the next day Bonaparte and his colleagues reported to the chamber that the pope had refused their request. He had said it was not necessary to do battle, because the territory of the church was inviolable and its exclusive possession by the pontiffs of Rome was a European right. He did not believe the Papal States were in danger and therefore he would not take exceptional measures to protect them. Even so, the chamber voted to authorize the defense of their country. The Roman army at that point was not impressive: it had been recruited from a large number of young and inexperienced volunteers and the officers had been chosen by mob acclamation in a public place. Earlier in the summer the army had gone to war as to a festival. After the first few reverses, all discipline had been lost and the chief officers unfairly accused of treason. At the meeting of 21 July 1848, Bonaparte hotly defended General Durando against this charge, pointing out that "we have in modern Rome generous judges of integrity, very different from the judges of ancient Carthage, who crucified their generals when they returned in defeat."[13]

In spite of the pope's April pronouncement against the war and his continued refusal to support it, the Piedmontese on their own continued to push back the Austrians. But the fatal blow to the Italian cause had come in mid-May when Ferdinand II of Naples withdrew his troops at a crucial moment. Their departure and the capture of General Durando's papal army at Vicenza in mid-July had enabled the Austrians to turn their entire force against the Piedmontese and defeat them at the town of Custoza toward the end of the month. A modern historian has stated, however, that "well before Custoza, Charles Albert's open policy of aggrandizement destroyed all the momentary wave of common purpose which had united patriots of all tendencies in the Italian states."[14] The war also failed for lack of popular support. It was hoped that the peasants would join the fight, but they had soon been alienated by the army's ruthless requisition of supplies in the countryside. For the peasants, putting food on their tables was a much more immediate and pressing concern than political independence or nationhood. After the battles they robbed the fallen Italian and Austrian soldiers indiscriminately. Dissatisfaction with the status quo did not always translate into active political or military support for change, and demands for local autonomy, fear of insurrection, and individual ambition often clashed with liberal ideals of national independence, constitutional government, and economic reform. Moreover, Mazzini's anticlericalism had alienated the rural clergy, who had enormous local influence and could have won peasant support for the national cause.[15] The writer/priest Gioberti observed that the beliefs, rituals, and language of the Catholic Church united Italians in ways that the idea of a secular nation could not.[16]

In the Council of Deputies, Bonaparte advocated that the representatives of the country take up the scepter of a fallen government [the pope's] and resist the inertia that was leading to disaster. Again, he was part of a committee selected to appear before Pio Nono and plead for his help in this matter of inaction. The deputation was to demand the mobilization of twelve thousand national guards and the recruitment of an equal number of volunteers, as well as the enrollment of a foreign legion and the release of money from the treasury. Before leaving the chamber, Bonaparte heard the minister of police report on a disturbance in the city in which the council president was insulted by a group of peasants. They had been severely dealt with, and the people of Rome would approve this police action, the minister said, because it was the people themselves who had been outraged in the person of the president. This was perhaps another instance of the peasant class, united by and devoted to the church, perceiving the new secular government as elitist and not representative of their age-old interests.

More sensitive than most to these issues, at the next session Bonaparte objected to a proposed loan to raise money for the troops. He thought a loan would bring considerable suffering on the poor and work to the advantage of the rich, for it would diminish the supply of money and cause interest to rise at a ruinous rate. The usurers alone would profit from this measure. At the same time, he urged the deputies to declare war against Austria. Such an action would not show ingratitude to the pope; on the contrary, he was the one who had taken the initiative on reform, and his warm allocutions had moved the masses at a moment when the propaganda of the liberals, the Carbonari, and Mazzini's Young Italy could not. "Is it not with the cry of 'long live Pius IX' that the cities of Palermo and Milan have accomplished their first, their glorious revolutions?" By evoking such memories, Bonaparte hoped to persuade the chamber. The war was a fact, he said, and Pope Pius had blessed the banners carried by the Roman troops across the Po River. (Bonaparte, shrewdly, did not mention that the pope had denounced General Durando for this action.) He proposed that the chamber declare war in the name of the Roman people, an honorable enterprise and justified by their constitution, because the religious office of their sovereign (Pius IX) denied him the right to declare war. But all Bonaparte's urging was not enough to move the reluctant chamber, and it was decided that the pope alone had the prerogative to declare war.

On 14 August the president announced with deep regret that Charles Albert had signed an armistice with Austria at Milan and that everything had been reestablished as it was before the Piedmontese offensive. In consolation, he wished to remind the Romans that various peoples—the Dutch, the French, the Americans—had won their independence only after prolonged struggle and many terrible defeats. To follow in the footsteps of these peoples to enjoy the emancipation they now enjoyed Italians must be ready to stand, or fall, together.

Two days later Bonaparte caused a great stir in the council by announcing that there were enormous abuses in the bureau of war. Much had been lost through the bad administration of this department, he said. A thousand pairs of shoes destined for the troops, first paid for by the Venetian government and then by the Roman, had been fraudulently resold. The soldiers never received a single pair, and many were now barefoot. He called the minister of war to account. Amid numerous angry shouts of "Prove what you say!" Bonaparte responded, "When I bring a fact of this nature to the tribunal, you can be quite certain that I can prove it." He had a number of questions to ask the war minister, but a deputy interrupted him and requested that he not continue. At this point Bonaparte's colleagues drowned him out with shouting, and the president declared that the discussion would continue the next day in secret session. To this decision Bonaparte objected heatedly: military affairs should be publicly debated, and nothing should be hidden. "Leave the Roman cardinals and the

Mohammedan viziers to concoct intrigues out of their shadowy politics within the four walls of a consistory or the length of a divan," he exclaimed; "a parallel situation is unworthy of us; it leaves us open to suspicion in the eyes of the country, and the loss of [the people's] confidence would be more detrimental [to our cause] than keeping our affairs secret."[17]

As August wore on there were conflicting reports about the progress of the fighting in other parts of Italy. When news came from the Vatican that the Austrians had pulled back and it was no longer necessary to send guns for the troops, Bonaparte sensed an undercurrent of malicious intrigue. He told his colleagues they were victims of a clandestine government (the Vatican) that paralyzed all the efforts of the best-intentioned ministers. When would an end be put to this flagrant unconstitutionality [not allowing the ministers to handle affairs that were in their province], which menaced the country with an approaching catastrophe? He demanded that all the money the Bolognese need be sent to them at once; he said that when he heard two cardinals had been dispatched as envoys to Bologna (part of the Papal States), he had thought this a strange choice, because he did not trust anyone connected with the church to give the Bolognese money to fight the Austrians. "I must tell the chamber, this caused me great anxiety; I was truly frightened by it."[18]

Several days later he read a letter sent to him privately by General Pepe, the Neapolitan commander who had disregarded the orders of his king, Ferdinand II, to return to Naples in the spring and instead had continued to fight the Austrians in the north. The general asked that the vessel *Roma*, which traveled between Venice and Ravenna, not be retired, because it was carrying arms to be stored in the Venetian arsenal. The men and women around him were making great sacrifices so that the "Queen of the Lagoons" would not fall to the Austrians. They lacked clothes, guns, ammunition—in fact, everything, except the resolution never to submit, which would be the irrevocable price of not sending these supplies. Bonaparte demanded that the *Roma* be kept in service. He offered a motion that the chamber allocate whatever was left of their resources to "the brave Italians shut up in Venice, who have taken an oath to be buried in the lagoons rather than to fall into the hands of their oppressors." Another deputy observed that the Sardinian fleet, on quitting the Adriatic, had left the Austrians masters of the sea, and he believed that they had captured the *Roma* along with other ships. Bonaparte answered that, even if the boat had fallen into enemy hands—and we don't know this for sure—it would be better to state that we would not retire it than to let their brothers believe that they had been abandoned and deprived of a last resort in their desperate circumstances. His proposal to send money to Venice was voted on and approved. At the end of this session, much to the dismay and consternation of all the deputies, a communication from the pope decreed the adjournment of the chamber until 15 November. The Commission of Finance alone was to remain in operation during the interval.[19]

In early November, since the Council of Deputies was in recess, Bonaparte traveled north to Leghorn, in Tuscany, to attend a meeting of republicans. Professor Carlo Pigli, governor of the city, opened the meeting by introducing the "great hero" Garibaldi, newly arrived from the far-off South America, as "an Italian refugee who, unable to fight for the independence of his own country has fought for that of other oppressed nations . . . this valiant man, this hero, is in your presence . . . honor, in person, the strongest defender of the Italian cause!" After introducing the Romeos, two heroes from Sicily and Calabria, the professor then turned to Bonaparte, who he said "was born at the foot of the most splendid throne of the world and was prince by blood, and stands before you . . . in only the uniform of a sergeant in the holy crusade of the Italian people." There were cries of "Viva Bonaparte!"

"Citizens," Pigli continued, "honor this bond of kinship which unites in his person the two greatest nations of the world, Italy and France . . . honor this link of the two greatest miracles of humanity: the empire of Napoleon and the emancipation of the people." After the applause died down, Bonaparte said he rejoiced with them that Leopold II (the Tuscan ruler) had become the first Italian king to embrace democracy; he had set a great example as an Italian monarch who both threw off the yoke of Austria and recognized the sovereignty of the Italian people. Turning to one of the young Romeos, he said that if it were not for physical infirmity he would follow him into battle. This was not an idle boast: he had proved his physical bravery on many occasions. There were renewed cries of "Viva Garibaldi!" "Viva Carlo Bonaparte!"[20]

At noon on 15 November, when the council reconvened, the deputies began to drift in and take their places on the benches of the meeting room in the Chancellery. Most arrived late and paid little attention to the first speaker, who lectured on legal procedures. The main event of the day was to be the appearance of the former ambassador from France to Rome, Count Pellegrino Rossi, the pope's rigidly restrictive, antidemocratic new minister of state, appointed on 15 September, who would address them on the politics of the pope's new cabinet. Rossi, born in Tuscany in 1787, had long been a voluntary exile from the Papal States for political activities in his youth. A French citizen, professor at the Sorbonne, and member of the Upper Chamber of the French government, he had so impressed Guizot that he had sent Rossi to Rome to negotiate for the suppression of the French Jesuits. Although Rossi's books were on the Index and he had a Protestant wife, the pope liked and trusted him and appointed him to replace Count Mamiani. Rossi was committed to preserving the pope's temporal power, not by concessions to the democrats but by economic reform and enlightened administration. His determination to protect the pope from the radicals of the war party had roused the various political clubs in Rome to put a price on his head.[21] Bonaparte, one of the most radical of the deputies, was particularly reluctant to welcome this man, who stood for the majority of principles he bitterly opposed.

The sound of horses' hooves on the stone pavement signaled that Rossi's carriage had entered the courtyard of the Chancellery. A large crowd pressed forward and held onto the horses. When the door was opened for the minister, the people began to hiss, whistle, and curse his name. As the count stepped down and started toward the deputies' council room, he turned to face them and with a sardonic smile waved his gloves playfully. At that instant someone pushed close to him and plunged a dagger into his throat. His piercing cry silenced the mob, who stood shocked and unmoving as two people lifted the dying man and carried him to the antechamber of Cardinal Gazzoli in the Chancellery. Doctors arrived almost at once, but Count Rossi was dead in minutes.[22]

Inside the council chamber, the deputies were told to remain at their posts, and—perhaps not strangely, considering the general hostility toward Rossi— the meeting continued without reference to the murder that had just occurred beneath the chamber's very windows. For the rest of the day the city remained oppressively quiet; everyone knew that the pontifical court was in turmoil. The following day the streets and squares filled with agitated crowds, enraged over the various men the pope had proposed to replace Rossi. Instead of the pontiff's choices, they wanted a minister more sympathetic to them and faithful to democratic principles. An inflamed mob, led by a few deputies—Bonaparte more than likely among them—marched to the Quirinal Palace, the pope's residence, demanding the convocation of a constituent assembly (an elected body representing various constituencies of Italy) and insisting on the deputies' right to decide whether the Papal States would participate in the war of national liberation. When the pope refused to grant their demands, the younger, more hotheaded insurgents threatened to burn down the palace and kill all its inhabitants, except the pope.[23] The Swiss guards stopped them from entering the Quirinal; a gun was fired and the guards instantly responded with a volley. In minutes the Roman police were on the scene and quelled the disturbance.

Five days passed before the deputies met again. Bonaparte opened the meeting by saying that the only urgent business of the day was to satisfy the needs of Italy. He decried the fact that brave Roman soldiers had been sent to Venice only to die of illnesses brought on by lack of food and clothing. He called for the convocation of a constituent assembly—a demand that had been put forth by proclamation to the people more than a month earlier—for all the Italian states "to draw up a federal compact with respect to the establishment of a single state . . . to secure the liberty, union, and absolute independence of Italy." Bonaparte would be elected vice-president of this assembly.

Then, on 25 November, eight days of complete governmental standstill came to a dramatic end when the minister of police announced officially that the pope had departed into exile, taking up residence in the town of Gaeta in the kingdom of Naples. He had named a committee, consisting of a cardinal, several princes, several marquis, and a general, with full power to govern and administer the Papal States in his absence, but the members of the commission declared their charge impossible to fulfill. Bonaparte incited his colleagues to do what was necessary. He invoked the example of the French Chamber of Deputies after the Revolution of 1830, which did not hesitate to nominate a king, Louis-Philippe, when the throne was left vacant and to impose their choice on the nation, although their official mandate did not give them the right to do so. "At this moment we must make real the difference that exists between the spiritual powers of Pius IX, head of Catholicism, and the temporal powers of Pius IX, king of a constituent regime," he said. "The diplomatic strategy that induced the pope to flight is as prejudicial to his own interests as it is opposed to the principles of the government that he himself established." Putting an adroitly diplomatic spin on the situation, he added, "For us Pius IX is only a prisoner of war, fallen into the hands of ambassadors who are our enemies."[24]

In early December Bonaparte again proposed a gathering in Rome of all the different principalities. Piedmont alone was prosecuting the war against Austria; Venice, isolated in the lagoons, was defending herself; Tuscany was too weak to do anything; and Sicily so far had declined to take an active part in the struggle. "What honor for us!" he urged. "What a benefit for our country if Rome should be the center where all forces, at this time so scattered, unite in one group against a common enemy, whose invasions are becoming more menacing every day."[25]

Two days later a telegraphic dispatch relayed the information that, when news reached France of the pope's flight, an immediate order had gone out for the embarkation of thirty-five hundred men on four state frigates, to be stationed at the port of Toulon. There was a strange contradiction in the order from the French government: France could not intervene between the pope and his subjects, but was dispatching troops to restore the pope to his powers. Fury and indignation broke forth in the Chamber of Deputies at Rome. The president, Mamiani, said that France was treating Italians with an undeserved contempt they would not tolerate, and Bonaparte renewed his pleas for a constituent assembly, in the hope that the continued reiteration of this idea would at last make an impression. The pope had never been denied the power to rule his church, he said. Should an outside power (France) be allowed to divest the Romans of their constitutional liberties? Never had a people been threatened with so unjust a war. He concluded, "This is not an isolated situation, I have seen all over Europe that nations who wish to unjustly crush other nations fall themselves under the tyranny of the man they designate to execute their iniquity. France is menaced with the same thing, and I must say that her enslavement is already accomplished if she gives her assent to the conduct of General Cavaignac [minister of war, a virtual dictator after the flight of Louis-Philippe; Cavaignac was popularly called "the butcher of the barricades"]. We protest immediately and wholeheartedly against the entrance of French troops into these states."

Bonaparte had been cruelly disabused of his belief that the French would assist the Italians in the war against Austria. His feelings about France would become even more complex and strained after the election of his cousin Louis Napoleon as president of the French Republic on 20 December. That same Louis-Napoleon who, with his brother Napoleon-Louis, Charlotte's husband, had fought against Pope Gregory XVI in 1831 as a revolutionary guerilla was now monarch of a country that seemed to be setting itself against Italy's struggle for freedom and nationhood.[26]

How conflicted Bonaparte's feelings were about the French! He had just received a warm letter from Geoffroy who addressed him as "Très cher et illustre collègue," thanked him for writing, and wanted to know the reason for his long silence. Their amiable correspondence had continued without a break from 1838 to 1847, wrote Geoffroy, and had all of a sudden been interrupted by Bonaparte. "Is it not a tribute to our friendship that I regret your silence so much? I will not hide from you that I have been and am distressed by it." "But," he added, "swamped by the great events in the midst of which we live and by which we are totally occupied and agitated, in the midst of the active role that you have been called upon to play for your country, it is natural that you only have a few rare moments!" He commented on the warm "chalereuse," patriotic discourse Bonaparte had sent him in his letter, setting aside all their differences of opinion, the sentiments he had expressed about Italy—that is, union being the common aim of everyone—were good ones. France, he said, was totally occupied with the election of its president. "When I say occupied, I am wrong; it is agitated. Will your cousin be elected president? God alone knows. But if he takes a crown, republicans of all types will be against him. Why have you not been here?—I know your right spirit and your sincere patriotism—the election of a Bonaparte as the second president of the Republic . . . is full of the glory of the emperor and all the heroes of the country."[27]

On 8 December Bonaparte proposed that the council appoint a junta to rule the Papal States. The pope's flight was a veritable abdication, as he had not left a regent to take charge of his affairs. The junta should consist of three Italians—one ecclesiastic and two laymen—to represent the executive and to fulfill the functions; it would be dissolved on the day Pius IX returned of his own free will to his states. This last was surely only a conciliatory move by Bonaparte, but the deputies agreed to the proposal.

The following day he continued to rally his colleagues to convoke a constituent assembly for all the Italian states, including Sicily and the free Venetian territories, to be charged with drawing up a pact of unification, liberty, and independence. There would be a delegate for every three thousand inhabitants. Rome would hold an election by universal suffrage; the other states would be invited to follow suit but free to choose their own method of election. "Rome is destined to be the capital of Italy," he said, "it is thus for us to take the initiative for all concerned in this great affair. I will not finish without recalling to our ministers that beautiful day of 18 November which carried them to power, and during which they heard the word Republic from every mouth."[28]

At that time Bonaparte's aims were even more radical than those of Mazzini, the leading intellectual of the Italian Risorgimento. Mazzini thought the immediate creation of a constituent assembly was unrealizable and insisted on the need to form a republic in the Roman states before convoking an Italian assembly. This would avoid creating a kingdom of central Italy, as the Florentine leader Giuseppe Montanelli wanted, while offering a republican base for the future assembly. He had thought Charles Albert, in particular, would not accept a unification initiative that came from Rome. In any case, the resolution for a constituent assembly was adopted on 9 December 1848.[29]

On 1 January 1849 Pius IX released a thunderbolt on the Papal States by excommunicating all members of the constituent assembly and the hundreds of thousands who had voted for them. Bonaparte had probably anticipated this move, but he and his colleagues did not hear it without feeling. His relations with his wife had been strained before; surely this latest event must have caused her great anguish and widened the breach between them. After all, she had promised Pius IX that she would use all her influence to calm her husband and to make him understand the necessity for moderation. And she had failed. Did she wonder, too, whether her husband had somehow been coerced into participating in the plot to kill Rossi? But if Zenaide was appalled and frightened by the decree of excommunication, it only increased Bonaparte's determination to end the pontiff's vindictive temporal rule.

When the roll was called at the meeting of the deputies on 5 February, with 140 present, Bonaparte answered his name with "Long live the republic!" Garibaldi, present as a deputy, spoke first and called for the immediate proclamation of the republic. "I support the proposition of General Garibaldi," Bonaparte rejoined, "with this modification, that first we proceed to the verification of powers; but when this is done, I believe, as he does, that no one should leave this place before the assembly has resolved on a constitution to govern us."[30]

Two days later Bonaparte, who had been named vice-president of the constituent assembly, announced an important note from the Piedmontese minister Gioberti offering to establish accord with Pius IX. Gioberti proposed that the pope send representatives to take part in the deliberations of the assembly. The court at Turin would place troops at the pope's disposition to protect him against "foreign betrayers and anarchists from within." This proposal astonished the assembly: the pope had already lost his temporal power, the deputies declared. Bonaparte, disillusioned with Charles Albert, said that speaking for himself alone he openly declared himself "the enemy of all princes or assemblies who would put the noble and generous Roman people under the pontifical tiara." He was ready for all sacrifices, he stated, even of his life, to prevent the return of that abhorred regime. The members of the assembly might believe they were committing a sacrilege, and their hands might tremble at the thought; they could assure their consciences that the true principles of religion were not compromised in this affair, and the church could only grow in dignity and influence by taking off the earthly crown that kings had forced upon its head.

Little as one might know of the history of the popes, he continued, one knew that their enthronement, even on the smallest of European states, had been an expedient of the great potentates, conceived with a view not to serving the church but to subjugating it to their own interests. From this had issued the diplomatic intrigues, the exclusions, the buying and selling of church offices—abuses renewed at each pontifical election, to the outrage of all honest souls. "And why have the great powers always gone along with these scandalous practices?" he asked. "You must agree that they do not attempt to elevate the dignity of the church, but to debase it, for fear that the successors of St. Peter, returned to primitive simplicity, would again, as in former times, be the necessary arbiters between the people and the kings. Do not hesitate then, *Signori*, to declare the divorce of the spiritual and the temporal; it is one of the greatest satisfactions you could give to sincere religious hearts."[31] Had he tried these arguments on Zenaide also? Perhaps. Had she accepted them? One suspects not.

Some of the deputies spoke against France, but Bonaparte suggested that

Figure 36. Uniform of the Roman Republic, 1849. Central Museum of the Risorgimento, Rome.

the clumsiness of their own Italian agents might be partly at fault for bad relations with the French government. He avowed that France would never engage in a "fratricidal war" against the newborn Roman republic. "There is so much more I could say on the subject," he concluded, "but it is necessary to be short, because threatening events demand a prompt solution. Time presses—the moment has come!" At that instant, a dull rumbling of thunder was heard. "What?" he exclaimed, ever quick to make the most of a theatrical opportunity. "Do you yourselves not feel the sacred earth tremble under your feet? It is the spirit of your ancestors, quivering with impatience, who cry to you through my voice. Long live the Roman Republic!"[32]

At the meeting on 22 February Bonaparte spoke in favor of electing Mazzini, "the illustrious writer," to lead them, and of making him a citizen of Rome. This proposal was heartily welcomed and he was elected amid cries of "Viva Mazzini!" "Viva, Bonaparte!" Several weeks later, on 6 March, Mazzini took his seat beside the president of the assembly. Surprisingly, Mazzini had never before been in Rome, but the deputies instantly made him a Roman citizen. "It is with joy that I see Mazzini here," Bonaparte declared as the first speaker. "Today he has become our fellow citizen and our colleague in the assembly. The city of Rome, the object of his choice for the capital of Italy, must make amends to him for twenty years of exile and persecutions, during which he has never ceased to be the indefatigable champion of Italian regeneration. His presence here is a matter of pride for us; and for him, he must find it a matter of satisfaction and encouragement to see his principles, so eminently Italian and republican, incarnated in the majority of the members of this assembly."[33]

Mazzini took the floor. In the course of twenty years of service to the republican cause, he said, he had met many men who believed that a republic was a utopia, unrealizable in the corruption of present times. But the danger to the Italian republic did not come from within; it came from without, from Austria. The time had come to help Venice and to drive the barbarous invaders from Lombardy. "The Roman people, in setting an example of accord, will save the Venetian republic and will render a great service to the cause of liberty and of civilization." Afterward, Bonaparte rose and quoted Mazzini as saying he had felt elevated on entering Rome. "In return," Bonaparte told his colleagues, "you tell him through your applause for his beautiful words that, by his presence, Rome vividly recalls its ancient grandeur and is encouraged to its renewal."[34]

Toward the end of March there was much discussion in the assembly concerning the new constitution and its laws. The issue had gained particular urgency when the Austrians defeated Piedmont at the battle of Novara (23 March) and Charles Albert was forced to abdicate in favor of his son Victor Emmanuel. In addition to heavy war indemnities, the Austrians had demanded that the liberal Piedmontese constitution be abolished (though this demand was subsequently withdrawn). It was therefore vital that the Roman constitution be implemented as soon as possible as a show of Italian strength. An example of an old law that Bonaparte wished to replace was that which cut off a war widow's pension if she remarried. Often a defender of women's rights, he objected to this law because the woman might still be impoverished after her second marriage. He cautioned the deputies about losing sight of what they wanted to achieve. "Our intention, is it not, is to encourage men to go to war. Do you not wish to encourage volunteers and to ensure them that their families will be cared for? . . . In conclusion, I say that your law must accord to military widows a poor morsel of bread, without condemning them to celibacy for the rest of their lives." His suggestion was adopted.[35]

All such proceedings came to a sudden halt, however, on 24 April, when Mazzini made an urgent announcement: he had just received word that the French were sending an expeditionary force of thirteen thousand men to land on the coast near Rome. Did France propose to be the oppressor of a republican friend? he asked. Bonaparte cautioned his colleagues about passing judgment too quickly on the expedition. "You know that you have not been recognized by France . . . to what should we attribute that? To bad will? To the hypocrisy of the French government? Or to the clumsiness of your agents? I leave you to decide, perhaps the faults are on both sides." Here are the facts, he said:

Piedmont has prostituted itself to Austria; the king of Naples represses and bloodies Sicily; Tuscany is in full reaction. Here is the sad state to which our holy cause of independence and liberty is reduced! France has been informed of these events and is not ignorant of what they mean. Suppose for a moment that she has been moved by the rapid succession of our disasters and wishes to stop them. In this case, . . . would she not send an expeditionary force to occupy by her valiant army one of the parts of Italian territory still free to protect against the invasion of reactionary Europeans? [This was exactly the argument his cousin Louis-Napoleon would use to justify the French invasion.] [France] is free to follow a policy of generosity; that is, French, because for me the two words [French and generosity] are synonymous. Wait for positive information and documents.

He added that they must leave it to Mazzini to watch over the honor and welfare of the republic that they had confided to him. There was lively applause and many deputies left their seats to shake Bonaparte's hand.[36]

Although it may seem at hindsight that Bonaparte was playing a double game, clearly his colleagues were aware that he was sympathetic to France because of his heritage—he had said as much in his speech at Lyon—and willing to give the French government the benefit of the doubt. His own cousin Louis-Napoleon, after all, was president of France and had once been a guerilla in Italy fighting for freedom from a repressive pope.

Several days later an emergency meeting was held at night. Mazzini announced that an advance guard of the French expedition had landed at Civitavecchia. Bonaparte quickly advised:

Be calm my colleagues. Calm at a time of danger is the true proof of great courage. A people as inflammable as the Romans easily explodes in indignation. It is necessary to restrain our first impulse. As for me, I have need of a double, of a triple [his brother Pierre, and cousins Prince Napoleon (Plon-Plon) and Lucien Murat in the French assembly—he does not include Louis-Napoleon] effort to hold back the indignation that I feel today; however, I must do it in the interest of the Republic. We must do our duty. I call to witness again the sacred soil that we tread; I call to witness the souls of your ancestors, already evoked by me in that memorable night when we proclaimed our Republic.

Bonaparte did not want to see the Italians and the French fight a war that he believed was against nature, that is, fratricidal. The deputy Sterbini remarked that it was fine to distinguish France from its government, but since the French government had indeed attacked Rome they were obliged to view the French as invaders.[37]

In spite of Bonaparte's ingenuous belief in the benevolence of the French, the army arrived in Rome on the evening of 29 April 1849, and a fierce battle ensued the following morning. Much to General Oudinot's surprise, Garibaldi's volunteers overwhelmed his troops and took three hundred captives, which Mazzini quickly released as a gesture of good will. Garibaldi had been eager to pursue the French and defeat them, but Mazzini restrained him. According to the historian Denis Mack Smith, Garibaldi never forgave Mazzini for this, "but the decision was politically justifiable, especially as many French politicians were strongly opposed to Napoleon's war policy."[38] Bonaparte's brother Pierre was among them. He proposed to the French assembly that they declare the independence of the Roman states inviolable and insisted that the French troops should only continue to occupy them in order to protect their independence.[39] Many French deputies thought General Oudinot had overstepped his powers. In the face of opinion, Louis-Napoleon took the stance that he had sent French troops to Rome to defend the Italians against the Austrians, but that Garibaldi had fired on them and thus started a war. The radical French deputies bitterly rejected this explanation and called for the impeachment of Louis-Napoleon, but they were quickly suppressed and their leaders fled the country. The result was that an envoy, the young Ferdinand de Lesseps, who would later make his name on the Suez Canal, was sent to Rome to negotiate a peace treaty.

On 15 May Bonaparte, acting as president of the assembly in the absence of Mamiani, told his colleagues that word had arrived from Paris that hostilities were to be suspended. "One can no longer believe that [France] pardons per-jurers," he said, referring to those who claimed that Rome had been taken over by a mad rabble, "neither that she permits a general to set aside his instructions in order to crush the liberty of all Romans and plunge two nations into a frat-ricidal struggle."[40]

Mazzini signed an armistice with de Lesseps on 31 May that allowed French troops to remain outside Rome, the pope to return to the Vatican, and the democratically elected assembly of the Roman republic to continue in office. But Louis-Napoleon, already planning to become emperor and in need of Catholic and right-wing support, recalled de Lesseps to Paris and reneged on the treaty. General Oudinot, without waiting for word from France, moved his troops to the Villa Corsini outside the walls of Rome and began shelling the city on 4 June 1849.

At the assembly meeting of 15 June, held at night, an architect told the deputies that the Chancellery was unsafe; the roof and the entire structure had been weakened by bullets and debris had fallen into the meeting room itself. The building was not in imminent danger of collapse, but it was unsafe to remain there for it appeared to be a target. A move to another building was sug-gested. Bonaparte objected, saying they could only move to a more crowded part of the city, and if the guns were indeed aimed at them, they would be putting more citizens in danger. "We must continue to promulgate our laws in the midst of the noise of battle, as in a former time Moses gave the tablets of law to his people in the midst of the lightning and thunder of Sinai."[41]

The next day a letter was read from Mazzini formally announcing that the French government had canceled the agreement with de Lesseps and recalled him. The new negotiator, de Courcelles, stated that France had only one goal and that was to maintain the liberty of the head of the church, the liberties of the Romans, and the peace of the world. Bonaparte protested:

This is a new instance of a faction of French extremism that dishonors French diplomacy as it has already dishonored military power, formerly so glorious. This infamous conduct toward us uses violence and fraud alternately . . . they want nothing less than the restoration of the pope and his government of priests; and, following the maxim of the Jesuits, this beautiful end justifies the means ignominiously employed against us. Without doubt, the absolution of *the good fathers* has been acquired in advance for the pious frauds of Oudinot and Courcelles. But they [Oudinot and Courcelles] can be sure that for our part, faithful to the principles of honor, we will fight them to the end.

Loud and violent applause greeted his speech.[42]

Even with the bombardment going on all around and above them, the deputies persisted in their attempt to establish a constitution for the Roman republic. Bonaparte was adamant that church and state be separated. "In voting for my amendment you will confirm once again the condemnation of that abhorred regime which certainly will never be reestablished, in spite of Austrian bayonets." At that very moment a bomb fell on the building, but without missing a beat he added, "in spite of French bombs." "At Rome," he continued, unperturbed, "in this center of Catholicism—*fetishism, convulsions, anabaptism, bloody flagellations* and all cruel and extravagant practices will not be allowed in public . . . Each adores God in his own way, and each must respect the manner in which another cult is practiced [but apparently with major exceptions]." When someone asserted that other religions should not be allowed, Bonaparte replied hotly that only if ancient paganism should be revived and with it the scandalous spectacle of a bacchanal, performed in a public place by idolatrous priests, would he object. But even that would be a matter for the police, not something set down in law to control morality.[43]

On 30 June Mazzini resigned: it was no longer possible to defend Rome, and no conditions could be made with General Oudinot. As the French soldiers poured through one gate of the city, Garibaldi and his army left by another, to continue the struggle in Tuscany. At the final meeting of the assembly, with all hope gone and only a few idealists left refusing to flee, those remaining called on Bonaparte to seek assistance from Italy's powerful friends England and the United States. Shortly thereafter, a detachment of French troops, headed by officers, entered to evacuate the room. With full Napoleonic force and dignity, Bonaparte stood straight as an arrow and upbraided them for this act of violence; soldiers might be excusable for obeying orders, but generals and statesmen could never be forgiven in the eyes of posterity. Those words, coming from a member of the Bonaparte family, created a sensation among the troops, but they were compelled to carry out their assignment.

From then on the deputies' lives were in serious danger. In fact, several who remained in Rome after the pope's return would be branded dire threats to the state and executed. Because Bonaparte took so seriously his mission to alert foreign powers to the tragedy in Rome, as well as the threat to his life, he obtained a passport from the American consul and escaped under cover of nightfall to Civitavecchia, where he boarded a ship for Marseilles.

13

THE DEAN OF
FRENCH EXILES

"Le prince démocrate erre en proscrit: le monde
savant ouvre ses bras au naturaliste."

Dr. Henri Roger, anonymous newspaper clipping,
possibly early 1850

BEFORE LEAVING CIVITAVECCHIA Bonaparte dashed off a note to Zenaide, beginning: "Ma chérie amie." He is furious that he was prevented from leaving on the steamboat *Bull Dog* with all the others. This was apparently because of General Oudinot, from whom he would demand satisfaction if it were possible. He will spare her the details. She is to write to his mother, embrace all the children, begin at once to write to him in Paris, and not to forget any of the numerous suggestions he made to her on parting. "My head boils," he says, "excuse the discourse of this letter that speaks of absurdities and perhaps not of essential things." He signs it in his old way: "Ton bon Zig."[1]

After landing at Marseilles he left at once for Paris. But two-thirds of the way there, in Bourges, he was handed an order of expulsion from France; his now hated cousin the prince-president would not allow him into the country. Incredibly, he was still banished from France, even though another Bonaparte was the French head of state. Disregarding the order, he continued on to Orléans. But he was stopped again and this time told that he would be escorted under guard to the port of Le Havre.

Before leaving Orléans, Bonaparte penned a letter to his old acquaintance Dupin, president of the French Chamber of Deputies: "Citizen president, I left freely from Rome, the 6th of this month and with a legal passport. It was only at the very end that I left the post of representative confided to me by the Roman people. Earlier, acting in the name of the Constituent Assembly nominated by the people and dissolved by the force of bayonets, I had the honor to place in the hands of the commander of French troops, who had invaded the capital, the protest of which I send you a copy today." He goes on to say that in spite of the unfortunate turn of events he would never have dreamed of leaving the city and abandoning his family if he had not received a mission from the dying republic to the governments of France, England, and America. "All other sentiments fell apart before the necessity of this mission," he says, "honor and duty ordered me to brave all perils; to fulfill it, then, I left Rome and embarked at Civitavecchia for France . . . debarking at Marseilles, I arrived quickly and without difficulty at Bourges. But as I tried to leave this city, I was stopped in a manner I will abstain from describing but that history will stigmatize, and I will not stoop to complain of, because the attitudes of the republicans of Bourges and of Orléans have been for me a sweet compensation."

His mission, he adds, is tied up with the honor and the interests of the French and Italian peoples, who are so well suited to love and aid one another, and thus he must exhaust all means to return to Paris. He must make his aim known to the legislative assembly and give it the greatest publicity possible. "I will not undertake here to defend my cause which is in the domain of history.

Other voices more eloquent than mine will know how to crush the lies of adversaries under the weight of evidence, and we are able to furnish authentic documents if necessary." As a representative of the Italian people, Bonaparte makes an appeal to the sentiments of justice and liberty innate to the hearts of the French: that these generous people not be the instrument of restoring papal absolutism, "the worst of all absolutisms." "Respect for religion, eternal hatred for the government of priests!"—these phrases he had heard from the "heroic Romans" as he was leaving them. Europe, he says, must recognize that the defense of Bologna, Ancona, and Rome had no other motive than the profound hatred of the populations for theocratic government, which now is reestablished, with all its abuses. He cautions that reestablishing the temporal power of the popes will guarantee revolutionary unrest in Italy and pose an obstacle to European peace.

Bonaparte concludes his letter to Dupin by saying that a "post-chaise accompanied by gendarmes" has just arrived to conduct him, against his will, to Le Havre. "This is very difficult for me, a Bonaparte, exiled from France since my birth and persecuted by a succession of governments down to the present day. It is France, who must defend indefeasible and sacred rights such as truth and eternal reason. Permit me, *Monsieur le Président*, to count on your personal support, because of my just cause, and a little for the old friendship and kindness you have always given proof of to the dean of French exiles."[2]

From Le Havre Bonaparte sailed to England to seek the sanctuary his father had found there some forty years earlier (though nominally Lucien had been a prisoner). The English in general were more sympathetic than the French to the Italian cause—Mazzini had lived in England for some twenty years prior to his recent return to Italy. Natural science, fortunately, is usually apolitical, so Bonaparte was heartily welcomed by his friends and colleagues.

But some, like George Ord, took a dim view of Bonaparte's activities. After he heard of Rossi's murder, the outraged Ord, himself a devout Catholic, wrote his English Catholic friend Waterton: "This rebellion is of a piece with all those insurrections which have reduced France and Germany from a state of unexampled prosperity to that of misrule and misery. Our thoughtless people call these uprootings *Revolutions*! . . . so the poor old Pope is a prisoner in his own domicile; and the *canaille* are shouting Hallelujahs for their victory, signalized by the blood of . . . a Prime Minister murdered in the face of day! And the hand of the accursed assassin, who plunged his knife into the throat of Count Rossi, is termed *blessed*! I must forbear—my whole frame is convulsed with horror."[3]

In March 1849 Ord told Waterton that he had heard nothing "about our kind friend Bonaparte" except what he read in the newspapers. "The celebrated naturalist" Agassiz was there in Philadelphia, he said, and "expressed his

sorrow that his good friend, Prince Charles, had abandoned the peaceful pursuits of natural history for the turmoil of politics." Ord concluded: "May God
enable him to open his eyes to the folly or madness of his conduct!"[4]

If Bonaparte had hoped to find a receptive ear in America for the cause of
the Roman republic, he was speaking to the wrong one. In Ord he had a staunch
opponent, and Ord was, unfortunately, his primary link to the American intellectual community, through his position in the American Philosophical Society.
When Waterton informed him that Bonaparte had arrived in England, Ord
replied that he hoped he would be able to stay there, because he should never
be allowed to return to Rome. "His participation in the late rebellion was an act
which cannot be justified, especially when one takes into view the deference
which was paid him by the Papal government, and the protection which was
afforded him after the banishment of his whole family from France. We cannot
here get a correct account of the true situation of political parties at Rome: Your
English papers, like our own, seem intent on misleading the public as to the
true cause of the pretended revolution, which I am constrained to believe was
brought about by a combination of thieves and cut-throats."[5] Even Edward
Everett, an American diplomat and one to whom Bonaparte might have
appealed for help, would caution him: "I do not write to you on political
events."[6]

His faithful friend Geoffroy Saint-Hilaire, in Paris, was decidedly more
sympathetic, although he too was unwilling to discuss politics and therefore
could offer Bonaparte no help in mustering French support. "My thoughts have
turned to you since these terrible events," he wrote, when he read in the newspapers that Bonaparte was in London. "Friendship is not devoted if it is not sincere. I will speak to you openly, as always, as when I wrote you I had voted for
Agassiz (I loved and esteemed you twice as much when I read with what nobility you heard and accepted this declaration)." He thinks Bonaparte has had an
"ultra-reaction" to the French occupation of Rome and that they will have to
separate out all political thoughts from their friendship and only be occupied
with science. "If you write me a letter purely academic and non-political, it will
be welcome," he specifies, adding that he will not communicate anything political to the French Institute. "If you are devoted to the end to your vision of the
Roman republic, history will judge your efforts, which are composed of passion, justice, disinterestedness, and courage. I wish the world could hear your
eloquent protests—those who accuse you of having fought against our army,
those who confuse you with the barricaders of yesterday in Paris. When you
write that you have always been French—you prove it by this *élan* so entirely
French, [and] from your heart. Let a little time pass: those who are the most

opposed to you today, without coming round to your opinions, have sympathy for you nevertheless."

He has seen Bonaparte's brother Louis-Lucien, who gives him news of his mother in Paris, and of "Madame Zénaïde" in Rome, but nothing of him. Bonaparte and his wife must be reunited, says Geoffroy, and Charles must resume his place in the field of natural science. This last is the double desire of his brother and all his colleagues. "It is mine above all," he concludes, "and I will count among the happiest hours of my life when you take your place next to me at the Academy."[7]

This would not happen for quite some time, however. For over a year Bonaparte would be a man without a country.

When he reached England on 22 July, he had written to Zenaide, "Thank God I am at last in London . . . in freedom!" His agent Kraus had brought him her letters of the eighth and ninth, which gave him more pleasure than she could imagine, he said, because he was so dejected, "so beaten down in heart and spirit," barely able to muster the energy he so badly needed. Until he received her letters, he had been rereading an old one from their son Joseph he had found by chance in his bag. "Would you believe it? This letter gave me such joy! . . . You and Joseph know how I loved him even when he left for America! . . . but the tears stain my paper . . . happiness depends on getting news of all of you in my solitude and my feeling of abandonment! . . . My Augusta! . . . My beautiful Marie! . . . Bathilde! . . . Joseph! . . . Lucien!! . . . Napoleon!!! . . . embrace them all for you and for me." He is writing to her from his modest room in the Hotel Lincoln, which "is not fashionable! . . . *for shame*!!!" But it is near Gould, the British Museum, the College of Surgeons, and Owen, with whom he has dined, or rather eaten roast beef and "pudding," "a kind of soup." He debarked in Brighton dressed as he had been at Le Havre and reached London only two hours later. He has seen Gray, Gould, and Lord Minto as well as Cobden, Rothschild, Baring (the banker), and the American ambassador. The way he was treated in France has certainly not enhanced Louis-Napoleon's image: "What articles, good God!"[8] (The English press had apparently been in Charles's favor.).

He continues that it is not probable that he can earn any money; therefore his principal resource must be Zenaide's thrift, and he is sure to be soon back in Rome. She doesn't need four carriages; three are really useless, therefore she should sell them, if she can get a good price. In spite of all the privations he will impose on himself, he will need a lot of money in London. The cabriolets are very expensive, but because of his bad legs they are indispensable, for he cannot use the omnibus. And the shops as well are "horribly" expensive. Canino is in the hands of Valentini (his sister Marie's husband), so she is not to worry about that, but she is to try to claim payment for the damages to the villa (presumably from the French). He ends the letter, "adieu! adieu! adieu! I have no time to lose."

Several weeks later, also writing from London, he thanks Zenaide for the tender thoughts in her last letter, which made him weep. But, he says, apparently in answer to her inquiry about their whole family moving to England, "we must not think of it—that would ruin our children."9 Perhaps he means that it would disrupt the children's lives if they were transplanted to a foreign country. But more likely he himself was not planning to stay in England: France was still his goal.

In a letter of the following month, written from Birmingham, where he had gone to attend a meeting of the British Association for the Advancement of Science, he reveals a different attitude. He is in a state of depression over money worries and the "torment" in his legs, and says that his projected voyage to America will depend on what he hears from (Louis) Mailliard, since after reading her letter he has decided at last to write Mailliard. "I say it and I repeat it," he says in despair, "that I want to be alone! . . . alone!! . . . alone!!! . . . Would to God that I might always have been!"10 Is it possible that Zenaide had suggested he go to America for a time to regain his balance? It is hard to say. He was clearly in extremely low spirits—nearly at his wit's end—and certainly did not mean to be taken literally about his wish to be alone. He had always been theatrical when excited or upset, and his legs were so badly inflamed he had had to stay in bed. But that Thursday he was scheduled to depart, for "Edinburgh? . . . London? . . . Lord Darby (Knowsley)? . . . Jardine?" In the end, he went to Scotland, to stay for several weeks with Sir William Jardine, who had just received a collection of rare birds from the Himalayas.

It was becoming more and more obvious that Bonaparte's mission to secure aid for the moribund Roman republic was doomed. He had thrown himself headlong into politics when it seemed he could effect change by bringing together scientists from all over Italy to share their ideas and research. But now that France had squashed the Roman republic, he must have felt that the cause of unity and independence was, for the time being, impossible. Natural science had always been his first interest, so when his political efforts proved futile, he abandoned them and turned back to science, where his heart had been all along. After leaving Italy, his passion for the country's future was replaced with his old passion for science. He was not among those who continued to fight for the cause on foreign soil, and this may explain why he has not figured in the history of the Risorgimento.

On his arrival in England, he spent time at the Zoological Society of London and wrote several notes for its *Proceedings*. His studies were far-ranging: one paper, for example, concerned a species of elephant originally from Sumatra.[11] After a few weeks in London, he crossed the channel to Brussels, probably to visit his revered elderly friend Professor Drapiez. Because he was exhausted and suffering from the gout in his legs, he spent part of the time at Spa, Belgium, to recover his health. But in so doing he may also have lost part of his wallet. Some years before, James Fenimore Cooper had described Spa to a friend as "the famous hard-drinking, dissipated, gambling, intriguing Spa; where so much foly [sic] has been committed, so many fortunes squandered, and so many women ruined! How are the mighty fallen!"[12]

Bonaparte went back to England in mid-September to attend the meeting in Birmingham. Then, after his visit with Sir William Jardine in Scotland, he returned for the month of October to London, where he had many invitations to meet with colleagues. Some of these occasions had a character all their own. The distinguished but eccentric Oxford geologist William Buckland invited him to breakfast one morning to meet Sir Walter Trevelyan, "one of our best Naturalists who is full of facts about the clairvoyant who has seen Sir John Franklin."[13] Franklin, a famous arctic explorer, had disappeared on his fourth voyage.

At the beginning of November Bonaparte left for Holland. He had decided that in his exile he would write the book he had been thinking about for twenty years: a synopsis of the birds. All his notes, his books, and his collections were of course in Rome, but the great Rijksmuseum van Natuurlijke Historie in Leiden had twelve thousand bird specimens, mostly unstudied, and these would provide him months of fascinating work. On this visit to Leiden he stayed with his old mentor Temminck, who welcomed him with open arms. Temminck's *Manuel d'ornithologie* had been so influential in determining his career as an ornithologist. At once Bonaparte set to work on his last great work, *Conspectus generum avium*, written in Latin to emphasize its international significance and his own world citizenship. The book "was intended to include all known species of birds and to facilitate a survey by its arrangement of small, closely related groups." Hermann Schlegel, Temminck's second in command at the museum, gave him the impetus to embark on this enormous project and would be his consultant on difficult distinctions. Bonaparte would live with Schlegel and his family for most of his stay in Holland.[14]

Perhaps it was at this time—the letter is undated—when he was "desolate in his solitude," that he wrote with deep feeling to tell his wife that he had just immortalized her name. "Zenaide lives! A proof of this is in the sweet Zenaida dove, *Columba Zenaida* Bonaparte. It is at all times so delightful to think that a

224 *Zenaida Dove*
Columbiformes Columbidae *Zenaida aurita*

Figure 37. *Zenaida Dove* by J. J. Audubon. From Audubon, *Birds of America*, edited by Roger Tory Peterson and Virginia Marie Peterson (New York: Abbeville Press, 1981). Photo credit: Lisa Tyson Ennis.

thousand years from now this mark of my esteem and of my tenderness will live on with this lovely species. I take the occasion to make known to the world that it is in your honor that I have bestowed this name. At this moment I can only love you on paper—what truly interests me in the world is you."[15]

Bonaparte thought constantly of his return to France, for he planned to have his family join him there. He wrote to Geoffroy repeatedly about it. Geoffroy responded that he had spoken to Count (Henri-Georges) Boulay de la Meurthe (vice-president of the republic), "a true friend of yours," who promised that "one of these days" he would arrange a meeting with the president at the Elysée Palace to discuss Bonaparte's situation. "You must have a spirit of reconciliation, although without concessions on your opinions or sentiments," Geoffroy advised him, "but without aggression." He said that M. Boulay understood all that he had said to him about the moral necessity of immediately securing permission for Bonaparte's reentry into France. It was painful for all Frenchmen, he said, to see this situation of an eminent savant who seemed to be a citizen of all countries except his own.[16]

Three days later Geoffroy wrote again to say that he had spoken to Victor Hugo as well as M. Boulay, and that the former would do what he could to get Bonaparte permission to come to France. Geoffroy had also received Bonaparte's letter that he wished forwarded to "Madame of Canino." The arch-republican Bonaparte had apparently dispensed with titles at this point, not only for himself but for his wife as well. Geoffroy expressed his delight with the *Cerorhinca* (a Rhinoceros Auklet from the Pacific coast of North America) that Bonaparte had sent—he had no doubt gotten Zenaide to ship it to him from Rome—and asked permission to present it to the academy. He was also pleased, he said, that Bonaparte had chosen him to speak to Louis-Napoleon on his behalf, for it touched him as a mark of friendship. At the same time he exclaims: "An exile of 45 years! What infamy! How history will stigmatize these bureaucrats! Alas! Alas! Why is it necessary that the name of France be placed in the middle of these horrors?"[17] Two weeks later he suggested that Bonaparte himself write to Victor Hugo, whom Geoffroy would be going to see the next Sunday, and perhaps also to M. Henri Milne-Edwards (a prominent Belgian zoologist and professor at the Museum of Natural History), who might be helpful. As for Bonaparte's brother Louis-Lucien, he could probably do nothing.[18]

Several weeks later Geoffroy heard from Victor Hugo, who expressed his fond sentiments for Bonaparte and said that his old affection (*vieille cordalité*) was at Bonaparte's service and would not fail him.[19] It was a perfect time to request help from the great writer, because of his sympathy with the Roman people and his belief that their liberties should be restored. But he was not the ideal spokesman to approach Louis-Napoleon. In a speech before the French assembly in late October 1849, Hugo had said that France had asked the pope to grant an amnesty to the Roman insurgents—which was true, but later denied by the French government—instead of which he had decreed mass proscriptions. Hugo had advised Pius IX to try to understand his people and the times in which he lived. As for the French invasion of Rome, he had thundered: "What is *not* possible is that France should commit her honour, pour out her money—the money of her suffering people—and shed the glorious blood of her soldiers, all for nothing . . . no, I am wrong, I ought rather to say for a policy of shame."[20] That speech was the beginning of Victor Hugo's rupture with Louis-Napoleon—whom he had once supported but who had seriously disappointed him—a rupture that led to his twenty-year self-imposed exile on the Channel Island of Guernsey.

While Bonaparte was attempting to return to France himself, Mailliard was putting pressure on him to have his father-in-law brought back as well. "It is unquestionably without doubt that the mortal remains of King Joseph cannot be cared for as well in Florence as in Paris," he wrote Bonaparte in September. "But above all his wish must be fulfilled [to be buried in France], and you must put all your effort into that . . . we will see if the French government will dare to refuse your request and prevent your family from carrying out the duty owed to the brother of Napoleon!"[21] Six weeks later he again addressed Bonaparte on the subject: "Many friends of King Joseph ask me why we should not profit by the presidency of a Napoleon to [bring him] back to France as his will asked his children to do. I reply to them that you are actively occupied [with this question] and it is for that you wished to go to Paris."[22] This was hardly the case, but Bonaparte may have pacified the old man by saying so.

Since the beginning of his exile Bonaparte had been in financially reduced circumstances; his letters to Zenaide are filled with his concern over money. He had therefore conceived the idea of selling the immense collection of specimens he had left behind him in Rome. He approached John Edward Gray, head of the British Museum, putting a slightly different slant on his motives. "Now my dear friend I am more decided than ever, after the kind proposition I received *not to return to Rome*—where another summer would completely finish my poor birds—I have quite made up my mind to sell them." He will sell them cheaply to a public institution "where they can always be consulted for my types [the actual birds from which his descriptions were taken and their names given]." He hopes the British Museum will buy them so he can always enjoy seeing them, but if not he will give them away to his friends.[23] But the museum was not interested. Gray told him that there was no use recommending this idea to the trustees: they would not buy a collection that was not in England, where it could be arranged [checked on in advance?], and anyway they would already have all the specimens. He suggested that Bonaparte approach Edward Wilson.[24] Wilson was an American, living in Paris, who acted as agent for his wealthy brother Thomas, an avid enthusiast for natural science and a benefactor of the Academy of Natural Sciences of Philadelphia. When he heard of it, Thomas Wilson was delighted with the opportunity to buy Bonaparte's collections and authorized his brother to go ahead with the transaction. What a sense of irony Bonaparte must have felt after all his anger and disgust at the Academy in 1825, to have his treasured bird types and numerous other specimens end up there! Yet the academy was where he had met most of the men who became his closest American friends: Say, Hays, Haines, Godman, Peale, and several others. And, after all, it was the oldest extant natural history institution in the Western hemisphere.

To his friend Waterton in England, George Ord wrote with delight of Wilson's purchase for the academy. He said that Bonaparte had been "compelled to dispose of his treasures in order to obtain the means of support in his exile" and that the price amounted to about thirty-five hundred dollars. Apparently somewhat mollified toward the renegade naturalist, Ord declares, "How rejoiced would the members of the Academy be, one and all, to behold our old *confrère* once more among us!" Then he adds, "But I doubt whether it would give him any pleasure to revisit those scenes which would too forcibly remind him of his fallen estate."[25] Ord could afford to be generous to a disgraced prince.

Toward the end of November, Edward Wilson, from his house in the rue de Lille in Paris, wrote to Bonaparte that when his catalog of birds was made up in Rome—this job may have fallen to Zenaide, who had always helped her husband with his scientific pursuits—a margin should be left in which Bonaparte could make notes of anything that would be of interest "on the other side of the water." The more information he could give on his types, the more valuable they would be to naturalists in America. Bonaparte is "perfectly welcome to retain the skunk and the rattlesnake and any of the dried specimens of North American animals, reptiles, or fish that would already be in the academy's museum," since Wilson does not want to go to the expense of "sending coals to Newcastle." The mammals should be taken off their stands and packed tightly in boxes, and the bottles of fish and reptiles should be counted.[26] When Wilson wrote again at the end of December, he advised sending the specimens in regular merchant ships rather than in "vessels of war," which often took many months to return to the United States. He was glad to hear Bonaparte was working so hard in Leiden, and he looked forward to gaining some knowledge of the rich treasures of its museum. "You must have got on the right side of Mr.

Temminck to be allowed the facilities you appear to have there to progress in your study," he said.[27] Temminck had a reputation for being difficult at the least of times, and increasingly intransigent as he grew older. In a later letter Wilson remarks: "Temminck is so very jealous of Schlegel that it would be difficult I expect for the latter to attempt to publish the Birds in the Leyden Museum which have not yet been described or figured."[28]

Temminck did allow Bonaparte to publish descriptions of previously undescribed species represented in the museum's collection, however, and the latter took particular satisfaction in naming a beautiful bird of paradise *Lophorina respublica*. Writing of the *respublica*, Bonaparte permitted his wit free rein against his nemesis, Louis Napoleon:

There are those who are much inclined to name their most beautiful species for princes; since I am not in the least enamored of the authority of any princes, I have adorned this extraordinarily beautiful bird of paradise with the name of Republic: of that Republic which would be a Paradise, if it had not been made into a Tartarus by the evil intrigues and the ambition of Republicans who are unworthy of the name they have taken. But since there is not to be a paradisiacal Republic, there shall at least be a republican bird of paradise.[29]

When Geoffroy read this comment, he wrote Bonaparte that he agreed the name did not apply to the present republic in France but to an abstract republic, "personified in one of the illustrious founders, or in one of your Roman heroes."[30]

As his stay in Leiden lengthened, Bonaparte became increasingly absorbed by his *Conspectus*. At various stages of the project he often sent what he had done to Wilson, then in England, and to others as well. Wilson forwarded the pages to his brother so that he could profit as quickly as possible from Bonaparte's researches, and said that he would write to Gould about the birds from his collection that Bonaparte wanted to include. He feared, though, that Gould would be too jealous to lend his assistance. "He has amassed together nearly all the Indian collections in the Kingdom, and I expect he will hold on to them." Wilson continued to wonder at Bonaparte's success with the director of the Leiden museum: "Princes have charms which common mortals know not—you have astonished everyone to find how you manage Temminck. If poor Kaup had been only a *baron*, he perhaps might have got on better than he did at Leyden. I hope you may continue your fascination over the Master of the Leyden treasures until we have at any rate got all we want out of them and that you may progress with your Conspectus which will certainly be your greatest scientific work."[31]

Bonaparte needed information from many sources. To John Edward Gray he wrote, "You know it is the bad habit (one of the worse) of we catholics to address God *almighty* through his saints! . . . Having treated you in the same way through Gould, Prince, Mitchill, and your own brother and *wife* (under whose protection I intend to remain) I now write directly in order that in the interest of Science you should let me have *immediately* what you can of your Batrachians [frogs and toads], printed sheets or even Ms., being sure that I will make good and friendly use of it!"[32] By February he could write Gray that he was engaged in writing several works and was being published in Italy, America, Paris, Brussels, Amsterdam, Leiden, and elsewhere. "I work 19 hours every day and go to bed only every two nights . . . as I am always afraid to be taken on a sudden from my dear *studies!*" He signs himself simply "Ch. Bonaparte."[33] This fear of being taken suddenly from his work may have been focused more on assassination than on sudden illness. He had just had word of a terrible event in Rome.

Before the city's yearly carnival took place—that February 1850—in a famous festival featuring throngs of people in fantastic masks and costumes, political radicals had sent threatening letters to various individuals warning them away from the Corso, the main thoroughfare through which the aristocracy in fine carriages were accustomed to parade slowly with great pomp. Young Joseph and his sister Marie had paid no attention to these threats and rode down the Corso in their elegant coach as they had done every year at the carnival, dodging the continuous barrage of flower bouquets thrown in all directions by the populace as was the custom. When Joseph leaned to pick one up that had landed at his feet, he noticed that it was especially heavy. A moment later it exploded, temporarily blinding him and causing serious wounds in his hand, leg, and stomach. Marie was also hurt, but not so badly. Both were carried at once to a nearby palazzo, where a French military doctor attended them. Marie soon recovered, but Joseph, in great pain, had to undergo several operations and was left with a damaged thumb and a permanent scar on his face. Their sister Julie thought the attack was the work of a "Mazzinian sect."[34]

Bonaparte was frantic when he heard the news. He scratched out a note to Zenaide: "Is it me they want to reach? —Ah! they have succeeded . . . I find again all my energy! Ah! they want war . . . *eh bien* . . . they will have it . . . I too can throw bombs! Although the bomb has not touched me, I feel my muscles torn and my bones broken. Poor woman! Poor Mother! After all you do not reproach me . . . I love you more than ever . . . and I am working hard for our prompt and absolutely necessary reunion."[35] How devastating it must have been for Bonaparte to be unable to join his family in their time of crisis. But he was forbidden under threat of death to return to Rome.

Many friends who read about the attack in the newspapers wrote him solicitous letters: Edward Wilson inquired about the injuries Joseph and Marie had sustained from "a most diabolical attempt at assassination." He wants to know if "the assassins" have been caught, but he supposes that in the "present unfortunate state of Rome" justice had been "trampled underfoot."[36]

Shortly afterward, Bonaparte received a long, reassuring letter from Zenaide that surely lightened his feelings of anger and frustration. The letter began with an account of a visit she had just had from a Duchess Cesarini, who solicited Marie's favor for a young Englishman who had seen her at the carnival and was madly in love ("éperdument amoureux") with her. The duchess described him as "fort noble, fort riche," of an excellent character, well educated, and of "liberal opinions." Zenaide asks Charles to avail himself of his many friends in England to inquire about the young man's relatives, "the Duchess of Cleaveland and Lord Harry Vare." When Marie recovers, her suitor will be allowed to visit her. She is better and is now lying on the sofa in the Chinese salon, has a good appetite, and drinks plenty of Bordeaux wine to restore her strength. Joseph has only three open wounds; the others have closed. He eats well, has visitors all day, and is in excellent humor. The doctors give him permission for a carriage ride, but he wants to trade the ride for a night at the Théâtre Français. They both send him a thousand tender regards; their first thought after the assassination attempt was of the grief it would cause him, and they have never ceased to think of it.

Zenaide adds that the pope has been so angry against the French for pardoning Cernuschi (a revolutionary deputy) that he will not return to Rome while they are masters there. It is believed that only those considered innocent (which would certainly not have included her husband) have been allowed to flee. She thinks the pope will not remain away for long, and that undoubtedly he will be escorted back by the Austrians. "It will be realized, but too late," she says, "what a mistake it was not to have negotiated with France." She understands that Charles has been a long time without a letter from her, even though she has written him without interruption. No doubt the frightful roads impede the couriers, for she too has been a long while without news of him. She closes briefly—"Adieu mon ami" and without a signature.[37] She loved him and she was a faithful wife, but his politics had caused her a great deal of grief. And it appears that her sympathies had always lain with France.

Although the forced separation from his family weighed heavily on him, Bonaparte felt driven to continue his work, and this was just as well. He began the *Conspectus Generum Avium* with the classification of parrots and published the first part of this study in the meeting reports (*Comptes rendus des séances*) of the French Academy of Sciences for 11 February 1850.[38] Shortly afterward, a French professor devoted an entire newspaper column to Bonaparte's undertaking. He said that "Monsieur le Prince de Canino" had profited by his exile at Leiden and "the leisure given him by the French army" to arrange the museum's specimens into a great work on the world's birds, beginning with the parrots, the "monkeys" of the bird world. Two hundred seventy-five different species are divided into two families, one of which consists of only one extremely rare species on the edge of extinction, the nocturnal parrot of New Zealand, remarkable for its affinities with owls. The author of the article congratulates Bonaparte for renouncing demagogy for science and concludes, "The democrat prince is outlawed: the intellectual world opens its arms to the naturalist."[39] Bonaparte's articles for the French academy followed each other in rapid succession: in early March he published one on *Accipitres* (hawks and eagles), in April, one on *Trochilides* (hummingbirds), in September, and two more on new species of *Passerines* (grosbeaks, finches, and sparrows) and on *Parides* (titmice and chickadees).

Several ornithologists came to see him in Leiden. Professor Carl Reinwardt brought him his own work on the birds of Java, and the director of the Brussels Museum came to call, accompanied by a baron who had once been Bonaparte's guest in Rome.[40] His favorite visitor was John Gould, who was touring the continent to obtain subscribers for his *Birds of Asia*. When Gould returned to London, he wrote Bonaparte that he had distributed all the copies of the *Conspectus* he had given him. He also said that when he saw Prince Maximilian in Germany, the latter told him he would "rejoice" if Bonaparte would pay him a visit. He concludes his letter with a note of concern: "I was very anxious as to the safety of your own health when I saw you working incessantly night and day—and I sincerely hope you will not strain the cord too tightly and make yourself ill. I saw in you during the few days I was in Holland a striking instance of the energy and determination of character so conspicuous in many members of the Napoleon clan and I doubt not when your work appears we shall be all astonished at the amount of labour which has been devoted to the subject."[41]

One of the naturalists to whom Gould had given Bonaparte's *Conspectus* was Richard Owen, who wrote to the prince complaining that he had been "worked to death with Lectures, Industry Exhibitions [for the upcoming World's Fair], Commissions, Reports on Water-Supply to London . . . all coming in at once, with the beginning of Parliament, and an accumulation of correspondence is the result, of which the first to be repaid is yours. A good many answer themselves after a few weeks, but yours make one think: you place a broad picture of Nature before the eye of the mind."[42]

It was heartening to hear from George Robert Gray as well, who wrote that he often looked at Bonaparte's portrait (probably the pencil drawing made in London in 1849 by T. H. McGuire, which brought out Charles's striking resemblance to Napoleon[43]) and wished that the original was in "old England, that land of true freedom," so that they could converse on their favorite subject, natural history.[44] As to Bonaparte's *Conspectus*, the arrangement of it differs from any ordering of the birds that Gray knows of and he cannot yet offer an opinion. However, even though he finds himself demurring at some points, he is willing to admit that Bonaparte may be right and that it is his own "unfortunate want of a correct and brilliant conception of a natural arrangement that blinds" him.[45]

Bonaparte had written Gray's brother, John Edward, in early May about returning a proof of the *Conspectus* from London, addressing him playfully as "old Gray head Zoologist." A mutual friend had returned to Leiden without the expected proof, and Bonaparte did not hesitate to badger Gray about it, in his usual imperious style. "Now do send it back *as it is* if you have not time or friendship enough to satisfy my wishes in the interest of science and your own!"[46] The dignified director of the British Museum responded with equal candor. "I did not send back the former proof because I hoped that you would yourself see that such manufacturing of names would not add to your reputation as a Naturalist and [I hoped] that you would not produce any more such tables—any person with common industry may make a dozen a week. Hoping that you will some day give us some nearly useful scientific work such as you formerly did, believe me, ever your most sincere . . ."[47] As Gray might have anticipated, this brutal critique would be the last communication between them for years.

Gray was not alone in protesting Bonaparte's plethora of new names. Years later the American ornithologist Elliott Coues would write that he thought Bonaparte's usefulness to the science had ended by 1850. "Scheme followed scheme, tableau tableau, conspectus conspectus, with perpetual changes," he said, "incessant coining of new names, often in mere sport—it was nothing but turning a kaleidoscope. It may have been fun for him, but it was death to the subject."[48] However, Erwin Stresemann, a renowned ornithologist from our own time, dismisses Coues's complaint as "of secondary importance"; Bonaparte's *Conspectus* is "not a product of literary diligence but the precipitate of experience which is often consulted even today by systematists."[49]

Johann Jacob Kaup wrote to Bonaparte from Darmstadt that his work on *Fringillidae* (grosbeaks, buntings, finches, and sparrows) "will be without doubt the best work we have until now in this branch." "But," he continues, voicing a caution that must have crossed Bonaparte's mind too at one time or another, "what will be your fate and what your recompense my Prince when some future ornithologist, in redoing the numerous species you have changed to their true genera, perhaps rejects a good number of those you have created? Would you not then have the sadness to see your great work, without speaking of your immense preparatory studies and of your sacrifices, serve only to make your illustrious name shine as a momentary flash in the annals of science [*d'un éclat passager dans les fastes de la science*]? For whom are you working and sacrificing, my Prince, for the present moment, or for the future?" He goes on with what might have been veiled criticism of Bonaparte's efforts: "What do we see men of science doing in the age in which we live? We see them cut, separate, disperse nature in a thousand pieces; take all the trouble possible to have the greatest number of divisions, sub-divisions etc, as if the study of, and the spirit's joy in, the work of God, consisted in assembling the greatest number of Greek or Latin technical terms. We do not see a single zoologist who undertakes to assemble these separate morsels."[50] Kaup would not have long to wait for that ideal zoologist to make himself known, for Charles Darwin had already assembled the separate morsels and in nine years (1859) would publish that synthesis as *The Origin of Species*. But, in fairness to Bonaparte, his first task was to marshal the vast amount of avian information into some sort of order. Only then could he have gone on to the task of interpretation and synthesis.

In May Bonaparte traveled with Schlegel to Berlin to check on the nomenclature of various species in the museum's collection, then visited naturalists in other German cities, including Poeppiq in Leipzig and Naumann in Ziebigk. They journeyed to Frankfurt, Darmstadt—where they undoubtedly saw Kaup—and Mainz, and spent several days with Prince Maximilian in his castle at Neuwied. One day, while shooting with Maximilian, on emerging from a marsh they were surprised to see a small crowd gathered to watch them. An aged veteran of the Grande Armée with a wooden leg spotted Bonaparte and confused him with his uncle. With tears in his eyes, he cried, "Vive l'empereur! Vive l'empereur!" Delighted, Bonaparte emptied the contents of his pockets into the old man's hat.[51]

While traveling, he and Schlegel coauthored a *Monographie des loxiens* (*Monograph of Crossbills*), which evaluated what they had seen in the Berlin and Frankfurt museums. Bonaparte dedicated the work to "Her Majesty the Queen of the Low Countries . . . who I found to have republican virtues."[52] His daughter Julie said that Queen Sophie was "educated, spiritual, and liberal" and was a great friend of her father's who found her charming.[53] The book, with fifty-four colored plates, would be published in Leiden and Dusseldorf that year (1850).

He wrote Zenaide from Frankfurt at the end of May that he had heard from Mailliard, "always as unreasonable as in the past!" The idea of going to

America had by now apparently been abandoned, but the need for money was as pressing as ever, and Bonaparte had wanted Mailliard to send him directly the income from Joseph's American investments. Mailliard must have refused. "Thank God I am not dependent on anyone," he tells Zenaide defiantly. "I know *suffering* and *work*... luxury is comparative ... but above all I want something to sacrifice my life for!" The two letters of Joseph and Augusta have given him great pleasure; the children's letters always do him much good, and "God knows I need it."[54] Several months later, Mailliard would reply to Bonaparte's request about finances that Joseph's money (his income from his American investments) should be paid directly to Zenaide during her lifetime, and if she should die before her husband, then he would get half and the other half would be divided equally among his eight children.[55]

At last, in mid-summer 1850, came the long-awaited word that Charles Bonaparte was permitted to return to France; Louis-Napoleon hoped to consolidate his power by gathering as much family around him as he could. Bonaparte had told his brother Louis-Lucien in January that from the country where he was born he had been exiled under a continuous succession of governments, beginning with that of his uncle and ending with that of his cousin— "from my cradle to my tomb," as he phrased it. He avowed that at all times— and his numerous friends led by Isadore Geoffroy Saint-Hilaire, could attest to it—he had tried to return to France. In his enthusiasm for the July Revolution, he had even addressed Louis-Philippe himself on the subject. Until his last breath, he said, he would fight for the cause of progress, of enlightenment, and of liberty in this land.[56]

Now, at last, after all these years, he could return to his native city; the man without a country would be welcomed in the one place he wanted to be above all others, especially because of its resources for the study of natural history. The great Jardin des Plantes, with its marvelous collections and its library, would be open to him, and his close friend Geoffroy was in charge of the zoological garden. Since he was forbidden to live with his family in Rome, they must, of course, come to him in Paris.

He was therefore distressed to receive word from his son Luciano that he planned to buy a house in Rome. He wrote back at once saying that it was absurd to think of such a thing when Italy was closed to his father and France called the family back more and more insistently every day. Actually, he writes (perhaps to fire his son's imagination), the fortunes of the Bonapartes might fare even better in America than in Europe. In a different vein and with an eye to economy (much on his mind at the time), he cautions Luciano about the marriage contract he is arranging for Marie with Count Paul Campello, since

Figure 38. *Luciano Bonaparte* (Charles-Lucien's son) by Andrea Belloli, 1850. Watercolor. Courtesy of the Museo Napoleonico, Rome. Luciano would become a cardinal of the Roman Catholic Church.

he thinks it gives too much away. (Marie, apparently, had rejected her English suitor.) "But whether you persist in your ideas or abandon them," Bonaparte adds, switching to what is more important, "I pray that you make it possible for Mama to come quickly to France. And if she absolutely refuses to come, in spite of my pleading and remonstrance, at least send two of my other children, even Napoleon and Bathilde, with Charlotte and Primoli [her husband], whom I await eagerly." He adds that Luciano's stubbornness in wishing to live far from him is incomprehensible, and his chagrin increases when he sees the precautions he is taking to insure that Marie's marriage takes place in Rome (rather than in Paris where her father is) and that she will live in Rome as well. He concludes that, if at his age and in spite of his infirmities, and without having been invited (he is jokingly referring to the papal government), he undertakes a voyage (to Italy?) with the only object—that is, in the sole hope—of embracing his son, then Luciano should come to France. "I hope, my dear son, that you will not do me the injury of not listening to me."[57]

Bonaparte could not go back to Rome, but perhaps he could have gone to Florence—a city outside the Papal States—although at some risk of arrest. In any case, he may have attempted to meet Luciano in Florence—because Geoffroy wrote him at the end of July: "I see you have left Leyden but where have you gone? M. Clary [Bonaparte's cousin Joachim] tells me you have gone to Tuscany to see your family."[58] If he went, however, the visit was a short one, since Geoffroy wrote again three weeks later to say that he "hears with joy" of Bonaparte's return to Paris.[59]

14

PARIS

"Quand on pense que c'est notre cousin qui trône la-dedans
et que nous sommes ici mêlés a la foule . . ."

Bonaparte to his brother Pierre,
30 January 1853

A S IT HAPPENED, Bonaparte arrived in the French capital amidst a maelstrom of angry protest and disgust directed at his brother Pierre. This hot headed ne'er-do-well, all his life embroiled in one serious scrape after another, had deserted his battalion in Algeria at a crucial time in France's war against Arab insurgents. He claimed that as a representative in the French assembly his return to Paris was more important than his role in the Foreign Legion. And he insisted that he had not needed anyone's authorization to leave Africa. The government took a different view, and in mid-October Pierre received his dismissal from the army, signed by his cousin the president. The next morning, *Le Moniteur Universel* published Louis-Napoleon's decree on its first page, and the affair took on a measure of importance. Foolishly, Pierre brought the subject up in the assembly, declaring that the treatment he had received had changed his sentiments toward his cousin, although not toward the president of the republic. However, this back-handed assurance of loyalty did not win him the support of his colleagues.[1] It was indeed fortunate for Charles Bonaparte that he had been granted permission to return to France prior to his brother's malfeasance and the negative publicity attending it.

The two brothers had never been close. It is probable that Pierre had for years been jealous of the advantages Charles received as the oldest son. At one point he even attempted to unseat him from his position. When Alexandrine was on the point of selling Canino to Charles in 1844, Pierre, who had transferred to his mother a small portion of the land he had inherited from Lucien in exchange for a minimal income, panicked that this flow of cash would cease. He wrote his younger brother Antoine that it was possible, since Charles was born before their parents' marriage—and this his mother had told him for sure—that Charles was actually the son of Jouberthou and not of their father, Lucien. Pierre thought that he and his siblings could challenge Charles's inheritance of Canino in court. Nothing came of the idea, however, after Alexandrine paid Pierre's many debts and raised his allowance.[2]

A reconciliation of sorts had occurred when Pierre, as a representative in the French assembly, learned of his brother's plight in the besieged Roman republic and spoke out against France's interference. A professed republican, Pierre was sympathetic to Charles's fight to free Italy from Austrian domination and furious at France's refusal to allow him into the country. When Charles reached Paris a year later, Pierre, then being vilified by the press, was no doubt glad to have his brother nearby. But for Charles the proximity of such a brother as Pierre proved a mixed blessing.

From Turin, Luigi Masi wrote Bonaparte that he had seen in the Italian newspaper, the *Risorgimento*, that his "dearest prince [*carissimo principe*]" was fully reconciled with his cousin and had attended certain festivities at the Elysée Palace. At the event, Bonaparte had reportedly spoken for a long time with the prefect of police, who had been in charge of his expulsion from France the previous year. Surely, the irony of this was not lost on Masi, especially since he ended his letter, "remember me to General Pepe with respects."3 General Pepe was the Neapolitan commander who defied Ferdinand II, and continued to fight the Austrians with a small contingent even after the king had recalled the troops. Politically, General Pepe was a republican who had fought for Italian freedom and represented for Bonaparte something quite different from the prince-president, who had destroyed the Roman republic and with whom Bonaparte was now, at least ostensibly, on good terms. Bonaparte's personality, and thus, his life, had been full of contrasts and this was yet another.

But if he was ambiguous with his cousin Louis-Napoleon, with his old mentor Temminck he was completely sincere. On New Year's Day 1851, he wrote his host in Holland:

Happily, there are times when overdue debtors can give thanks to creditors without [creating] too much surprise. The turning of this mid-century year offers me the occasion to pay you a tribute of gratitude that is no less sincere for having been so long contained in my heart. Yes, my dear friend, in the midst of a thousand occupations not nearly so agreeable as those I had at Leyden, not a single day has passed that I have not thought of the generous hospitality I always experienced during my prolonged stay . . . and without reproaching me for waiting so long to thank you. Many events have passed since I began my Odyssey of which it would be impossible to give you details . . . although some are quite good without doubt, but it would be difficult to forget the many agreeable moments passed [at your house]. I will never forget the herbed butter, the first strawberries, the little broiled fish etc. . . . the books and colored engravings beautifully bound and arranged so scientifically. And the advice given with generosity and conviction from which I have so benefited . . . and of which I hope to continue to prove to you that I was at least worthy through my conscientious desire to do well. But I do not want to bore you too much after having risked appearing forgetful and ungrateful.4

Temminck answered him at once and thanked him for his fond memories, above all for the hours they had spent together devoted to their favorite studies. "You and I accept that we see things differently," he said, "but I flatter myself that although different there is no hindrance to our friendship; make genera by the bushel, without being angry at me if I don't adopt them. My taste for criticism, even when I have the chance of success on my side, is completely passed." He was not entirely sincere. Later in his letter, he pointed out that if Bonaparte adopted his (Temminck's) "barbarous" name of *Kalikikili* instead of the *Great*

Figure 39. *Coenraad Jacob Temminck.* Courtesy of the Rijksmuseum Van Natuurlijke Historie, Leiden, Holland.

Lafayette for a certain bird, then "for sure" he was not "a good democrat" and he would be abandoning "*republican virtues* on the throne of kings."5 Perhaps Temminck had read in the papers of Bonaparte's reception at the Elysée Palace and, like Geoffroy and all liberals, was suspicious of France's allegedly republican government.

Bonaparte's oldest daughter, Julie, and her husband Alessandro del Gallo had arrived in Paris in December 1850 to stay with him. At first they all lived at the Hôtel Chaltham, but in early January they moved to a house at 107 rue de Lille, the same street where Edward Wilson was established. Julie said her husband searched all the shops in Paris to furnish their house. It was important that the rooms be elegant, because she particularly wished to shine in the social life of the Elysée Palace. It was not long before she invited Louis-Napoleon for dinner, along with the vice-president M. Boulay de la Meurthe; Leon Faucher, minister of the interior; Fialin de Persigny, the president's aide de camp; cousin Mathilde, Jerome's daughter; and Count Nieuwerkerke, superintendent of the Louvre6 and reputed to be Mathilde's lover. In a short time Bonaparte would be at odds with most of these people, for a variety of reasons.

He tried repeatedly to persuade Zenaide to join him in Paris, but she was reluctant to leave Rome. Her memories of the French capital were undoubtedly unhappy ones: after the battle of Waterloo, her father and uncles had had to flee for their lives from France, and she (then fourteen), her mother, and Charlotte had gone to Germany, and then to Belgium. To act as intermediary between himself and his wife, Bonaparte enlisted the aid of Adolph, Louis Mailliard's son, from whom he received a report at the end of April. Although he realized that the princess regarded his intervention, quite rightly, as presumptuous and lacking in proper deference, Adolphe had nevertheless tried five or six times to see her since his arrival in Rome, and at last she had granted him an interview. But he had not prevailed with her: she was not willing to leave her married children, nor the tranquillity she was enjoying in Rome (due to Bonaparte's absence?). "I doubt, Prince, that you will succeed in persuading the Princess to leave Rome before the time she has set for herself in 1852. A little patience will arrange things better and more quickly than all other methods."7

Not one to give up easily, Bonaparte asked that the French ambassador to Rome obtain permission for him to spend fifteen days in the city in order to bring his wife back to France. "The motive for this request is strange," wrote a French newspaper columnist in May 1851, "because it is known that the Princess has never associated herself with the political opinions and conduct of her husband [that Bonaparte's motive was suspect because Zenaide would not be willing to go into exile with her spouse]." The writer expresses his astonishment that the president of the republic has authorized such a request: when M. Charles Bonaparte arrived in France after the fall of the Roman republic, the president ordered him to leave French territory; now he is appealing on Bonaparte's behalf to the pontifical government. The two acts seem contradictory. In permitting Bonaparte to live in France (after being assured that his presence would not favor revolutionary projects), the president fulfilled all his duties to his family; to do more would be to fail in his duties to France's foreign relations. It has certainly been unpleasant for the diplomatic corps to meet face to face with the ex-president (Bonaparte) of the Roman Constituent Assembly in the salons of the Elysée. "The request made to the pontifical government in favor of M. Charles Bonaparte," the columnist warns, "proceeds evidently from the same family spirit as the request to the assembly of 250,000 francs for Marshal Jerome. The unfortunate consequences these petitions will have for the future is good reason for the president to guard against weaknesses which could have no importance in his private life but great significance in his eminent situation."[8]

If the French press made good use of this bit of news, it got more fuel from Bonaparte the following month. In early June, while he was dining at the Café d'Orsay with the vice-president of the republic, M. Boulay, a young man approached their table and demanded to speak to Bonaparte. When the intruder refused to give his name, Bonaparte told him he did not respond to those who would not identify themselves. Then, as he left the restaurant, the young man accosted him again. "You are the prince of Canino," he said between his teeth. When Bonaparte affirmed this, the man struck him in the face and shouted, "You are an assassin and a scoundrel [canaille]—I am the son of Count Rossi!" Of course, a duel followed this encounter. The seconds were Zenaide's cousin Justinien-Nicolas Clary and Baron Charles Lepic, the president's ordinance officer. Nieuwerkerke had been asked but refused, which prompted the irascible Pierre to challenge him to a duel. (It was also rumored that Nieuwerkerke had made improper advances to one of Bonaparte's daughters, so Pierre had two reasons for the challenge.) Neither Bonaparte nor Rossi's son seems to have been injured in the duel, but Pierre stabbed Nieuwerkerke in the thigh.[9] Cousin Mathilde, believing in her lover's faithfulness, was so furious that she rushed to the president to demand a warrant of imprisonment (lettre de cachet) against Pierre. But Louis-Napoleon reportedly told her, "You must be joking, my dear, a lettre de cachet in our day and age?"[10] This whole fracas unquestionably stirred up other angry emotions, because Bonaparte had an argument with his son-in-law Alessandro, after which he and Julie moved out of the house in the rue de Lille and into a furnished apartment. Julie recounted in her memoirs that many people, enemies of her father, including her cousin Mathilde, approved of her departure, but several others counseled her to return. Several days after leaving she went to see him. Bonaparte entreated her to come back, but Julie told him frankly that if he wished to make peace with her husband he would have to allow her dowry (possibly tied up in investments) to be sent to her from America. "Papa did nothing," she noted with regret, and soon afterward, she and Alessandro left for the World's Fair in London.[11] A sad irony that Bonaparte made difficulties over Julie's dowry as Lucien had over Zenaide's, and with the same embittering result.

Bonaparte too went to London for the fair, and especially to see the great Crystal Palace that had been built in Hyde Park. He told a friend in Leiden that he had had "an indigestion of Science at Ipswich and at the British Museum" and was "now enjoying the delights of the exposition." He planned to return in a few days to Paris, to begin again his "political-scientific life."[12]

Politics were heating up in Paris. As the fall of 1851 progressed, the political climate in France became charged with rumors of a coup d'état. Since the constitution stipulated that no president could be elected for a second term, Louis-Napoleon sought to extend his term of office to ten years. The conservatives and the radicals both opposed him, the first group resistant to all change and the second afraid of seeing too much power invested in one man. The long-anticipated coup took place on 2 December. Again, as in 1830 and 1848, barricades, manned by radicals, went up in various parts of Paris. They were soon dismantled however, and without the loss of life that had occurred in the previous uprisings. Bonaparte and Plon-Plon (as republican in his politics as Charles), dressed in workmen's clothes, toured the city's suburbs in an attempt to arouse the workers against their cousin's power grab, but they were recognized and had to give up the attempt.[13]

After the coup d'état, one of the president's first decrees, on 22 January, was to renounce all financial claims of the Bonaparte family. This was a particular blow to Pierre, who had attempted to reclaim the large sum, never repaid, that their father loaned Napoleon during the Hundred Days.[14] The decree affected Charles too, still plagued with an insufficiency of income. Then, in late August, he got a letter from Louis Mailliard announcing that "the Princess of Canino" had ordered him to send the revenues from [Joseph's] inheritance directly to her in Rome. "She would prevent you from changing anything that I must conform to," he said.[15] Bonaparte was both vexed and disappointed. By this time word of his debts and various duels and quarrels had undoubtedly reached Zenaide, and she was becoming more and more disenchanted with her demanding, contentious husband. Was she moved to pity, one wonders, when her daughter Marie, who had come to Paris with her husband, Count Paul Campello, shortly after their marriage, wrote in early October that Masi (who was in Paris living with Charles) had said her father was sad and depressed and that he was no longer angry at Julie's departure?[16]

Bonaparte's low spirits stemmed in part from the fact that Zenaide had refused to allow his unmarried children to come and live with him in Paris. She was a devoted mother, so it is perfectly reasonable that she would have wanted to keep her young children with her in Rome. As for Charles, perhaps it would be cynical to suggest that the need for money, as much as love of his wife and children, was an equally pressing incentive for him to bring Zenaide back to Paris where they could both live on her income. But his persistence, in the face of her continued refusal, makes it difficult to dispel this suspicion entirely. Bonaparte's Corsican family feeling was strong—but he was also extremely short of cash.

Because he finally had the backing—albeit reluctant—of the French government (though not the pope's permission) to return to Italy, Bonaparte set out for Civitavecchia in March 1852. On arrival at the port of Rome, he wrote Zenaide:

If anything could soften the bitterness that floods my soul, it would certainly be the visit of Souveni [a family friend?], whom I have loved and esteemed for years and whom I would wish to appreciate and understand me as I appreciate and understand him. But why is he alone? How is it that you yourself are not beside me since you know that my most hideous and perhaps most terrible [?] fear is still that Rome closes its doors against me, in spite of the President's [Louis-Napoleon's] wish and that the excuse is that my own family desires this estrangement which has now gone on for all of three years! . . . Are you no longer my wife? She who has given me twelve children? . . . Is it possible that you are preoccupied with the *chimerical* anxiety of the loss of [certain moneys, no doubt through gambling] at a time so crucial for our family? . . . As for myself, I am not occupied with similar miseries but think only of a provisional reunion at Civitavecchia that would prepare for a permanent one. I have come to revoke the unfair [*indigne*] sentence that by a breach of faith flies in the face of all French and Roman laws. As soon as Sauveur [M. de Saint-Sauveur, a French diplomat] is safe [i.e., out of the Papal States?] I will offer him a disinterested arrangement, and you, I trust, will no longer deprive me of my children who ought to be already in my arms! . . . I have not the courage to respond to your last letter . . . and I do not wish to raise again the feelings that relate to it. I believe I have a right to another sentiment than commiseration. And the daughter of King Joseph will understand a little [because Joseph was a self-sufficient person?] that it is only to myself that I am responsible for the only position that I aspire to [a loving husband and father] the only one which *now and always* suits her husband, unfairly scoffed at but always tender and loving.

He signs himself simply, "Charles Bonaparte."[17]

A week later, still in Civitavecchia, he wrote the French ambassador a long letter thanking him for all the trouble he has taken on his behalf, even though it has only served to "increase the audacity" of his enemies. He understands that the ambassador has left Rome under the gravest circumstances and that he has only left because he was unable to bring Bonaparte his children. The Papal government is as immoral as it is weak. And what can you do with a man as false as Cardinal (Giacomo) Antonelli (secretary of state), who has had the cynicism to dine with the French ambassador and make up to his (Bonaparte's) family, while all the time he was in the camp of the Austrians? "How can I hope to respect human laws when they bend under the weight of divine laws—of which [the cardinals] are supposedly the interpreters?" he asks. "How to struggle against the wickedness of Pigliacelli [?]—more powerful than the French ambassador and who paralyzes his noble efforts ... or the priest to whom I took my children for confession! ... or the secret agents of Cardinal Antonelli? It is he who must be made responsible before God and before France for the abduction [*l'enlèvement*] of my family; it is he who I would wish to bring before the Tribunal! I will only withdraw from Civitavecchia to render justice to myself and I will be the judge of the moment and the manner that I quit the shore, satisfied that I have been a true Bonaparte ... at least no one will accuse me of hiding my thoughts."[18]

The moment did at last come, and the *Journal des Faits* in Paris reported that the prince of Canino's departure from Civitavecchia was as extraordinary as his arrival. He had embarked as a simple sailor on the commercial steamboat *L'Industrie*, bound for Marseilles. The paper states that the French authorities had done all in their power to help settle the prince's domestic affairs, which (they had assured the Italians) had nothing to do with politics. "But what was the nature of these domestic affairs?" asks the reporter. Apparently a letter sent to a religious journal in Piedmont by a priest, who seems to have visited the princess at her Roman palace, stated that the prince was in debt to an American for approximately 250,000 francs. To free himself from this debt, he had wished to sell his cabinet of zoology specimens and his gallery of paintings. Since the family opposed the last idea, he had asked French permission to go to Rome, which had been granted on condition that he remain in Civitavecchia. "However," concludes the writer, "if the Princess of Canino, learning of her husband's arrival at Civitavecchia, left for Perugia, it was not to avoid a settlement; she did it to take away her child [Napoleon-Grégoire] who the prince wanted with him in France."[19]

The journey to Italy was a total failure. Bonaparte returned to Paris without his son or his paintings, and without having seen his wife or his other children. *La Maga*, a newspaper in Genoa, published a pair of amusing cartoons entitled "Arrival of a Troublesome Diplomat," showing a portly, heavily bearded Bonaparte wearing a frock coat and the Phrygian cap of a revolutionary as he disembarks at Civitavecchia. Angry priests threaten him and point the way back to France, while French soldiers, looking dubious and apprehensive, wait in the landing boat. Bonaparte, holding his right arm in a Napoleonic gesture, presents with his left hand a paper inscribed "Credentials of the French Government." In the second cartoon, he is shown entering Rome by the Porta del Popolo (the People's Gate), still carrying the same document but this time at the head of determined-looking French soldiers with fixed bayonets. The chagrined priests, carrying their belongings and one of them shaking his fist at Bonaparte, leave by the gate that points the way to Gaeta, the town near Naples where the pope had taken refuge in 1849. Of course, this did not happen, but

Figure 40. "Arrivo d'un Diplomatico Importuno: Sbarco a Civitavecchia" (Arrival of a Troublesome Diplomat: Disembarking at Civitavecchia). Cartoon of Charles-Lucien Bonaparte attempting to land at Civitavecchia in 1852. From *La Maga*, Genoa. Courtesy of the Museo Napoleonico, Rome.

Genoa—once an independent republic, but for many years included in the kingdom of Piedmont/Sardinia—clearly hoped at the time that it would.[20]

Masi wrote to him from Paris that he was profoundly afflicted to hear of Bonaparte's treatment in Italy. He said that the newspapers had all given the slant of a diplomatic mission to his journey (perhaps having to do with France's relations with the Papal States). Masi was disappointed that Bonaparte had not communicated with him directly, to give him the truth behind all these vague rumors. But he conveyed the affectionate greetings of all the prince's friends.[21]

Back in Paris, Bonaparte continued his desperate attempts to have his

Figure 41. "Arrivo a Roma" (Arrival at Rome). Cartoon of Charles-Lucien Bonaparte imaginatively entering Rome in 1852. From *La Maga*, Genoa. Courtesy of the Museo Napoleonico, Rome.

minor children brought to him: Augusta, sixteen; Napoleon-Grégoire, thirteen; and Bathilde, twelve. (Marie had married Count Campello over a year earlier, in March 1851, and Charlotte had been the wife of Pierre, Count Primoli, since the fall of 1848.) He enlisted the help of his mother. In mid-July he wrote to Alexandrine in an apprehensive mood: "Your excellent letter of the 4th informed me that I still have a misfortune to fear! Take care, my dear Mother, and let me hope to see you in Paris with my children. This request cannot be refused you, given my rights and since you take charge of them with the blessing of the French ambassador. I have only one hope . . . to soon receive your news that I can no longer do without." He warns that she must not use Kraus (his agent in Paris) as an intermediary, because he has betrayed him despite all that Charles has done for him in the past. All his affairs and those of his wife must be taken out of Kraus's hands, or he will bring him before the tribunal as a forger. He has tried to arrange his affairs so that his heirs will be satisfied and will bless his memory. "Above all," he concludes bitterly, "because of their regard for the *vil métal*, which all of a sudden has become the idol to which they sacrifice everything, beginning with their husbands and father, who at the same time is your son, nearly stupefied by his misfortunes but always tender and devoted."[22] Not surprisingly, Bonaparte's own regard for the *vil métal*, a regard—if not a positive need—inherited from both his extravagant parents, had filtered down to some of his offspring.

Marie was now acting as a go-between. In May she wrote to her mother: "I have done all I can to get Papa to send you your painting right away. Among other things he assures me that he already did it several days ago—that he gave the Murillo to M. Mailliard [Adolph?], but I know the painting is still there in the salon, and I know with pain that Papa listens to no one. I believe that the only method to get him to do it right away would be for me to speak to the President and get him to make Papa send you your painting."[23] Bonaparte had no doubt planned to sell the valuable Murillo. In June, Marie had a further bit of bad news for Zenaide: "Two words hurriedly to tell you that Papa told me he sold the palace [in the Piazza Venezia] to the Princess Borghese. I cannot believe it and you know that Papa says these things sometimes to shock. But nevertheless I tend to believe it . . . I hope, my dear Mother that if this is unhappily true, you will be able to remedy it in advance."[24]

Around this same time Masi wrote a letter (unsigned, but the handwriting is his, although scrawling and agitated) to Count Primoli, Charlotte's husband, in answer to a letter Bonaparte had received from the count that had caused the prince "astonishment, sorrow [*dolore*], and indignation." Masi sets forth various points that Bonaparte dictated to him: That he had never thought seriously of selling or leasing the palace ("but if he had wished to, no one could have stopped him"), nor had he thought to mortgage it. That he was shocked at the infamous calumny that he had thought to sell anything of the princess's without her formal consent. That it was treacherous to withdraw his power of attorney and to give clandestine orders to his agents. That it was punishment for a father to be deprived of his children or any of his family and the education of minor children should always belong to the father. That he would repay the sum that was lost (the gambling money?) and would have nothing to do with the impudent lawyers who treated him with so little respect; the value of Canino was sufficient to pay all his debts. At the end of the letter, Masi adds his own view of "il Principe." Bonaparte is very far from showing hostility to his family, says Masi, rather, he is disposed to render them not only justice but sacrifice. It has been "immoral" for the princess to stir up in the children such feelings against their father, and he should at least be given the power of attorney. "Those who know the character of the prince," he concludes, "know that he will not give way to insults or threats. He spends little or nothing on himself—I should say on us—and his family can be certain that they will profit now and always from his economy."[25]

If Zenaide blocked the sale of the palace in Rome—and she apparently did; after all, the building had been left to her by her father—she could do nothing about Canino which belonged to Charles and which he sold to the Torlonia family the following year, in the fall of 1853. With the estate went the title, which he no longer prized, since it was a Papal title. In Paris, as his republicanism slowly wore off, he began to call himself Prince Charles Bonaparte. His father had been given this prefix by Napoleon in gratitude for Lucien's help during the Hundred Days, and Charles, as the oldest son, was legal heir to it.

In spite of his need for money, or perhaps because of it, Bonaparte was living high. Isaac Lea, an American friend from Philadelphia traveling in Europe, wrote George Ord describing the "sumptuous entertainment" Bonaparte had given in his honor in mid-July. The dinner party was "dignified by some of the conspicuous savants of Paris, Counts, colonels etc.," and at one point Bonaparte called for a hundred-year-old bottle of port with which to drink the health of "Mr. Ord of America." Lea said that he had been under the impression when he arrived in Paris that Charles Bonaparte was the director of the natural history museum with a salary of twenty-five thousand francs, but Bonaparte told him that he had refused the appointment.[26] This was not the case, however. He applied for the position two years later, in 1854, but was turned down.[27]

At another dinner that summer, described by Julie, who was enlisted to act as hostess, the guests were the radicals Victor Hugo, Giuseppe Montanelli (an Italian dissident of the Risorgimento), and Prince Napoleon (Plon-Plon).

Figure 42. *Portrait of Napoleon-Joseph-Charles-Paul Bonaparte, Prince Napoleon (1822–1864) (Plon-Plon) by Hippolyte Flandrin, 1860.* Oil. Courtesy of the Musée du Château de Versailles. On loan to the Musée d'Orsay, Paris.

When Louis-Napoleon's minister of the interior was announced, Plon-Plon promptly left. Later, in reference to this incident, Julie said that her father described his salon as neutral territory where he wished to entertain all celebrities regardless of their opinions.[28] A chastened Bonaparte was treading lightly on political issues and trying not to offend the highly placed persons on whose favor he depended. Soon it would be dangerous to speak out too strongly against the president, who was tightening his grip on the nation. Victor Hugo, among others, would be forced to evade arrest through exile, after his seditious tirades against Louis-Napoleon and the publication in London of his book *Napoleon le petit.*

In September Bonaparte traveled to Germany. He revisited the museums of Mainz and Frankfurt to get information he needed for the second volume of his *Conspectus,* and at a meeting in Wiesbaden he lectured to a large group of naturalists and physicians. Shortly after his return, he received a letter from an American ornithologist, John Cassin. George Ord had informed Cassin that Bonaparte was preparing a work on the birds of North America not included in former studies. "I beg the liberty of representing to you, Sir," Cassin said, "that I am also at present unfortunately engaged in a similar enterprise—in the shape of a supplement to the octavo edition of Audubon's *Birds of America*—and have made extensive collections and arrangements with special reference to such a publication." Cassin proposed that they pursue this project jointly, as Temminck and Schlegel had done with their *Fauna japonica.* He could supply 150 specimens not found in the books of former naturalists. "What could I do in France?" he asked, anticipating that Bonaparte might suggest that he cross the ocean. "I have to make a living out of natural history—a bad business in America!"[29]

While Bonaparte was in Germany politics had been left behind, but on his return, he would have been well aware of the drift toward the Second Empire. As Louis-Napoleon traveled around France, crowds often greeted him with shouts of "Vive l'Empereur! Vive Napoleon III!" Finally, on 6 November, the senate passed an act establishing the empire and declaring Louis-Napoleon emperor. His son would succeed him, but if he had no heir he could name any descendant of Napoleon I to continue the line. The act was put to a referendum, and an overwhelming majority voted in its favor. On 2 December, the anniversary of Napoleon the First's coronation and exactly one year after the coup d'état, Louis-Napoleon signed the decree creating the Second Empire.

From Darmstadt, Johann Jacob Kaup wrote Bonaparte, perhaps a bit facetiously: "If in the middle of the splendor that since the 2nd of December 1852 surrounds the return of the Bonaparte name, already brilliant with titles, your *altesse sérénissime* [most serene highness] has not forgotten your old collabora-

Figure 43. *Emperor Napoleon III* by Franz Xavier Winterhalter. Courtesy of the Museo Napoleonico, Rome.

tors in Ornithology—I send you my best wishes on the occasion of this great event."[30]

From America, Ord, who as usual had his own definite opinion of events, wrote his friend Waterton, "When I reflect upon the magnificent farce which is now enacting in France, I can hardly conceal a burst of indignation against a great and gallant nation, which has permitted itself to be trampled under foot by an insignificant impostor." Ord understands that "at this juncture" Louis-Napoleon, still a bachelor, is in a quandary over the imperial succession. Ord says that Bonaparte is doubtless "looking to his piece of the cake [*part au gâteau*]." "Should he consult me," says the curmudgeonly old man, "I should promptly advise him to touch not, to taste not, what must prove to be a deadly poison."[31] Actually Ord was not far off the mark. There had once been talk of Louis-Napoleon adopting Bonaparte's youngest son Napoleon-Grégoire and naming him as his heir,[32] an interesting twist in view of Napoleon's hostile attitude to Lucien's children: Louis-Napoleon, himself of questionable paternity, making Charles Bonaparte's son next in line for the Napoleonic succession. To his credit, Bonaparte was against this adoption, and nothing came of it

Yet for other reasons Bonaparte wanted Napoleon-Grégoire to be sent to him in Paris. In March, Marie wrote her mother that she had spoken to the emperor about Zenaide's anguish at the thought of being separated from Napoleon, and she was sure the emperor had spoken to her father on the subject. Marie did not think her father would pit himself against the emperor, if the latter took up Zenaide's cause.[33] Marie also reported on a talk she had had with Luigi Masi. "The poor man came to tell me that he was very upset at all Papa makes him write—I know that he is always in opposition to Papa and I believe he will not stay here long."[34] The patience of this loyal, devoutly republican friend was at last wearing thin; he must have been as astonished at Bonaparte's abrupt political about-face as Ord was. Ord wrote Waterton in the spring of 1853 that he had received a parcel from Bonaparte, and on it was written in beautiful letters: "Son altesse impériale le Prince Charles Lucien Bonaparte." "Here was an announcement that hit me like a clap of thunder," said Ord. "Truly, this change of title was unknown to me; and when I addressed my letter simply to Monsieur the Prince of Canino it appears that I committed a fault against the laws of propriety that people of great *dignité* would not know how to excuse!"[35]

Actually, Charles was not allowed to use "impériale" with his name. All

Lucien's descendants had a lesser rank at Louis-Napoleon's court than other Bonapartes. Shortly after becoming emperor, Louis-Napoleon had declared that Lucien's descendants were not part of his private, but only of his civil, family. Charles protested vehemently, saying that he would not be part of a family "si vile!" and the emperor changed his decree to "not having rank at court."[36] Because Charles and his siblings were descended from a brother of Napoleon I who was older than Louis-Napoleon's father, Louis, they were considered an indirect threat to the emperor's ambitions.[37] It was particularly important to keep Charles, the oldest of the cousins, in his place. This was underscored when Louis-Napoleon married Eugénie del Montijo on 29 January 1853: none of Lucien's descendants were invited to the wedding ceremony at Notre Dame, or to the grand festivities afterward at the Tuileries. That night Pierre and his wife dined with Charles, and after dinner they all strolled through the immense crowds on the rue de Rivoli and stood outside the brilliantly lit palace crowded with dignitaries. Charles could not help remarking with resentment, "To think it is our cousin who is enthroned in there, while we are outside here with the mob."[38] Surely, he would not have wanted to trade places with Louis-Napoleon. But the contrast in their positions at that moment must have rankled, particularly when he reflected that had Napoleon not declared him illegitimate, he would have been the next in succession rather than this cousin, whose Bonaparte blood had always been in question.

On 17 March he had even more reason to be roiled, for *Le Moniteur* printed a decree from the emperor stating that the imperial livery could only be used by the grand-marshal of the palace. This edict was aimed directly at Bonaparte, and everyone knew why. At the time, he was having an affair with the famous actress of the Comédie Française, Rachel Félix—as were Plon-Plon and several others—and sent his four-horse carriage, manned by footmen in the imperial livery, to parade the great tragedienne at Longchamps. As she swept by, the public thought she was Eugénie and cried out "Vive l'Impératrice!" Amused by this, Rachel deliberately had her coachman drive through the empress's private passage in the Arc de Triomphe. Eugénie was furious when she heard of the incident and immediately initiated the decree prohibiting the use of the livery. Rachel was quoted as commenting dryly that "it was most unpleasant to be mistaken for the empress."[39]

This may have been Bonaparte's first dalliance; no evidence has been found to the contrary. It is probable that he had met Rachel when she was still very young, some years before in England. She was already famous in the early 1840s. In the summer of 1841, London's *Morning Post* reported on a performance she had given at "Her Majesty's Theater": "It was not without a feeling of regret that we went to look our last on the accomplished actress who has

Figure 44. *Rachel* (1820–1858) in the role of Camille (*Horace* by Pierre Corneille) by
Edouard Dubufe. Collection of the Comédie-Française.

astonished and delighted the English public during the last six weeks. One has been long accustomed to consider French tragedies and *ennui* as synonymous, but it was reserved for Mlle Rachel to dispel the illusion, for all who went to scoff remained to praise; and even the most caustic critics of the age have come forward unanimously and contributed glowing eulogisms on her acting and declamation."[40]

Bonaparte had grown up with a love of the theater promoted by both his parents. The theatricals staged by Lucien at his Roman palace in the Bocca di Leone were a vivid part of Charles's childhood. When he was in London in the summer of 1847, Rachel was playing at the St. James Theater throughout August. Both Plon-Plon and Louis-Napoleon, also in London, were reputedly enjoying her charms. More than likely, Plon-Plon introduced his cousin to his mistress.

Bonaparte seems to have sought out famous women, just as he had made it a point to cultivate the acquaintance of famous men. It was also around this time (the spring of 1853) that Geoffroy sent him a note saying he had written the young artist Rosa Bonheur, presumably at Bonaparte's request, and she had replied that "she would see them on Friday" and "would be charmed to receive Bonaparte's visit."[41] Bonheur was a fine painter of animal subjects, known for the accuracy of her drawing, and a thoroughly unconventional woman. At home she wore trousers and smoked cigarettes, and at one time kept a lioness as a pet. Such nonconformity in such a talented individual was bound to have appealed to him. He himself had not conformed to his father's idea of a career or to his wife's concept of religious devotion. He had been a radical in politics, a squanderer of money through his gambling, and, essentially, a nonconformist in science, by taking the other side from Agassiz and the majority of others at the time, in believing in the evolutionary development of living things.

In the spring Bonaparte's daughter Charlotte and her husband, Count Pierre Primoli, came to stay temporarily with him in Paris. Charlotte was only twenty-one but had already been married for five years. Her son Joseph, born in Paris in 1852, would become a great promoter of French and Italian relations, which would have pleased his grandfather immensely. Joseph Primoli would found the Museo Napoleonico in Rome, in his elegant mansion facing the Tiber where he housed his immense collections of paintings, drawings, miniatures, sculpture, and memorabilia having to do with the Bonaparte family. His library of books and manuscripts would become the Fondazioni Primoli, located on the second floor above the Museo Napoleonico.

Bonaparte had health problems throughout the summer, and in

September he went to a spa in Hamburg "to take the waters," in the hope of relieving the excruciating pain in his legs. In need of money as always and unable to resist an old temptation, he again indulged in gambling to pay his debts. It seems that by using the method of a M. Grégoire, a professor of mathematics who had devised a system for beating the odds, Bonaparte won 600,000 francs at a Hamburg casino.[42] Nevertheless, given his penchant for gambling, it is possible he quickly lost this sum in subsequent play.

Whatever his gains or losses at the gaming tables, his luck with his family was running out, and relations with them continued to erode. Julie, who had temporarily returned to Italy, wrote in September, "I strongly believe that a family such as ours must not be a prey to lawyers and to the Tribunal, who could only add venom to these things." Knowingly but sadly adding to her father's bitterness, she announced that her brother Luciano was going to enter the priesthood.[43] This last bit of news must have been a stab to the heart because Luciano would serve the pope Bonaparte had lost faith in when Pio Nono refused to surrender his temporal power. Fortunately, Bonaparte would never know that Luciano, on becoming a cardinal, would take Cardinal Fesch's title of S. Lorenzo in Lucino; an honor Charles would surely have denied his despised uncle. Once, he had written his friend, William Cooper, in America, that he was glad to hear that Cooper had a son with "a strong taste for our amiable science! God has denied me that blessing, none of my numerous children attending to Nat[ural] Hist[ory]."[44] He himself must have disappointed all his children when he sold Canino the following month; Joseph particularly would have regretted the sale, for in the absence of his father he had become the third and last prince of Canino.

Bonaparte attempted to enlist Louis Mailliard to intercede for him with Zenaide, as he had once used Mailliard's son. But the old man refused the role. After rereading letters from the princess in which she had asked him to remain silent on the subject as far as her husband was concerned, he found his position untenable and trusted the prince to appreciate this. "I must remain outside your family differences, my position, my attachment command me to act accordingly and I do not doubt that you appreciate my just reasons."[45]

This family strife was playing out against a background of political turmoil in the drift toward the Crimean War. France, Britain, and Turkey were lined up against Russia, whose tsar sought to defend the rights of Christians in the Turkish Empire. France and England wanted to control Constantinople (Istanbul) and thus the Mediterranean Sea. On 30 November 1853, Russia had attacked Turkish (Muslim) ships at anchor in the port of Sinope on the Black Sea, sinking nearly the whole fleet, with great loss of life. War was declared against Russia on 28 March 1854. It would be two years before the allied victors would sign a peace treaty establishing the neutrality of the Black Sea and imposing a joint European protectorate over the Ottoman Christians.

France and its allies won the Crimean War. But Bonaparte's all-out efforts to win back his wife were to no avail. In the spring of 1854 his marriage of thirty-two years came to an official end by an imperial decree from Louis-Napoleon. In a letter to Charlotte, Zenaide mentions two letters she has sent to "their Majesties" thanking them for the separation decree; she was undoubtedly the one who requested it. In concluding her letter, she says she has seen a little brochure announcing that her son-in-law Primoli has been chosen as "godfather to a bird." "This is proof that he is in the highest favor with his father-in-law, who shows this gallantry to those he loves *for the moment*," she says, with uncharacteristic sarcasm.[46] Zenaide was remembering with bitter nostalgia that once she had been immortalized in the name of a beautiful dove. By August of that year, she would be dead of diphtheria in Naples.

15

A RACE AGAINST

DEATH

"The more I have to put up with, the more I work."

Bonaparte to Gustav Hartlaub,
Paris, June 1857

ZENAIDE had been Bonaparte's "douce Colombe," his Zenaida Dove, the mother of his eight living children and the four they had buried. She had helped him for years with his researches, making fair copies of his manuscripts and translating German letters and papers. And though their political and religious views had been different he had never ceased to love her. The legal separation had not been his idea; throughout the time of their estrangement he had always sought their reconciliation. Now the spirit of the plump little bride he had once been so delighted with, of the cousin who looked more like his sister than his wife, had flown away forever.

Zenaide died on 8 August 1854 of a heart attack brought on by diphtheria. Praising her beloved mother, Julie said she had had an education rare for a woman of her time and a mastery of language, a correctness and elegance in style, that had been a great help to her husband in his work.[1] She was only fifty-three when she died, and her youngest children were still at home. Because she had entrusted them to her cousin the emperor, Louis-Napoleon put these minors under the protection of the duke of Cambacérès, once a page of the first Napoleon and now grand master of ceremonies to the third emperor. The Hôtel Montholon in the rue de Grenelle was provided as a residence for all Bonaparte's children. Julie and Augusta, with their husbands, stayed there throughout the Second Empire, as did Napoleon-Grégoire until he married, although his mother had willed him the Villa Paolina in Rome. Luciano, the future cardinal, alternated between Paris and Rome, as did Marie and Count Campello; Charlotte and Count Primoli bought their own *hôtel*. Joseph, who never got over mourning his mother's death and never married, remained in Rome.[2]

Zenaide's death made Bonaparte acutely aware that his own time was limited, especially since he had been unwell for years, with severe bouts of swelling and ulceration of the legs, possibly an indication of diabetes. A new urgency entered his life, propelling him onward with his work at even greater intensity, although he had already been driving himself more than was good for him. A year earlier, when Richard Owen visited him at the Jardin des Plantes, he had already found "much evidence of your indomitable powers of zoological labour."[3]

In the same letter, written in October 1853, Owen tells Bonaparte about his forthcoming monograph on the gorilla and the astonishment with which he had seen "the features of that formidable ape in the well-stuffed specimen" at the natural history museum. The gorilla was a fascinating novelty at the time, only recently discovered (1846) by Thomas Savage, an American Episcopalian missionary who came across a skull of the huge ape in the Gabon region. Owen

Figure 45. *Joseph Bonaparte* (1824–1865) (Charles-Lucien's son) by Andrea Belloli, 1852. Watercolor. Courtesy of the Museo Napoleonico, Rome.

named the beast after Savage, but the name Isadore Geoffroy Saint-Hilaire had already given it took priority. Today it is called *Gorilla gorilla*.[4] The creature would have had great interest for Bonaparte, as it had for other naturalists, because of the intense debate over its similarity to man, a debate at the heart of the transmutation of species. A few months earlier Owen had informed him that another original drawing of the dodo, painted in 1613 by Guimare, had been found, in excellent condition, in the collection of the duke of Northumberland at Syon House. "But I know how quickly you have all the best scientific news from here & elsewhere," he said, "so forgive this gossip from yours truly."[5] Bonaparte was situated at the hub of the scientific world at the time, the Jardin des Plantes.

Bonaparte was eager to distribute his own books and papers and often sent copies of them to John Gould for the purpose. A Belgian friend took six copies of his *Loxiens* to England in May, and Bonaparte asked Gould to sell them at the price of four pounds each. He also wanted Gould to send him all his papers about trogons, woodpeckers—of which Bonaparte had 250 specimens—and "Cuccus." The trogon notes would especially be welcome, "but if quickly sent!"[6]

Gould wrote back that knowing Bonaparte was anxious to see the "introductory matters" of his work on toucans, he had sent off an uncorrected proof to him at the rue de Lille. "I trust you will approve of it as I have paid every possible attention to the subject . . . a fine copy shall be sent off to the binders for you immediately. I have nothing new in the way of Trogons and Cuckoos, nor I believe of Woodpeckers, otherwise I would gladly communicate them to you."[7]

In November Gould sent him a "very fine handsomely bound copy" of his work on the "Odontophorinae" (*Tetraonidae*, grouse), which he had dedicated to Bonaparte. He hoped that the prince would see that "neither pains nor expense have been spared," for he thinks it is "by far" the best of his monographs. "The Genera are all well defined and distinct—of this, however, no one is a more competent judge than yourself. I still regard it merely as a pioneer to works of greater importance which will at some future period become necessary, when the vast country of America shall be more intimately known to us."[8]

In early December Bonaparte was laid up for several weeks, possibly by a fall from his horse. Owen heard of this "painful accident" and that Bonaparte had borne it "heroically." "Had the fracture been received on the field of battle, your cool demeanour would have been the subject of one of the enduring anecdotes of War," he wrote him. He hoped that some day in the following summer he and Masi would visit his "cottage" and "again receive the cordial welcome of yours truly."[9]

There was no doubt that Bonaparte had warm friends and that he cared about them and treated them kindly. He had tried to find his German friend Johann Jacob Kaup a position in the scientific field in Paris and apparently offered him room and board as well. "Could I follow only my heart, I would hasten upon wings of love and friendship to you," wrote Kaup in mid-December 1854. "Such a kind invitation never in my life have I received, and I am quite proud to have such a friend. In the moment I can only go with help of a stick, because I have lumbago, what sickness we call witch's-shoot." He says he can only accept on one condition, however, and that is if he can work half of the time for Bonaparte. He could be of some use; he could "correct some little mistakes," and if Bonaparte would give him "some little monographs to exe-cuting," he would be "the happiest man in Paris . . . thousand thanks for your kindness and generosity."[10]

For Owen, Bonaparte took over the task of seeing his "*Principes d'ostéolo-gie comparée*" through the press in Paris. Owen told him in February 1855 that he was having difficulty getting it printed and he knew his friend would "sym-pathize with a fellow-author."[11] Bonaparte told him he was certain his "hard pushes against the printer & publisher" had been of some use toward Owen's long expected publication. He himself was anxious to receive in turn "new information & new orders" from his friend "in relation to a business in which science is so much interested." He needed Owen's assistance in a matter of which "little is known & Prof. Owen master of that little." Bonaparte was plan-ning to print a notice about fossil ornithology, "a science yet to be founded"; wanted to know about the actual state of that science in its "cradle, old England" and Owen's opinion about various genera, listed in detail. Bonaparte planned to prepare a table of genera and species something like the one pub-lished the previous year "in the *Annals* of [Henri] Milne-Edwards," a copy of which Bonaparte had sent to Owen. Their mutual friend (Joseph) Pentland "will soon cross the Channel" bringing Owen the cast of a very curious bone, along with Bonaparte's projected table of fossils. But he wants to hear from Owen before sending the table, so that he could "arrange things better accord-ing to your philosophical views."[12]

Owen replied that he would attempt to answer some of Bonaparte's queries, but that he didn't deserve the confidence in his ornithological knowl-edge with which Bonaparte honored him. He expected to spend two or three weeks in Paris in June and would give him then any information on fossil birds that he wanted, though he would probably be charged by his government with some "little duties" in connection with the Paris Exhibition. "You see that you have been leaning on a poor reed in confiding for light and help on me."[13]

Bonaparte had also written to his old friend, illustrator, and occasional bête noir Titian Peale, enclosing one of his monographs and requesting a copy of Peale's report from the U.S. government's expedition to the Antarctic and Pacific Oceans (1838–42). Peale answered that by "legislative error" only one hundred copies were ordered by Congress for foreign distribution and only a few of these had actually been sent when the rest were accidentally destroyed in a fire at the Library of Congress. Since he had differed with "the parties in power," he had been deprived of the means of publishing his work. "But original observations . . . never lose their value, and I entertain a hope of again having access to the material collected . . . when it is my intention to publish much that remains unnoticed." He adds, "We have long hoped to see you again in this country—but now I suppose we must abandon that hope. Should you however come, none I can assure you will be more pleased to see you than the subscriber who remains respectfully and truly yours."[14]

Bonaparte heard again from Kaup, who sent him the skins of three rare birds, one of which had been a present from "old Lord Derby." He hoped the prince would incorporate these birds into his collection as a sign of his "deepest thanks and highest respect." He would probably not be coming to Paris, because he has had the "misfortune" while in London to buy cheaply the "excellent conserved skeleton" of a mastodon. Now he is forced to set up these gigantic bones: the grand duke and duchess are curious to see the creature. He is happy to hear the prince's children will soon be near him, and he understands quite well "that your heart has no place for a foreign person [meaning that Bonaparte would not want Kaup to visit him now that Bonaparte is so preoccupied with his children]."[15]

Several weeks later Kaup wrote again to say he had heard that M. (Georges-Louis) Duvernoy (director of the Jardin des Plantes) had died and he would like to take his place. His present situation in Darmstadt was not at all suited to his talents, and "the false pride and ignorance" of the duke's favorite, "a city born tailor," renders his situation quite unbearable. Kaup did not realize that his competition for this job was Bonaparte himself, but he was soon put off. In a week he wrote back: "It is a thousand pities that such a high civilized nation like the French is in scientifical affairs not cosmopolitan. I was for a moment happy in the hope to receive by your high protection a position in which I could work as never before. Now I see I am damned to persevere and to suffer to the end. My only wish is that this excellent position receives a man who is worthy to be the successor of G[eorges] Cuvier. De Blainville was a fancy-monger and Duvernoy a good old man."[16]

More than likely Bonaparte's explosive personality worked against his appointment to this most important post. An unsigned, undated statement refers to an unfortunate occurrence at the Academy of Sciences that would no doubt have spoiled his chances. The writer speaks of a quarrel that Charles Bonaparte, the prince of Canino, has had with his colleagues: "The last meeting of this Academy was widely troubled by an outburst [*incartade*] from this member of the imperial family. The scandal has been so great that one of the most illustrious members of the Academy, M. Biot, has been obliged to introduce a rule that would remove the prince of Canino from the right to attend future meetings. M. Charles Bonaparte is not the head [*titulaire*] but only a simple corresponding member. It remains to be seen if the prince of Canino will submit to this expulsion."[17] Of course, he would never submit.

These outbursts with his family had been frequent for years, and now that he was living apart from them he was particularly sensitive to their behavior toward him. Because Charlotte was the only one who did not show up for a family reunion in the spring of 1855, he did not answer her letters for several months, and then wrote to her husband that he could not explain his feelings or forget her offense. "My destiny, my fatality would have been understood by the ancients, but not by the modern world!" he exclaims, somewhat theatrically. He asks Primoli to embrace Charlotte for him—even though she has lost a little in the highest parental esteem, will lose more if she does not join the "family caravan," and will go down to zero if she is not persuaded to come to the arms of her especially loving father.[18]

"Fatality" soon visited Bonaparte in another way, when his mother died of cholera on 12 July 1855 at her summer place in Sinigallia, on the Adriatic coast. She was seventy-seven. Julie eulogized her "remarkably beautiful" grandmother as a woman of intellect, who had been interested in literature all her life, had written numerous lines of poetry, and had corresponded with Balzac and Stendhal.[19] Although there is no proof of a correspondence with Stendhal, it is highly probable, because Stendhal had visited Canino on several occasions when he was a customs officer at Civitavecchia (1831–41). The great writer was known to have been intensely interested in archaeology and surely would have been fascinated with the Etruscan artifacts Lucien and Alexandrine were uncovering. Julie also noted that her grandfather had married for love, but says nothing of how that decision determined the course of his life and that of his descendants.

In September Bonaparte put his troubles temporarily behind him and went to London with his daughter Marie and her husband Paul Campello. Owen reciprocated the hospitality Bonaparte had shown him in Paris by inviting them all for dinner with him and his wife at their home in Richmond Park. The following month Bonaparte went to Scotland to visit Sir William Jardine at Jardine Hall, and afterward stayed with several other Scottish naturalists. He wrote Charlotte—whom by now he had completely forgiven—that the weath-

er was beautiful and the kindness of his friends was keeping him from returning to the "fracas of Paris." Marie had been quite a hit, and this had been very
useful to him on the trip. One always had to dress for dinner, which was the fifth
or sixth meal of the day, and since he only had one outfit, he could not appear
elegantly attired. However, the hunting had been a great success.[20]

On returning to Paris he received a warm letter from Owen thanking him,
in his idiosyncratic diction, for "the instructive evidence" of his "unabated
energy" in the advancement of zoology and for his "admirable and piquant
sketch of excursions amongst continental museums." Since Bonaparte had
again sought Owen's help in gaining a membership he had coveted for years,
the latter answered him, "With regard to our Royal Society, you comprehend its
republican constitution; and by virtue of the rotation of its governing body, the
influence which a member may one year possess is neutralized by his removal
from the council, at the next election, when an opposite party may have the
majority." No doubt Owen knew that his candidate would not stand a chance
of election, in spite of his high reputation in science, because he was known to
be so contentious. But Owen ends his letter with heartfelt sympathy for
Bonaparte's now chronic illness. "Mrs. Owen and our son most sincerely griev-
ed, with me, to read your allusion to your own state of health: you bear up
bravely, and set a noble example of power of work and devotion to your adopted science. I could not help remarking that the spirit of the true Bonaparte
flashes forth from more than one passage of a letter which I shall always
value."[21]

Gould wrote him that he had received, only a few days after Bonaparte
returned to Paris, specimens of both sexes of a new hummingbird. For some
time Gould had wanted to name a bird after the French empress and so took
the opportunity to call this one *Eugenia Impératrise*. He had had duplicate
drawings made of this "fine species" and sent the specimen so that Bonaparte
might exhibit the bird at the Institute, "if you think it proper to do so [since
Bonaparte was not friendly with Eugénie]." After this, he "would deem it a
great favor" if Bonaparte's daughter, or any other member of his family, would
submit it to the empress, "but this I leave entirely to your Highness to do or not
as you think best."[22] Because Bonaparte refused to appear at Louis- Napoleon's
court, and was accordingly not invited, the hummingbird may only have been
shown to members of the Institute.

Even though he boycotted the imperial court, his stationery bore the
imprint "Cabinet de Monseigneur Le Prince Bonaparte." The designation
Monseigneur can be translated as "your Royal or Imperial Highness." To disdain
the pomp of monarchy while claiming royal status for himself was typical of the
contradictions in his character. Although he snubbed the court, he did sur-

round himself with the scientific intelligentsia of the city. Julie mentions in her memoirs that she dined at her father's house on several occasions in the fall of 1855 and met many distinguished men, including Alfred Moquin-Tandon, naturalist; Chevreul, chemist and member of the Institute; Claude de Bernard, physicist; Pierre-François Rayer, doctor and professor of comparative medicine; Giuseppi Filippo Baruffi, voyager, writer, and popularizer of scientific culture; Joseph Pentland, English geologist; Charles-Joseph Giraud, professor of Roman law at the Sorbonne; Elie de Beaumont, geologist and perpetual secretary of the Academy of Sciences since 1853; as well as Isadore Geoffroy Saint-Hilaire; General Pepe; and Giuseppe Montanelli, the distinguished Tuscan writer.[23]

But despite his noteworthy connections, his membership in the Institute, and his high standing as a naturalist, Bonaparte had been unable to secure the position he coveted: the directorship of the Jardin des Plantes. Aside from his problematic personality, he had had a serious disagreement with the administration of this great museum of natural history. It seems he wanted to establish a large department devoted solely to French fauna. Because the idea was not accepted, Bonaparte planned to publish a work in twenty-four volumes (!), one to appear every three months beginning in 1858, that would cover the subject. The prospectus for *Faune française, ou histoire naturelle générale et particulière des animaux qui vivent en France,* is primarily an indictment of the museum for not creating the vast exhibit he had proposed. Even so, he made elaborate plans for the book: woodcuts, interspersed in the text, would show particular characteristics of the animals, while numerous colored plates would give exact portraits of the species and depict their habitats and the vegetation on which many of them depended. Since country dwellers, hunters, and fishermen were "gifted with a spirit of observation and rich in knowledge not found in books," Bonaparte and his coauthor, Victor Meunier, solicited their reports from the field. The prospectus stated that: "Unfortunately, the professors of the Museum of Paris, whose task it is to raise this monument [the exhibit], have defaulted, and they will be jealous of the glory of such a work, not having dreamt of the success of these displays. The scientific usefulness and the patriotic character of a collection exclusively French appears to have entirely escaped them. . . . One thing only is lacking in the scientific cosmopolitanism of the professors: *patriotism.*" The national collections, as well as many others, were for the most part buried in the museum's storerooms, and not even the administrators knew what they contained. Bonaparte suggested (facetiously) that those who commissioned explorers to bring back specimens could save a great deal of money by simply sending them to explore the museum's forgotten holdings. And the country would be enriched by founding a center in the capital for studying the flora and fauna of the provinces. "It is the work of the Jardin des Plantes that we are going to do [by putting all this information into the twenty-four volumes]." In the last paragraph of the prospectus Bonaparte invited naturalists from all across the country, as well as professors and conservators, to help erect this "monument," "which will not be unworthy of our dear France, and will contribute to the love and knowledge of the zoological riches nature has given us."[24]

Bonaparte's nationalism had been honed in the fires of the Risorgimento, and the embers of his passionate republicanism—reflected in his invitation to the common man to contribute to this great work—were still glowing beneath the imperial trappings of "Monseigneur." Surely he was aware, however, that too little time was left to him for such an enormous undertaking. The prospectus was really only a device to express his ideas—and perhaps his bitterness. The atmosphere of contention that surrounded his birth and that followed him throughout his life continued to hover about him during his final years.

In the winter of 1856 Bonaparte at last realized a long-held desire to visit Spain and Portugal. He left shortly after his twenty-year-old daughter Augusta married her cousin Prince Placide Gabrielli, the son of Bonaparte's oldest half-sister Charlotte. The wedding took place on 2 February in the chapel of the Tuileries Palace, with the emperor and empress in attendance. Under the circumstances of Bonaparte's relationship with the court, more than likely, he had had nothing to do with the arrangements.

By the third week of February he reached Alicante on the Spanish Mediterranean coast, where he ascended the "famous citadel of the city," the Castillo de Santa Barbara, extensive fortifications crowning the summit of an isolated hill that dominated the town and provided panoramic views. From Alicante he proceeded along the coast to Cartagena, a navel base in ancient times, and then to Almeria, once the most important city in Moorish Spain, where he had a fine view across the bay to Gibraltar. The next day he reached Algeciras—surprisingly fast for someone traveling by horse-drawn carriage across bumpy dirt roads. Once before he had been in Algeciras, when he returned from Europe from America in 1828. How much had happened to him since then! The birth and death of children, the intense ten-year work on the *Fauna italica*, the scientific congresses, the Roman republic, his escape and exile, the frantic study in Holland, the final return to the city of his birth, and the recovery of his French citizenship in February 1851. Now the children were mostly grown and nearly all the girls were married; Zenaide was dead and he himself was in precarious health. But he was an optimist, with a great deal left to do. He traveled on to Cadiz, a principal seaport of Spain and one of the oldest towns in Europe. From there he set sail for Lisbon.[25] In that historic city, he met with the young king of Portugal, who delighted him with his enthusiasm for natural history. By the end of March he was back in Paris.[26]

His race against time did not allow him to stay long in one spot, however. Two months later he traveled to Germany to survey collections of bird specimens in various museums for his *Conspectus*. His first destination was Köthen and a meeting of the German Ornithological Society (Deutsche Ornithologen-Gesellschaft) in early June. The topic under discussion was "What is a species, particularly in ornithology?" Although the leading German specialists, including J. F. Naumann, C. L. Brehm, and Eduard Baldamus, were present, only Bonaparte could grapple with the question in a fundamental way. As a disciple of Isadore Geoffroy Saint-Hilaire, only he "understood existing species as the result of a long evolution, the product of a struggle between the conservatism of heredity and the modifications of environment."[27] He addressed the meeting:

> Will one oppose to our obvious theory of limited mutation the theory of successive creations and the theory of the so-called transmission of acquired characteristics? And are the creatures that died out a long time ago supposed to have left no progeny at all, though we see creatures like them everywhere? No! We will state with unanimous conviction that the antediluvian crocodiles, elephants, and rhinoceroses were the ancestors of those living in our day; and these animals would not have been able to continue to exist without the manifold mutations that their systems produced to adapt themselves to the environment, and that became second nature to their descendants. I say manifold mutations, because clearly the number of species seems more likely to increase than to decrease.... If the environment remains the same, so do the species. The stabilizing influence is then by itself all-powerful. The mutating influence can succeed in opposing it only when the whole world surrounding the species changes.... But races, however different in characteristics they may be, vanish entirely or at least do not long survive as soon as the environment that produced them ceases to be the same.... The transitions between the different races and their type are the best evidence that we can supply to set aside putative species, which are to be relegated to races, with which the painstaking zoologist must nevertheless occupy himself just as earnestly."[28]

From Köthen he traveled north to Berlin. There, in the Zoological Museum, he compared established species of birds with possible new ones. As he examined a magnificent blue macaw from Brazil, he realized that it was a new species, and named it Lear's Macaw (*Anodorhynchus leari*) in honor of his talented artist friend Edward Lear. Lear had published a beautiful watercolor of this bird in his book on parrots some years before, not knowing that it was different from another Brazilian species that it closely resembled. In Bonaparte's work at the Berlin museum, he was aided by the director, Heinrich Liechtenstein, and his assistant, the excellent ornithologist Jean Cabanis. Although the erudite Professor Liechtenstein had amassed an ornithological collection that rivaled that of the Leiden museum, systematic evaluation was not his forte. He tended to ignore anatomical criteria and even bartered or sold specimens before they were thoroughly studied.[29] Cabanis was editor of the *Journal für Ornithologie* in which Bonaparte's remarks at the Ornithological Society were published, as well as his naming of Lear's Macaw (1856).[30]

On the next leg of his journey Bonaparte visited Brunswick, Leipzig, Dresden, Strasbourg, and Frankfurt, where he saw his old friend Rüppell. Then it was on to Neuwied to pay another visit to the enthusiastic Prince Maximilian. In the course of his travels Bonaparte somehow received a letter from Kaup, who thought Bonaparte was in Hamburg and who was himself on the coast of southern France. It must have been gratifying to Bonaparte to learn that Kaup had been able to obtain a copy of the *Fauna italica* from the library in Montpellier, as well as to hear Kaup's praise of his *Catalogo methodica* (of fish), for which he asked permission to arrange a second edition.[31] In Bremen Bonaparte saw Gustav Hartlaub, a brilliant and cultured man specializing in exotic ornithology, who had a fine library and a large collection of bird specimens, classified scientifically. Hartlaub was discovering undescribed species in his collection and studying them intently, and had done some work, with Temminck's permission, at the Leiden museum. Bonaparte's subsequent stops of course included Leiden, where he saw his dear friends Temminck and Schlegel. He visited the natural history museums of Wiesbaden, Antwerp, Brussels, and Ghent.[32] On his return to Paris he was busier than ever incorporating all the new material he had collected into the next part of his *Conspectus*.

In September, he gave his permission for his youngest daughter Bathilde to marry Louis, count of Cambacérès, although he may have had misgivings about this decision since the bride was not quite sixteen. In any case, the wedding took place the following month in the Tuileries. Julie spoke tenderly of this little sister, describing her as "beautiful, good, and affectionate."[33] Five years later Bathilde would die in childbirth.

In mid-January Julie noted in her diary that her father was very ill and she was afraid he would not recover. "He was only fifty-four years old!" She read newspapers to him and had just begun a novel as well, *Deux amours* by Mme de Girardin (Delphine Gay, who had been one of his good friends). He was so grateful for everything Julie did for him, and it broke her heart when he exclaimed, "What torment to live this way!" "I love my father so much and I shudder at the idea that I will lose him," she wrote.[34]

In spite of his illness (terrible edema—probably the result of heart trouble—in his ulcerated legs), he was still working as hard as humanly possible, even trying to keep up with his correspondence. George Robert Gray wrote in February that Bonaparte's brother Louis-Lucien—who divided his time between London and Paris—had kindly offered to convey any packet Charles wanted. Gray says that he is sending a catalog of fish but he doesn't know if

Figure 46. *Prince Charles-Lucien Bonaparte* by F. Bocourt, 1858. Pencil drawing. Posthumous portrait. courtesy of the Museo Napoleonico, Rome.

Bonaparte still takes an interest in this class of animals. He adds, "May I express a hope that you are enjoying better health than you have done of late."[35]

He was not. By May he was completely bedridden. Still he worked on, his bedside table covered with books, bird specimens wrapped in straw, and proofs waiting for correction. "The more I have to put up with, the more I work," he told Hartlaub, during one of his last visits. The German ornithologist had found him writing in his bathtub, the only place where he was reasonably comfortable.[36] Julie recorded that he told her "with vehemence" in his voice that he loved science for science's sake and not for honors, celebrity, or money. And he only cared about those colleagues who loved the study of nature as he loved it. She said that her father wrote in a clear and original style, that his brilliant wit (*esprit*) was combined with a superior intelligence and a broad education, and that he could speak and write fluently in English, French, and Italian. Her cousin Prince Napoleon (Plon-Plon) had said to the Empress Eugénie: "Charles is one of the most amusing men I know, I could stay with him for two hours without being bored."[37] Julie also felt that he had not been treated in life with the respect he deserved. After his death she would write: "My father was slighted, not understood, not appreciated enough! I wish I had the talent to write his story; in depicting his character, in retracing his life, one could make a very interesting book."[38]

Julie spent the evening of 7 July with her father and Giuseppe Montanelli, his old friend and ally in the fight for the independence of Italy, whom she described as having "a distinguished intelligence and a great heart." During the course of the evening, she saw with the deepest sadness how much illness had aged her "Papa."[39]

On 13 July Bonaparte wrote to the American naturalist John Cassin, who had once suggested collaborating with him. He praised Cassin's interesting volume on the birds of Texas and California and said that he himself, though hovering between life and death, had new works forthcoming, of which Cassin would receive samples. "If heaven gives me life," he concludes, "I hope that our future relations will be closer and such that they benefit our beloved science."[40] This was not to be, however; in fact, this letter to Cassin was among the last he would ever write. On 29 July 1857, at 2:30 in the afternoon, with Julie beside him, Bonaparte lost his race with death.[41]

Lost, too, was the chance to finish his *Conspectus*. The work still lacked auks, loons, and grebes, as well as ducks and geese, rails, grouse, and pheasants. And this study had been intended only as the precursor of a comprehensive ornithology in many volumes, which other zoologists looked forward to with high hopes.[42] However, Erwin Stresemann, a distinguished ornithologist of our own day, wrote that "Bonaparte's achievements in ornithological systematics ensure him an outstanding place in history. His work left deep and indelible marks."[43] Because he had visited more collections in more countries than any of his contemporaries, his knowledge of bird species was extensive enough for the ambitious synopsis he had undertaken. Stresemann adds that "his arrangement of genera and their relationship to families and orders differs from our 'modern' system less than other contemporary efforts," because he was "already inspired by the theory of evolution" and the years he had spent in comparative studies had trained him to recognize essential differences.[44]

The Linnean Society of London said in its *Proceedings* that through his labors he had contributed largely to "our knowledge of the faunas of Europe and North America in particular" and "to the improvement of their systematic arrangement, to the establishment of many well-marked genera, and to the distinction and description of a multitude of new or imperfectly known species." His death was attributed to "dropsy of the chest" (what today would be described as congestive heart failure).[45]

Hermann Schlegel wrote of him that "without doubt this remarkable man found the right way into the profoundest depths of science, because of his all-penetrating perception and his almost excessively intense activity. To the highest degree pleasant in company, fonder of children than most men, and in his family circle the most amiable and unreserved imaginable; in politics he was by contrast what the French call a 'farouche [fierce] républicain.' But he was wild only in speech and not in action."[46] Two months before Bonaparte died, another devoted colleague, Isadore Geoffroy Saint-Hilaire, wrote to thank him for his efforts in raising funds for the completed statue of Isadore's father Etienne: "It is to you, dear prince, and exalted friend that we must give our thanks. You have been a great part of the monument, which makes it even more dear to me. I will always love the memory that connects all that you have done to the memory of my father, who had a sincere and deep affection for you."[47]

Etienne Geoffroy Saint-Hilaire had been one of the gifted men who accompanied Napoleon on his militarily disastrous expedition to Egypt and through his brilliant scientific discoveries he had brought glory to the future emperor. Would Charles Bonaparte's powerful uncle have cast such a negative eye on him had he known the respect in which men like Geoffroy and his son would hold the naturalist prince? And yet, had Napoleon not barred Charles from the succession, Bonaparte might never have devoted his life to the study of natural science.

With Plon-Plon and two of his sons-in-law present, he was buried in the Bonaparte graveyard at Ajaccio, Corsica. The man without a country for so long, was at last laid to rest in the land of his ancestors.

His life had been full of tumult, often stirred up by the contrasts within his own personality, conflicting forces that not only tossed him about but often perplexed or angered others. Being a Bonaparte and a prince had certain social advantages, but often worked against him in intellectual circles. Those who were not aware of the depth of his erudition regarded him as a dilettante, an aristocratic dabbler.

Bonaparte's energy and enthusiasm were tremendous, but they sometimes led him into immoderate behavior that alienated the very people whose help he needed to advance his goals. He fervently loved his wife and children but often caused them grief through his petulant demands and self-indulgence. He was a man of great strength and courage, who could fall prey to petty weaknesses, such as the gambling of his later years. He was sincerely dedicated to the unification and independence of Italy, as well as to republican and humanitarian principles that even today would be considered progressive. Yet he was easily enough seduced by high society and the good life, and after the defeat of the Roman republic, he seems to have done little to promote the Italian cause. In short, Charles Bonaparte was a brilliant, fascinating, and complicated man.

But above all, he was a student of the natural world. His energy and drive advanced ornithology further than any other naturalist in the first half of the nineteenth century, by bringing scientific principles of classification to a welter of disorganized data. His contributions to natural history in his own time can be ranked with those of his better known contemporaries—Huxley, Gould, Owen, Agassiz. Shut out from the imperial succession that was, in fact, his birthright as Napoleon's oldest nephew, Charles Lucien Bonaparte was nevertheless a figure of international importance and a great scientist—one of the first to understand how birds fit into the vast empire of nature.

NOTES

CHAPTER 1

1. *Le prince Lucien Bonaparte et sa famille* (Paris: Librairie Plon, 1889), 53.

2. Quoted in Michael Allin, *Zarafa: A Giraffe's True Story, from Deep in Africa to the Heart of Paris* (New York: Walker and Company, 1998), 130.

3. A. Hilliard Atteridge, *Napoleon's Brothers* (London: Methuen, 1909), 99.

4. Bonaparte, *Memoirs of the Private and Political Life of Lucien Bonaparte, Prince of Canino*, trans. from the French, 2 vols. (London: H. Colburn, 1818), 1: 163.

5. Atteridge, 99.

6. Ibid., 100.

7. *Memoirs of Lucien*, 1: 108.

8. The Duchess D'Abrantes (Madame Junot), *Memoirs of Napoleon, His Court and Family* (London: Richard Bentley, 1836) 1: 267.

9. *Le prince Lucien Bonaparte*, 40.

10. Fiorella Bartoccini, "Il Principe di Canino e i congressi degli scienziati," *Sui congressi degli Scienziati*, Quaderni del Risorgimento 2 (Roma: Edizioni dell'Atteneo, 1952), 6.

11. *Le prince Lucien Bonaparte*, 51.

12. August Friedrich Ferdinand von Kotzbue, *Travels from Berlin to Paris in the year 1804* (London, 1805), 3: 174–81; quoted in Marina Natoli, "Le residenze di Luciano Bonaparte a Roma, nel Lazio e in Italia (1804–1840)," *Luciano Bonaparte: le sue collezioni d'arte, le sue residenze a Roma, nel Lazio, in Italia (1804–1840)* (Rome: Libreria dello Stato, 1995), 380, n.20.

13. Alan Schom, *Napoleon Bonaparte* (New York: HarperCollins, 1997), 238.

14. Mina Gregori, "La collezione dei dipinti antichi," in Natoli and Gregori, 266.

15. Vincent Cronin, *Napoleon Bonaparte* (New York: William Morrow, 1972), 261.

16. Atteridge, 101.

17. Gregori, 264.

18. Memoirs of Lucien, 2: 18.

19. Monica Stirling, *Madame Letizia: A Portrait of Napoleon's Mother* (New York: Harper, 1962), 142.

20. Natoli, 390.

21. *Memoirs of Lucien*, 1: 247.

22. Ibid., 1: 253.

23. Atteridge, 174.

24. Napoleon Bonaparte to Joseph, Milan, December 17, 1807. *Napoleon Bonaparte, The Confidential Correspondence of Napoleon Bonaparte with His Brother Joseph, Sometime King of Spain* (New York: Mason Brothers, 1857), 1: 282.

25. Bonaparte, "Cenni Autobiografici di Carlo Giulio Lorenzo Luciano Principe Bonaparte" (manuscript, del Gallo family archives), 59.

26. Atteridge, 175.

27. D'Abrantes, 144.

28. *Memoirs of Lucien,* 1: 236.

29. *Memoirs of Lucien,* 2: 26. Also *Le prince Lucien Bonaparte,* 72.

30. An anecdote told to the author by Monsignore Luigi del Gallo Roccagiovine, a great-great grandson of Charles-Lucien Bonaparte.

31. W. H. Oswald to Samuel Mifflin, Malta to Cadiz, 22 August 1810 (Library Company Collection, HSP).

32. Giovanni Bonello, LL.D., "Malta in the Life of Four Bonapartes," pt. 2, *Sunday Times* (Malta), 24 April 1994.

33. Cartoon in the Bonaparte collection (Houghton Library).

34. Atteridge, 262.

35. Ibid., 263.

36. Ibid., 307.

37. "Autobiografici," 60.

38. Ibid., 61.

39. Natoli, 397, n.61.

40. "Autobiografici," 60.

41. Ibid., 61.

42. *Memoirs of Lucien,* 2: 35.

43. "Autobiografici," 62.

44. Obituary, *Journal of the Proceedings of the Linnean Society* 3 (London, 1859): xli–xliv.

45. Erwin Stresemann, *Ornithology from Aristotle to the Present,* trans. Hans J. Epstein and Cathleen Epstein (Cambridge, Mass.: Harvard University Press, 1975), 154.

46. Natoli, 390.

47. "Autobiografici," 62–63.

48. Ibid., 63.

49. The full French spelling is Zénaïde; see Note on Names.

50. Barbara Mearns and Richard Mearns, *Biographies for Birdwatchers: The Lives of Those Commemorated in Western Palearctic Bird Names* (London: Academic Press, 1988), 77.

51. Gabriel Girod de l'Ain, *Joseph Bonaparte: le roi malgré lui* (Paris: Librairie Académique Perrin, 1970), 365, n. 4.

52. Ibid., 366.

53. Atteridge, 362–63.

54. David received 6,000 francs on 25 June 1821 for an original and two copies of the painting, the latter undoubtedly executed by his Belgian students. One copy was sent to Joseph in America, the second may have been the portrait sent to Charles and Lucien, Julie perhaps retained the original. Today the original is at the Getty Museum in California, one copy is at the Museo Napoleonico in Rome, and the second copy is at the Musée de Toulon. Girod de l'Ain, 364 n.1.

55. Bonaparte to Julie Clary Bonaparte, Canino, 19 December 1821 (Fondazioni Primoli).

56. Zenaide Bonaparte to Lucien Bonaparte in a letter of Julie Clary Bonaparte to Lucien, Brussels, 22 December 1821 (Fondazioni Primoli).

57. Girod de l'Ain, 368.

58. "Autobiografici," 64.

59. Letter not found. Contents taken from Charles Bonaparte to Lucien Bonaparte, 4 October 1822 (Fondazioni Primoli).

60. Bonaparte to Lucien Bonaparte, 4 October 1822 (Fondazioni Primoli).

61. Bonaparte to Lucien Bonaparte, 28 February 1823 (#8390, Fondazioni Primoli).

62. Lucien Bonaparte to Charles written on the back of the letter from Charles to Lucien, Rome, 28 February 1823 (#8390, Fondazioni Primoli).

63. Bonaparte to Lucien Bonaparte, Rome, 12 February 1823 (Fondazioni Primoli).

64. Pierre-Augustin-Joseph Drapiez to Bonaparte, Brussels, 28 February 1923 (MNHN).

65. Bonaparte to Lucien Bonaparte, *Croce di Bianco*, [Bologna], 14 May 1823 (#8392, Fondazioni Primoli).

CHAPTER 2

1. *Poulson's American Daily Advertiser*, 12 September 1823.

2. Charlotte Bonaparte to Julie Clary Bonaparte, New York, 28 August 1823 (del Gallo family archives).

3. Bonaparte to Coenraad Jacob Temminck, 1 October 1823 (MS 2612, MNHN).

4. Vincent Cronin, *Napoleon Bonaparte: An Intimate Biography* (New York: William Morrow, 1972), 430.

5. Alexander Wilson, *American Ornithology or, The Natural History of the Birds of the United States* (Philadelphia: Bradford and Inskeep, 1808–13), 2: 387.

6. Ibid., 388.

7. Edward Biddle, "Joseph Bonaparte as Recorded in the Private Journal of Nicholas Biddle," *Pennsylvania Magazine of History and Biography* 55, 14 (1931): 208.

8. E. M. Woodward, *Bonaparte's Park and the Murats* (Trenton, N.J.: MacCrellish and Quigley, 1879), 42.

9. Weymer Jay Mills, *Historic Houses of New Jersey* (Philadelphia: J. P. Lippincott, 1903), 302.

10. Reuben Haines to Ann Haines, added to a letter from Jane Haines, Germantown, 3 July 1825 (Wyck Papers).

11. Charlemagne Tower, "Joseph Bonaparte in Philadelphia and Bordentown," *Pennsylvania Magazine of History and Biography* 4 (1918): 305.

12. Zenaide Bonaparte to Julie Clary Bonaparte, Point Breeze, 1 November 1824 (Fondazioni Primoli).

13. Woodward, 42; Anthony Hobson, "The Escorial," *Great Palaces*, intro. Sacheverell Sitwell (New York: Spring Books, 1964), 157.

14. Woodward, 43.

15. Owen Connelly, *The Gentle Bonaparte: The Story of Napoleon's Older Brother* (New York: Macmillan, 1968), 252.

16. John F. Watson (manuscript diary), "Trip to Pennsbury & to Count Survilliers, 1826" (Library of the Henry Francis Du Pont Winterthur Museum).

17. Woodward, 44–45.

18. Gabriel Girod de l'Ain, *Joseph Bonaparte: le roi malgré lui* (Paris: Librairie Académique Perrin, 1970), 380.

19. Biddle, 215.

20. "A Sketch of Joseph Bounaparte," *Godey's Lady's Book*, April 1845, 185.

21. J. M. Thompson, "Lucien Bonaparte, Napoleon's Ablest Brother," *History Today* (London) 5, 5 (May 1955).

22. *Niles Weekly Register* new series 11, no.15 (14 December 1822).

23. Edwin Wolf 2nd, *Philadelphia: Portrait of an American City* (Harrisburg, Pa.: Stackpole Books, 1975; reprint Philadelphia: Camino Books, 1990), 127.

24. Russell F. Weigley, ed., *Philadelphia: A 300-Year History* (New York: W. W. Norton, 1982), 245.

25. *Poulson's American Daily Advertiser*, 12 July 1823.

26. Ibid., 22 Aug. 1823.

27. Ibid., 12 Sept. 1823.

28. Bonaparte, "Cenni Autobiografici di Carlo Giulio Lorenzo Luciano Principe Bonaparte" (manuscript, del Gallo family archives), 66.

29. Charles Bonaparte to Alexandrine Bonaparte, Point Breeze, 1 November 1823 (Fondazioni Primoli).

30. Biddle, 215.

31. Bonaparte to Alexandrine Bonaparte, Point Breeze, 1 November 1823 (Fondazioni Primoli).

32. Ibid.

33. Watson, diary.

34. Fiorella Bartoccini, "Il principe di Canino e i congressi degli scienziati," Bartoccini and Silvana Verdini, *Sui congressi degli scienziati*, Quaderni del Risorgimento 2 (Rome: Edizioni dell'Atteneo, 1952), 5. The description of Charles-Lucien is "dai contemporanei, concordi solo sulla sua bella faccia napoleonica."

35. Lucien Bonaparte, *Memoirs of the Private and Political Life of Lucien Bonaparte, Prince of Canino*, trans. from the French, 2 vols. (London, 1818), 1: 179.

36. Erwin Stresemann, *Ornithology from Aristotle to the Present*, trans. Hans J. Epstein and Cathleen Epstein (Cambridge, Mass.: Harvard University Press, 1975), 157.

37. Bonaparte's manuscript notebook (MS 2548, MNHN).

38. Watson, diary.

39. Ibid.

40. Bonaparte to Pierre-Augustin-Joseph Drapiez, 7 April 1824, fair copy in Bonaparte's notebook (MS 2549, MNHN).

41. Joseph Bonaparte to Julie Bonaparte, Philadelphia, 13 February 1824 (Prince and Princess Napoleon archives).

42. "Autobiografici," 67.

43. Dr. Caspar Wistar (1761–1818) was the first professor of anatomy at the University of Pennsylvania, a friend of Thomas Jefferson and an influential presence in the early republic. During his lifetime, the Wistar parties were held at his home.

44. Biddle, 209.

45. Bonaparte, "An Account of Four Species of Stormy Petrels. Read January 13th, 1824," *Journal of the Academy of Natural Sciences of Philadelphia* 3, 1 (Philadelphia: J. Harding, 1823 [sic]): 227–33.

46. *Minutes of the Academy of Natural Sciences of Philadelphia*, 24 February 1824 (ASP).

47. Ibid., Saturday, 25 January 1812.

48. Ibid., 30 December 1817, 26 May 1818.

49. Bonaparte, "Observations on the Nomenclature of Wilson's Ornithology," *Journal of the Academy of Natural Sciences of Philadelphia* 3, 2 (1824): 340–71.

50. Bonaparte, "Observations on the Nomenclature of Wilson's Ornithology," *Journal of the Academy of Natural Sciences* 4, 1 (1824): 26.

51. Charles Lucian (sic) Bonaparte, *American Ornithology; or, the Natural History of Birds Inhabiting the United States, not given by Wilson* (Philadelphia: Carey, Lea & Carey, 1825), 1.

52. Ord to Bonaparte, Philadelphia, 2 June 1824 (MS 2608, MNHN).

53. Ord to Bonaparte, 5 June 1824 (MS 2608, MNHN).

54. James Forester to Charles Bonaparte, New York, 9 January 1824 (del Gallo family archives).

55. Forester to Bonaparte, New York, 10 February 1824 (del Gallo family archives). The Red- and White-winged Crossbills (*Loxia curvirostra* and *Loxia leucoptra*) are mainly found in the conifer forests of New Hampshire.

56. Forester to Bonaparte, New York, 10 June 1824 (del Gallo family archives).

57. Reuben Haines to Bonaparte, Philadelphia, 6 December 1825 (MS 2603, MNHN).

58. Forester to Bonaparte, New York, 9 September 1824 (del Gallo family archives).

59. Jessie Poesch, *Titian Ramsay Peale, 1799–1885, and His Memoirs of the Wilkes Expedition*, Memoirs of the American Philosophical Society 52 (Philadelphia: American Philosophical Society, 1961), 49.

60. Paul Lawrence Farber, *The Emergence of Ornithology as a Scientific Discipline: 1760–1850*, Studies in the History of Modern Science 12 (Dordrecht: D. Reidel, 1982), 108.

61. Charles Bonaparte to Lucien Bonaparte, Point Breeze, 15 August 1825 (Fondazioni Primoli).

62. Quoted in Bernard Jaffe, *Men of Science in America: The Role of Science in the Growth of Our Country* (New York: Simon and Schuster, 1944), 235.

63. George H. Daniels, *American Science in the Age of Jackson* (New York: Columbia University Press, 1968), 19.

64. Thomas Jefferson to an unknown correspondent, September 28, 1821, quoted in Silvio A. Bedini, "Jefferson: Man of Science," *Frontiers: Annual of the Academy of Natural Sciences of Philadelphia* 3 (1981–82): 21.

65. *Journal of the Academy of Natural Sciences* 1, pt. 1 (May 1817).

66. Thomas Jefferson to George Wythe, 16 September 1787, quoted in Silvio A. Bedini, *Thomas Jefferson: Statesman of Science* (New York, Macmillan, 1990), 180.

67. *Journal of the Academy of Natural Sciences of Philadelphia* 1, pt.1 (May 1817), introduction.

68. Alice Ford, *John James Audubon* (Norman: University of Oklahoma Press, 1964)

69. Ford, 142–43.

70. Frank L. Burns, "Miss Lawson's Recollections of Ornithologists," *The Auk: A Quarterly Journal of Ornithology* 341 (1917): 281.

71. Ford, 145.

72. Ford quotes Charles Waterton in a letter to George Ord, 4 August 1840 (p. 374): Waterton, on a visit to Rome, had asked Bonaparte whether Audubon had studied with David; Bonaparte replied that he had asked David, and David had denied it.

73. Bonaparte to Lucien Bonaparte, Point Breeze, 19 November 1824 (#8395, Fondazioni Primoli).

74. Zenaide to Julie Clary Bonaparte, Point Breeze, 1 November 1824 (#9079, Fondazioni Primoli).

75. James D. Magee, *Bordentown 1682–1932: An Illustrated Story of a Colonial Town* (Bordentown, N.J., 1932), 77.

76. Ibid., 80.

77. Ibid., 78.

78. Daniels, 19.

CHAPTER 3

1. Bonaparte to Thomas Say, Point Breeze, 15 October 1824 (Thomas Say Papers, APS).

2. T. S. Palmer, "Names of Persons Whose Names Appear in the Nomenclature of California birds," *Condor* 30 (1928): 69.

3. Witmer Stone, "Some Philadelphia Collections and Collectors," *The Auk: A Quarterly Journal of Ornithology* 16 (April 1899).

4. Bonaparte, *American Ornithology; or, The Natural History of Birds Inhabiting the United States, Not Given by Wilson* (Philadelphia: Carey, Lea & Carey, 1825), 1: Preface.

5. Bonaparte to Say, Point Breeze, 15 October 1824 (Say Papers, APS).

6. Bonaparte, "Observations on the Nomenclature of Wilson's Ornithology," *Journal of the Academy of Natural Sciences of Philadelphia* 4, 1 (1824): 167–68.

7. Ibid., 168.

8. Bonaparte to Temminck, Point Breeze, 15 May 1824 (MS 2612, MNHN).

9. Bonaparte to Isaac Hays, Philadelphia, Tues. evening [probably August 1824] (Isaac Hays Papers, APS).

10. Bonaparte, *Continuation of Wilson*, 37.

11. Frank L. Burns, "Miss Lawson's Recollections of Ornithologists," *The Auk: A Quarterly Journal of Ornithology* 34 (1917): 279.

12. Ibid., 281.

13. Ord to Bonaparte, Philadelphia 9 September 1825 (MS 2608, MNHN).

14. John James Audubon to Bonaparte, Beech Woods, Louisiana, 14 April 1825 (MNHN; film 542, APS).

15. Audubon to Reuben Haines, Bayou Sarah, 5 May 1825 (Quaker Collection, Haverford College).

16. Bonaparte to Audubon, Saratoga, 28 July 1825 (MS 2598, MNHN). This is Bonaparte's draft copy of the letter. The fair copy he sent Audubon is in the Morris Tyler Collection (Gen. MSS 85m, Box 3, Beinecke Library).

17. Audubon to Bonaparte, Bayou Sarah, 1 October 1825 (MNHN; film 542, APS).

18. Bonaparte to Audubon, Point Breeze, 24 December 1825 (in French) (Morris Tyler Collection, Gen. MSS 85, Box 3, Beinecke Library).

19. Charles Bonaparte, "Descriptions of Ten Species of South American Birds. Read April 19, 1825," *Journal of the Academy of Natural Sciences of Philadelphia* 4, 2 (1825).

20. Bonaparte, *American Ornithology*, 1: 20.

21. Ibid., 69.

22. Bonaparte to Say, 15 October 1825 (Say Papers, APS).

23. Bonaparte to Hays, Philadelphia, [probably August 1824] (Isaac Hays Papers, APS).

24. Bonaparte to Temminck, Point Breeze, 15 May 1824 (MS 2612, MNHN).

25. Drapiez to Bonaparte, Brussels, 28 May 1824 (MNHN).

26. Bonaparte to Hays, Point Breeze, Tues. evening, n.d. [probably July 1824] (Isaac Hays Papers, APS).

27. Bonaparte to Hays, Point Breeze, n.d. (Isaac Hays Papers, APS).

28. Bonaparte to Hays, New York, 2 August 1824 (Isaac Hays Papers, APS).

29. Bonaparte to Hays, Saratoga Springs, N.Y., Tuesday, July 27? [probably 1825] (Isaac Hays Papers, APS).

30. Jean Lavrey, *Madame Mère* (Paris, 1982).

31. John Godman to Bonaparte, Philadelphia, 15 May 1825 (del Gallo family archives).

32. James E. DeKay to Bonaparte, New York, 17 March 1825 (MNHN; film 542, APS).

33. Fiorella Bartoccini, "Il Principe di Canino e i congressi degli scienziati," Bartoccini and Silvana Verdini, *Sui congressi degli scienzati*, Quaderni del Risorgimento 2 (Rome: Edizioni dell'Atteneo, 1952), 5–6.

34. Zenaide Bonaparte to Julie Clary Bonaparte and Charlotte Bonaparte, Philadelphia, 5 January 1825 (#8833, Fondazioni Primoli).

35. Bonaparte to Lucien Bonaparte, Point Breeze, 15 August 1825 (#8396, Fondazioni Primoli).

36. Say to Bonaparte, Columbus, Ohio, 13 July 1826 (MNHN; film 542, APS).

37. Say to Nicholas M. Hentz, Philadelphia, 12 October 1825 (Museum of Comparative Zoology Archives, Harvard University).

38. Charles Bonaparte to Lucien Bonaparte, Point Breeze, 15 August 1825 (#8396, Fondazioni Primoli).

39. Bonaparte to Hays, New York, 9 February 1826 (Isaac Hays Papers, APS).

40. Bonaparte to Hays, New York, 14 January 1826 (Isaac Hays Papers, APS).

41. Bonaparte to Hays, New York, 22 February 1826 (Isaac Hays Papers, APS).

42. Bonaparte to Hays, New York, 14 January 1826 (Isaac Hays Papers, APS).

43. Audubon to Reuben Haines, Bayou Sarah, 25 December 1825 (Wyck Papers, APS).

44. Bonaparte to William Cooper, "on board the Baltimore steamboat headed for Washington," 9 March 1826 (William Cooper Papers, film 514, APS).

45. Ibid.

46. Cooper to Bonaparte, New York, 20 March 1826 (film 1514, APS).

47. Bonaparte to Zenaide Bonaparte, "on board the steamboat United States between New Castle and Baltimore," 9 March 1826 (Prince and Princess Napoleon archives).

48. Bonaparte to Hays, Washington, 18 March 1826 (Isaac Hays Papers, APS).

49. Bonaparte to Hays, Washington, 20 March 1826 Isaac Hays Papers, APS.

50. Bonaparte to Zenaide, Washington, 11 March 1826 (Prince and Princess Napoleon archives).

51. Bonaparte to William Cooper, Point Breeze, 27 March 1826 (film 1514, APS).

52. Bonaparte to Cooper, Point Breeze, 12 April 1826 (film 1514, APS).

53. Quoted in Alan Taylor, *William Cooper's Town: Power and Persuasion on the Frontier of the Early American Republic* (New York: Knopf, 1995), 411.

54. James Fenimore Cooper, *The Letters and Journals of James Fenimore Cooper*, ed. James Franklin Beard (Cambridge, Mass.: Belknap Press of Harvard University Press, 1968), letter to the Princess Galitzin Souvarof, Paris, 22 October [1826], 6 :292. The princess was apparently making a collection of autographs.

55. Taylor, *William Cooper's Town*, 400.

56. Owen Connelly, *The Gentle Bonaparte: The Story of Napoleon's Elder Brother* (New York: Macmillan, 1968), 259–61.

57. Zenaide to Julie Bonaparte, New York 13 August 1826 (Prince and Princess Napoleon archives).

58. Bonaparte to William Cooper, Point Breeze, 2 April 1826 (film 1514, APS). The reference to "my list" is to "The Genera of North American Birds, and a Synopsis of the Species found within the territory of the United States; systematically arranged in Orders and Families," *Annals of the Lyceum of Natural History of New York* 2 (1828): 7–128, 293–451.

59. Thomas Say to Isaac Hays, Yellow Springs, Ohio, 29 June 1826 (Isaac Hays Papers, APS).

60. Bonaparte to Hays, Point Breeze, April 1826 (Isaac Hays Papers, APS). Count François Miot de Melito had been known to Joseph Bonaparte since his days in Corsica when Miot had been sent as the French Directory's representative.

61. Bonaparte to William Cooper, Point Breeze, 15 May 1826 (film 1514, APS).

62. *Contributions of the Maclurian Lyceum to the Arts and Sciences*, 1, 1 (1827).

63. Say to Bonaparte, New Harmony, 6 January 1828 (MNHN; film 542, APS).

64. Bonaparte to Hays, Point Breeze, "last of June," 1826 (Isaac Hays Papers, APS).

65. Godman to Bonaparte, Philadelphia, 8 June 1826 (del Gallo family archives).

66. Godman to Bonaparte, Phila., 16 June 1826 (del Gallo family archives).

67. Bonaparte to Hays, Point Breeze, 8 June 1826 (Isaac Hays Papers, APS).

68. Bonaparte to William Cooper, Point Breeze, 6 October 1826 (film 1514, APS).

69. List of paintings in Bonaparte's handwriting in the del Gallo family archives.

CHAPTER 4

1. Audubon to Bonaparte, Edinburgh, 16 December 1826 (Correspondence of Charles Lucien Bonaparte from American Scientists, MNHN; film 542, APS).

2. Bonaparte to Isaac Hays, London, 19 December 1826 (Isaac Hays Papers, APS).

3. William Swainson to Bonaparte, St. Albans, 2 November 1829 (MNHN).

4. David Elliston Allen, *The Naturalist in Britain: A Social History* (Princeton, N.J.: Princeton University Press, 1994), 36.

5. Bonaparte, "Cenni Autobiografici di Carlo Giulio Lorenzo Luciano Principe

Bonaparte" (manuscript, del Gallo family archives), 68.

6. Bonaparte to Cooper, Point Breeze, 12 April 1826 (film 1514, APS)

7. Christine E. Jackson, *Prideaux John Selby: A Gentleman Naturalist* (Northumberland: Spredden Press, 1992), 142.

8. Sampson Batard & Co., London, 29 December 1826 (del Gallo family archives).

9. Erwin Stresemann, *Ornithology from Aristotle to the Present*, trans. Hans J. Epstein and Cathleen Epstein (Cambridge, Mass.: Harvard University Press, 1975), 109.

10. Quoted in Stresemann, 156–57. Cretzschmar was planning to found a society of German ornithologists and to publish, with the participation of foreign experts, a "Synopsis" of world birds.

11. "Autobiografici," 69.

12. Bonaparte, *Specchio comparativo delle ornithologie di Roma e di Filadelfia* (Pisa: Dalla Tipografia Nistri, 1827), iii.

13. Ibid. 78–79.

14. *Niles Weekly Register*, 20 September 1823.

15. "Autobiografici," 69.

16. "Autobiografici," 69.

17. Bonaparte to Julie Clary Bonaparte, Dublin, 30 June 1827 (Fondazioni Primoli).

18. Jasper Ridley, *Napoléon III and Eugénie* (New York: Viking Press, 1979), 58.

19. Bonaparte to Julie Clary Bonaparte, Dublin, 30 June 1827 (Fondazioni Primoli).

20. Quoted in Hans Naef, *Die Bildniszeichnungen von J.-A.-D. Ingres* (Bern: Benteli Verlag, 1977), 530.

21. Bonaparte to Julie Bonaparte, Liverpool, 2 July 1827 (Fondazioni Primoli).

22. Maria R. Audubon, *Audubon and His Journals*, 2 vols. (New York: Charles Scribner's Sons, 1897; reprint New York: Dover, 1994), 1: 256.

23. Ibid., 257.

24. Bonaparte to William Cooper, Point Breeze, 11 September 1827 (film 1514, APS).

25. Ibid.

26. John D. Godman, *American Natural History: Part 1—Mastology* (1826–28; 3rd ed. Philadelphia: R. W. Pomeroy, 1842), 1: vii.

27. Bonaparte to William Cooper, Point Breeze, 24 September 1827 (film 1514, APS).

28. Benjamin Leadbeater to Bonaparte, London, April 1828 (MS 2605, MNHN).

29. John F. Watson, "Trip to Pennsbury & to Countsurvilliers, 1826" (manuscript diary, Library of the Henry Francis Du Pont Winterthur Museum).

30. "Autobiografici," 70.

31. Bonaparte to Cooper, Point Breeze, 23 (?) October 1827 (film 1514, APS). Cooper was a member of the publishing committee of the New York *Annals*.

32. Bonaparte to Cooper, Point Breeze, Friday morning, (late October?) 1827 (film 1514, APS).

33. Bonaparte to Cooper, Point Breeze, 8 (?) November 1827 (film 1514, APS).

34. Cooper to Bonaparte, New York, 16 November 1827 (MNHN; film 542, APS).

35. John Godman to Bonaparte, New York, 21 November 1827 (del Gallo family archives).

36. Bonaparte, *American Ornithology*, 2: 8–9.

37. Cooper to Bonaparte, New York, 23 November 1827 (MNHN; film 542 APS).

38. Bonaparte to Cooper, Point Breeze, 13 November 1827 (film 1514, APS).

39. Bonaparte to Cooper, Point Breeze, 19 November 1827 (film 1514, APS).

40. Bonaparte to Cooper, Point Breeze, n.d. December 1827 (film 1514, APS).
41. Bonaparte to Cooper, Point Breeze, 2 December 1827 (film 1514, APS).
42. Ibid.
43. Bonaparte to Cooper, Point Breeze, 8 December 1827 (film 1514, APS).
44. Ibid.
45. Cooper to Bonaparte, New York, 31 December 1827 (MNHN; film 542, APS).
46. Bonaparte to Cooper, Philadelphia, 22 December 1827 (film 1514, APS).
47. Bonaparte to Cooper, Washington, 29 December 1827 (film 1514, APS).
48. Bonaparte to Cooper, Point Breeze, 24 December 1827 (film 1514, APS).
49. Reuben Haines to Bonaparte, Germantown, 26 December 1827 (MNHN; film 542, APS).
50. Bonaparte to Cooper, Washington, 29 December 1827 (film 1514, APS).
51. Bonaparte to Cooper, Washington, 9 January 1828 (film 1514, APS).
52. Bonaparte to John Edward Gray, Washington, 30 December 1827 (Correspondence, Foreign Letters, vol.1, in Keeper of Zoology's Room, Natural History Museum, London).
53. Edward Everett to Bonaparte, Washington, 25 December 1827 (del Gallo family archives).
54. Monica Stirling, *Madame Letizia: A Portrait of Napoleon's Mother* (New York: Harper, 1962), 266.
55. Bonaparte to Cooper, Baltimore, 20 January 1828 (film 1514, APS).
56. "Autobiografici," 70.
57. Bonaparte to Cooper, "on board the Delaware," 18 February 1828 (film 1514, APS).

CHAPTER 5

1. Bonaparte to Cooper, Leghorn from the Lazareth [lazaretto], 14 April 1828 (film 1514, APS).
2. Bonaparte, "Cenni Autobiografici di Carlo Giulio Lorenzo Luciano Principe Bonaparte" (manuscript, del Gallo family archives), 71.
3. Ibid.
4. Bonaparte to Hays, "on board the *Delaware* in sight of Leghorn (but with a provoking head wind)," 9 April 1828 (Isaac Hays Papers, APS).
5. Bonaparte to Cooper, Leghorn, 14 April 1828 (film 1514, APS).
6. Ibid.
7. Bonaparte to Hays, 9 April 1828 (Isaac Hays Papers, APS).
8. Bonaparte to Cooper, Leghorn, 20 April 1828 (film 1514, APS).
9. Mary Swainson to John Parkes, 3 June 1828, quoted in William Swainson, *William Swainson, F.L.S., F.R.S., Naturalist and Artist: Family Letters & Diaries 1809–1855, Final Destiny New Zealand*, ed. Geoffrey M. Swainson (Palmerston North, N.Z.: published by Geoffrey Marshall Swainson, 1992), 17–18.
10. Audubon to Bonaparte, London, 10 May 1828 (MNHN; film 542, APS).
11. Audubon to Lucy Audubon, London, 6 February 1828, *Letters of John James Audubon, 1826–1840*, ed. Howard Corning, 2 vols. (Boston: Club of Odd Volumes, 1930; reprint New York: Kraus, 1969), 1: 59.

12. "Autobiografici," 72.

13. Bonaparte to Cooper, Florence, 3 July 1828 (film 1514, APS).

14. William Swainson to Audubon, London, 29 January 1830 (Morris Tyler Collection, Beinecke Library).

15. Audubon to Bonaparte, London, 29 April 1828 (MNHN; film 542, APS).

16. Ibid.

17. Audubon to Bonaparte, London, 18 April 1828 (MNHN; film 542, APS).

18. Audubon to Bonaparte, London, 10 May 1828 (MNHN; film 542, APS).

19. Audubon to Bonaparte, London, 29 May 1828 (MNHN; film 542, APS).

20. Bonaparte to Cooper, 26 August 1828 (film 1514, APS). The United States Exploring Expedition did not leave for ten more years, until 1838.

21. Isaac Lea to Bonaparte, Philadelphia, 14 August 1828 (MS 2605, MNHN).

22. Edward Everett to Bonaparte, Boston, 14 June 1828 (del Gallo family archives).

23. Bonaparte to Audubon, Florence, 14 October 1828 (in English) (Morris Tyler Collection, Gen. MSS 85, Box 3, Beinecke Library).

24. Audubon to Bonaparte, London, 3 November 1828 (MNHN; film 542, APS).

25. Bonaparte to Audubon, Rome, 19 March 1829 (in English) (Morris Tyler Collection, Gen. MSS 85, Box 3, Beinecke Library).

26. Thomas Say to Bonaparte, New Orleans, 6 January 1828 (MNHN; film 542, APS).

27. Say to Bonaparte, New Harmony, December 1828 (MNHN, film 542, APS).

28. Reuben Haines to Bonaparte, Germantown, 29 January 1830 (MS 2603, MNHN).

29. Bonaparte to Isaac Hays, Point Breeze, 11 November 1826 (Isaac Hays Papers, APS).

30. "Autobiografici," 66.

31. Hans Naef, *Die Bildniszeichnungen von J.-A.-D. Ingres* (Bern: Benteli Verlag,1977), 530.

32. Bonaparte to Cooper, Rome, 20 January 1829 (film 1514, APS).

33. Bonaparte to Cooper, Rome, 15 April 1829 (film 1514, APS).

34. Ibid.

35. Bonaparte to Cooper, 27 August 1829 (film 1514, APS).

36. Charles Lucien Bonaparte, *American Ornithology; or the Natural History of the Birds of the United States, not given by Wilson* (Philadelphia: Carey, Lea & Carey, 1828), 56–57.

37. Ibid., 32, 34.

38. Swainson to Bonaparte, St. Albans, 1 July 1829 (MS 2612, MNHN).

39. Swainson to Bonaparte, St. Albans, 26 June 1830 (MS 2612, MNHN).

40. Naef, 528.

41. Cooper to Bonaparte, New York, 8 December 1829 (MNHN; film 542, APS).

42. Carlo Luciano Bonaparte, Principe di Musignano, "Sulla seconda edizione del *Regno Animale* del Barone Cuvier," *Nouvelles annales des sciences naturelles de Bologne* (Bologna: Tipografia Marsigli, 1830).

43. Say to Bonaparte, New Harmony, 19 October 1830 (MNHN; film 542, APS).

44. Baron Georges Cuvier, *The Animal Kingdom Arranged According to Its Organization* (London: Willam S. Orr & Co., 1854), 12.

45. "Autobiografici," 67.

46. Bonaparte to Cooper, Florence, 5 October 1829 (film 1514, APS). Peale found the Reddish Egret in its white phase, not realizing that it has a totally different phase of neutral gray with a rusty-colored head and neck.

47. Cooper to Bonaparte, New York, 19 October 1830 (MNHN; film 542, APS).

48. Bonaparte to Cooper, Rome 19 December 1830 (film 1514, APS).

49. Audubon to Bonaparte, London, 5 May 1829 (MNHN; film 542, APS).

50. Audubon to Bonaparte, London, 14 July 1830 (MNHN; film 542, APS).

51. Audubon to Robert Havell Jr., Birmingham, 29 June 1830, *Letters*, 1: 112.

52. Bonaparte to Audubon, Rome, 6 December 1830 (Missouri Historical Society).

53. Bonaparte to Cooper, Florence, 9 July 1831 (film 1514, APS).

54. Cooper to Bonaparte, New York, 28 September 1831 (MNHN; film 542, APS).

55. Robert V. Bruce, *The Launching of Modern American Science: 1846–1876* (New York: Knopf, 1987), 10.

56. Swainson to Bonaparte, St. Albans, 12 August 1830 (MS 2612, MNHN).

57. Nicholas Vigors to Bonaparte, London, 11 January 1831 (MS 2613, MNHN).

58. Bonaparte to Cooper, Rome, 2 July 1830 (film 1514, APS).

59. Stresemann, 123–24.

60. Bonaparte to Cooper, Florence, 9 July 1831 (film 1514, APS).

61. Ibid.

62. Audubon to Bonaparte, Edinburgh, 2 January 1831 (MNHN; film 542, APS).

63. Swainson to Bonaparte, St. Albans, 1 July 1829 (MS 2612, MNHN).

64. Bonaparte to Swainson, Florence, 30 July 1829 (Archives of the Linnean Society of London).

65. Swainson to Bonaparte, St. Albans, 26 June 1830 (MS 2612, MNHN).

66. Swainson to Bonaparte, St. Albans, 1 September 1831 (MS 2612, MNHN).

67. Bonaparte to Audubon, Rome 10 April 1831 (Morris Tyler Collection, Gen. MSS 85, box 3, Beinecke Library).

68. Bonaparte to Cooper, Rome, 8 December 1831 (film 514, APS).

69. Ibid.

70. Bonaparte to Swainson, Rome, 23 July 1830 (Archives of the Linnean Society of London).

71. Swainson to Bonaparte, St. Albans, 3 January 1832 (MS 2612, MNHN).

72. Swainson to Bonaparte, St. Albans, 26 February 1832 (MS 2612, MNHN).

CHAPTER 6

1. William Cooper to Bonaparte, New York, 10 February 1833 (MNHN; film 542, APS).

2. Bonaparte to William Swainson, Rome, 19 March 1833, William Swainson, *William Swainson, F. L. S., F. R. S., Naturalist & Artist: Family Letters & Diaries 1809–1855, Final Destiny New Zealand,* ed. Geoffrey M. Swainson (Palmerston North, N.Z.: Geoffrey Marshall Swainson, 1992), 40.

3. Bonaparte, "Cenni Autobiografici di Carlo Giulio Lorenzo Luciano Principe Bonaparte" (manuscript, del Gallo family archives), 72; Bonaparte to Julie Bonaparte, 14 March 1832 (#8295, Fondazioni Primoli).

4. Bonaparte to Cooper, Rome, 26 June 1833 (film 1514, APS).

5. Bonaparte to Cooper, Rome, 18 April 1832 (film 1514, APS).

6. Richard Harlan to William Swainson, Philadelphia, 20 October 1829 (Linnean Society of London).

7. Gabriel Girod de l'Ain, *Joseph Bonaparte: le roi malgré lui* (Paris: Librairie Académique Perrin, 1970), 389.

8. Zenaide Bonaparte to Julie Bonaparte, Philadelphia, 1 January 1824 (Prince and Princess Napoleon archives).

9. Owen Connelly, *The Gentle Bonaparte: The Story of Napoleon's Older Brother* (New York: Macmillan, 1968), 282.

10. Bonaparte to Cooper, Rome, 26 June 1833 (film 1514, APS).

11. Bonaparte to Cooper, Florence, 9 September 1833 (film 1514, APS).

12. James E. DeKay to Bonaparte, New York, 2 March 1829 (MNHN; film 542, APS).

13. Cooper to Bonaparte, Troy, N.Y., 25 August 1832 (MNHN; film 542, APS).

14. John Godman to Bonaparte (courtesy of Rembrandt Peale), Germantown, 29 October 1828 (del Gallo family archives).

15. Cooper to Bonaparte, New York, 11 October 1833 (film 542, APS).

16. Ibid.

17. Cooper to Bonaparte, New York, 30 October 1833 (film 542, APS).

18. Bonaparte to Cooper, Florence, 29 December 1833 (film 1514, APS).

19. Cooper to Bonaparte, New York 10 February 1833 (MNHN; film 542, APS).

20. Maximilian, Prince of Weid, Neuweid sur Rhine, to Bonaparte, 16 February 1835 (MNHN; film 542, APS).

21. Patricia Trenton and Peter H. Hassick, *The Rocky Mountains: A Vision for Artists in the Nineteenth Century* (Norman: University of Oklahoma Press, 1983), 30.

22. "Autobiografici," 66–67.

23. Bonaparte to Louis Agassiz, Rome, 27 April 1834 (in Zenaide's handwriting) (Louis Agassiz Papers, Houghton Library).

24. Bonaparte to Agassiz, Rome, 8 July 1835 (Louis Agassiz Papers, Houghton Library).

25. Audubon to Bonaparte, London, 24 April 1835 (MNHN; film 542, APS).

26. Audubon to Bonaparte, London, 25 May 1835 (MNHN; film 542, APS).

27. Charlotte Brontë to Ellen Nussey, 4 July 1834, quoted in Juliet Barker, *The Brontës* (New York, St. Martin's Press: 1995), 220.

28. Bonaparte to Cooper, Ariccia near Rome, 27 September 1835 (film 514, APS).

29. Prince Maximilian to Bonaparte, 30 October 1835 (MNHN; film 542, APS).

30. Audubon to Bonaparte, London, 1 January 1836 (MNHN; film 542, APS).

31. Audubon to Bonaparte, London, 7 February 1836 (MNHN; film 542, APS).

32. "Autobiografici," 72.

33 Audubon to Bonaparte, London, 23 February 1836 (MNHN; film 542, APS).

34. Bonaparte to Alexander Lawson, 2 July 1836, quoted in Frank L. Burns, "Miss Lawson's Recollections of Ornithologists," *The Auk: A Quarterly Journal of Ornithology* 34 (1917): 282.

35. Audubon to Bonaparte, London, 16 March 1836 (MNHN; film 542, APS).

36. Eugénie de Grèce, *Pierre-Napoléon Bonaparte, 1815–1881* (Paris: Hachette, 1963), 135.

37. Desmond Seward, *Napoleon's Family: The Notorious Bonapartes and Their Ascent to the Thrones of Europe* (New York: Viking, 1986), 196.

38. Bonaparte to Zenaide Bonaparte, Mannheim, 13 September 1837 (MS 2598, MNHN).

39. Connelly, 288.

40. A statement signed by Joseph Bonaparte, Count of Survilliers, London, 16 October 1837 (#8371, Fondazioni Primoli).

41. Bonaparte to Cooper, Liverpool, 31 October 1837 (film 1514, APS).

42. Audubon to John Bachman, London, 4 October 1837, John James Audubon, *Letters of John James Audubon, 1826–1840*, 2 vols., ed. Howard Corning (Boston: Club of Odd Volumes, 1930; reprint New York: Kraus, 1969), 2: 182.

43. Louis-Lucien Bonaparte to Zenaide Bonaparte, London, n.d. (Museo Napoleonico).

44. Audubon to Bachman, London, 8 October 1837, *Letters*, 2: 185–86.

45. Audubon to Bachman, London, 20 December 1837, *Letters*, 2: 190–91.

46. Bonaparte, *A Geographical and Comparative List of the Birds of Europe and North America* (London: John Van Voorst, 1838), preface.

47. Ibid.

48. Audubon to Bachman, London, 14 April 1838, *Letters*, 2: 200.

49. Richard Owen to the Secretary of the Linnean Society, Royal College of Surgeons, 6 December 1837 (Linnean Society of London).

50. Bonaparte, "A New Systematic Arrangement of Vertebrated Animals," *Transactions of the Linnean Society of London* 18 (1841): 247–304. This paper, read at a meeting of the society on 7 November 1837, divided placental mammals into two sub-classes, based on the structure of the nervous system. This means of classification had also been of prime importance to Cuvier.

51. John Edward Gray to Bonaparte, London, 14 December 1837 (MS 2603, MNHN).

52. "Autobiografici," 74.

53. Ibid., 75.

54. Jasper Ridley, *Napoléon III and Eugénie* (New York: Viking Press, 1980), 14–15.

55. Etienne Geoffroy Saint-Hilaire to Bonaparte, Paris, 13 January 1838 (MS2602, MNHN).

56. Marie-Noelle Bourguet et al., *Il y a 200 ans, les savants en Egypte*, catalogue of an exhibition (Paris: Muséum National d'Histoire Naturelle, 1998), 7. Geoffroy believed that nature has only one plan of construction, the same in principle, but varied in its accessory parts.

57. "Autobiografici," 75–76. Prince Victor Masséna, duke of Rivoli and prince of Essling, was the son of Napoleon's general Marshal André Masséna, who distinguished himself in the battle of Rivoli, near Turin, in 1796 and at the battle of Essling, near Vienna, in 1809. Prince Masséna's entire collection of bird specimens was eventually bought by Thomas B. Wilson and presented to the Academy of Natural Sciences of Philadelphia.

58. "Autobiografici," 76.

59. Bonaparte to Julie Bonaparte, Rome, 27 March 1838 (#8310, Fondazioni Primoli).

60. Bonaparte to Cooper, Florence, 14 April 1838 (film 1514, APS).

61. Ibid.

62. Prince Maximilian to Bonaparte, 25 May 1838 (MNHN; film 542, APS).

63. Bonaparte to Hermann Schlegel, Rome, 3 July 1844 (Natural History Museum, Leiden, courtesy of Dr. L. B. Holthuis).

64. Wilhelm Peter Eduard Simon Rüppell (1794–1884) to Bonaparte, Frankfurt, 18 March 1838 (MS 2610, MNHN).

65. Rüppell to Bonaparte, 3 June 1838 (MS 2610, MNHN).

66. Bonaparte to Swainson, Leghorn, 19 July 1838 (Swainson Correspondence, Linnean Society of London).

67. Swainson to Bonaparte, August 1838 (Swainson Correspondence, Linnean Society of London).

68. Rüppell to Bonaparte, Milan, 30 September 1838 (MS 2610, MNHN).

CHAPTER 7

1. Bonaparte, "Cenni Autobiografici di Carlo Giulio Lorenzo Luciano Principe Bonaparte" (manuscript, del Gallo family archives), 77.

2. Ibid., 77.

3. Ibid., 79.

4. Ibid., 79.

5. Ibid., 80.

6. Antonio Pace, "The American Philosophical Society and Italy," *Proceedings of the American Philosophical Society* 90, 5 (December 1946): 402.

7. Isadore Geoffroy Saint-Hilaire to Bonaparte, Paris, 10 October 1838 (MS 2602, MNHN).

8. Ibid.

9. Bonaparte to Richard Owen, Rome, 26 February 1839 (Richard Owen Papers, Natural History Museum, London).

10. Bonaparte to John Edward Gray, Florence, 31 March 1839 (John Edward Gray Papers, Natural History Museum, London).

11. Joseph Valynseele, *Le sang des Bonapartes* (Paris: 26 Boulevard de Magenta, 1954), 35.

12. Gabriel Girod de l'Ain, *Joseph Bonaparte: le roi malgré lui* (Paris: Librairie Académique Perrin, 1970), 390.

13. "Autobiografici," 82.

14. Bonaparte to Julie Clary Bonaparte, Philadelphia, 29 December 1823 (Fondazioni Primoli).

15. Bonaparte to Charlotte and Napoleon Bonaparte (cousins, so with the same surname although not yet married), New York, 12 January 1826 (Fondazioni Primoli).

16. Frank L. Burns, "Miss Lawson's Recollections of Ornithologists," *The Auk: A Quarterly Journal of Ornithology* 34 (1917): 280.

17. Patricia T. Stroud, "The Founding of the Academy of Natural Sciences of Philadelphia in 1812 and Its *Journal* in 1817," *Archives of Natural History* (London) 22, 2 (1995): 221–33.

18. Bonaparte to Joseph Bonaparte, Florence, 30 March 1839 (#8397, Fondazioni Primoli).

19. Zenaide to Joseph Bonaparte, Ariccia, 19 August 1839 (#10743 [letter draft], Fondazioni Primoli).

20. "Autobiografici," 83.

21. Geoffroy Saint-Hilaire to Bonaparte, Paris, 2 April 1839 (MS 2602, MNHN). Dominique François Jean Arago (1786–1853) discovered the principle of the development of magnetism by rotation.

22. Ibid.

23. Geoffroy to Bonaparte, Toulon, 26 May 1839 (MS2602, MNHN).

24. Geoffroy to Bonaparte, Chaville, France, 19 September 1839 (MS2602, MNHN).

25. Circular for the first Italian scientific congress to be held in Pisa on 15 October 1839 (Richard Owen Papers, Natural History Museum, London).

26. Bonaparte to Richard Owen, Rome, 16 April 1839 (Richard Owen Papers, Natural History Museum, London).

27. Pace, 403.

28. Edward Lear to Bonaparte, Via Felice, Rome, 19 July 1839 (MS 2603, MNHN).

29. Joseph Bonaparte to Zenaide, London, 10 October 1839 (del Gallo family archives).

30. *Notice sur les travaux zoölogiques de M. Charles-Lucien Bonaparte* (Paris: Bachelier, Imprimeur-Libraire de l'Ecole Polytechnique et du Bureau des Longitudes, 1850), 28.

31. Autobiografici, 85.

32. Fiorella Bartoccini, "Il principe di Canino e i congressi degli scienziati," Bartoccini and Silvana Verdini, *Sui congressi degli scienziati,* Quaderni del Risorgimento 2 (Rome: Edizioni dell'Atteneo, 1952), 9.

33. Geoffroy to Bonaparte, Toulon, 26 May 1839 (MS 2602, MNHN).

34. Fiorella Bartoccini, "Il principe de Canino e i congressi degli scienziati," Bartoccini and Verdini, 8–9.

35. "Autobiografici," 86.

36. Ibid., 88.

37. George Robert Gray to Bonaparte, British Museum, 13 March 1840 (MS 2603, MNHN).

38. Swainson to Audubon, London, 1 May, 1830 (Morris Tyler Collection, Beinecke Library). Swainson had spent two years (1816–18) collecting specimens in Brazil.

39. " Autobiografici," 89.

40. Zenaide to Joseph Bonaparte, Rome, 1 July 1840 (#10747 [letter draft], Fondazioni Primoli).

41. Edward Everett to Bonaparte, Florence, 28 November 1840 (del Gallo family archives).

CHAPTER 8

1. Silvana Verdini, "I congressi degli scienziati nei documenti vaticani (1839–1846)," Fiorella Bartoccini and Verdini, *Sui congressi degli scienziati,* Quaderni del Risorgimento 2 (Rome: Edizioni dell'Atteneo, 1952), 29.

2. Ibid., 29–30.

3. Ibid., 30–31.

4. Bonaparte, "Cenni Autobiografici di Carlo Giulio Lorenzo Luciano Principe Bonaparte" (manuscript, del Gallo family archives), 91.

5. Stuart Woolf, *A History of Italy, 1700–1860: The Social Constraints of Political Change* (London and New York: Routledge, 1979), 350–51.

6. "Autobiografici," 91.

7. Antonio Pace, "The American Philosophical Society and Italy," *Transactions of the American Philosophical Society* 90, 5 (December 1946): 402.

8. "Autobiografici," 92.

9. Bonaparte to Edward Everett, Rome, 15 December 1840 (Massachusetts Historical Society).

10. Everett to Bonaparte, Careggi (near Florence), 15 June 1841 (del Gallo family archives).

11. Bonaparte to Jean-Marie Dupin, Rome, 8 December 1840 (#300AP/50, Archives of France).

12. Dupin to Bonaparte, Paris, 4 January 1841 (#300AP/50, Archives of France).

13. Isadore Geoffroy Saint-Hilaire to Bonaparte, Hyères, 6 January 1841 (MS 2602, MNHN).

14. Edward Everett to Bonaparte, London, 13 March 1845 (del Gallo family archives).

15. Edward Everett to Bonaparte, London, 7 July 1845 (del Gallo family archives).

16. Bonaparte to Agassiz, Rome, 30 March 1841 (Louis Agassiz Papers, Houghton Library).

17. Bonaparte, *Iconografia della fauna italica per le quattro classi degli animali vertebrati*, 30 parts in 3 vols. (Rome: Dalla Tipografia Salviucci, 1832–41), preface.

18. Elie de Beaumont, *Notice sur les travaux scientifiques de son altesse le prince Charles-Lucien Bonaparte* (Paris: Imprimerie Seringe Frères, 1866), 5.

19. Ibid.

20. Bonaparte, *Iconografia della fauna italica*, no page numbers.

21. Ibid., *Mus tectorum*.

22. Ibid., *Vespertilio bonapartii*.

23. Ibid., copy in the author's possession.

24. Bonaparte to John Edward Gray, Rome, 1 April 1841 (John Edward Gray Correspondence #247, Natural History Museum, London).

25. Geoffroy to Bonaparte, Paris, 7 May 1841 (MS 2602, MNHN).

26. Geoffroy to Bonaparte, Paris, 27 May 1841 (MNHN).

27. "Autobiografici," 97.

28. Ibid., 101–6.

29. Hugh Edwin Strickland to Bonaparte, Worcestershire, 18 May 1841 (MS 2612, MNHN).

30. "Autobiografici," 107–8.

31. Quoted in the *Morning Post* (London), 29 June 1841.

32. "Autobiografici," 110–11.

33. George Ord to Charles Waterton, Philadelphia, 18 September 1841 (Ord Papers, APS).

34. Bonaparte to Cooper, Point Breeze, 2 April 1826 (film 514, APS).

35. "Autobiografici," 111.

36. Geoffroy St. Hilaire to Bonaparte, Paris, 16 July 1841 (MS 2602, MNHN).

37. John Gould to Bonaparte, 2 July 1841 (MS 2603, MNHN).

38. "Autobiografici," 114–15.

39. Charles Dickens, *Pictures from Italy* (1846; reprint London: Oxford University Press, 1908), 106.

40. "Autobiografici," 115-16.

41. Ibid., 116-17. François-Pierre-Guillaume Guizot (1787-1874) was appointed minister of foreign affairs by Louis Philippe in 1840. He upheld the principle of a *juste milieu* between monarchy and republicanism and strengthened the Conservative Party. He had opposed Napoleon.

42. Ibid., 119.

43. Ibid., 123.

44. Ibid., 122-24.

45. *Atti della terzo riunione degli scienziati italiani, tenuta in Firenze nell'settembre del 1841* (Firenze: Galileiana, 1841), 6-8.

46. "Autobiografici," 125.

47. Fiorella Bartoccini, "Il principe di Canino e i congressi degli scienziati," Bartoccini and Verdini, 6. Bonaparte's credo quoted on page 16, translated by the author.

48. Ibid., 21, nn.9, 8.

49. Loreto Santucci to Cardinal Luigi Lambruschini, Florence, 20 August 1841, Verdini, 59.

50. Verdini, 34.

51. Ibid.

52. *Notice sur les travaux zoölogiques de M. Charles-Lucien Bonaparte* (Paris: Bachelier, Imprimeur-Libraire de l'Ecole Polytechnique et du Bureau des Longitudes, 1850), 19, 33-34. All Bonaparte's papers at this meeting were later published in the *Atti della terza diunione*.

53. Paul Lawrence Farber, *The Emergence of Science as a Scientific Discipline, 1760-1850*, Studies in the History of Modern Science 12 (Dordrecht: D. Reidel, 1982), 83.

54. *Atti della terza riunione*, 332-33.

55. Bonaparte, "Observations on the State of Zoology in Europe as Regards the Vertebrata," read at the third meeting of the Italian Congress of Science, Florence, 1841, trans. for the Ray Society by H. E. Strickland, *The Ray Society, Reports on the Progress of Zoology and Botany* (Edinburgh: Ray Society, 1845), 3-18.

56. Ibid., 22.

57. Ibid., 25.

58. Erwin Stresemann, *Ornithology from Aristotle to the Present*, trans. Hans J. Epstein and Cathleen Epstein (Cambridge, Mass.: Harvard University Press, 1975), 236.

CHAPTER 9

1. Bonaparte, "Cenni Autobiografici di Carlo Giulo Lorenzo Luciano Principe Bonaparte" (manuscript, del Gallo family archives), 134-35.

2. Bonaparte to Richard Owen, Florence, 3 May 1842 (Natural History Museum, London).

3. Agassiz to Bonaparte, 1 December 1841 (MS 2592, MNHN).

4. Agassiz to Bonaparte, Neuchâtel, 28 February 1842 (MS 2592, MNHN).

5. Zenaide to Bonaparte, Florence, 25 November 1841 (del Gallo family archives).

6. John Gould to Bonaparte, London, 16 August 1842 (MNHN).

7. Bonaparte to Edward Prince, Genoa, 21 July, 1841 (courtesy of Maureen Lambourne, England, from her private collection).

8. Ibid.

9. "Autobiografici," 135.

10. Bonaparte to Louis Agassiz, Florence, 2 April 1842 (Louis Agassiz Papers, Houghton Library).

11. Bonaparte to Agassiz, Florence, 7 June 1842 (Louis Agassiz Papers, Houghton Library).

12. Bonaparte to Edward Everett, Rome, 15 December 1840 (quoted in Antonio Pace, "The American Philosophical Society and Italy," *Proceedings of the American Philosophical Society* 90, 5 (December 1946): 413.

13. "Autobiografici," 136.

14. Ibid.

15. Francesco Buranelli, "Gli scavi a Vulci (1828–54) di Luciano ed Alexandrine Bonaparte Principi de Canino," Marino Natoli and Mina Gregori, *Luciano Bonaparte: le sue collezioni d'arte, le sue residenze a Roma, nel Lazio, in Italia* (Rome: Libreria dello Stato, 1995), 81.

16. D. H. Lawrence, *Etruscan Places* (1932; reprint London: Olive Press, 1994), 125–26.

17. Bonaparte to Alexandrine Bonaparte, Rome, 18 June 1845 (Fondazioni Primoli).

18. *Canino: arte, storia e tradizioni* (Canino: CO.AR. Turismo, n.d.), 17.

19. "Autobiografici," 137.

20. Bonaparte to Agassiz, 7 June 1842, Florence (Louis Agassiz Papers, Houghton Library).

21. Bonaparte to J. K. Kane, Secretary of the American Philosophical Society, Florence, 29 July, 1842 (quoted in Pace, 415).

22. Bonaparte to Agassiz, 7 June 1842, Florence (Louis Agassiz Papers, Houghton Library).

23. Agassiz to Bonaparte, n.d. [July 1842?] (MS 2592, MNHN).

24. Erwin Stresemann, *Ornithology from Aristotle to the Present*, trans. Hans J. Epstein and Cathleen Epstein (Cambridge, Mass.: Harvard University Press, 1975), 163.

25. Bonaparte to Agassiz, Florence, 10 July 1842 (Louis Agassiz Papers, Houghton Library).

26. Agassiz to Bonaparte, Glacier of the Aar, 1 September 1842, quoted in *Louis Agassiz: His Life and Correspondence*, ed. Elizabeth Cary Agassiz, 2 vols. (Boston: Houghton Mifflin, 1886), 1: 356–58.

27. Paul Lawrence Farber, *Discovering Birds: The Emergence of Ornithology as a Scientific Discipline, 1760–1850* (Baltimore and London: Johns Hopkins University Press,1997), 114–15.

28. Ibid., 115.

29. Barbara Means and Richard Mearns, *Audubon to Xantus: The Lives of Those Commemorated in North American Bird Names* (London: Academic Press, 1992), 417.

30. Stephen Jay Gould, "An Awful, Terrible Dinosaurian Irony," *Natural History* (February 1998): 25.

31. Maximilian to Bonaparte, Neuweid, 4 January 1839 (MNHN; film 542, APS).

32. Bonaparte to Hermann Schlegel, Marseilles, 11 September 1841 (Natural History Museum, Leiden).

33. Maximilian to Bonaparte, Neuweid, 10 May 1839 (MNHN; film 542, APS). Titian Peale spent from 1838 to 1842 working as naturalist on the United States South Seas Surveying and Exploring Expedition.

34. Bonaparte to Ord, Florence, 5 September 1842, quoted in George Ord to Charles Waterton, Philadelphia, 21 November 1842 (Ord Papers, APS).

35. Ibid.

36. Pace, 404.

37. George Ord to Bonaparte, Philadelphia, 11 September 1842 (MS 2608, MNHN).

38. Ord to Bonaparte, Philadelphia, 30 November 1842 (MS 2608, MNHN).

39. "Autobiografici," 138.

40. Ibid.

41. Maximilian to Bonaparte, Neuweid, 13 February 1842 (MNHN; film 542, APS).

42. Silvana Verdini, "I congressi degli scienziati nei documenti vaticani (1839–1846)," Fiorella Bartoccini and Verdini, Sui congressi degli scienziati, Quaderni del Risorgimento 2 (Rome: Edizioni dell'Atteneo, 1952), 35.

43. Ibid., 61.

44. Fiorella Bartoccini, "Il principe de Canino e i congressi degli scienziati," Bartoccini and Verdini, 15–16.

45. Ibid. 16.

46. Geoffroy Saint-Hilaire to Bonaparte, Paris, 24 May 1843 (MS2602 MNHN).

47. Bonaparte to Julie Clary Bonaparte, Rome, 25 March 1843 (#8315, Fondazioni Primoli).

48. Agassiz to Bonaparte, Neuchâtel, 3 April 1843 (Louis Agassiz Papers, Houghton Library).

49. Ibid.

50. Bonaparte to Agassiz, Rome, 13 August 1843 (Louis Agassiz Papers, Houghton Library).

51. Strickland to Bonaparte, Cracombe House, Evesham, Worcestershire, 15 May 1843 (MS 2612, MNHN).

52. John Edward Gray to Bonaparte, London, 9 August 1843 (MS 2603, MNHN).

53. Audubon to Bonaparte, New York, 26 February 1843 (MNHN; film 542, APS).

54. Ibid.

55. Bernardo Tirabassi to Cardinal Luigi Lambruschini, Florence, 7 October 1843, quoted in Verdini, "I congressi degli scienziati," 68.

56. David Stacton, The Bonapartes (New York: Simon and Schuster, 1966), 313.

57. Verdini, 69.

58. Bonaparte to Alexandrine Bonaparte, Rome, 9 November 1843 (#8329, Fondazioni Primoli).

59. Ibid.

CHAPTER 10

1. Agassiz to Bonaparte, Neuchâtel, 15 January 1844 (MS 2595, MNHN). I have not succeeded in locating this portrait.

2. Agassiz to Bonaparte, Neuchâtel, 20 February 1844 (MS 2595, MNHN).

3. Bonaparte's fascination with uniforms stemmed from his childhood when his mother dressed him as an officer in the Roman cavalry. As a grown man, he had once

asked permission to wear a uniform of the pontifical guard, on the grounds that he had worn it as a child! Fiorella Bartoccini, "Il principe di Canino e i congressi degli scienziati," Bartoccini and Silvana Verdini," *Sui congressi degli scienziati,* Quaderni del Risorgimento 2 (Rome: Edizioni dell'Atteneo, 1952), 23, n.27.

4. Ibid., 13.

5. Bonaparte to Alexandrine, Rome, 13 April 1844 (#8331, Fondazioni Primoli).

6. Maximilian to Bonaparte, Neuweid, 23 February 1844 (MNHN; film 542, APS).

7. John Edward Gray to Bonaparte, London, 21 February 1844 (MS 2603, MNHN).

8. Bonaparte to Gray, Rome, 12 May 1844 (John Edward Gray Papers, Natural History Museum, London).

9. *Catalogue des manuscrits,* 2e supplement (2528–3270), 23 (MNHN).

10. Owen Connelly, *The Gentle Bonaparte: The Story of Napoleon's Older Brother* (New York: Macmillan, 1968), 296.

11. Luigi Masi to Bonaparte, Florence, 29 July 1844 (Fondazioni Primoli).

12. Edward Lear to Bonaparte, Rome, 22 July 1844 (MS 2605, MNHN).

13. *Le Siècle* 216 (Paris), 7 August 1844, 2 (MS 2594, MNHN).

14. Bonaparte to Alexandrine Bonaparte, Rome, 31 October 1844 (#8317, Fondazioni Primoli).

15. Bartoccini, 37–38.

16. Bonaparte, *Notice sur les travaux zoölogiques de M. Charles-Lucien Bonaparte* (Paris: Bachelier, Imprimeur-Librairie de l'Ecole Polytechnique et du Bureau des Longitudes, 1850), 12, 20, 29, 32.

17. Eduard Rüppell to Bonaparte, Milan, 20 October 1844 (MS 2610, MNHN).

18. Alexander von Humboldt to Bonaparte, Berlin, 22 September 1844 (MS 2604, MNHN).

19. Bonaparte to Alexandrine Bonaparte, Rome, 31 October 1844 (#8317, Fondazioni Primoli).

20. Bonaparte to Alexandrine, Rome, 4 November 1844 (#8318, Fondazioni Primoli).

21. Zenaide to Alexandrine, November 1844 (#8318, Fondazioni Primoli).

22. Agassiz to Bonaparte, Neuchâtel, 19 November 1844 (MS 2595, MNHN).

23. Constantine Samuel Rafinesque to Bonaparte, Germantown, 6 August 1826 (MS 2610, MNHN).

24. Rafinesque to Bonaparte, Philadelphia, 10 September 1839 (MS 2610, MNHN).

25. Agassiz to Bonaparte, Neuchâtel, 10 December 1844 (MS 2595, MNHN).

26. Agassiz to Bonaparte, Neuchâtel, 7 February 1845 (MS 2595, MNHN).

27. Agassiz to Bonaparte, Neuchâtel, 7 March 1845 (MS 2595, MNHN).

28. Gould to Bonaparte, London, 26 November 1844 (MS 2603, MNHN).

29. Gould to Bonaparte, London, 22 April 1845 (MS 2603, MNHN).

30. Ord to Bonaparte, Philadelphia, 20 April 1845 (MS 2608, MNHN).

31. Julie Bonaparte, *La princesse Julie Bonaparte Marquise de Roccagiovine et son temps: mémoires inédits (1853–1870),* ed. Isa Dardano Basso (Rome: Edizioni di Storia e Literature, 1975), 10.

32. Zenaide to Alexandrine, Rome, 23 April 1845 (#8335, Fondazioni Primoli).

33. George Ord to Bonaparte, Philadelphia, 13 August 1845 (MS 2608, MNHN).

34. Louis Maillard to Zenaide Bonaparte, Bordentown, 14 May 1845 (del Gallo family archives).

35. Zenaide to Alexandrine Bonaparte, Rome, 23 April 1845 (#8359, Fondazioni Primoli).

36. Agassiz to Bonaparte, Neuchâtel, 30 June 1845 (MS 2595, MNHN).

37. Zenaide to Alexandrine Bonaparte, Rome, 23 May 1845 (#8336, Fondazioni Primoli).

38. Bonaparte to Hermann Schlegel, Rome, 14 July 1845 (Fondazioni Primoli).

39. Ord to Bonaparte, Philadelphia, 13 August 1845 (MS 2608, MNHN).

40. Silvana Verdini, "I congressi degli scienziati nei documenti vaticani (1839–1846)," Bartoccini and Verdini, 39.

41. Bonaparte, *Notice sur les travaux zoölogiques*, 34.

42. Bonaparte, *Iconografia della fauna italica per le quattro classi degli animali vertebrati*, 30 parts in 3 vols. (Rome: Dalla Tipografia Salviucci, 1832–41), Intro. to Class IV: Pesci.

43. Julie Bonaparte, *La princesse Julie Bonaparte*, 11.

44. Richard Owen to Bonaparte, Milan, 27 October 1845 (MS 2608, MNHN).

45. Owen to Bonaparte, Royal College of Surgeons, London, 18 May 1846 (MS 2608, MNHN).

46. Bonaparte to Richard Owen, Rome, 29 June 1846 (Richard Owen Papers, Natural History Museum, London).

CHAPTER 11

1. Richard P. McBrien, *Lives of the Popes: The Pontiffs from St. Peter to John Paul II* (San Francisco: HarperSanFrancisco, 1997), 336.

2. Ibid., 344.

3. Julie Bonaparte, *La princesse Julie Bonaparte, marquise de Roccagiovine et son temps, mémoirs inédits*, ed. Isa Dardano Basso (Rome: Edizioni di Storia e Literature, 1975), 12.

4. Frank J. Coppa, *The Origins of the Italian Wars of Independence* (London and New York: Longman, 1992), 23.

5. Coppa, 24.

6. Fiorella Bartoccini, "Il principe di Canino e i congressi degli scienziati," Bartoccini and Silvana Verdini, *Sui congressi degli scienziati*, Quaderni del Risorgimento 2 (Rome: Edizioni dell'Atteneo, 1952), 14.

7. Edward Everett to Bonaparte, Cambridge, 24 July 1846 (del Gallo family archives).

8. George Ord to Bonaparte, Philadelphia, 26 July 1846 (MNHN).

9. Isadore Geoffroy Saint-Hilaire to Bonaparte, Paris, 10 January 1840 (MS 2602, MNHN). Georges Cuvier maintained the invariability of species, while Etienne Geoffroy Saint-Hilaire believed that, owing to the conditions of life, the same forms had not been perpetuated since the origin of all things, although it was not his belief that existing species are becoming modified.

10. A. Brignole Sale to Cardinal Pasquale Gizzi, Genoa, 17 September 1846, quoted in Silvana Verdini, "I congressi degli scienziati nei documenti vaticani (1839–1846)," Bartoccini and Verdini, 73.

11. Coppa, 25.

12. "Rapporto per la sezione di zoologia del Segretario Principe Bonaparte letto

nell'ultima assemblea generale dell'ottavo Congresso Scientifico Italiano," 29 September 1846 (Museo Napoleonico).

    13. George Ord to Bonaparte, Philadelphia, 31 October 1846 (MS 2608, MNHN).

    14. Julie Bonaparte, 13.

    15. Hugh Strickland to Bonaparte, Oxford, 23 March 1847 (MS 3398, MNHN).

    16. George Robert Gray to Bonaparte, London, 10 March 1847 (MS 2603, MNHN). By the late 1840s, Audubon was turning over much of the drawing for the *Quadrupeds of North America* to his second son, John Woodhouse Audubon.

    17. Janet Browne, *Charles Darwin: Voyaging* (Princeton, N.J.: Princeton University Press,1995), 492.

    18. Zenaide to Alexandrine Bonaparte, n.d. (June 1847?), Rome? (#8338, Fondazioni Primoli).

    19. Hugh E. Strickland to Bonaparte, Oxford, 2 June 1847 (MS 3398, MNHN).

    20. Strickland to Bonaparte, Oxford, 1 July 1847 (MS 3398, MNHN).

    21. Charles to Zenaide, Oxford, 24 June 1849 [postmarked 1847] (MS 2598, MNHN). The first British railway, between London and Greenwich, had opened only thirteen years earlier in 1836.

    22. Browne, 476.

    23. Charles to Zenaide, Oxford, 26 June 1847 (MS 2598, MNHN).

    24. Charles to Zenaide, Oxford, 29 June 1847 (MS 2598, MNHN).

    25. Strickland to Bonaparte, Oxford, 5 July 1847 (MS 3398, MNHN).

    26. Bonaparte, "Nouvelles espèces d'oiseaux méxicains," *Proceedings of the Zoological Society of London* (1838), and "Sur le quezalt des méxicains, *trogon paradisoeus*," *Magazin de Zoölogie* (1838).

    27. Told to the author by Maureen Lambourne, a direct descendent of Gould's wife Elizabeth.

    28. Charles to Zenaide, Copenhagen, 15 July 1847 (MS 2598, MNHN).

    29. Ibid.

    30. Concert program, 11 July 1847 (MS 2598, MNHN).

    31. Mary Jane Philips-Matz, *Verdi: A Biography* (New York and London: Oxford University Press, 1996), 229.

    32. Charles to Zenaide, Lund (Sweden), 22 July 1847 (MS 2598, MNHN).

    33. Charles to Zenaide, Stockholm, 27 July 1847 (MS 2598, MNHN).

    34. Julie Bonaparte, 100. The author was privileged to be shown this cup and saucer in Rome by Monsignore Luigi del Gallo di Roccagiovine, a direct descendent of Charles-Lucien Bonaparte.

    35. Bonaparte to Zenaide, Vienna, 6 August 1847 (MS 2598, MNHN).

    36. Ibid.

    37. Bonaparte to John Edward Gray, Vienna, 7 August 1847 (John Edward Gray Papers, Natural History Museum, London).

    38. Julie Bonaparte, 14.

    39. Bartoccini, 19.

    40. Ibid.

    41. Zenaide to Bonaparte, Rome, 17 September 1847 (MS 2598, MNHN).

    42. Ibid.

    43. Bonaparte, *Discours, allocutions et opinions de Charles-Lucien Prince Bonaparte dans le Conseil des députés et l'Assemblée constituante de Rome en 1848 et 1849 avec un*

appendice contenant des documents historiques et des pièces diverses, traduits de l'Italien d'après le *Moniteur* et autres journaux et documents officiels (Leiden, 1857), 430–31.

44. Bartoccini, 19.

45. Ibid., 25, n.54.

46. Bonaparte to John Edward Gray, Rome, 18 October 1847, enclosed in a letter to William Prince (Natural History Museum, London).

47. Geoffroy to Bonaparte, Muséum d'Histoire Naturelle, Paris, 27 September 1847 (MS 2602, MNHN).

48. Bonaparte, *Discours,* 442.

49. Ibid., 444–46.

50. Quoted in Denis Mack Smith, *Mazzini* (New Haven, Conn.: Yale University Press, 1994), 51–52.

51. Francis Bowen, "The Reforms of Pius IX," in *The Great Events by Famous Historians,* ed. Charles Francis Horne, John Rudd, and Rossiter Johnson (New York: National Alumni, 1904), 17: 120.

52. Coppa, 27–29.

53. Ibid., 31.

54. Mack Smith, *Mazzini,* 55.

55. Phillips-Matz, *Verdi,* 190, 153.

56. Ibid., 212.

57. Bonaparte to Alexandrine Bonaparte, Point Breeze, 1 November 1823 (Fondazioni Primoli).

58. Mack Smith, *Mazzini,* 54–55.

CHAPTER 12

1. Isadore Geoffroy Saint-Hilaire to Bonaparte, Paris, 2 February 1848 (MNHN).

2. Charles F. Horne, "An Outline Narrative: The Triumph of Democracy," *The Great Events by Famous Historians,* ed. Horne, John Rudd, and Rossiter Johnson (New York: National Alumni, 1904), 17: xvi.

3. Bonaparte, *Discours, allocutions et opinions de Charles-Lucien Prince Bonaparte dans le Conseil des députés et l'Assemblée constituante de Rome en 1848 et 1849 avec un appendice contenant des documents historiques et des pièces diverses,* traduits de l'Italien d'après le Moniteur *et autres journaux et documents officiels* (Leiden, 1857), 10. Much of this chapter is taken from Bonaparte's speeches and formal written opinion, because they reveal a great deal about his character. It is odd that these documents survive, so far as I can discover, only in French translation.

4. John Bierman, *Napoleon III and His Carnival Empire* (New York: St. Martin's Press, 1988), 63.

5. Bonaparte, *Discours,* 25.

6. Virgil, *The Aeneid,* trans. Robert Fitzgerald (New York: Random House, 1983), book VI, 11, 851-53, p.190. Bonaparte, *Discours,* 26-27.

7. Bonaparte, *Discours,* 30.

8. Ibid., 35-37.

9. Ibid., 48.

10. Ibid., 56.

11. Ibid., 58.

12. Ibid., 100-101.

13. Ibid., 115.

14. Stuart Woolf, *A History of Italy, 1700-1860: The Social Constraints of Political Change* (London and New York: Routledge, 1979), 382.

15. Lucy Riall, *The Italian Risorgimento: State, Society, and National Unification* (London: Routledge, 1994), 73.

16. Ibid., 79.

17. Bonaparte, *Discours*, 195-96.

18. Ibid., 213.

19. Ibid., 218.

20. Ibid. 414.

21. Frank J. Coppa, *The Origins of the Italian Wars of Independence* (New York: Longman, 1992), 52.

22. Clipping from an unidentified French newspaper in Bonaparte's papers (MS2592, MNHN).

23. Coppa, 52.

24. Bonaparte, *Discours*, 239.

25. Ibid., 243.

26. Ibid., 255.

27. Geoffroy Saint-Hilaire to Bonaparte ("République Française" printed on letterhead), Paris, 19 November 1848 (MS2602, MNHN).

28. Bonaparte, *Discours*, 266.

29. Woolf, 398-99.

30. Bonaparte, *Discours*, 297.

31. Ibid., 299-301.

32. Ibid., 302-3.

33. Ibid., 340.

34. Ibid., 347.

35. Ibid., 362-63.

36. Ibid., 370.

37. Ibid., 375.

38. Denis Mack Smith, *Mazzini* (New Haven, Conn.: Yale University Press, 1994), 70.

39. *Le prince Lucien Bonaparte et sa famille* (Paris: Librairie Plon, 1889), 158-59.

40. Bonaparte, *Discours*, 383.

41. Ibid., 385.

42. Ibid., 392.

43. Ibid., 402.

CHAPTER 13

1. Bonaparte to Zenaide, Civitavecchia, 7 July 1849 (Prince and Princess Napoleon archives).

2. Bonaparte to Jean-Marie Dupin, Orléans, July 1849. *Discours, allocutions et opinions de Charles Lucien Prince Bonaparte dans le Conseil des députés et l'Assemblée constituante de Rome en 1848 et 1849 avec un appendice contenant des documents historiques et des pièces diverses,* traduits de l'Italien d'après le *Moniteur* et autres journaux et documents officiels (Leiden, 1857), 502–4.

3. George Ord to Charles Waterton, Philadelphia, 17 December 1848 (Ord Papers, APS).

4. Ord to Waterton, Philadelphia, 4 March 1849 (Ord Papers, APS).

5. Ord to Waterton, Philadelphia, 3 September 1849 (Ord Papers, APS).

6. Edward Everett to Bonaparte, Boston, 12 February 1852 (del Gallo family archives).

7. Isadore Geoffroy Saint-Hilaire to Bonaparte, Paris, 29 August 1849 (MS 2602, MNHN).

8. Bonaparte to Zenaide, London, 22 July 1849 (Prince and Princess Napoleon archives).

9. Bonaparte to Zenaide, London, 9 August 1849 (Prince and Princess Napoleon archives).

10. Bonaparte to Zenaide, Birmingham, 17 September 1849 (Prince and Princess Napoleon archives).

11. Bonaparte, *Notice sur les travaux zoölogiques de M. Charles-Lucien Bonaparte* (Paris: Bachelier, Imprimeur-Libraire de l'Ecole Polytechnique et du Bureau des Longitudes, 1850), 13.

12. James Fenimore Cooper to Samuel F. B. Morse, Spa, Belgium, 31 July–3 August 1832; quoted in catalog 67, "Early American Literature, Medicine & Science, Thought, Reform & History" (M&S Rare Books, Inc., Providence, R.I.), 19.

13. William Buckland to Bonaparte, 15 October [1849?] (MS 2598, MNHN).

14. Erwin Stresemann, *Ornithology from Aristotle to the Present*, trans. Hans J. Epstein and Cathleen Epstein (Cambridge, Mass.: Harvard University Press, 1975), 160.

15. Bonaparte to Zenaide, scrap of a letter draft, Leiden? n.d. (probably early fall of 1849), (MS2598, MNHN).

16. Geoffroy to Bonaparte, "République français," Paris, 6 November 1849 (MS 2602, MNHN).

17. Geoffroy to Bonaparte, Paris, 9 November 1849 (MNHN).

18. Geoffroy to Bonaparte, Paris, 22 November 1849 (MNHN).

19. Geoffroy to Bonaparte, Paris, 7 December 1849 (MNHN).

20. André Maurois, *Victor Hugo*, trans. Gerard Hopkins (London: Jonathan Cape, 1956), 302.

21. Louis Mailliard to Bonaparte, Bordentown, 27 September 1849 (del Gallo family archives).

22. Mailliard to Bonaparte, Bordentown, 11 November 1849 (del Gallo family archives).

23. Bonaparte to John Edward Gray, Leiden, 1 February 1850 (MNHN).

24. John Edward Gray to Bonaparte, London, 16 February 1850 (MNHN).

25. George Ord to Charles Waterton, Philadelphia, 6 October 1850 (Ord Papers, APS).

26. Edward Wilson to Bonaparte, 105 rue de Lille, Paris, 22 November 1849 (MS 2613, MNHN).

27. Wilson to Bonaparte, Paris, 28 December 1849 (MNHN).

28. Wilson to Bonaparte, Pembrokeshire, 14 January 1850 (MNHN).

29. Translated from the Latin and quoted in Stresemann, 160–61. The author was shown this bird—a Bonaparte type specimen—by Dave Agro, curator of the ornithology collection at the Academy of Natural Sciences of Philadelphia.

30. Geoffroy to Bonaparte, Paris, 12 January 1850 (MNHN).

31. Wilson to Bonaparte, Pembrokeshire, 5 February 1850 (MNHN).

32. Bonaparte to John Edward Gray, Leiden, 2 January 1850 (John Edward Gray Papers, APS).

33. Bonaparte to John Edward Gray, Leiden, 28 February 1850 (J. E. Gray Papers, Natural History Museum, London).

34. Julie Bonaparte, *La princesse Julie Bonaparte marquise de Roccagiovine et son temps, mémoires inédits (1853–1870)*, ed. Isa Dardano Basso (Rome: Edizioni di Storia e literature, 1975), 18–19.

35. Bonaparte to Zenaide Bonaparte, Leiden, 22 February 1850 (MS 2598, MNHN).

36. Wilson to Bonaparte, Pembrokeshire, 2 March 1850 (MNHN).

37. Zenaide to Bonaparte, Rome, 26 February 1850 (Fondazioni Primoli). The letter is addressed to M. T. Kraus (for the Prince of Canino), rue St. Hyacinthe St. Honoré, Paris.

38. Charles-Lucien Bonaparte, "Nouvelles éspeces zoölogiques—première partie: perroquets," *Comptes rendus des séances de l'Académie des Sciences*, séance du 11 February 1850.

39. From a newspaper fragment sent to the author by Dr. L. B. Holthuis at the Rijksmuseum van Natuurlijke Historie, Leiden.

40. Stresemann, 161.

41. John Gould to Bonaparte, London, 30 January 1850 (MNHN).

42. Richard Owen to Bonaparte, London, College of Surgeons, 6 May 1850 (MNHN).

43. The Irish painter and lithographer T. H. Maguire was commissioned by the Ipswich Museum to produce a series of portraits of the leading scientists of the time. These included Darwin, Henslow, Gould, Bonaparte, and Owen.

44. George Robert Gray to Bonaparte, London, 1 January 1850 (MS 2603, MNHN).

45. Gray to Bonaparte, London, 15 March 1850 (MNHN).

46. Bonaparte to Gray, Leiden, 1 May 1850 (J. E. Gray Papers, Natural History Museum, London).

47. Gray to Bonaparte, London, 6 May 1850 (MNHN).

48. Elliott Coues, "Third Installment of American Ornithological Biography," *Bulletin of the U.S. Geological and Geographical Survey* 5 (1880): 677. Quoted in Stresemann, 168.

49. Stresemann, 169.

50. Johann Jacob Kaup to Bonaparte, Darmstadt, 25 June 1850 (MS 2604, MNHN).

51. Barbara Mearns and Richard Mearns, *Audubon to Xantus: The Lives of Those Commemorated in North American Bird Names* (London: Academic Press, 1992), 99.

52. Bonaparte and Hermann Schlegel, *Monographie des loxiens* (Leiden and Dusseldorf: Arnz, 1850).

53. Julie Bonaparte, 368.

54. Bonaparte to Zenaide, Frankfort, 27 May 1850 (Prince and Princess Napoleon archives).

55. Louis Mailliard to Bonaparte, Bordentown, N.J., 15 July 1850 (del Gallo family archives).

56. Bonaparte to Louis-Lucien (?) Bonaparte (the letter is headed "Mon cher Frère"), Leiden, 9 January 1850, Centre d'Accueil et de Recherche des Archives

Nationales (CARAN).

57. Bonaparte to Lucien Bonaparte (son), Paris, 16 September 1850 (#8122-XX, Fondazioni Primoli).

58. Geoffroy to Bonaparte, Paris, 29 July 1850 (MS 2602, MNHN).

59. Geoffroy to Bonaparte, Paris, 20 August 1850 (MS 2602, MNHN).

CHAPTER 14

1. Eugénie de Grèce, *Pierre-Napoleon Bonaparte, 1815–1881* (Paris: Librairie Hachette, 1963), 237.

2. Ibid., 175.

3. Luigi Masi to Bonaparte, Turin, 4 January 185[1] (Fondazioni Primoli).

4. Bonaparte to Temminck, Paris, 1 January 1851 (Temminck Papers, Nationaal Natuurhistorisch Museum).

5. Temminck to Bonaparte, Leyden, 8 January 1851, Temminck's own copy, letter copybook, p.100, #2 (Temminck Papers, Nationaal Natuurhistorisch Museum).

6. Julie Bonaparte, *La princesse Julie Bonaparte marquise de Roccagiovine et son temps*, ed. Isa Dardano Basso (Rome: Edizioni di Storia e Literature, 1975), 21.

7. Adolph Mailliard to Bonaparte, Rome, 28 April 1851 (del Gallo family archives).

8. Newspaper clipping entitled "Le prince de Canino" and signed Am. Pellier, dated May 1851 (Bonaparte Papers, Nationaal Natuurhistorich Museum).

9. Horace de Viel-Castel, *Mémoires du Comte Horace de Viel-Castel sur le règne de Napoléon III (1851–1864)*, 2 vols. (1883–84; reprint Paris: Guy Le Prat, 1957), 1: 75–76.

10. Eugénie de Grèce, 277.

11. Julie Bonaparte, *La princesse Julie Bonaparte*, 24–26.

12. Bonaparte to an unidentified correspondent, London, 19 July 1851 (Bonaparte Papers, Nationaal Natuurhistorich Museum).

13. Barbara Mearns and Richard Mearns, *Biographies for Birdwatchers: The Lives of Those Commemorated in Western Palearctic Bird Names* (London: Academic Press, 1988), 81.

14. Eugénie de Grèce, 178, 242.

15. Louis Mailliard to Bonaparte, Bordentown, 26 August 1851 (del Gallo family archives).

16. Marie Campello to Zenaide, Paris, 8 October 1851 (Fondazioni Primoli).

17. Bonaparte to Zenaide, Civitavecchia, 24 March 1852 (Fondazioni Primoli).

18. Bonaparte to the French Ambassador, Civitavecchia, 31 March 1852 (Fondazioni Primoli).

19. *Journal des Faits*, Paris, 15 April 1852 (Museo Napoleonico).

20. *La Maga*, Genoa, 30 March 1852 (Museo Napoleonico).

21. Luigi Masi to Bonaparte, Paris, 6 April 1852 (Fondazioni Primoli).

22. Bonaparte to Alexandrine Bonaparte, Paris, 15 July 1852 (Fondazioni Primoli).

23. Marie Campello to Zenaide, Paris, 27 May 1852 (Fondazioni Primoli).

24. Marie Campello to Zenaide, Paris, 3 June 1852 (Fondazioni Primoli).

25. Document in Luigi Masi's (?) handwriting to Pietro Primoli, n.d. (1852?) (#8256 Fondazioni Primoli).

26. George Ord to Charles Waterton, Philadelphia, 7 October 1852 (Ord Papers, APS).

27. Barbara Mearns and Richard Mearns, *Audubon to Xantus: The Lives of Those Commemorated in North American Bird Names* (London: Academic Press, 1992), 100.

28. Julie Bonaparte, *La princesse Julie Bonaparte*, 26.

29. John Cassin to Bonaparte, Philadelphia, 25 November 1852 (MNHN).

30. Johann Jacob Kaup to Bonaparte, Darmstadt, 28 January 1853 (MNHN).

31. Ord to Waterton, Philadelphia, 12 December 1852 (Ord Papers, APS).

32. Julie Bonaparte, *La princesse Julie Bonaparte*, 32, n.4.

33. Marie Campello to Zenaide, Paris, 2 March 1853 (Fondazioni Primoli).

34. Marie Campello to Zenaide, Paris, 30 May 1852 (Fondazioni Primoli).

35. George Ord to Waterton, Philadelphia, 17 April 1853 (Ord Papers, APS).

36. Julie Bonaparte, *La princesse Julie Bonaparte*, 268, n.2.

37. Eugénie de Grèce, 258.

38. Ibid., 260. There is irony in this scene. Nearly twenty years later, in 1870, Pierre's acquittal after murdering the journalist Victor Noir would contribute significantly to discrediting the regime of Louis-Napoleon in the public's opinion and would lead to the emperor's downfall.

39. Viel-Castel, 1: 174–75. Theo Aronson, *The Golden Bees: The Story of the Bonapartes* (New York: New York Graphic Society, 1964), 299–300.

40. *Morning Post*, London, Saturday, 17 July 1841.

41. Isadore Geoffroy Saint-Hilaire to Bonaparte, Paris, 5 April 1853 (MNHN).

42. Fragment of an undated newspaper article (in French) (Bonaparte Papers, Nationaal Natuurhistorich Museum).

43. Julie del Gallo Roccagiovine to Bonaparte, Cantalupe, 16 September 1853 (Fondazioni Primoli).

44. Bonaparte to William Cooper, Rome, 12 September 1843 (film 1514, APS).

45. Louis Mailliard to Bonaparte, Paris, 17 January 1854 (del Gallo family archives).

46. Zenaide to Charlotte Primoli, Rome, 28 April 1854 (Fondazioni Primoli).

CHAPTER 15

1. Julie Bonaparte, *La princesse Julie Bonaparte, marquise de Roccagiovine et son temps, mémoires inédits, 1853–1870*, ed. Isa Dardano Basso (Rome: Edizioni de Storia e Literature, 1975), 206.

2. Ibid., 34, n.10.

3. Richard Owen to Bonaparte, London, 15 October 1853 (MNHN).

4. Nicolaas A. Rüpke, *Richard Owen: Victorian Naturalist* (New Haven, Conn.: Yale University Press, 1994), 261–62.

5. Richard Owen to Bonaparte, London, College of Surgeons, 3 June 1853 (MNHN).

6. Bonaparte to Gould, Paris, 4 May 1854 (Gould Papers, Natural History Museum, London).

7. Gould to Bonaparte, London, 10 May 1854 (MNHN).

8. Gould to Bonaparte, London, 10 November 1854 (MNHN).

9. Richard Owen to Bonaparte, College of Surgeons, London, 15 December 1854 (MNHN).

10. Johann Jacob Kaup to Bonaparte, Darmstadt, 15 December 1854 (MNHN).

11. Richard Owen to Bonaparte, London, 6 February 1855 (MNHN).

12. Bonaparte to Owen, Paris, 15 March 1855 (Owen Papers, Natural History Museum, London).

13. Owen to Bonaparte, London, 15 March and 9 April 1855 (MNHN).

14. Titian R. Peale to Bonaparte, Washington, 26 June 1855 (MNHN).

15. J. J. Kaup to Bonaparte, Darmstadt, 23 February 1855 (MNHN).

16. J. J. Kaup to Bonaparte, Heidelberg, 11 March, and Darmstadt, 19 March 1855 (MNHN).

17. Unsigned, undated handwritten note (Bonaparte Papers, Nationaal Natuurhistorich Museum).

18. Bonaparte to Primoli, Paris, 3 June 1855 (#8264, Fondazioni Primoli).

19. Julie Bonaparte, *La princesse Julie Bonaparte*, 36, 8,n18.

20. Bonaparte to Charlotte Primoli, Brodrick Castle, Scotland, 4 October 1855 (Fondazioni Primoli).

21. Richard Owen to Bonaparte, British Museum, 16 September 1855 (MNHN). Unfortunately, the author was unable to locate the letter Bonaparte wrote Owen that prompted his reference to Napoleon.

22. Gould to Bonaparte, London, 13 June 1856 (MNHN).

23. Julie Bonaparte, *La princesse Julie Bonaparte*, 38.

24. Bonaparte et Victor Meunier, *Faune française ou histoire naturelle générale et particulière des animaux qui vivent en France*, Prospectus 2–8.

25. Bonaparte to Charlotte Primoli, Alicante, 21 February 1856 (Fondazioni Primoli).

26. Julie Bonaparte, 44.

27. Erwin Stresemann, *Ornithology from Aristotle to the Present*, trans. Hans J. Epstein and Cathleen Epstein (Cambridge, Mass.: Harvard University Press, 1975), 165–66.

28. Bonaparte, *Journal für Ornithologie* 4 (1856): 258, 259. Quoted in Stresemann, 165–66.

29. Barbara Mearns and Richard Mearns, *Biographies for Birdwatchers: The Lives of Those Commemorated in Western Palearctic Bird Names* (London: Academic Press, 1988), 243.

30. Lear's Macaw was thought to be extinct, but a small number were found in northeastern Brazil in the 1970s. Information about Lear's Macaw was given the author by Robert McCracken Peck, fellow of the Academy of Natural Sciences of Philadelphia, who is writing a book on Edward Lear.

31. Johann Jacob Kaup to Bonaparte, Cette (Sete), France, 15 July 1856 (MNHN).

32. Stresemann, 166.

33. Julie Bonaparte, *La princesse Julie Bonaparte*, 47.

34. Ibid., 54.

35. George Robert Gray to Bonaparte, London, 13 February 1857 (MNHN).

36. Stresemann, 167.

37. Julie Bonaparte, *La princesse Julie Bonaparte*, 70.

38. Ibid. 272
39. Ibid., 72.
40. Bonaparte to John Cassin, Paris, 13 July 1857 (Houghton Library).
41. Julie Bonaparte, *La princesse Julie Bonaparte*, 73.
42. Stresemann, 167.
43. Ibid. 168.
44. Ibid. 169.
45. Obituary, *Journal of the Proceedings of the Linnean Society* 3 (1859): xli–xliv.
46. Stresemann, 168.
47. Geoffroy to Bonaparte, Paris, 4 May 1857 (MNHN).

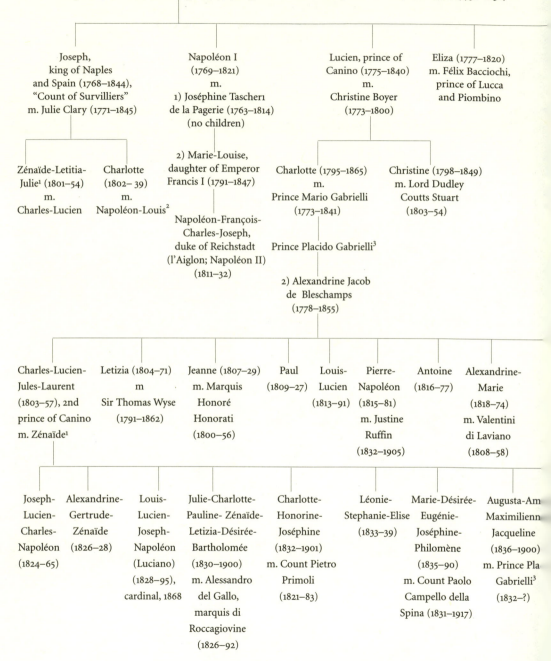

Charles Bonaparte (Carlo Maria Buonaparte) (1746–85) m. Marie-Laetitia (Maria-Letizia) Ramolino (1750–1836)

Joseph,
king of Naples
and Spain (1768–1844),
"Count of Survilliers"
m. Julie Clary (1771–1845)

Napoléon I
(1769–1821)
m.
1) Joséphine Tascheri
de la Pagerie (1763–1814)
(no children)

Lucien, prince of
Canino (1775–1840)
m.
Christine Boyer
(1773–1800)

Eliza (1777–1820)
m. Félix Bacciochi,
prince of Lucca
and Piombino

Zénaïde-Letitia-
Julie[1] (1801–54)
m.
Charles-Lucien

Charlotte
(1802– 39)
m.
Napoléon-Louis[2]

2) Marie-Louise,
daughter of Emperor
Francis I (1791–1847)

Napoléon-François-
Charles-Joseph,
duke of Reichstadt
(l'Aiglon; Napoléon II)
(1811–32)

Charlotte (1795–1865)
m.
Prince Mario Gabrielli
(1773–1841)

Christine (1798–1849)
m. Lord Dudley
Coutts Stuart
(1803–54)

Prince Placido Gabrielli[3]

2) Alexandrine Jacob
de Bleschamps
(1778–1855)

Charles-Lucien-
Jules-Laurent
(1803–57), 2nd
prince of Canino
m. Zénaïde[1]

Letizia (1804–71)
m
Sir Thomas Wyse
(1791–1862)

Jeanne (1807–29)
m. Marquis
Honoré
Honorati
(1800–56)

Paul
(1809–27)

Louis-
Lucien
(1813–91)

Pierre-
Napoléon
(1815–81)
m. Justine
Ruffin
(1832–1905)

Antoine
(1816–77)

Alexandrine-
Marie
(1818–74)
m. Valentini
di Laviano
(1808–58)

Joseph-
Lucien-
Charles-
Napoléon
(1824–65)

Alexandrine-
Gertrude-
Zénaïde
(1826–28)

Louis-
Lucien-
Joseph-
Napoléon
(Luciano)
(1828–95),
cardinal, 1868

Julie-Charlotte-
Pauline- Zénaïde-
Letizia-Désirée-
Bartholomée
(1830–1900)
m. Alessandro
del Gallo,
marquis di
Roccagiovine
(1826–92)

Charlotte-
Honorine-
Joséphine
(1832–1901)
m. Count Pietro
Primoli
(1821–83)

Léonie-
Stephanie-Elise
(1833–39)

Marie-Désirée-
Eugénie-
Joséphine-
Philomène
(1835–90)
m. Count Paolo
Campello della
Spina (1831–1917)

Augusta-Am
Maximilienn
Jacqueline
(1836–1900)
m. Prince Pla
Gabrielli[3]
(1832–?)

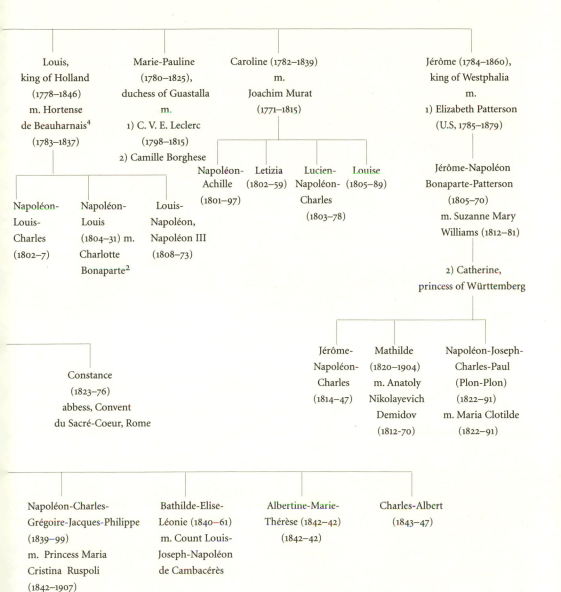

Louis,
king of Holland
(1778–1846)
m. Hortense
de Beauharnais[4]
(1783–1837)

Marie-Pauline
(1780–1825),
duchess of Guastalla
m.
1) C. V. E. Leclerc
(1798–1815)
2) Camille Borghese

Caroline (1782–1839)
m.
Joachim Murat
(1771–1815)

Jérôme (1784–1860),
king of Westphalia
m.
1) Elizabeth Patterson
(U.S, 1785–1879)

Napoléon-
Achille
(1801–97)

Letizia
(1802–59)

Lucien-
Napoléon-
Charles
(1803–78)

Louise
(1805–89)

Jérôme-Napoléon
Bonaparte-Patterson
(1805–70)
m. Suzanne Mary
Williams (1812–81)

Napoléon-
Louis-
Charles
(1802–7)

Napoléon-
Louis
(1804–31) m.
Charlotte
Bonaparte[2]

Louis-
Napoléon,
Napoléon III
(1808–73)

2) Catherine,
princess of Württemberg

Jérôme-
Napoléon-
Charles
(1814–47)

Mathilde
(1820–1904)
m. Anatoly
Nikolayevich
Demidov
(1812-70)

Napoléon-Joseph-
Charles-Paul
(Plon-Plon)
(1822–91)
m. Maria Clotilde
(1822–91)

Constance
(1823–76)
abbess, Convent
du Sacré-Coeur, Rome

Napoléon-Charles-
Grégoire-Jacques-Philippe
(1839–99)
m. Princess Maria
Cristina Ruspoli
(1842–1907)

Bathilde-Elise-
Léonie (1840–61)
m. Count Louis-
Joseph-Napoléon
de Cambacérès

Albertine-Marie-
Thérèse (1842–42)
(1842–42)

Charles-Albert
(1843–47)

BIBLIOGRAPHY

MANUSCRIPT COLLECTIONS

American Philosophical Society Library, Philadelphia (APS)
Archives of the Linnean Society of London
Bibliothèque Centrale, Muséum National d'Histoire Naturelle (MNHN), Paris, Charles L. Bonaparte Papers.
Centre d'Accueil et de Recherche des Archives Nationales (CARAN), Paris.
Fondazioni Primoli, Rome, Bonaparte Papers.
Library of the Academy of Natural Sciences of Philadelphia.
Historical Society of Pennsylvania (including the collection of the Library Company).
Houghton Library, Harvard University
Massachusetts Historical Society
Missouri Historical Society
Morris Tyler Collection, Beinecke Rare Book and Manuscript Library, Yale University
Museo Napoleonico, Rome
Nationaal Natuurhistorisch Museum, Leiden (courtesy of Dr. L. B. Holthuis)
The Natural History Museum, London.
Private archives of the del Gallo family, Rome
Private archives of the Prince and Princess Napoleon, Switzerland

WRITINGS BY CHARLES-LUCIEN BONAPARTE

Bonaparte, Carlo L. *Catalogo metodico dei pesci europei.* Napoli: Stamperia e Cartiere de Fibreno, 1846.
Bonaparte, Carolo Luciano, Principe di Musignano. *Saggio di una distribuzione metodica degli animali vettebrati.* Roma: Presso Antonio Boulzaler, 1831.
——. "Sulla seconda edizione del *Regno Animale* del barone Cuvier." *Nouvelles annales des sciences naturelles de Bologne.* Bologna: Tipografia Marsigli, 1830.
Bonaparte, Charles Lucian, Prince of Musignano. *A Geographical and Comparative List of the Birds of Europe and North America.* London: John Van Voorst, 1838.
——. *American Ornithology; or, The Natural History of Birds Inhabiting the United States, Not Given by Wilson.* 4 vols. Philadelphia: Carey, Lea & Carey, 1825–33.
——. "The Genera of North American Birds and a synopsis of the species found within the territory of the United States." *Annals of the Lyceum of Natural*

History of New-York (1828): 293–451. New York: printed by J. Seymour, John Street.

Bonaparte, Charles-Lucien. "An Account of Four Species of Stormy Petrels. Read January 13th, 1824," *Journal of the Academy of Natural Sciences of Philadelphia* 3, 1 (1823 [sic]): 227–33.

———. "Account of a New Species of Petrel." *Journal of the Academy of Natural Sciences of Philadelphia* 3, 2 (1824): 227–32.

———. "Cenni Autobiografici di Carlo Giulio Lorenzo Luciano Principe Bonaparte." Manuscript, del Gallo family archives.

———. *Conspectus Generum Avium.* Lugduni Batavorum, apud E. J. Brill, 1850–57.

———. "Descriptions of Ten Species of South American Birds. Read April 19, 1825." *Journal of the Academy of Natural Sciences of Philadelphia* 4, pt. 2 (1825): 370–87.

———. *Discours, allocutions et opinions de Charles Lucien Prince Bonaparte dans le Conseil des députés et l'Assemblée constituante de Rome en 1848 et 1849 avec un appendice contenant des documents historiques et des pièces diverses.* Traduits de l'Italien d'après le *Moniteur*, et autres journaux et documents officiels. Leiden, 1857.

———. *Iconografia della fauna italica per le quattro classi degli animali vertebrati.* 30 parts in 3 vols. Roma: Dalla Tipografia Salviucci, 1832–41.

———. *Iconografia des pigeons non figurés par Mme. Knip.* Paris: P. Bertrand, 1857.

———. *Manuel d'ichthyologie italienne.* 1840.

———. *Monografie des loxiens.* Leiden and Dusseldorf: Arnz & Comp., 1850.

———. "A New Systematic Arrangement of Vertebrated Animals." *Transactions of the Linnean Society of London* 18 (1841): 247–304.

———. *Notice sur les travaux zoölogiques de M. Charles-Lucien Bonaparte.* Paris: Bachelier, Imprimeur-Librairie de l'Ecole Polytechnique et du Bureau des Longitudes, 1850.

———. "Nouvelles espèces d'oiseaux méxicains." *Proceedings of the Zoological Society of London* (1838).

———. "Nouvelles espèces zoölogiques—première partie: perroquets," *Comptes Rendus des Séances de l'Académie des Sciences*, séance du 11 February 1850.

———. "Observations on the Nomenclature of Wilson's Ornithology." *Journal of the Academy of Natural Sciences of Philadelphia* 3, 2 (1824): 340–71; 4, 1 (1824): 25–66, 163–200.

———. "Observations on the State of Zoology in Europe as Regards the Vertebrata." Trans. for the Ray Society by H. E. Strickland. *The Ray Society, Reports on the Progress of Zoology and Botany.* Edinburgh: Ray Society, 1845. 3–18.

———. *Report on the Progress of Zoology and Botany, 1841–1842.* Edinburgh: Ray Society, 1845.

———. *Specchio comparativo delle ornithologie di Roma e di Filadelfia.* Pisa: Dalla Tipografia Nistri, 1827.

———. "Sur le quézalt des méxicains, *trogon paradisoeus*," *Magazin de Zoölogie* (1838).

Bonaparte, Charles-Lucien and Victor Meunier. *Faune français ou histoire naturelle générale et particulière des animaux qui vivent en France.*

Bonaparte, Charles Lucien and Hermann Schlegel, *Monographie des loxiens.* Leiden and Dusseldorf: Arnz, 1850.

GENERAL

Abbot, John S. C. *History of Louis Philippe, King of the French.* New York and London: Harper & Bros., 1899.

Abrantès, Laure Junot, duchesse d'(Duchess D'Abrantès). *Memoirs of Napoleon, His Court and Family.* 2 vols. London: Richard Bentley, 1836.

Agassiz, Elizabeth Cary, ed. *Louis Agassiz: His Life and Correspondence.* 2 vols. Boston: Houghton, Mifflin, 1886.

Allen, David Elliston. *The Naturalist in Britain: A Social History.* Princeton, N.J.: Princeton University Press, 1994.

Allin, Michael. *Zarafa: A Giraffe's True Story, from Deep in Africa to the Heart of Paris.* New York: Walker, 1998.

Aronson, Theo. *The Golden Bees: The Story of the Bonapartes.* Greenwich, Conn.: New York Graphic Society, 1964.

Atteridge, A. Hilliard. *Napoleon's Brothers.* London: Methuen, 1909.

Atti della terzo riunione degli scienziati Italiani, tenuta in Firenze nell'settembre del 1841. Firenze: Galileiana, 1841.

Aububon, John James. *Audubon's Birds of America.* Ed. Roger Tory Peterson and Virginia Marie Peterson. New York: Abbeville Press, 1981.

——. *Letters of John James Audubon, 1826–1840.* 2 vols. Ed. Howard Corning. Boston: Club of Odd Volumes, 1930. Reprint New York: Kraus, 1969.

Audubon, Maria R. *Audubon and His Journals.* 2 vols. New York: Charles Scribner's Sons, 1897. Reprint New York: Dover, 1994.

Baatz, Simon. *Knowledge, Culture and Science in the Metropolis: The New York Academy of Sciences 1817–1970.* New York: New York Academy of Sciences, 1990.

Barber, Lynn. *The Heyday of Natural History, 1820–1870.* New York: Doubleday, 1980.

Barker, Juliet R. V. *The Brontës.* New York: St. Martin's Press, 1995.

Bartoccini, Fiorella. "Il principe di Canino e i congressi degli scienziati," Bartoccini and Silvana Verdini, *Sui congressi degli scienzati,* Quaderni del Risorgimento 2. Rome: Edizioni dell'Atteneo, 1952.

Beaumont, Élie de. *Notice sur les travaux scientifiques de son altesse le prince Charles-Lucien Bonaparte.* Paris: Imprimerie Seringe Frères, 1866.

Bedini, Silvio A. "Jefferson: Man of Science." *Frontiers, Annual of the Academy of Natural Sciences of Philadelphia* 3 (1981–82): 10–23.

——. *Thomas Jefferson: Statesman of Science.* New York: Macmillan, 1990.

Biddle, Edward. "Joseph Bonaparte as Recorded in the Private Journal of Nicholas Biddle." *Pennsylvania Magazine of History and Biography* 55, 14 (1931): 208–24.

Bierman, John. *Napoleon III and His Carnival Empire.* New York: St. Martin's Press, 1988.

——. *Biographie du prince Charles Bonaparte, Prince de Canino, fils de Lucien.* Trans. from Italian J. F. Jules Pautet. Beaune, 1844.

Blumenthal, Henry. *American and French Culture, 1800–1900: Interchanges in Art, Science, Literature, and Society.* Baton Rouge: Louisiana State University Press, 1975.

Bonaparte, Julie. *La princesse Julie Bonaparte, marquise de Roccagiovine et son temps:*

.

mémoires inédits, 1853–1870. Ed. Isa Dardano Basso. Rome: Edizioni di Storia e Literature, 1975.

Bonaparte, Lucien. *Memoirs of the Private and Political Life of Lucien Bonaparte, Prince of Canino.* Translated from the French. 2 vols. London: H. Colburn, 1818. Translation of *Mémoires de Lucien Bonaparte, prince de Canino, par lui-même.*

Bonaparte, Napoléon. *The Confidential Correspondence of Napoléon Bonaparte with His Brother Joseph, Sometime King of Spain.* 2 vols. New York: Mason Brothers,1857.

Bonello, Giovanni. "Malta in the Life of Four Bonapartes." Part 2. *Sunday Times* (Malta), 24 April 1994.

Bourguet, Marie-Noelle et al. *Il y a 200 ans, les savants en Egypte.* Catalogue of an exhibition. Paris: Muséum National d'Histoire Naturelle, 1998.

Bowen, Francis. "The Reforms of Pius IX." In *The Great Events by Famous Historians.* 20 vols. Ed. Charles Francis Horne, John Rudd, and Rossiter Johnson. New York: National Alumni, 1904–14. vol. 17.

Bowlby, John. *Charles Darwin: A New Life.* New York: W.W. Norton, 1992.

Bowler, Peter J. *Evolution: The History of an Idea.* Berkeley: University of California Press, 1984.

Brodhead, Michael J. "The Work of Charles Lucien Bonaparte in America." *Proceedings of the American Philosophical Society* 122, 4 (18 August 1978): 198–203.

Brook-Shepherd, Gordon. *The Austrians: A Thousand-Year Odyssey.* New York: Carroll & Graf, 1996.

Browne, Janet. *Charles Darwin: Voyaging.* Princeton, N.J.: Princeton University Press: 1995.

Brownstein, Rachel M. *Tragic Muse: Rachel of the Comédie-Française.* Durham and London: Duke University Press, 1995.

Bruce, Robert V. *The Launching of Modern American Science: 1846–1876.* New York: Knopf, 1987.

Buranelli, Francesco. "Gli scavi a Vulci (1828–1854) di Luciano ed Alexandrine Bonaparte Principi de Canino" in Marina Natoli and Mina Gregori, *Luciano Bonaparte: le sue collezioni d'arte, le sue residenze a Roma, nel Lazio, in Italia.* Rome: Libreria dello Stato: 1995.

Burns, Frank L. "Miss Lawson's Recollections of Ornithologists." *The Auk: A Quarterly Journal of Ornithology* 34 (1917): 275–82.

Canino: arte, storia e tradizioni. Canino: CO.AR. Tursimo.

Connelly, Owen. *The Gentle Bonaparte: The Story of Napoleon's Older Brother.* New York: Macmillan, 1968.

Contributions of the Maclurian Lyceum to the Arts and Sciences 1, 1 (January 1827). Philadelphia: Maclurian Lyceum.

Cooper, James Fenimore. *The Letters and Journals of James Fenimore Cooper,* vols. 1–6. Ed. James Franklin Beard. Cambridge, Mass.: Belknap Press of Harvard University Press, 1968.

Coppa, Frank J. *The Origins of the Italian Wars of Independence.* London and New York: Longman, 1992.

Corsi, Pietro. *The Age of Lamarck: Evolutionary Theories in France.* Berkeley: University of California Press, 1983.

Cronin, Vincent. *Napoleon Bonaparte: An Intimate Biography*. New York: William Morrow, 1972.

Cuvier, Georges. *The Animal Kingdom Arranged According to Its Organization*. London: William S. Orr & Co., 1854.

Daniels, George. *American Science in the Age of Jackson*. New York: Columbia University Press, 1968.

Dennis, George. *The Cities and Cemeteries of Etruria*. London: J. Murray, 1878. Reprint Princeton, N.J.: Princeton University Press.

Dickens, Charles. *Pictures from Italy*. 1846. Reprint London: Oxford University Press, 1908.

Farber, Paul Lawrence. *The Emergence of Ornithology as a Scientific Discipline, 1760–1850*. Studies in the History of Modern Science 12. Dordrecht: D. Reidel, 1982.

Flaubert, Gustave. *Sentimental Education, or, the History of a Young Man*. New York and London: M. Walter Dunne, 1904.

Ford, Alice. *John James Audubon*. Norman: University of Oklahoma Press, 1964.

Gentling, Scott, John Graves, and Stuart Gentling. *Of Birds and Texas*. Fort Worth, Tex.: Gentling Editions, 1986.

Gill, Frank B. *Ornithology*. New York: W. H. Freeman, 1990.

Gillespie, Neal C. *Charles Darwin and the Problem of Creation*. Chicago: University of Chicago Press, 1979.

Girod de l'Ain, Gabriel. *Joseph Bonaparte: le roi malgré lui*. Paris: Librairie Académique Perrin, 1970.

Godman, John D. *American Natural History: Part 1—Mastology*. 3 vols. (1826–28). 3rd ed. Philadelphia: R.W. Pomeroy, 1842.

Gould, Stephen Jay. "An Awful, Terrible Dinosaurian Irony." *Natural History* (February 1998); 24, 26, 61–68.

Eugénie de Grèce. *Pierre-Napoléon Bonaparte, 1815–1881*. Paris: Hachette, 1963.

Gregori, Mina. "La collezione dei dipinti antichi." In Marina Natoli and Gregori, *Luciano Bonaparte: le sue collezioni d'arte, le sue residenze a Roma, nel Lazio, in Italia (1804–1840)*. Rome: Libreria dello Stato, 1995.

Himmelfarb, Gertrude. *Darwin and the Darwinian Revolution*. Garden City, N.Y.: Doubleday, 1959. Reprint Chicago: I. R. Dee Elephant Paperback, 1996.

Hobson, Anthony. "The Escorial." *Great Palaces*, intro. Sacheverell Sitwell. New York: Spring Books, 1964.

Horne, Charles F. "An Outline Narrative: The Triumph of Democracy." In *The Great Events by Famous Historians*, ed. Horne, John Rudd, and Rossiter Johnson. New York: National Alumni, 1904. 17: xvi.

Jackson, Christine E. *Prideaux John Selby: A Gentleman Naturalist*. Northumberland: Spredden Press, 1992.

Jaffe, Bernard. *Men of Science in America: The Role of Science in the Growth of Our Country*. New York: Simon and Schuster, 1944.

Journal of the Academy of Natural Sciences of Philadelphia 1, pt.1 (May 1817).

Kotzbue, August Friedrich Ferdinand von. *Travels from Berlin to Paris in the year 1804*. London, 1805.

Kragh, Helge. *An Introduction to the Historiography of Science*. Cambridge: Cambridge University Press, 1987.

Langle, Fleuriot de. *Alexandrine Lucien Bonaparte, princesse de Canino (1778–1855)*. Paris: Librairie Plon, 1939.

Lavrey, Jean. *Madame Mère*. Paris, 1982.

Lawrence, D. H. *Etruscan Places*. 1932. Reprint London: Olive Press, 1994.

Longford, Elizabeth. *Queen Victoria: Born to Succeed*. New York: Harper and Row, 1964.

Ludwig, Emil. *Napoleon*. Trans. Eden and Cedar Paul. New York: Boni & Liveright, 1926.

Mack Smith, Denis. *Mazzini*. New Haven, Conn.: Yale University Press, 1994.

Magee, James D. *Bordentown 1682–1932: An Illustrated Story of a Colonial Town*. Bordentown, N. J.: 1932.

Manzoni, Alessandro. *I promessi sposi (The Betrothed)*. New York and London: Limited Editions Club, 1951.

Maurois, André. *Victor Hugo*. Trans. Gerard Hopkins. London: Jonathan Cape, 1956.

Mayr, Ernst. *This Is Biology: The Science of the Living World* (Cambridge, Mass.: Belknap Press of Harvard University Press, 1997.

McBrien, Richard P. *Lives of the Popes: The Pontiffs from St. Peter to John Paul II*. San Francisco: HarperSanFrancisco, 1997.

Mearns, Barbara and Richard Mearns. *Audubon to Xantus: The Lives of Those Commemorated in North American Bird Names*. London: Academic Press, 1992.

——. *Biographies for Birdwatchers: The Lives of Those Commemorated in Western Palearctic Bird Names*. London: Academic Press, 1988.

Mills, Weymer Jay. *Historic Houses of New Jersey*. Philadelphia: J. B. Lippincott, 1903. Reprint Union City: Books About New Jersey, 1977.

Minutes of the Academy of Natural Sciences of Philadelphia. 25 Jan. 1812, 30 Dec. 1817, 26 May 1818. Academy of the Natural Sciences of Philadelphia.

The Morning Post (London). 29 June 1841.

Naef, Hans. *Die Bildniszeichnungen von J.-A.-D. Ingres*. Bern: Benteli Verlag, 1977.

Natoli, Marina. "Le residenze di Luciano Bonaparte a Roma, nel Lazio e in Italia (1804–1840)." In Natoli and Mina Gregori, *Luciano Bonaparte: le sue collezioni d'arte, le sue residenze a Roma, nel Lazio, in Italia (1804–1840)*. Rome: Libreria dello Stato, 1995.

Natoli, Marina and Mina Gregori. *Luciano Bonaparte: le sue collezioni d'arte, le sue residenze a Roma, nel Lazio, in Italia (1804–1840)*. Rome: Libreria dello Stato, 1995.

Niles Weekly Register (Baltimore) (new series). 11, n. 15 (14 December 1822); (20 September 1823).

Obituary. *Journal of the Proceedings of the Linnean Society* 3 (London, 1859): xli–xliv.

Oddie, E. M. *The Bonapartes and the New World*. London: Elkin Mathews and Marrot Ltd., 1932.

Osborn, Henry Fairfield. *From the Greeks to Darwin: An Outline of the Development of the Evolution Idea*. New York: Macmillan, 1908.

Pace, Antonio. "The American Philosophical Society and Italy." *Proceedings of the American Philosophical Society* 90, 5 (Dec. 1846): 400–416.

Phillips-Matz, Mary Jane. *Verdi: A Biography*. New York and London: Oxford University Press, 1996.

Poesch, Jessie J. *Titian Ramsay Peale, 1799–1885, and His Journals of the Wilkes Expedition.* Memoirs of the American Philosophical Society 52. Philadelphia: American Philosophical Society, 1961.

Poulson's American Daily Advertiser. 12 July 1823, 22 August, 1873, 12 September 1873, .

Le prince Lucien Bonaparte et sa famille. Paris: Librairie Plon, 1889.

Riall, Lucy. *The Italian Risorgimento: State, Society, and National Unification.* London: Routledge, 1994.

Ridley, Jasper. *Napoleon III and Eugénie.* New York: Viking Press, 1979.

Ritvo, Harriet. *The Platypus and the Mermaid and Other Figments of the Classifying Imagination.* Cambridge, Mass.: Harvard University Press, 1997.

Rossi, Joseph. *The Image of America in Mazzini's Writings.* Madison: University of Wisconsin Press, 1954.

Rupke, Nicolaas A. *Richard Owen: Victorian Naturalist.* New Haven, Conn.: Yale University Press, 1994.

Sauer, Gordon C. *John Gould the Bird Man: A Chronology and Bibliography.* Lawrence: University of Kansas Press, 1982.

Schom, Alan. *Napoleon Bonaparte.* New York: HarperCollins, 1997.

Le Siècle (Paris). 7 August 1844.

Seward, Desmond. *Napoleon's Family: The Notorious Bonapartes and Their Ascent to the Thrones of Europe.* New York: Viking, 1986.

"A Sketch of Joseph Buonoparte." *Godey's Lady's Book,* April 1845.

Stacton, David. *The Bonapartes.* New York: Simon and Schuster, 1966.

Stendhal (Marie-Henri Beyle). *The Charterhouse of Parma.* New York: Limited Editions Club, 1955.

———. *Rome, Naples et Florence.* Sceaux: Jean-Jacques Pauvert, 1955.

Stevens, Peter F. *The Development of Biological Systematics: Antoine-Laurent de Jussieu, Nature, and the Natural System.* New York: Columbia University Press, 1994.

Stirling, Monica. *Madame Letizia: A Portrait of Napoleon's Mother.* New York: Harper, 1962.

Stresemann, Erwin. *Ornithology from Aristotle to the Present.* Trans. Hans J. Epstein and Cathleen Epstein. Cambridge, Mass.: Harvard University Press, 1975.

Stroud, Patricia Tyson. "The Founding of the Academy of Natural Sciences of Philadelphia in 1812 and Its *Journal* in 1817." *Archives of Natural History* (London) 22, 2 (1995): 221–33.

———. *Thomas Say: New World Naturalist.* Philadelphia: University of Pennsylvania Press, 1992.

Swainson, William. *William Swainson, F.L.S., F.R.S., Naturalist & Artist: Family Letters & Diaries 1809–1855, Final Destiny New Zealand.* Ed. Geoffrey M. Swainson. Palmerston North, New Zealand: Geoffrey Marshall Swainson, 1992.

Taylor, Alan. *William Cooper's Town: Power and Persuasion on the Frontier of the Early American Republic.* New York: Knopf, 1995.

Thompson, J. M. "Lucien Bonaparte, Napoleon's Ablest Brother." *History Today* (London) 5, 5 (May 1955).

———. *Napoleon Bonaparte.* London: Oxford University Press, 1952.

Tower, Charlemagne. "Joseph Bonaparte in Philadelphia and Bordentown."

Pennsylvania Magazine of History and Biography 42, 4 (1918): 289–309.

Tree, Isabella. *The Ruling Passion of John Gould: A Biography of the British Audubon.* New York: Grove Weidenfeld, 1991.

Trenton, Patricia and Peter H. Hassrick. *The Rocky Mountains: A Vision for Artists in the Nineteenth Century.* Norman: University of Oklahoma Press, 1983.

Valynseele, Joseph. *Le sang des Bonapartes.* Paris: 126 Boulevard de Magenta, 1954.

Verdini, Silvana. "I Congressi degli scienziati nei documenti vaticani (1839–1846)." In Fiorella Bartoccini and Verdini, *Sui Congressi degli scienzati.* Quaderni del Risorgimento 2. Rome: Edizioni dell'Atteneo.

Viel-Castel, Horace de. *Mémoires du comte Horace de Viel-Castel sur le règne de Napoléon III (1851–1864).* 6 vols. Paris: Chez tous les Libraires, 1883–84. Reprint, 2 vols. Paris: Guy Le Prat, 1957.

Virgil. *The Aeneid.* Trans. Robert Fitzgerald. New York: Random House, 1983.

Watson, John Fanning. "Trip to Pennsbury & to Count Survilliers, 1826." Manuscript diary. Library of the Henry Francis Du Pont Winterthur Museum.

Weigley, Russell F., ed. *Philadelphia: A 300-Year History.* New York: W.W. Norton, 1982.

Welker, R. H. *Birds and Men: American Birds in Science, Art, Literature, and Conservation.* Cambridge, Mass.: Belknap Press of Harvard University Press, 1955.

Wilson, Alexander. *American Ornithology, or, The Natural History of the Birds of the United States.* Philadelphia: Bradford and Inskeep, 7 vols. 1808–13.

Wilson, George. *Stephen Girard: America's First Tycoon.* Conshohocken, Pa.: Combined Books, 1995.

Wolf, Edwin 2nd. *Philadelphia: Portrait of an American City.* Harrisburg, Pa.: Stackpole Books, 1975. Reprint Philadelphia: Camino Books, 1990.

Woodward, E. M. *Bonaparte's Park and the Murats.* Trenton, N. J.: MacCrellish and Quigley, 1879.

Woolf, Stuart J. *A History of Italy, 1700–1860: The Social Constraints of Political Change.* London and New York: Routledge, 1979.

INDEX

Aar glacier, 189–90

Abeele, J. S. van den, plates 10, 11

Academy of Baltimore, 96

Academy of Natural Sciences of Philadelphia,
xiv, 37, 41, 47–48, 49, 52, 54, 56, 75, 79–81, 98,
105; Bonaparte's specimens, 269. See also
Journal of the Academy of Natural Sciences

Academy of Sciences, Turin, 158

Academy of Sciences of France, 140, 150, 202,
222, 306–7, 309, 330n53; Bonaparte's reports,
272–73, 343n38; Bonaparte's membership, 154,
202

Accademia Nazionale dei Lincei, 203, 220, 223,
225

Accipiter cooperii (Cooper's Hawk), 91

Accipitres (hawks and eagles), 273

Adams, John Quincy, 42, 59, 76, 96

Adams, Louisa Catherine, 43

Adriatic coast: collecting specimens, 127; death
of Alexandrine, 307; visit with parents, 87, 103

Agassiz, (Jean) Louis (Rodolphe), xv, 54, 124,
130, 131 fig., 139, 145, 146, 148, 181, 184–85, 196,
202, 316; asks Bonaparte for loan, 209–10;
French Academy, 155; glacier study, 167, 189;
Oxford, 223

Ajaccio, 159, 315

Albany, New York, 71

Alessandro. *See* Roccagiovine

Alessandro, marchese del Gallo di Roccagiovine
(Belloli), 227

Alexandrine de Bleschamps Bonaparte (Fabre), 7

Alfieri, Count Vittorio, 178

Algeciras, 310

Alicanti, 310

Allertz, Dr., 151, 174

Almería, 310

American Academy of Arts and Sciences, 219

American Antiquarian Society, 219

American Entomology (Say), 67, 108, 191

American Natural History (Godman), 81, 90,
324n65

American Ornithology, or, The Natural History of

the Birds of the United States (Wilson), 56,
104, 221

*American Ornithology; or, The Natural History
of Birds Inhabiting the United States, Not
Given by Wilson* (Bonaparte), 50, 62, 66, 67, 73
95, 114, 117, 189, 321n51, 322nn3, 38, 335n22;
completion of two volumes, 91, 325n30; copy
for Pope Leo XII, 87; disagreement with
Audubon, 75–76; editing of second volume,
110; gift for Agassiz, 196, 336n49; illustrations,
109; specimens for, 132; volume five, 128,
329n11; volume four, 116, 117–18, 120, 129

American Philosophical Society, xiv, 40, 46, 48,
124, 156, 262; copy of *Fauna italica*, 193; copy
of *Genera of Birds*, 96

Amici, Giovanni Battista, 156

Andromeda racemosa, 45

The Animal Kingdom (Cuvier). See *Règne animal*

Annals of Natural History of Bologne, 112

*Annals of the Lyceum of Natural History of New
York*, 90

Antinori, Vincenzio, 156

Antonelli, Cardinal Giacomo, 287

Antwerp, 312

Arago, Dominique-François-Jean, 154, 155

Arc de Triomphe, 296

Arenenberg, 148

Ariccia, 134, 157

"Arrivo a Roma" (cartoon), 289

"Arrivo d'un Diplomatico Importuno: Sbarco a
Civitavecchia" (cartoon) 288

Assiniboin Indians, 129, 13

Atrium of the Villa Paolina (Abeele), plate 10

Audouin, Jean-Victor, 158

Audubon (Syme), 57

Audubon, John James, xiv, 55, 56, 57 fig., 65 fig.,
66, 67–68, 76, 89, 102, 103, 106, 115–16, 120, 130,
134–38, 197–98, 266 fig., 321n68, 322n16,
326n11, plate 16; *Birds of America*, 84; *Genera
of Birds*, 96; Great Crow Blackbird, 64–65;
Ornithological Biography, 118; sons of, 135, 136,

221; voyage to Florida, 116
Audubon, John Wodehouse, 135, 221
Audubon, Lucy, 102
Audubon, Victor, 135, 136
Austrian army, 232, 242

Bachman, the Reverend John, 136, 197
Bald Eagle, 120, 328n67
Baldamus, Eduard, 311
Balzac Honoré de, 307
Band-tailed Pigeon (*Columba fasciata*), 68
Bartoccini, Fiorella, 317n10
Bartram, William, 63
Baruffi, Giuseppi Filippo, 309
Bats, 143, 168, 169 fig., 170, 181
Battle of Waterloo, 21
Beagle (ship), 105
Beaumont, (Jean-Baptiste-Armond-Louis-
    Léonce) Elie de, xiii, 309
Belloli, Andrea, 226 fig., 227 fig., 277 fig.
Berlin, 225, 311
Bernadotte, Jean-Baptiste-Jules, 224
Bernard, Claude de, 309
Bertrand, General Henri-Gratien, 25, 139, 140
The Betrothed (Manzoni), 233
Bibliothèque universelle, 190
Biddle, Nicholas, 39, 42–43, 59, 320n19
Bingham & Hilliard, 134
Binomial nomenclature, 85, 324n4. *See also*
    Linnaeus
Biot, Jean-Baptiste, 307
Birds, 42, 45–46, 49, 86, 95–96, 110–11, 117,
    273–75, 305, 315, 346n44; California, 314; com-
    parative anatomy, 180; Cuba and Caribbean
    islands, 52–53; Florida, 52–53; fossil, 305; gen-
    era, 91, 272–75, 304, 305; Germany, 311, 312;
    Himalaya, 124, 264; Holland, 265; Java, 273;
    Mexico, 223; North America, 111; Philadelphia,
    86–87; plumage stages, 49; Rome, 86–87;
    Texas, 314; Say expedition, 48–49. See also
    Conspectus generum avium
The Birds of America (Audubon), 65 fig., 84, 90,
    103, 107, 266 fig.; copies for Bonaparte, 101,
    135, 329n35; drawings for, 104; supplement,
    293
Birds of Asia (Gould), 273
Birds of Australia (Gould), 185–86
Birds of Europe (Gould), 124
Birch, Thomas, plate 6
Black River, New York, 79
Black Sea, 299, 300
Black-winged Kite, 86

Blackfoot Indians, 129, 132
Blainville, Henri-Marie Ducrotoi de, 48, 139, 143,
    222, 306
Blue Grouse (*Dendragapus obscurus*), 110
Boat-tailed Grackle, 63
"Boatload of Knowledge," 74
Bocca di Leone, 87, 298
Bocourt, F. 313 fig.
Bodmer, Charles, 35 fig., 129
Bohemian Silk-tail, 93
Bohemian Waxwing, 93
Boisduval, 141
Bologna, 29, 30
Bombycilla cedrorum. See Cedar Waxwing
Bonaparte, Albertine-Marie-Thérèse, 186
Bonaparte, Alexandrine Jacob de Bleschamps
    Jouberthy de Vamberthy, 1, 2, 4, 7 fig., 10, 22
    fig., 43,134, 290; death, 307, 346n19; Etruscan
    vases, 187; family, 7, 317n11; payment of
    Pierre's debts, 280, 344n2; as proprietor of
    Canino, 199–200, 206
Bonaparte, Alexandrine-Gertrude-Zénaïde, 79,
    102, 110
Bonaparte, Anna, 14
Bonaparte, Antoine, 280
Bonaparte, Augusta-Amélie-Maximilienne-
    Jacqueline, 136, 290, 302, 310
Bonaparte, Bathilde-Elise-Léonie, 175, 290, 312
Bonaparte, Caroline, 14, 135, 154, 238
Bonaparte, Charles-Albert, 195, 225
Bonaparte, Charles-Lucien-Jules-Laurent, 2, 10,
    11, 12 fig., 28 fig., 14, 124, 171 fig., 313 fig.;
    Academy of Brussels, 193; achievements in
    retrospect, 314–16 arrest, 231; Ariccia, 134;
    arrival in America, 34; aviary, 114; birth, 2,
    317n1; birth of daughters, 79, 136, 175, 186;
    birth of sons, 46, 109, 153, 195; bust, 44 fig., 87;
    childhood and youth, 2, 12, 14, 19, 23–24; chil-
    dren, 134, 271–72, 295, 298, 302; classifying
    American birds, 57–58, 60; congresses, 194–95;
    death, 314, 315, 347n41; deputy during war,
    238, 248, 249; enemies, 158; in England, 87–88,
    263, 307; European trip, 84; excluded from
    succession, 140, 316; exile, 260–78; family
    deaths, 110, 157, 160–61, 188, 307, 332n39; fami-
    ly relations, 112, 287, 290, 299, 300; fascination
    with fauna, 124; father of descriptive
    ornithology, 62; financial difficulties, 200,
    264, 268–69, 276, 291, 299; France, 135, 139,
    260, 276; French Academy, 202; gambling,
    299, 345n42; health, 109–10, 212, 298–99, 302,
    312–15, 347n39; honeymoon, 29; honored by

Queen of Denmark, 224; last correspondence, 314, 347n40; mammals, reptiles, fishes, 44–45, 120, 320n39; marriage, 25, 27, 29; and Napoleon III, 296; natural science, 19, 24, 42, 54, 264–65, 314, 316; as nonconformist, 298; plants, 45, 320n39; personality, 71–72, 158, 178–79, 281, 300, 306, 309, 315–16; physical description, 43, 202, 320n33; and planned escape of Louis- Napoleon, 198; political efforts, 220–58, 264; president of section of zoology and comparative anatomy, 198, 208, 229; prince of Canino, 164, 168, 291; "prince of Musignano," 31, 51, 97, 319n61; problems with mother, 185; Venice, 230; return to Italy, 100–102, 107–8; Rome, 128, 194; seeking help from father, 72, 74; shipwreck, 174–75; speech to Italian parliament, 239–40; speech to council, 250–51, 253, 254, 255; threats against, 257–58; visit with Audubon, 136–37; visiting parents, 87; relations with Zenaide, 287, 290, 291, 299, 300, 302, 345n46

Bonaparte, Charles-Napoléon, 6, 58

Bonaparte, Charlotte (daughter of Joseph, sister of Zenaide, m. Napoleon-Louis), 27, 34, 40, 44, 56, 58, 72, 77, 102, 103 fig., 151–54, 152 fig., 207 fig.

Bonaparte, Charlotte (daughter of Lucien, m. Mario Gabrielli), 8, 10, 14, 21, 124, 310

Bonaparte, Charlotte-Honorine-Joséphine, 128, 290, 307; birth of son, Joseph Primolo, 298

Bonaparte, Christine, 8, 10, 14, 21, 89, 135

Bonaparte, Hortense de Beauharnais, 4, 140

Bonaparte, Jeanne, 14, 21, 74, 112

Bonaparte, Jérôme, 11, 77, 87, 228, 283

Bonaparte, Joseph, "Count of Survilliers," 4, 5 fig., 25, 27, 36–40, 39 fig., 43, 46, 58, 59, 78, 79, 124, 135, 136, 173; assists Charles-Lucien's family, 72, 73; death, 203–4, 337nn10, 13; health, 172, 184; heir to throne, 127; reunion with wife and daughter, 176

Bonaparte, Joseph-Lucien-Charles-Napoléon, 46, 72, 128, 303 fig.; after mother's death, 302; birth, 46, 320n41; injured by explosion, 271–72, 343n34; trip to America, 211–12

Bonaparte, Joséphine, 4

Bonaparte, Julie-Charlotte-Pauline-Zénaïde-Letizia-Désirée-Batholomée, 188, 225, 226 fig.; after mother's death, 302; during Charles-Lucien's illness, 312, 314; eulogy of Alexandrine, 307; eulogy of Zenaide, 302; as hostess, 215, 291–92, 338n43; marriage, 225, 283; memoirs of Charles-Lucien, 284–85, 299,
309; visit with Alexandrine, 186–87

Bonaparte, Julie Clary, 26 fig., 27, 29, 79, 88, 204; death, 211–12; health problems, 204–5; separation from Joseph, 58

Bonaparte, Léonie-Stephanie-Louise, 128, 157

Bonaparte, Letizia (Charles's sister), 14, 21, 89

Bonaparte, Letizia Ramolino (Madame Mère), 22, 29, 46, 71, 89, 109; and Charles-Lucien, 31, 71; death, 102, 132; visit with, 31; will of, 141

Bonaparte, Letizia-Julie, 128

Bonaparte, Louis, king of Holland, 4, 58, 124, 198, 204

Bonaparte, Louis-Lucien (Charles-Lucien's brother), 21

Bonaparte, Louis-Lucien-Joseph-Napoléon (Luciano), 109, 128, 135, 136, 157, 172, 198, 277 fig., 312; after mother's death, 302; decision to remain in Rome, 276; as priest, 299, 345n43; visit with Alexandrine, 186–87

Bonaparte, Louis-Napoléon (Napoleon III), 127, 204, 249, 268, 276, 283, 284, 293, 294 fig., 298; emperor of France, 140, 293; escape, 198, 336n55; exile to United States, 148; feelings toward family, 296, 302; legitimacy, 140; marriage, 296, 345n38; president of French Republic, 249, 255, 256, 285; succession, 293, 295

Bonaparte, Luciano. See Bonaparte, Louis-Lucien-Joseph-Napoléon

Bonaparte, Lucien, prince of Canino, 2, 4, 6, 10, 13 fig., 16 fig., 18–19, 24, 135; arrest, 14–15, 21; Canino, 12–19; death, 160–61, 332n39; disagreement with Charles-Lucien, 29–30, 31; exile, 15–21; financial difficulties, 58, 135–36; French surveillance, 13–14, 16–17; Legion of Honor, 21; reconciliation with Napoleon, 21; return to Italy, 21; Rome, 8–11

Bonaparte, Marie-Désirée-Eugénie-Joséphine-Philomène, 136, 276, 278, 285, 290, 295, 302, 307; injured by explosion, 271–72, 343n34

Bonaparte, Mathilde, 227, 283, 284

Bonaparte, Napoléon (Napoleon I), 2, 3 fig., 21, 25, 149, 166; impact on Charles-Lucien, 315

Bonaparte, Napoléon-François-Charles-Joseph, duke of Reichstadt, 127

Bonaparte, Napoléon-Charles-Grégoire-Jacques-Philippe, 153, 225, 287, 290, 295, 302, 344n19

Bonaparte, Napoléon-Grégoire. See Bonaparte, Napoléon-Charles-Grégoire-Jacques-Philippe

Bonaparte, Napoléon-Joseph-Charles-Paul (Plon-Plon), 285, 291, 292 fig., 293, 298, 314,

315; on Charles-Lucien, 314, 346n37

Bonaparte, Napoleon-Louis, 58, 72, 127, 102, 249

Bonaparte, Paul, 14, 21, 41, 74, 97–98

Bonaparte, Pierre-Napoléon, 21, 135, 255, 280, 284, 285, 296

Bonaparte, Zénaïde-Letitia-Julie, 25, 98, 151, 207 fig., 295; Ajaccio house, 206–7; assists with Charles-Lucien's book, 46; birth of children, 46, 79, 109, 136, 153, 175, 186, 195; children's injuries, 272; custody of children, 302; death, 300, 302, 345nn1, 2; death of daughters, 110, 157, 188; death of sister, 153–54; dowry, 25, 29–30, 58, 136, 318n52, 319n57, 324n57; excommunication, 250; health problems, 72; marriage, 25–27, 285–87, 290, 291, 299, 300, 302, 318n49, 345n46; marriage of daughter, 225; mortgage on Canino, 135–36, 161; reunion with father, 176; translation of German, 144, 208

Bonaparte-Patterson, Jérôme-Napoléon, 77

Bonaparte's Gull (*Larus Bonapartii*), xiii, 111, 327n39

Bonaparte's Gull (Audubon), plate 16

Bonelli, Franco Andrea, 86, 121

Bonheur, Rosa, 298, 345n41

Book distribution, 84, 124, 125, 130, 134

Bordentown, New Jersey, 35–36, 35 fig., 59, 319nn7, 8. *See also* Bonaparte, Joseph

Borghese, Pauline, 9, 74, 102, 154

Botany, 24; nomenclature, 195

Boulay de la Meurthe, Count Henri-Georges, 267, 283, 284

Boyer, André, 14

Brachiopoda, 214

Brehm, Christian Ludwig, 311

Bremen, 312

Brescia, Maurizio da (Fortunato Antonio Malvestiti), 14, 19, 20 fig., 74, 212

British Association for the Advancement of Science, 190, 210, 221, 264

British Museum of Natural History, 85, 97, 121, 136, 139, 151, 159, 268, 170

Brontë, Charlotte, 130, 329n27

Brueghel, Pieter, 82, 324n69

Brunswick, 312

Brussels, 86, 312

Buckland, William, 265

Bufalini, Maurizio, 156

Buffon, Comte Georges-Louis Leclerc de, 63, 70

Bufo (Quattrocchi), 125

Buonaparte, Luciano. *See* Bonaparte, Louis-Lucien

Burrowing Owl (*Athene cunicularia*; *Strix cunicularia*), 68

Burrowing Owl (Peale), 69

Bust of Charles-Lucien Bonaparte (Trentanove), 44 fig.

Byron, Lord George Gordon, 18, 145, 318n36

Cabanis, Jean, 312

Cadiz, Spain, 310

Cadwallader, General Thomas, 59

Café d'Orsay, 284

Café Florian, 230

Café Pedrocchi, 194

Cagliari, Sardinia, 14–15

Cambacérès, Comte Louis-Joseph-Napoléon, 302, 312

Campello, Count Paul, 276, 285, 290, 307

Canada (ship), 84

Candolle, Augustus Pyramus de, 148

Canino, 21, 23, 24, 74, 110; expenses of, 199–200; mortgage, 58, 136, 161, 188, 330n40; purchase, 9, 317n21; sale, 299

Canis Melanogaster (wolf), 168

Canova, Antonio, 9, 178

Capalti, Alexander, 124

Capitoline Hill, 24, 157

Carbonari, 244

Carey & Lea Publishers, 110, 114, 126, 128, 130

Carlos IV, 8, 317n13

Carret, James, 59

Cartagena, 310

Cassin, John, 293, 314;

Castel Gondolfo, Italy, 134

Castel St. Angelo, Rome, 135, 179, 334n48

Castillo de Santa Barbara, Spain, 310

Catalogo methodica (of fish) (Bonaparte), 312, 346n31

Catesby, Mark, 63, 120, 322n6

Catherine, princess of Württemberg, 77

Cavaignac, General Louis-Eugène, 249

Cedar Waxwing (*Bombycilla cedrorum*), 50

"The Cenci" (Byron), 145

A Century of Birds Hitherto Unfigured from the Himalaya Mountains (Gould), 117, 124, 328n57

Cernuschi, Enrico (Henri), 272

Cerorhinca (Rhinoceros Auklet), 267

Cesarini, Duchess, 272

Chamant-Plessis, 4

Chamber of Deputies, France, 141, 149, 166, 241–42, 248, 260, 340n12

Charlemagne (poem), 10, 18

Charles Albert, 236, 251; abdication, 253; as god-

father, 186; permission to enter Genoa, 172, 173, 176; problems with Austria, 219–20, 233, 237, 238, 243; signing of armistice, 244
Charles X, xiii, 114, 155
Charles-Lucien Bonaparte (Châtillon), plate 4
Charles-Lucien Bonaparte (Liverati), 171
Charles-Lucien Bonaparte (Maguire), frontispiece
Charles-Lucien Bonaparte as a Child (Wicar), 12
Charles-Lucien Bonaparte as a Young Man (de Châtillon), 28
Charles-Lucien Bonaparte with Zenaide at the Harp (Châtillon), plate 5
Charleston, South Carolina, 54
Charlotte Bonaparte (Robert), 152
Charpentier, Father, 19
The Charterhouse of Parma (Stendhal), 19, 234
Château of Ham, 204
Châteaubriand, François-Auguste-René, 9
Châtillon, Count Charles de, 14, 16 fig., 18, 19, 24, 25 fig., 28 fig., 29, plate 4, plate 5
Chaumont, Count de, 78–79
Chestnut Street Theater, Philadelphia, 40
Chevreul, Michel-Eugène, 309
Children, John George, 85, 89
Cicero, 9
Ciuffa, Father Leandro, 24, 318n43
Civitavecchia, 14, 151, 156, 160, 172, 176, 219, 257–58, 260, 286–88, 307
Clairmont, Jane "Claire," 87
Clary, Désirée, 224
Clary, Joachim, 141
Clary, Juliette, 141
Clary, Justinien-Nicolas, 284
Clausel, General Bertrand, 59, 322n75
Clay, Henry, 59, 104
Cleaveland, duchess of, 272
Cobden, Richard, 221
Cock of the Plains. *See* Sage Grouse
Coenraad Jacob Temminck, 282 fig.
Collegio Clementino, 24
Collins, Zacheus, 80
Columba fasciata. See Band-tailed Pigeon
Columba migratoria, 44, 320n37
Columba Zenaida. See Zenaida Dove
Columbia River, 110
Columbian Jay, 120
A Comparative Register of the Ornithology of Rome and Philadelphia (Bonaparte), 86
Congresso Scientifico Italiano, 148, 155–56, 178, 180–81, 331n1; Bonaparte contributions to, 194–95, 205–6; Genoa, 219; Milan, 205;

Naples, 214; Padua, 180, 189, 193, 194, 335n25; precursor of troubles in Naples, 214, 338n40; purpose, 149–50, 331n6; Santa Croce, 178; surveillance, 164; suspicions about Bonapartes, 198
Conspectus generum avium (Bonaparte), 265, 270, 272–74, 293, 312, 314, 343nn31, 38; copies distributed, 272–74, 343n38, 347n42
Constantinople, 209, 299
Contributions of the Maclurian Lyceum, 80–81, 324n62
Conwell, Bishop Henry, 46
Cooper, James Fenimore, 78, 265, 324n51
Cooper, William, 76, 78, 80, 81, 94–95, 98, 101, 105, 109, 116, 131–32, 326n45; Audubon, 77; *American Ornithology*, 114, 129; 126; bats, 143; *Fauna italica*, 126; fish, 118; hawks, 91–92
Cooper's Hawk (*Falco cooperii; Accipiter cooperii*), 91, 109
Copenhagen, 223
Corréa da Serra, José Francisco, 39
Coues, Elliott, 274, 343n48
Council of Deputies, 238, 243, 246, 257–58
Council of Five Hundred, 6
Count de Survilliers. *See* Bonaparte, Joseph
Coup d'état, 6, 148, 285
Courrier de Lyon, 174
Cozzens, Samuel Woodworth, 110, 126
Crested Coot (*Fulica cristata*), 180
Cretzschmar, Dr. Philip Jacob, 86, 98, 144, 146
Crimean War, 299, 300
Crosswicks Creek, New Jersey, 38
Crystal Palace, 285
Cuckoo, 304
Cuvier, Georges, 48, 106, 112–14, 113 fig., 306, 338n9; *Règne animal*, 112
Cybium bonapartii (fish), 220

D'Abrantes, Laure, duchesse de (Madame Junot), 6, 11, 317n8
D'Azeglio, Massimo, 221
Darmstadt, 275, 293, 306
Darwin, Charles, 4, 105, 159,189, 191, 223; Down House, 105; *Origin of Species*, 189, 223; *Zoology of the Voyage of the Beagle*, 181, 334n55
Darwin, Erasmus, 102
Dasybates fullonica (ray), 180
David, Jacques-Louis, 3 fig., 27, 56, 318n54
David, Pierre-Jean, 219
Dejean, General, 141
DeKay, Dr. James Ellsworth, 52, 72, 128
Delaware (ship), 94–95 fig., 96, 98, 100

Delaware River, 36, 40
Derby. *See* Stanley
Deutsche Ornithologen-Gesellschaft, 311
Deux amours (de Girardin), 312
Dinosauria, 191, 335n30
Dodo, 222, 304
Drapiez, Pierre-Augustin-Joseph, 29, 45, 68, 70, 139, 265, 323n18
Dresden, 312
Dubufe, Edouard, 297 fig.
Duel, 284, 344n9
Dumas, Alexander, 221
Duméril, André-Marie-Constant, 155
Dupin, Jean-Marie, 141, 166, 260
Durando, General Giovanni, 237, 242, 243
Durazzo, Marchese Carlo, 148, 220
"Dusky Grous," 110
Duvernoy, Georges-Louis, 306

Eastern Pewee, 63
Egret Heron (*Ardea pealii*), 114
Egypt, 2
Elba, 21, 173, 318n41
Elephant, 265, 342n11
Elysée Palace, 267, 281, 283, 284
Emperor Napoleon III (Winterhalter), 294
Etruria, 4
Etruscan vases, 187, 307
Eugénia Impératrise (hummingbird), 308
European Nuthatch (*Sitta europa*), 168
Everett, Edward, 97, 161, 165; ambassador to Great Britain, 167; editor of *North American Review*, 106; president of Harvard University, 219
Evolution, theory of, 4, 105, 189, 222–23, 315

Fabre, F. X., 7 fig., plate 2
Falco columbarius. *See* Pigeon Hawk
Falco cooperii. *See* Cooper's Hawk
Falcon (ship), 32, 34
Farini, Luigi Carlo, 232
Faucher, Léon-Léonard-Joseph, 283
Fauna italica. See *Iconografia della fauna italica*
Fauna japonica (Temminck and Schlegel), 293
Faune française (Bonaparte), 309
Félix, Rachel, 296–98, 297 fig., 345n39, 345n40
Ferdinand II, 173, 214, 236, 243, 245, 281
Ferdinand VII, 27
Ferrara, Italy, 228, 232, 242
Fesch, Cardinal Joseph, 9, 11, 29, 30, 79, 141, 318n26, 319n58; death of, 154, 332n20; gallery of paintings, 159, 205, 213

First Consul. *See* Bonaparte, Napoléon (Napoleon I)
Fish, 117–18, 121, 122, 130, 134, 188, 205, 312
The fishes & fisheries of North America (Rafinesque), 209, 337n24
Flandrin, Hyppolyte, 292 fig.
Flaubert, Gustave, 236
Florence, 86, 176
Florida, 53, 54, 63, 66–67, 75, 116. *See also* St. Augustine
Fondazioni Primoli, xiv, 298
Forester, James, 51, 52, 167, 321n54
Fort Ricasoli, 15
France, 4, 6; Bonapartes barred from, 135, 139; exile of Napoleon I, 21; return of Charles-Lucien, 139. *See also* Academy of Sciences; Chamber of Deputies; French Revolution
France, Dr. Henri de, 19
Frankfurt, 44, 86, 275, 293, 312
Franklin, Benjamin, 40
Franklin, Sir John, 111, 265
Franklin's Gull (*Larus Franklinii*), 111, 327n39
Frascati, Italy, 18, 24
Frederick William IV, 236
Freiburg, 146, 148
French Revolution, 6, 114
Fringilla amoena. *See* Lazuli Finch
Fringilla albicollis. *See* White-throated Sparrow
Fringilla purpurea. *See* Purple Finch
Fringillidae (grosbeaks, buntings, finches, sparrows), 274

Gabrielli, Mario, 11
Gabrielli, Placide, 310
Gaeta, 248, 288
Gallo, del. *See* Roccagiovine
The Garden of the Palazzo Serristori at Florence (Napoleone), 142
Garibaldi, Giuseppe, xiii, 218, 234, 245, 251, 255, 256, 257, 340n5, 341nn30, 38
Gates, Dr. H., 128
Gay, Delphine, 312
Gazzoli, Cardinal, 247
Genè, Gíuseppe, 148, 165
Geneva, 148, 149
Genoa, 148, 173, 176
Geoffroy. *See* Saint-Hilaire, Etienne Geoffroy de
A Geographical and Comparative List of the Birds of Europe and North America (Bonaparte), 138, 144
Gérard, Baron François-Pascal-Simon, 36, 133 fig.

German Ornithological Society. *See* Deutsche Ornithologen-Gesellschaft
Ghent, 312
Gilliams, Jacob, 80, 108
Gioberti, Vincenzo, 218, 220, 243, 251, 341n16
Giorgini, Gaetano, 156
Giovine Italia (Young Italy), 179, 232, 340n50
Girard, Stephen, 41, 59, 96, 97
Giraud, Charles-Joseph, 309
Giulio-Romano. *See* Romain, Jules
Giusti, Giuseppe, 198
Gizzi, Cardinal Pasquale, 218
Gluck, Christophe Willibald, 8, 317n15
Godman, John D., 62, 71, 78, 81, 91, 98, 322n4
Golden Plover, 64
Gorilla gorilla, 302, 304, 345n4
Gould, Elizabeth, 185
Gould, John, xiv, 117, 124, 137, 138, 175, 181, 185–86, 203, 210, 223, 273, 304, 308, 316
Goya, Francisco José, 8
Gracula barita, 65, 67, 322n15, 322n17. *See also* Great Crow Blackbird
Gray, Asa, 220
Gray, George Robert, 172, 221, 273; correspondence, 159, 312–13
Gray, John Edward, 85, 97, 170, 172, 197, 268–69; correspondence, 203; gains Bonaparte access to France, 139, 140
Great Crested Flycatcher, 63
Great Crow Blackbird, 63, 64, 65 fig., 67
Great Crow Blackbird (Audubon and Rider), 65 fig.
Grégoire, M. (math professor), 299
Gregory XVI, pope, 160, 164, 216, 218, 241, 249, 341n26
Grouchy, Emmanuel de, 59, 322n75
Guernsey, 268
Guimare (artist), 304
Guizot, François-Pierre-Guillaume, 177, 232, 236, 246

Haines, Reuben, 36–37, 52, 65, 76, 96, 108, 126
Hamburg, 299
Harlan, Richard, 71, 78, 126
"Harmony fever," 129
Harrison, George, 107
Hartlaub, Gustav, 213, 314
Harvard University, 219
Havell, Robert, Jr., 115, 132, 134, 328n51
Hays, Dr. Isaac, 63, 71, 74–75, 76, 80, 81, 96; editor of the *Journal*, 70, 323n28
Heckel, Johann Jakob, 220

Henslow, John Stevens, 191
Hercules (ship), 14
Herschel, John Frederick William, 18, 212
Heule, Dr., 148
Historical Society of Pennsylvania, xiv
History of the Fresh Water Fishes of Central Europe (Agassiz), 167
History of the Indian Tribes of America (McKenney and Hall), 192
Homburg, Father Eugenio di, 24, 318n43
Honorati, Marchese Honoratio, 112
Hopkinson, Joseph, 59
Hôtel Chaltham, 283
Hôtel de Brienne, 8
Hôtel des Invalides, 149, 204
Hôtel Montholon, 302
Howe, Dr., 97, 98
Hugo, Victor, 127, 221–22, 233, 267, 291; self-imposed exile, 268, 293, 342n20
Humboldt, Alexander von, xiv, 88, 206, 225
Hume, Joseph, 172
Hundred Days, 285, 344n14
Huxley, Thomas, xiv, 316
Hyères, 206, 337n18

Ichthyology, 145, 180, 214. *See also* Fish
Iconografia della fauna italica per le quattro classi degli animali vertebrati (Bonaparte), 120, 124, 128, 130, 132, 134, 159, 167, 170, 184, 191, 196, 214, 332n37, 334n1; American Philosophical Society, 193; Ireland, 197; Montpellier, 312; science and politics, 168, 333n20
Iconography. *See Iconografia della fauna italica*
Icterus spurius. See Orchard Oriole
Illiger, Johann Carl Wilhelm, 130
Independence Hall, Philadelphia, 41
Indiana, 73, 74. *See also* New Harmony
Ingres, Jean-Auguste-Dominique, xiv, 21 fig., 23
Insectes en Afrique & en Amérique (Beauvois), 48
Insects, 24, 42
Institute of Cairo, 219
Isard of the Pyrennees (*Rupicapra pyrenaica*), 205
Isis (journal), 181
Italy, 195: closed to Charles-Lucien, 276; nationalism, 178, 218; politics, 220. *See also* Garibaldi; Giovine Italia; individual places

Jardin des Plantes, xiv, 140, 141, 143, 276, 304, 309; director, 219, 306; visit with Sir Richard Owen, 302
Jardine, Sir William, 124, 181, 222, 264, 307;

Jardine Hall, 307

Jefferson, Thomas, 6, 40, 55, 321n66

Joseph Bonaparte (Belloli), 303

Jouberthou de Vamberthy, Alexandrine Jacob de Bleschamps. *See* Bonaparte, Alexandrine

Jouberthou de Vamberthy, Anna, 22

Jouberthou de Vamberthy, Gian Francesco Ippolito, 4, 317n5

Journal des Faits (Paris), 287

Journal für Ornithologie, 312

Journal of the Academy of Natural Sciences, 50, 54–55, 153, 321n64, 331n17; article by Ord, 63; articles by Bonaparte, 48, 57–58, 64, 67, 75, 77; editors, 68, 70

Julie Bonaparte, marchesa del Gallo di Roccagiovine (Belloli), 226

Julie Clary Bonaparte, Queen of Spain, and her daughter Zenaide (Lefèvre), 26

Junot, General Andoche, 6, 317n8

Junot, Madame. *See* D'Abrantes

Jussieu, Antoine-Laurent de, 48

Kaup, Johann Jakob, 274, 293, 305, 306, 312

Keating, William, 80

Köthen, 311

Kraus, M. T., 290

La Farge, John, 79

La Maga cartoon, 287, 288–89 figs.

La Spezia, 110

Lacoste, Emilie, 38, 58, 88

Lacoste, Félix, 38, 59, 320n18

Lafayette, Marquis de, 59

Lake Trasimeno, 180

Lallemand, General Charles, 59, 322n75

Lamarck, Jean-Baptiste-(Pierre-Antoine) de Monet de, 48

Lark Finch/Sparrow (*Fringilla grammaca*; *Chondestes grammacus*), 62

Larus Franklinii. See Franklin's Gull

Larus philadelphia, 111

Larus pipixcan, 111

Latham, John, 63

Latreille, Pierre-André, 48

Lawrence, D. H., 187

Lawson, Alexander, 56, 74–75, 95–96, 322n70, 326n46; *American Ornithology*, 56

Lawson, Miss (Alexander's daughter), 63, 71, 114, 116, 153

Lazuli Bunting/Finch (*Passerina amoena/Fringilla amoena*), 68, 132

Le Conte, John Lawrence, 77, 112

Le Havre, 260, 261

Le Moniteur Universel, 280, 296

Lea, Isaac, 105, 291

Leach's Storm Petrel (*Oceanodroma leucorhoa*), 34

Leadbeater, Benjamin, 91, 97, 104, 221

Lear, Edward, 117, 136, 157, 205 fig., 311

Lear's Macaw (*Anodorhynchus leari*), 311, 312, 346n30

Lefebvre-Desmouettes, Charles, 59, 322n75

Lefèvre, Robert, 5 fig., 26 fig.

Leghorn, 96, 100–102, 145, 151

Leiden, 86, 173, 265, 273, 312

Leipzig, 275, 312

Leo III, pope, 10

Leo XII, pope, 87, 110

Leopold II, 149, 167, 173, 176, 233, 236, 241

Lepic, Baron Charles, 284

Lesseps, Ferdinand de, 256

Lesueur, Charles Alexandre, 48, 56, 66, 98, 143; "school of industry," 73

Lethière, Eugène, 8, 317n14

Letizia Ramolino Bonaparte (Gérard), 133

Lewis and Clark expedition, 110

Library Company of Philadelphia, xiv

Liechtenstein, Heinrich, 312

Liguria, 220

Linnaeus, Carl, 50, 63, 80, 84, 85, 138, 324n5

Linnean Society of London, 84, 86, 138–39, 172, 335n50; Bonaparte's achievements, 315

Lisbon, 310–11

Lithography, 124

Liverati, C. E., 171 fig., 202

Liverpool, 84

Lizars, William H., 84, 89

London, 84, 87–88, 89, 135, 172, 263, 307

Long, Major Stephen, 62; expedition, 48, 62

Longchamps, 296

Lophorina respublica (bird of paradise), 270

Lottery, 241, 340n10

Louis Agassiz (Stuart), 131

Louis XVIII, xiii, 114, 155

Louis-Napoleon. *See* Bonaparte, Louis-Napoléon

Louis-Philippe, xiii, 114, 127, 135, 140, 148, 150, 155, 236, 248; welcome of Charles-Lucien, 140

Louisiana, 6, 66; Louisiana Purchase, 6, 317n9

Louvre, 283, 344n6

Lucca, 176, 198

Luciano Bonaparte (Belloli), 277

Lucien Bonaparte (Fabre), plate 2

Lucien Bonaparte and His Family at the Villa Rufinella (de Châtillon), 25
Lucien Bonaparte and His Family (Wicar), 13
Lucien Bonaparte with Charles-Lucien and other members of his ménage (de Châtillon), 16–17
Lyceum of Natural History of New York, 72, 78
Lyon, 149, 176–77

MacGillivray, William, 119, 181
Maclure, William, 48, 49, 54–55, 63, 81, 108; "school of industry," 73
Maclurian Lyceum, 80, 96
Madame Mère. *See* Bonaparte, Letizia Ramolino
Magpie Jay, 120
Mailliard, Adolphe, 211, 268, 283, 290
Mailliard, Louis, 211, 264, 285, 299
Mainz, 275, 293
Maison du Lac (Lake House), 38, 59
Malta, 15
Malvestiti, Fortunato Antonio. *See* Brescia, Maurizio da
Mamiani, Count Terenzio, 237–38, 247, 256
Mammals, 45, 205, 215
Manchester (ship), 90
Manin, Daniele, 236, 237
Mannheim, 135
Manor House of Joseph Bonaparte (Bodmer), 35
Manual of Fishes/Ichthyology. See Manuel d'ichthyologie
Manuel d'ichthyologie italienne (Bonaparte), 145, 148, 331nn66, 3
Manuel d'ornithologie (Temminck), 24, 265
Manzoni, Alessandro, 233
Maria Cristina, 176
Marseilles, 149, 172
Masi, Luigi, 134, 148, 157, 172, 218, 228, 280–81, 285, 289, 290, 295
Masséna, Victor, duc de Rivoli, 141
Mastodon, 306
Maurizio, Padre (Père Maurice). *See* Brescia, Maurizio da
Maximilian, prince of Wied-Neuweid, xv, 126, 132, 143–44, 181, 191, 192, 194, 203, 275, 312; Thomas Say, 129
Mayer, Enrico, 179
Mazzini, Giuseppe, xiii, 179, 232, 233, 234, 243, 244, 250, 253, 254–57, 340n54; People's International League, 233
McGuire, T. H., 274, 343n43
Mease, James, 55
"Messiah of Italy," 218
Metaxa, Count, 134

Metternich, Klemens von, 218, 232, 236, 236–37
Meunier, Victor, 309
Milan, 205, 237
Milne-Edwards, Henri, 267, 305
Miot de Melito, Count André-François, 80, n60
Missouri, 73; Missouri River, 62
Mogador (Morocco), 100
Mongibello (ship), 173, 174
Monograph of Crossbills. See Monographie des loxiens
Monographie des loxiens (Bonaparte and Schlegel), 275, 304
Montanelli, Giuseppe, 250, 291, 309, 314, 341n29
Monte Cristo, 221
Montecatini, 145, 176
Montenero, 145
Montijo, Eugénie del, wife of Napoleon III, 296, 345n38
Moquin-Tandon, Alfred, 309
Morning Post (London), 296
Mortfontaine, 223
Mount Cenis, 148
Mount Vernon, New York, 78
Müller, Johannes Peter, 220
Murat, Caroline. *See* Bonaparte, Caroline
Murat, Joachim, 2, 14, 40, 154
Murat, Lucien-Napoléon-Charles, 238
Murat, Napoléon-Achille, 40, 54, 127, 329n7
Murchison, Sir Roderick, 223
Murillo, Bartholomé Esteban, 82
Mus tectorum (rodent), 168
Museo Napoleonico, xiv, 20, 298
Muséum étrusque de Lucien Bonaparte, Prince de Canino (Lucien Bonaparte), 124, 187
Musical Fund Society, 40
Musignano, 10, 31, 317n22, 204 fig.

Naples, 213, 300; congress, 214
Napoleon III. *See* Bonaparte, Louis-Napoleon
Napoleon in His Study (David), xiv, 3
Napoleon le petit (Hugo), 293
"Napoleon of peace," 140, 148
Napoleone, Luigi B., 142 fig.
Napoleonic souvenirs, 167
Natterer, Johann (Jean), 144, 181, 194
Naumann, Johann Friedrich, 275, 311
Neuchâtel, 145, 148
Neue Wirbelthiere zu der Fauna von Abyssinien gehörig (Rüppell), 145
Neuwied, 132, 312
New Harmony, Indiana, 73, 74, 80, 108, 109, 129, 143, 324n59, 327n28

New York, 34, 71
Niagara Falls, 65, 71
Nieuwerkerke, Count Alfred-Emilieu, 283, 284
Night Blooming Cereus (*Cactus grandiflorus*), 41
Niles Weekly Regster, 40
Nomenclator zoologicus, 190
Nonsense Rhymes (Lear), 157
North American Review, 106
Northumberland, duke of, 304
Notre Dame, 296

Oakes, Hildebrand, 15
Oak (*Quercus*), 42, 320n29
"Observations on the Nomenclature of Wilson's
    Ornithology" (Bonaparte), 49, 64, 77
O'Connell, Daniel, 172
Odontophorinae (Gould), 210, 304, 337n28
Ohio River, 74
Oken, Lorenz, 146, 158, 181
Old Point, Virginia, 98, 326n56
Orange-crowned Warbler (*Sylvia celata*;
    Vermivora celata), 62
Orchard Oriole (*Icterus spurius*), 49–50
Ord, George, 174–75, 210–11, 220–21, 261–62, 269,
    295; Academy of Natural Sciences, 48, 50–51,
    63; Audubon, 192; disagreements with
    Bonaparte, 64, 77, 80; Wilson's *Ornithology*,
    50, 56
Origin of Species (Darwin), 189, 274–75
Orléans, duke of, 140
Ornithological Biography (Audubon), 118, 120
Ornithology, 4, 35–36, 45, 54, 86, 137, 191, 316;
    American, 56, 67, 73, 75–76; Bonaparte's
    achievements, 314–15, 316. *See also* Birds
Ornithology (Ord), 50
Ornitologia Romana (Bonaparte), 24, 318n45
Oudinot, General Nicolas-Charles, 255, 257, 260
Owen, Richard, xiv, 85, 139, 148, 172, 181, 191, 214,
    215, 302, 307, 335n30; on Bonaparte's achieve-
    ments, 316; *Principes d'ostéologie comparée*,
    305
Owen, Robert, 73, 74, 108, 109
Oxford University, 124, 222, 223

Padua, 180, 189, 193, 194
Palazzo Bonaparte, 102, 154, 157, 161
Palazzo della Cancelleria, 242
Palazzo di Brera, 205
Palazzo Lancelotti, 9
Palazzo Nuñez, 9, 12
Palazzo Torlonia, 9
Palazzo Verospi, 87, 102
Palisot de Beauvois, 48

Palmerston, Henry John Temple, 233
Pamphili, Filippo Doria, 124
Papal States, 179, 218, 237, 245, 246, 250
Parides (titmice and chickadees), 273
Paris, 140–41, 172
Paris Exhibition, 305, 346n13
Parliament, 85, 172
Parrots, 272, 273, 311
Passavant, Jean, 148, 331n2
Passerines (grosbeaks, finches, sparrows), 273
Passerini, Carlo, 86
Patterson, Dr. Dewees, 77
Patterson, Elizabeth, 11, 77
Peale, Angelica, 98
Peale, Charles Willson, 39 fig., 41, 47 fig., 48
Peale, Rembrandt, 113 fig.
Peale, Titian Ramsay, 48, 53 fig., 69 fig., 74–75,
    80, 105, 114, 305–6, plates 8–9; Florida expedi-
    tion, 53, 66–67
Pennsylvania Academy of the Fine Arts, 40, 153
Pentland, Joseph, 305, 309
People's International League, 233
Pepe, General Guglielmo, 245, 281, 309
Percides (fish), 180
Père Maurizio da Brescia (Wicar), 20
*Père Maurizio, Dr. de France, and Charles-Lucien
    Bonaparte* (Wicar), 20
Persigny, Jean-Gilbert-Victor Fialin, 283
Persimmon (*Diospyros virginiana*), 42
Perugia, 134, 180, 287, 344n19
"Petit Corporal" hawk, 120
Petrels, 34–35, 48
Philadelphia, 36, 40, 41, 56, 72
Philadelphus (mock orange), 45
Philip II, 37
Piazza di Spagna, 9
Piazza San Marco, 230
Piazza Venezia, 102, 132, 157, 161, 237, 290
Pickering, Dr., 193
Picta (woodpecker), 112
Pigeon, flightless, 222
Pigeon Hawk (*Falco columbarius*), 120
Pigli, Carlo, 246
Pigliacelli, 287
Pike, Zebulon, 41
Pisa, 86, 149
Pius VII, pope, 8, 9, 10, 12, 77, 218
Pius IX (Pio Nono), pope, 216, 218, 220, 223,
    228–29, 232, 233, 236, 237, 243, 244, 248, 250,
    341n24
Place de la Concorde, 167, 333n13
Place Vendôme, 166
Planches coloriées (Temminck), 24

Plon-Plon *See* Bonaparte, Napoléon-Joseph-Charles-Paul
Po River, 228
Poggia a Caiano, 149
Point Breeze, 36, 37, 59, 82, 90, 91, 96, 97; passed to Joseph-Lucien, 211
Point Breeze on the Delaware (Birch), plate 6
Pollux (ship), 174, 192, 333n31
Pomona (ship), 14–15
Pompeii, 213
Poppelsdorf, 4
Port-au-Prince, 4
Portrait of Alexandrine de Bleschamps Bonaparte (Viganoni), plate 3
Portrait of Georges Cuvier (R. Peale), 113
Portrait of the Family of Lucien Bonaparte (Ingres), 21–22
Portrait of Joseph Bonaparte (Lefèvre), 5
Portrait of Joseph Bonaparte (Peale), 39
Portrait of Napoleon-Joseph-Charles-Paul Bonaparte, Prince Napoleon (Flandrin), 292
Portugal, 310, 311
Potocki, Count, 151, 331n11
Powis, Lord, 18
President (ship), 15–17
Primoli, Count Pierre, 290, 298, 300, 302, 307
Primoli, Joseph, founder of Museo Napoleonico, 298
Prince Charles-Lucien Bonaparte (Bocourt), 313
Prince of Canino. *See* Bonaparte, Charles-Lucien
Prince of Musignano. *See* Bonaparte, Charles-Lucien
Princess Zenaide Bonaparte (Charlotte Bonaparte), 207
Principes d'ostéologie comparée (Owen), 305, 346n11
Purple Finch (*Fringilla purpurea*), 46

Quakers, 40, 46, 55
Quattrocchi, Petrus, 12, 124, 125 fig.,169 fig., plates 12, 13, 15
Querquedula agustirostris (duck), 180
Quezalts (quetzals), 223
Quirinal Palace, 247, 341n23

Rachel (Dubufe), 297
Radetsky, Count Johann Joseph Franz Karl, 236
Rafinesque, Constantine Samuel, 208, 209, 214
Ranzani, Professor, 124
Raphael, 8, 213, 317n15
Rathbone, William, 84
Rattlesnake, 42

Rayer, Pierre-François, 309
Recherches sur les poissons fossiles (Agassiz), 190
Red-breasted Nuthatch, 50
Reddish Egret (*Dichromanassa rufescens*), 114
Règne animal (Cuvier), 112
Reichstadt, duke of. *See* Bonaparte, Napoléon-François-Charles-Joseph
Reinwardt, Caspar George Carl, 273, 343n4
Rembrandt, 213
Reni, Guido, 8
Reptiles, 45, 191, 205
Republicanism, 6, 228, 310, 316
Rhododendron maxima, 45
Rhône River, 149
Riccioli, Italy, 110
Richardson, Dr. John, 111, 191
Rider, Alexander, 65 fig.,, 66, 67, 114, 116
Ridolfi, Marchese Cosimo, 165, 178
Rijksmuseum von Natuurlijke Historie, 86, 265, 273
Risorgimento, xiii, 213, 230, 232, 250, 264, 310
Risorgimento (newspaper), 280–81
Rivoli, duke of. *See* Masséna
Robert, Louis-Leopold, 151, 152 fig.
Roccagiovine, Alessandro, marchese del Gallo di, 224, 225, 227 fig., 283, 284–85
Roccagiovine, Luigi del Gallo, 318n30
Rocky Mountains, 48, 62, 68, 110, 129, 197, 323n20
Roma (ship), 245
Romain, Jules, 213, 225
Roman republic, 264
Rome, 102, 141, 218; bombing, 256–57
Rossi, Pellegrino, 233, 246–47, 284, 344n9; murder of, 247, 250, 261, 341n22, 342n3
Rossini, Gioacchino, 149
Rothsay, Lord Stuart de, 135, 329n36
Rothschild, Baron C. M., 124
Rothschild, Lionel, 241
Rovadies, Marquis, 118
Royal Academy of Turin, 186
Royal Society Club, 89, 116
Royal Society of London, 115, 116, 150, 308
Royal Zoological Museum, Turin, 148
Rubens, Peter Paul, 82
Rüppell, (Wilhelm Peter) Eduard (Simon), 144–45, 146, 220, 312; "System of Ichthyology," 206
Ruspi, Carlo (Carolus), 124, 184, plate 14
Ruspoli, Prince Alessandro, 124

Sablet, Jacques, 8, 317n14
Sage Grouse (*Centrocercus urophasianus*), 110,

132

St. Augustine, Florida, 54, 321n59

Saint Helena, 21, 25, 139, 149, 167

Saint-Hilaire, Etienne Geoffroy, 2, 48, 140, 155, 172, 219, 315, 338n9

Saint-Hilaire, Isadore Geoffroy, 141, 150, 154, 166–67, 170–71, 172, 175, 180–81, 236, 262–63, 267, 304, 309, 340n1; Jardin des Plantes, 276; last correspondence with Bonaparte, 315, 346n47

Saint Kilda, 34

Saint Malo, 7

Saint Mark's Cathedral, 237

The salon of the Villa Paolina with Zenaide and her child Augusta (Abeele), plate 11

Saluzzo di Menusiglio, Giuseppe Angelo Conte di, 165, 333n7

Sampson Batard & Co., 85

Santa Croce, 178, 179, 188, 203–4

Santo Domingo, 4, 38, 55

Saratoga, New York, 65, 71

Sarzana, 151

Savage, Annette, 79

Savage, Thomas, 302, 304

Savi, Paolo, 81, 86, 124, 156, 168

Say, Lucy, 108

Say, Thomas, 46, 47 fig., 48, 63, 68, 70, 75, 77, 80, 98, 108, 129–30, 329n22; *American Entomology*, 67; bird collection, 48; Bonaparte's book, 62; editor of *Journal*, 68; Long expedition, 48, 62; remarks on Cuvier, 112; Rocky Mountains, 48, 62; "school of industry," 73, 323n37

Say's Flycatcher (*Muscicapa saya*; *Sayornis saya*), 68

Scandinavian Association of Scientists, 222

Scarpellini, Feliciano, 203

Schlegel, Hermann, 124, 144, 173, 213, 265, 275, 312, 342n14, 343n52; on Bonaparte's achievements, 315, 346n46; *Fauna japonica*, 293

Schonbrunn Palace, 127

Schuylkill River, Philadelphia, 40

Scombrides (fish), 180

Scotland, 223, 264, 307

Scott, General Winfield, 59

Sebastiani, Dr., 24, 318n43

Second Empire, 293, 302

Seine River, 172

Selachorum tabula analitica (Bonaparte), 145, 148

Selby, John Prideaux, 107, 124, 181

Senckenberg Museum, Frankfurt, 86

A Sentimental Education (Flaubert), 236

Serristori Palace, 127, 141, 142 fig., 203

Sharp-tailed Grouse (*Pedioecetes phasianellus*), 132

Sharpless, Dr. John, 80

Shelley, Mary, 87

Shelley, Percy, 87

Sighton, Colonel, 19

Sinigallia, 103, 134, 307

The Sisters Zenaide and Charlotte Bonaparte, plate 7

Sitta canadensis, 50, 321n50

Sitta sulta, 50, 321n50

Sitta varia, 50, 321n50

Sketch of Musignano (Lear), 204–5

Skunk, 42

Slavonian Grebe (*Podiceps longirostris*), 180

Smith, Denis Mack, 255

Smith, James Edward, 84–85

Sorbonne, 309

Spa, 265

Specchio comparativo delle ornithologie di Roma e di Filadelfia (Bonaparte), 86

Species: birds, 85, 110–11, 119, 120, 137–38, 273–75, 305, 315, 346n44; splitting, 208; transmutation, 304, 311, unification, 168

Stanley, Lord Edward, earl of Derby, 124, 136, 306

Stendhal, 19, 307

Stockton, Richard, 59

Stokoe, Dr. John, 34

Strasbourg, 312; coup d'état, 148

Stresemann, Erwin, xiii, 182, 274, 314–15, 318n45, 346n43, 346n44

Strickland, Hugh Edwin, 172–73, 191, 197, 221

Strickland, William, 77

Strix asio (owl), 118

Strix noevia (owl), 118

Stuart, Lord Dudley, 89

Stuart, F. T., 131 fig.

Swainson, Mary, 102

Swainson, William, 84, 106–7, 111, 117, 119, 121, 126, 145–46; bird collection, 159

Sylvecola Swainsonii, 119

Syme, John, 57 fig.

Synopsis (Bonaparte), 116

Syon House, 304

"Systema Vertebratorum" (Bonaparte), 138–39, 194

Systema vegetabilum (Linnaeus), 19, 318n37

Temminck, Coenraad Jacob, 24, 34, 49, 63, 68, 70, 81, 86, 146, 181, 265, 281, 282 fig.; 312; book on India, 203; *Fauna japonica*, 293

Teniers, David, 82, 213

Tetraonidae (grouse), 304
Thames River tunnel, 87–88
Thomas Say in the Uniform of the Long Expedition (Peale), 47
Thornegrove, 18–19
Tiber River, 298
Titian Ramsay Peale (self-portrait), 53
Tivoli, Copenhagen, 223
Tivoli, Italy, 9
Torlonia, Alessandro, 233
Torlonia, Charles, 185
Torpedine (ray), 184
Toucans, 304
Toulon, 248
Treaty of Campo Formio, 240
Treaty of Valençay, 27
Trees, 42, 45
Trentanove, R., 44 fig., 87
Trenton, New Jersey, 36
Trevelyan, Sir Walter, 265, 342n13
Trochilides (hummingbirds), 273
Trogons, 304
Tuileries Palace, 296, 310, 312
Turin, 86, 148, 251
Turkish Empire, 299
Turtles, 118, 121
Tuscany, 101, 145, 331n64

"Universal Murderer of Domestic Happiness, or the Fraternal Tyrant" (cartoon), 18, plate 1
University of Bologna, 179
U.S.S. Delaware (painting), 94–95

Van Dyck, Anthony, 82, 213
Vare, Lord Harry, 272
Vatican, 164, 198, 233, 237, 245
Vaux, Robert, 80
Verdi, Giuseppe, 224, 233
Vernet, Joseph, 36
Vespertilio (Quattrocchi), 169 fig.
Vespertilio bonapartii (bat), 168–69
Vestiges of the Natural History of Creation, 222
Via Bocca di Leone, 9, 29, 317n18
Via del Corso, 87
Via Sistina, 151
Viburnum prunifolium, 45
Vicenza, 243
Victor Emmanuel I, 253
Victoria, 172, 333n28
Vieillot, Louis Pierre, 50, 63, 117, 328n58
Vienna, 127; revolt, 236–37
Viganoni, Carlo Maria, plate 3
Vigors, Nicholas Aylward, 85, 89, 90, 117, 157

Villa Borghese, 232
Villa Croce del Biacco, 29
Villa Paolina, 102, 103 fig., 132, 151, 154, 157, 159, 215, 225, 302, plates 10, 11
Villa Paolina (Charlotte Bonaparte), 103 fig.
Villa Rufinella, 9, 24, 317n20; 25 fig.
Viterbo, 9, 19, 160

Wabash River, 73
Wagler, Johann, 130
Washington Eagle, 120
Waterhouse, Benjamin, 172, 181
Waterton, Charles, 174–75
Watson, John, 38, 44, 320n38
Webster, Daniel, 59
Weisbaden, 293, 312
Western Phoebe, 68
White-throated Sparrow (*Fringilla albicollis*), 45
Wicar, Jean-Baptiste-Joseph, 12 fig., 13 fig., 20 fig.
Wild Turkey, 67
Wild Turkey (T. Peale), plate 8
Wilkes Expedition, 192, 336n33
William Tell (Rossini), 149
Wilson, Alexander, 34, 57, 63, 70, 137; *American Ornithology*, xiv, 49, 56, 321n49; classification of species, 49, 52, 62
Wilson, Edward, 269–70, 342n24
Wilson, Thomas, 269
Wilson's Storm Petrel (*Oceanites oceanicus*), 34
Winterhalter, Frans Xavier, 294 fig.
Wise, Dr., 59
Wistar, Caspar, 46, 320n43; Wistar parties, 46
Wolof, Edwin, 40
Woodpeckers, 304, 345n7
World's Fair, London, 285, 344n11
Wyse, Thomas, 89, 109, 172

Yarrell, William, 181

Zenaide. *See* Bonaparte, Zénaïde-Letitia-Julie
Zenaide and Charlotte Bonaparte (Ingres), xiv
Zenaida Dove, 265, 266 fig., 267, 300, 302
Zenaida Dove (Audubon), 266
Ziebigk, 275
Zoological Gardens, London, 136, 158
Zoological Museum, Berlin, 311
Zoological Society of London, 85, 90, 97, 117, 124, 172, 223, 265
Zoology, 121, 190–91, 195, 197, 215; anatomical, 139; systematic, 139
Zoology of the Voyage of the Beagle (Darwin), 181, 334n55